C0-BWY-367

AUSTRALIAN & NEW ZEALAND
Warships 1914-1945

AUSTRALIAN & NEW ZEALAND
Warships
1914—1945

Ross Gillett

GP
Sydney

This book is dedicated to my good friend and fellow Naval Historian Harold (Harry) Charles Adlam, whose attention to historical accuracy was second to none.

First published in 1983 by
Doubleday Australia Pty. Limited
This edition published 1987 by
Golden Press Pty Ltd, Incorporated in New South Wales,
Birkenhead Point, Drummoyne N.S.W. 2047, Australia.

Copyright © Ross Gillett 1983

All rights reserved. No part of this publication may be reproduced stored in a retrieval system, or transmitted in any form or by any means, electronic, mechanical, photocopying, recording or otherwise without the prior permission of the publisher.

Gillett, Ross, 1953 –
    Australian and New Zealand warships, 1914-1945.

    Bibliography.
    Includes index.
    ISBN 0 86824 095 8.

    1. Australia. Royal Australian Navy.
    2. New Zealand. Royal New Zealand Navy.
    3. Warships. I. Title.

359.3'25'0994

This book was created and produced —
by **Obelisk Press Pty. Ltd. N.S.W.**

Printing by arrangement with Imago Productions (FE) Pte Ltd, Singapore.

CONTENTS

PART I
AUSTRALIA

Preface

'Australian and New Zealand Warships, 1914–1945', traces the development of the two navies from the Great War, through to V-J Day, 15th August, 1945. The book highlights the technical aspects of the ships, including weapons carried and any special design or performance features.

As the story of these ships is inseparable from that of the navies, brief chronologies of the major events precede the main sections.

Part one describes the RAN during the Great War of 1914–1918, the years of peace 1919–1939, and the Second World War 1939–1945. The New Zealand Section, part two, lists in turn, vessels operated by the Government from 1914–1921, the New Zealand Division of the Royal Navy 1921–1941 and the RNZN from 1941 to 1945.

Every ship listed is classified by type, e.g. cruiser, patrol craft, support, etc., and then sub-divided as either built-for-the-purpose or requisitioned.

During 1914–18 Australia's Navy operated a total of 63 ships, of which 22 were requisitioned from private sources. The number of vessels reduced significantly during the mid-war period, only to swell again in the Second World War. Many privately owned craft were taken up for war service and by August, 1945, the number had reached 679. In comparison the 209 ships specifically acquired between 1939 and 1945 for fleet operations included ships on loan, e.g. N class destroyers, and those ordered prior to the outbreak of war but completed during the conflict, e.g. PARRAMATTA, WARREGO and KOALA.

Thus, during the years it was required to wage war, the RAN was in both eras a predominantly small ship force. In many cases it's ships were hurriedly modified to carry defensive armament to satisfy patrol and escort duties around Australia, New Guinea and the islands.

Kiwi involvement in naval actions was limited until the Second World War. At this time the new navy found itself in a similar position to that of the RAN. As few built-for-the-purpose warships were available, the Government turned to private concerns to satisfy early minesweeping, patrol and support requirements. Up to V-J Day, 45 vessels had been requisitioned for naval duties.

Many of the craft requisitioned by Australia and New Zealand for the 1939–45 conflict dated from the turn of the century; some were even older. Despite a lack of speed, insufficient space for armament and the fact that most were unsuitable for naval warfare, these Lilliputian fleets of requisitioned craft provided a force able to satisfy the immediate needs of the Fleet until the more specialised naval ships could be commissioned.

The largest warship classes constructed (trawler size and above), were the 56 unit Bathurst class Australian Minesweepers for the RAN and the 13-strong Castle class comprising four minesweepers and nine antisubmarine vessels for New Zealand. Local yards in both countries produced significant numbers of Fairmile B and Harbour Defence Motor launches which supplemented, and eventually replaced, a large percentage of the requisitioned boats.

Like many fleets, the need for afloat support and re-supply of forward bases was essential and a wide selection of requisitioned merchant craft filled the support role. The RAN supplemented these ships during the last years of the war by a variety of small support craft, such as motor stores lighters, tugs and air-sea rescue vessels. But, whereas new destroyers, frigates and minesweepers would eventually supplement older requisitioned tonnage, no large support craft was ordered and the Australian fleet continued to rely on its requisitioned ships and the surviving pre-war tonnage of PLATYPUS, KURUMBA, MORESBY, RIPPLE and KOORONGA.

The only losses of the Great War were the submarines AE1 and AE2. Thirty-eight ships were lost in the Second World War including 14 combatants and 24 requisitioned vessels; a loss rate of 3.03% from 1939 to 1945. At the end of hostilities, 39 vessels were under construction. Most of these were completed but laid up; others were disposed of immediately.

In New Zealand three vessels were lost up to 1945 including one corvette and two auxiliary minesweepers.

The trend of requisitioning privately owned tonnage then constructing built-for-the-purpose craft also applied to the marine sections of both the Australian Army and Royal Australian Air Force. Unlike the Navy, these forces concentrated primarily on small support craft, the only large new construction vessels being the Army's 300 tonners and AV2767 (CRUSADER), which was laid down in 1944.

To facilitate matters many new vessels built for the RAN, Army and RAAF, were of one design, but modified to suit the different requirements. This policy was adopted for various classes including the 120' motor lighters, 40' workboats and general purpose vessels. The Army and RAAF "fleets" reached peak strength in 1945, with over 2,700 under Army control and 300 plus operating with the R.A.A.F.

By V-J Day more than 3,790 known vessels had served or were active with the RAN, Australian Army and RAAF of which more than 1,830 were built-for-the-purpose.

HMAS SYDNEY; the funnels, mainmast and foremast have been camouflaged for New Guinea operations.

Acknowledgements

A small but enthusiastic band of friends assisted me in the compilation of Australian and New Zealand Warships 1914–1945. These included the late Harry Adlam, Peter Armstrong, Michael Askey, Peter Britz, Michael Burgess, Steve Given, Robert Head, Ken Hughes, John Jepperson, John Jeremy, John Mackenzie, John Mortimer, Doug Robertson, Lieut. Joe Straczek, RAN, Paul Webb, Peter Williams and Ron Wright.

Material was also kindly supplied by the Australian War Memorial, Cockatoo Island, C. W. Collins, Department of Defence (Navy), Ministry of Defence (N.Z.) and the Naval Historical Society of Australia.

Ross Gillett

Illustrations

Except where indicated, all photographs appearing in 'Australian and New Zealand Warships 1914–1945' are from official sources, i.e. Royal Australian Navy and Royal New Zealand Navy. Photographs from private collections are marked accordingly and those from the Australian War Memorial allotted a negative number, e.g. (11111).

Line-drawings are provided courtesy of the Naval Ship Design Section; Paul Webb of Webb Warships, Williamstown, Victoria; the Fleet Air Arm Museum, HMAS ALBATROSS; and Cockatoo Island Dockyard Pty. Ltd.

Specification tables

Throughout the book specification tables are presented in two formats; one for built-for-the-purpose and purchased vessels, and the second for requisitioned craft taken up for war duties.

Imperial measurements have been used as all ships were built and maintained in an era before metrification.

Dimensions presented; for example, length 25.8, should be read as 25 feet, 8 inches; construction time, 2y 5m as 2 years and 5 months.

Part I
Australia

The Great War 1914–1918

AUSTRALIA'S LARGEST and most prestigious warship of the Great War was, without doubt, the Indefatigable class battle-cruiser, AUSTRALIA. The 21,300 ton ship was fleet flagship and had been in commission a little over twelve months. On 4th October, 1913 she led the new RAN fleet unit into Port Jackson for the first time.

AUSTRALIA was sixth British-built battlecruiser to enter service after the three ship Invincible class. She was designed to use her high speed and large 12 inch guns to seek out and destroy enemy cruisers. This speed enabled her to remain clear of any more powerful capital ships.

As the war progressed it was found necessary to remove two of the ship's 4 inch guns and mount a single 4 inch anti-aircraft gun atop the after-superstructure. The cumbersome torpedo nets and booms originally fitted were also deleted.

First Lord of the Admiralty, Winston Churchill suggested that AUSTRALIA be deployed to the Atlantic Ocean, but the ship was retained in local waters from fear of Von Spee's squadron and its two armoured cruisers. AUSTRALIA's range of 6,300 miles at a speed of ten knots gave her sufficient radius of action in the search (albeit unsuccessful) for the German ships and on subsequent war patrols.

After sailing to Europe in January, 1915, AUSTRALIA served as flagship of the Second Battlecruiser Squadron of the Grand Fleet, returning home in June, 1919. With another two

Three units of the RAN fleet preparing to anchor in Farm Cove. From left, HMAS AUSTRALIA, HMAS MELBOURNE, and HMAS SYDNEY. (Photo – B. Alsop Collection).

years service as flagship of the RAN behind her, AUSTRALIA paid off to reserve and was scuttled on 12th April, 1924, in accordance with warship limitations imposed by the 1922 Washington Naval Treaty.

Cruisers

The only cruiser to operate with the Commonwealth Naval Forces between 1904 and 1911 was the former South Australian ship PROTECTOR. During this period she was the only suitable vessel for sea training and accordingly maintained a tight schedule.

By the outbreak of war in 1914, the RAN's cruiser force was a mixture of old and new construction. Two new light cruisers were in commission with another pair scheduled to join the fleet. Three were former Royal Navy ships transferred to Australia and another was requisitioned from the Pacific and Orient Steam Navigation Company for conversion to an auxiliary.

In addition to the thirty year old PROTECTOR, the oldest ships to partake in the war were the 1900 vintage Pelorus class light cruisers PIONEER and PSYCHE. The most heavily armed cruiser of the war was ENCOUNTER, fitted with eleven 6-inch guns. Next came the Town class which comprised SYDNEY, MELBOURNE and BRISBANE. Because of their youth and 'modern armament' the trio operated in most of the combat areas in which the RAN was called upon to assist.

The RAN's only auxiliary cruiser of the 1914–18 war, BERRIMA, was employed primarily as a troop-transport, although she had been designated an Armed Merchant Cruiser.

Torpedo-Boat Destroyers

Three British-built and three Australian-built torpedo-boat destroyers were introduced into service between 1910 and 1916. PARRAMATTA and YARRA were originally ordered for the Commonwealth Naval Forces and, along with the remnants of the former Colonial navies, were integrated into the RAN in 1911.

The River or 'I' class TBDs were the ninth destroyer class built for the Royal Navy. The third Australian unit, WARREGO, was built in sections by Fairfield in England and assembled at the Cockatoo Island Dockyard in Sydney to give experience to local shipbuilders.

During the course of the war the six Rivers operated in the Pacific Ocean, northern Australian waters and Mediterranean Sea, providing escort, patrol and search and destroy missions, as well as working with other allied naval units. PARRAMATTA, YARRA and HUON were fitted with captive balloons during May, 1918, when in the Adriatic Sea. The balloons were flown from the boats with observers aloft to detect submarines and direct the TBDs to the enemy. During one of these operations HUON and YARRA collided.

Despite extensive wartime service, the six Rivers remained in the post-war fleet, HUON surviving as a training ship until June, 1928. They were replaced in the fleet by the larger ANZAC and five S class destroyers. Ironically, ANZAC and the S boats saw little service and by 1937 had all been sold for scrap, only nine years after the vessels they replaced had been laid up.

Sloops

No new sloop entered service between 1914 and 1918. Only UNA (captured) and FANTOME (transferred from the Royal Navy) saw active service.

Submarines

Following the loss early in the conflict of both AE1 and AE2, submarine activity in the RAN came to an abrupt end. The depot ship PLATYPUS under construction in the United Kingdom, was retained in the European area and arrived in Australia with a new generation of boats in 1919.

Mine Warfare Ships

The laying of mines by the German raider WOLF in Australian coastal waters during the early war period led to the requisitioning of three tugs specially fitted for minesweeping, and three Castle class minesweeping trawlers belonging to the New South Wales Government.

Operations conducted along the New South Wales and Victorian coasts netted more than a dozen of the German mines. After sweeps by the vessels in late 1917/early 1918 and September/October, 1918, the patrol craft COOGEE joined the force off Gabo Island in January, 1919.

Neither the converted tugs nor Castle class trawlers were retained in the post-war fleet. However, in 1919 the RAN acquired the three Flower class minesweeping sloops as part of the 'Gift Fleet'.

Patrol Craft

Of the thirteen patrol vessels available for service in the Great War, only eight were actively employed. The others, primarily ex-colonial warships, were either restricted to patrols within Port Phillip, (COUNTESS OF HOPETOUN and CHILDERS), were too old (CERBERUS) or had been ordered for disposal (LONSDALE and NEPEAN).

Only GAYUNDAH, the former Queensland gunboat provided coastal surveillance to the fleet, operating on the eastern seaboard until 1918. The other patrol craft, either requisitioned locally or captured in German New Guinea gave varying lengths of service. MOURILYAN operated for only seven months but NUSA lasted seven years. Most of the requisitioned or captured ships were unsuitable for patrol work as they carried only a flimsy gun armament with no protection for crew members. A 3 pounder

HMAS AUSTRALIA in the North Sea, 1915.

gun was hastily mounted in SLEUTH's bow while the tiny NUSA was given one 12 pounder weapon.

MOURILYAN, COOGEE and SUMATRA, were capable of carrying additional weapons but because of short supply these could not be mounted.

Supporting the auxiliary patrol craft were four examination vessels, CAPTAIN COOK (II), working from Sydney, OTTER from Brisbane, AJAX from Newcastle and ALVINA from Melbourne. They were only required to stop and search ships entering port and so were not armed. A number of small craft were also employed in the role.

No new construction patrol-type vessels were ordered or acquired and by 1919 only two remained with the fleet, albeit in reserve. CAPTAIN COOK (II) survived to World War II when she was requisitioned by the Australian Army as a training ship. In 1945 she was used by cadets on Snapper Island until scuttled off Sydney in October, 1947.

Support

To assist the fleet on its early missions in the South Pacific and northern Australian waters, the RAN commenced the requisi-

tioning of sufficient numbers of privately owned merchant ships while instituting a new construction programme for a built-for-the-purpose fleet train comprising such ships as the collier BILOELA, depot ship PLATYPUS and oiler KURUMBA.

However, the majority of support ships were former merchant ships, some purchased outright by the RAN and others taken on only for short periods.

Eight ships were requisitioned as auxiliaries (including one conversion cancelled) and another three purchased. Former colonial vessels comprised another two ships. TINGIRA, HANKOW, RIPPLE and PENGUIN were already in service at the outbreak of the war. Generally the requisitioned tonnage served only six months to a year, the need for their services lessening in the mid war period after the major part of the fleet had transferred to the European theatre.

The Great War also saw the short career of the RAN's only hospital ship, GRANTALA, outfitted at Garden Island for service in New Guinea and Suva.

Four 1914–18 auxiliaries, PLATYPUS, KURUMBA, FRANKLIN and RIPPLE, survived the mid-war down-turn in the fleet to 'fight again' in the Second World War.

12-inch guns aboard the flagship,
HMAS AUSTRALIA.

1911

JULY

A ROYAL PROCLOMATION

The Royal Australian Navy was officially created on 10th July, 1911, when His Majesty, King George V, granted the title to the naval forces of the Commonwealth of Australia. It was decreed that all ships of the fleet would fly the White Ensign and be known as His Majesty's Australian Ships. The citizen naval forces received the official designation RAN Reserve.

OCTOBER

FLAGSHIP LAUNCHED

The RAN's first flagship, the battlecruiser AUSTRALIA, was launched at the shipyards of John Brown and Company on the Clyde on 25th October. At 21,300 tons she was the largest and most powerful warship ever built for the nation.

1912

APRIL

TRAINING AFLOAT

To fulfill the important task of training personnel to man the new fleet, the former clipper ship SOBRAON was purchased for use as a boys' training ship. She was renamed TINGIRA and commissioned on 25th April. About the same time Williamstown was selected as the receiving point for new recruits and to satisfy early training requirements.

The RAN's first flagship, the battlecruiser AUSTRALIA on the slipway prior to launching.

Vessels incorporated from the Colonial Fleets

Name	Colony	Type	Age	Status
Cerberus	Vic	Turret ship	41	Depot duties
Protector	S.A.	Light cruiser	27	Training
Gayundah	Qld	Gunboat	27	Training
Paluma	Qld	Gunboat	27	Laid up
Countess of Hopetoun	Vic	Torpedo boat (1st class)	19	Patrol
Childers	Vic	Torpedo boat (1st class)	27	Laid up
Lonsdale & Nepean	Vic	Torpedo boats (2nd class)	27	Hulks
Mosquito	Qld	Torpedo boat (2nd class)	27	Training
TB No 191	S.A.	Torpedo boat (2nd class)	27	Training/hulk
Gordon	Vic	Torpedo boat (turnabout)	27	Depot duties
Midge	Qld	Torpedo boat (turnabout)	24	Training

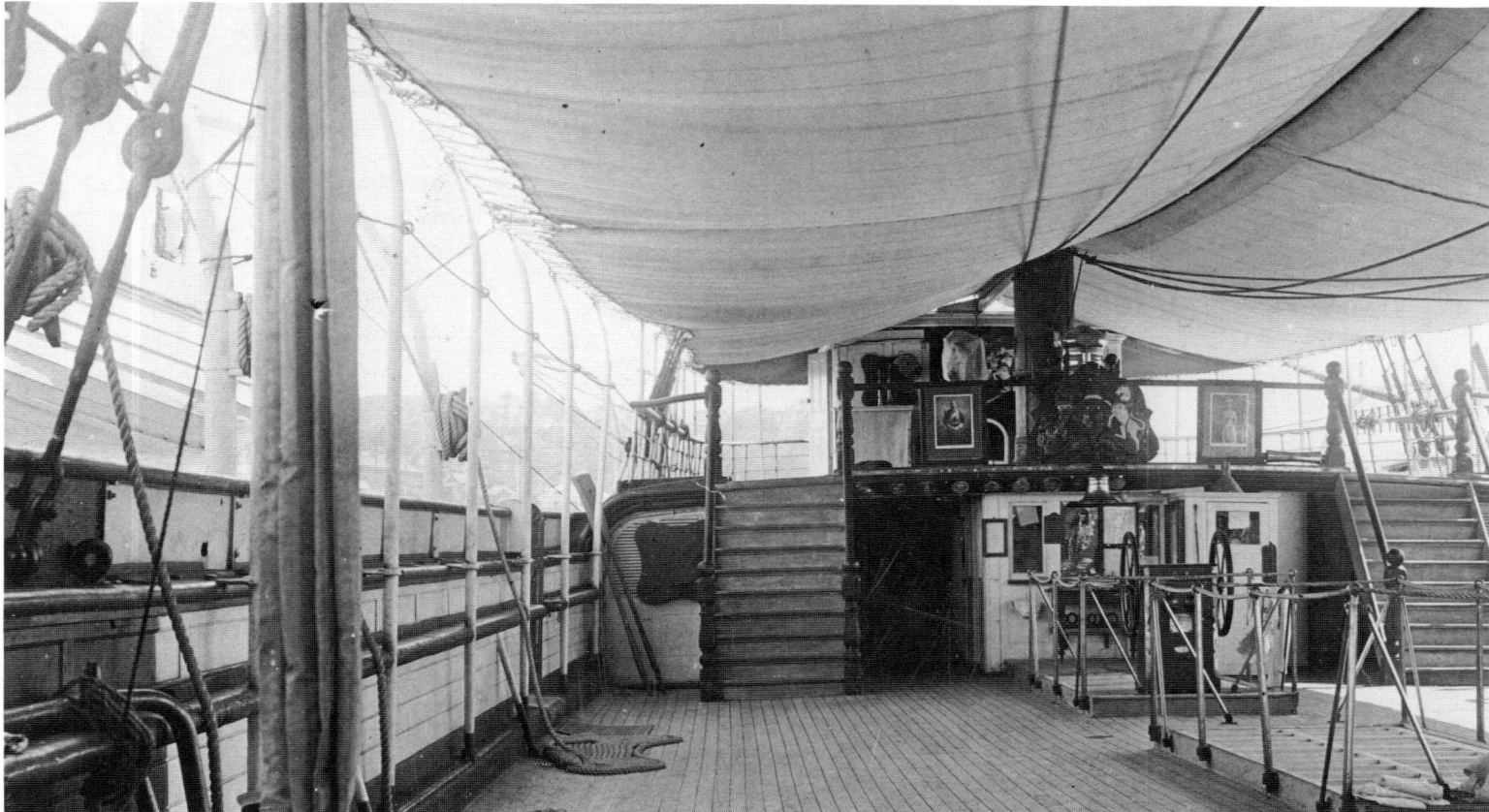
Aboard the boys' training ship HMAS TINGIRA. (Photo – J. Straczek).

JUNE

TORPEDO BOAT DESTROYERS

The most effective units of the RAN, PARRAMATTA and YARRA, were joined by the first Australian-built TBD, WARREGO, when she commissioned on 1st June. Originally built in the United Kingdom, the vessel was dismantled there and then re-assembled in Sydney.

JULY

'ENCOUNTER' ON LOAN

To assist in the training role and to fill the gap until the new construction BRISBANE was commissioned, the seven-year old light cruiser ENCOUNTER was transferred on loan from the Royal Navy.

1913

MARCH

NEW CRUISER TONNAGE

The 5,400 ton MELBOURNE, the first light cruiser to be constructed for the RAN, arrived in Fremantle from Britain on 10th March.

OCTOBER

ARRIVAL OF THE FLEET

Following completion of the flagship AUSTRALIA and a second light cruiser, SYDNEY, the two ships sailed for home in July, 1913, via St. Helena, Capetown and Mauritius.

The first ceremonial entry of the RAN into Sydney Harbour was on 4th October. Port Jackson was filled with craft of every type as the battlecruiser led the cruisers

HMCS PARRAMATTA as a unit of the Commonwealth Naval Forces. (Photo – B. Alsop Collection).

MELBOURNE, SYDNEY and ENCOUNTER and the torpedo-boat destroyers WARREGO, PARRAMATTA and YARRA into harbour as a complete fleet unit. Prime Minister Joseph Cook hailed the arrival as the Navy's coming of age.

SYDNEY immediately after launch, 29th August, 1912.

OUR SHIPS COME IN.

BRITANNIA: "Congratulations, daughter! It is a proud day for both of us."

Some fleet arrival propaganda.

1914

MAY

NEW ADDITIONS

The Australian fleet received its first submarines when AE1 and AE2 arrived in Sydney on 24th May. The two boats had reached Singapore with only minor troubles, but after leaving for home, AE1 lost all power and had to be towed by the accompanying cruiser SYDNEY. Later she was almost rammed by her sister ship AE2.

AUGUST

OUTBREAK OF WAR

'ZAMBESI' CAPTURED

The day after the outbreak of war on the 5th August, the training ship/light cruiser

RAN Fleet strength – 5th August 1914

Ships	Class	Type	Knots	Age	Principal Armament
Australia	Indefatigable	Battlecruiser	25	1	Eight 12 inch
Protector	Protector	Light cruiser	14	30	Two 4 inch
Encounter	Challenger	Light cruiser	21	8	Eleven 6 inch
Melbourne & Sydney	Town	Light cruisers	25	1	Eight 6 inch
Parramatta, Warrego & Yarra	River	Torpedo-boat destroyers	28	3	One 4 inch / Three 18 inch torpedoes
AE1 & AE2	Australian E	Submarines	15	.5	Four 18 inch torpedo tubes
Countess of Hopetoun	First	Torpedo boat	20	23	Three 14 inch torpedo tubes
Childers	First	Torpedo boat	20	30	One 14 inch torpedo tube
Gayundah & Paluma	Third	Gunboats	10	30	One 4.7 inch (Gay) / One 6 inch (Pal)
Lonsdale & Nepean	Second	Torpedo boats	16	30	Two 14 inch torpedoes
Tingira	–	Training	–	46	–
Penguin	–	Depot	–	37	–
Hankow	–	Collier	–	–	–

Fleet disposition – 5th August 1914

Ships	Location	Status
Australia	En route Sydney to Northern Australia	Active
Protector	Port Phillip to Port Jackson	Active
Encounter	Sydney	Refit
Melbourne	En route Sydney to Western Australia	Active
Sydney	Thursday Island	Active
Parramatta	En route Sydney to Townsville	Active
Warrego	Thursday Island	Active
Yarra	Thursday Island	Active
AE1	Sydney	Refit
AE2	Sydney	Refit
Cerberus	Williamstown	Alongside
Countess of Hopetoun	Port Phillip	Active
Childers	Port Phillip	Active
Gayundah	En route Sydney to Brisbane	Active
Paluma	Williamstown	Alongside
Lonsdale	Swan Island	For disposal
Nepean	Swan Island	For disposal
Tingira	Sydney	Alongside
Penguin	Sydney	Alongside
Hankow	Sydney	Alongside

ENCOUNTER sailed from Port Jackson to join the flagship AUSTRALIA in St. Georges Channel, New Guinea. Seven

ZAMBEZI; Captured at Rabaul by HMAS ENCOUNTER, 12th August, 1914.

days later she intercepted and captured the ZAMBESI, a British steamer which had been commandeered by Nauru's German administrator to carry materials to Rabaul for the completion of a wireless station. ZAMBESI was sent to Sydney as a prize.

SEARCHING FOR THE ENEMY

When war was declared the German Pacific Squadron, comprising the 11,600 ton cruisers GNEISENAU and SCHARNHORST (flagship of Admiral Von Spee), the cruisers EMDEN, LEIPZIG and NURNBERG, sloop KORMORAN and survey ship PLANET vanished from the sight of Australian and Royal Navy forces.

Admiral Patey, in charge of the Australian fleet, received intelligence reports that the Germans had established a coaling station at Simpson Harbour, New Britain. Accordingly, AUSTRALIA joined ENCOUNTER, SYDNEY and the three torpedo-boat destroyers for an attack on the harbour. Confident of finding the German fleet, SYDNEY led the three TBDs into Simpson Harbour, while YARRA investigated Matupi Harbour and her sister ships went on to Rabaul. No trace of the enemy was found.

SUCCESS FOR 'PIONEER'

August proved a very busy period for the cruiser PIONEER. On the 16th she captured the German liner NEUMUNSTER about eight miles west of Rottnest Island, Western Australia, and eight days later, ten miles south-west of the island, found the THURINGEN, which she captured and escorted to Fremantle.

GERMAN NEW GUINEA OCCUPIED

The force sent to occupy New Guinea was a combination of naval and military personnel. The former provided a contingent of 500 men comprising six companies.

The expedition sailed from Sydney on 19th August aboard the auxiliary cruiser BERRIMA to team up with the KANOWNA (an AUSN vessel) at Port Moresby. BERRIMA, escorted by SYDNEY, proceeded from Sandy Cape to Palm Island to await orders. Here the force was joined by ENCOUNTER on 23rd August, the store carrier AORANGI on 30th August and the submarines AE1 and AE2. The latter were accompanied by the light cruiser PROTECTOR and UPOLU a depot ship, both of which had been delayed and were ordered to join the convoy later at Simpson Harbour.

The convoy left for Port Moresby on 2nd September, but after sailing from that port crew members aboard KANOWNA mutinied and refused to take the ship any further. With a volunteer crew drawn from the troops onboard, she turned back. It was decided that the expedition should carry on using only BERRIMA and her embarked troops.

By 9th September the occupation force, including AUSTRALIA back from the occupation of Samoa, had come together. Rabaul and the area bounded on the southern shore of the St. Georges Channel were occupied and a naval party from the cruiser SYDNEY was detailed to locate and destroy the wireless station at Bita-paka.

The officer in charge managed to persuade the German defence force that his group was merely the scouting party for a large contingent of 800 men. The local Commander withdrew his forces inland then left only small parties of defenders behind. The German party eventually surrendered after being out-flanked by reinforcements from WARREGO.

KOMET returned to her hide-out at Komethafen. On being informed of the possibility that KOMET was in harbour, NUSA was detailed to locate and capture her. With the help of a local guide, NUSA proceeded to the hideout. Surprise was complete as she was able to sail within fifty yards of KOMET without detection. KOMET was sent to Rabaul and then on to Sydney for refitting at Cockatoo Dockyard, where she commissioned into the Royal Australian Navy as UNA, 'the only one'.

NOVEMBER

THE FIRST CONVOY

After many delays, the first transport convoy met at Fremantle in late 1914, with MELBOURNE, SYDNEY, MINOTAUR and the Japanese IBUKI as escorts. The convoy left the Western Australian port on 1st November.

During passage MINOTAUR was detached to the Cape Squadron as von Spee's fleet was reported to be proceeding to that area. The day following her departure the convoy was alerted by two radio messages, the first in an unknown code, which later proved to be from the German raider EMDEN to her collier, and the other from the Cocos Island wireless station reporting the presence of a three-funnelled warship.

MELBOURNE ordered SYDNEY to the island at full speed. Approximately two

A pre-war view of the German cruiser EMDEN. (Photo – P. Britz).

EMDEN; 'beached and done for', November, 1914.

hours later SYDNEY's lookouts sighted the island and the raider. Soon after sighting EMDEN, SYDNEY reduced speed. Firing opened at a distance of about six miles, with EMDEN commencing action at extreme range. Although EMDEN closed in, she was offered only a small target with SYDNEY, steaming head-on.

The Australian cruiser opened fire and scored her first hit with the third salvo. Aboard EMDEN, the German Captain realising his only chance of success was in rapid fire, sent off a salvo every six seconds. SYDNEY turned away slightly and, making full use of her superior speed and strength, scored further hits, damaging the raider's wireless room, steering gear, forward funnel, the voice pipes used to control the guns and both range finders. Soon after, the raider's second funnel was struck and her engine room set on fire. Further hits blew the third funnel overboard.

EMDEN was ordered to maximum speed so that she could be beached ashore on nearby Cocos Island. SYDNEY fired two further salvoes to render the German harmless and turned her attention to the enemy collier BURESK, which had arrived on the scene. However, before SYDNEY could take her, BURESK was scuttled by her own crew.

SYDNEY was soon ordered back to Cocos Island and requested EMDEN's surrender. When no reply was received SYDNEY opened fire. EMDEN surrendered promptly.

DECEMBER

SAILING THE SEPIK

Reports persisted of small German detachments, and auxiliary cruisers in the New Guinea region. In response YARRA, WARREGO and PARRAMANTTA sailed to Friedrich Wilhelm Harbour and blocked the mouth of the Sepik River. An expedition proceeded inland to clear out the missions and odd individuals remaining in the area.

The three destroyers subsequently searched the New Guinea coast and transported relief troops to the garrisons set up at Aitape and Angorum. The ships remained on this duty until February, 1915, when they left for Sydney.

1915

JANUARY

FLAGSHIP TO EUROPE

On New Year's Day, 1915, AUSTRALIA damaged her propellers while transitting the Straits of Magellan en route to England. With speed cut by fifty percent she made for the Falkland Islands for repairs. Not long after leaving the Falklands AUSTRALIA spotted a suspicious ship on the horizon, and gave chase. Although still hampered by the faulty propeller, AUSTRALIA was forced to open fire while still ten miles astern. However, the twelve inch salvoes soon brought the vessel to a halt. Upon boarding she was identified as ELEONORE WOERMAN, an auxiliary of the German raiders.

With insufficient crew to man the captured ship as a prize, AUSTRALIA took aboard the German crew and sank her.

AUSTRALIA visited St. Vincent before arriving at Plymouth on 28th January, 1915. Later she proceeded to Rosyth to join the 2nd Battlecruiser Squadron. During the following months she maintained patrols in the North Sea with the other ships of her squadron and the Grand Fleet.

FEBRUARY

EAST AFRICA

PIONEER arrived at Zanzibar, German East Africa, on 6th February, 1915, following Admiralty orders of 24th December,

HMAS WARREGO in the Sepik River, December, 1914.

1914, to operate as a blockade ship against the German cruiser KONIGSBERG. It had been intended to augment PIONEER with the escort PROTECTOR in these operations. However it was found unacceptable to mount modern 6-inch guns aboard the ship and ammunition for her old guns had been mostly destroyed.

En route from Fremantle PIONEER also inspected the wreck of EMDEN at Cocos Island.

Upon her arrival in Zanzibar, the RAN ship was given charge of the northern coastal areas and, with the Royal Navy cruiser HYACINTH, bombarded the mouth of the Rufugi River with over 600 6-inch shells, in an effort to drive KONIGSBERG out of hiding. The attack was resumed on 12th July and the German ship destroyed.

APRIL

THROUGH THE NARROWS

Following the loss of AE1, her sister AE2, was recalled from the Pacific and, after some indecision, offered for use to the Admiralty. The boat left Albany on 31st December 1914, under tow of BERRIMA, with a convoy heading for the Middle East.

AE2 arrived to find preparations under way for the forcing of the Dardanelles. Her one abortive foray resulted in her return to Malta for repairs to the hull.

Turkish torpedo boat SULTAN HISSAR.

The Australian submarine's attempt to reach the Sea of Marmora on 25th April, 1915, was however more successful. In the evening of 25th, a message from AE2 was received that she had passed through the Narrows. Five days later (30th) after an incredible series of adventures, AE2 was forced to the surface following repeated attacks by the Turkish torpedo boat SULTAN HISSAR. After scuttling the submarine the crew were taken prison by the Turks.

HMAS FANTOME.

JULY

FANTOME RECOMMISSIONED

The urgent need for suitable warships for patrol work in the Indian Ocean led to the re-activation of the old sloop FANTOME on 27th July. Originally ordered to the Persian Gulf, FANTOME was diverted to the Bay of Bengal to patrol with PSYCHE. Later in January, 1916, the sloop sailed to Sandakan in British Borneo.

1916
APRIL
COLLISIONS

AUSTRALIA arrived for North Sea Service in January, 1915, and became flagship of the 2nd Battlecruiser Squadron. On the night of 22nd April, the Grand Fleet was supporting a light cruiser sweep

The flagship in Scottish waters 1917.

in the Skagerrak when a series of mishaps took place. Three destroyers collided, a neutral merchant ship hit a battleship, and AUSTRALIA collided with NEW ZEALAND during zig-zagging. Both battlecruisers were damaged and had to return to port. Upon inspection it was found that AUSTRALIA required at least two months in dockyard. Accordingly she proceeded to Devonport to be drydocked.

Later on 12th December, 1917, AUSTRALIA was again damaged after colliding with the battlecruiser REPULSE. She then spent a further 3 weeks in dock under repair.

OCTOBER

PUNITIVE EXPEDITION TO NEW HEBRIDES

On 10th October, UNA sailed from Rabaul for Vila in the New Hebrides where she joined the French gunboat KERSAINT. Both ships landed troops at nearby Malikula where they were faced by rebellious natives. The expedition was abandoned after casualties to Australian, French and New Guinea personnel, and the ships sailed back to Vila. Here 40 percent of UNA's crew were struck down by malaria. UNA returned to Sydney on 26th November.

A subsequent expedition in late September, 1918, involved the French warship KERSAINT and FANTOME with the RAN ship landing 65 officers and men. Eventually the rebels were put down.

NOVEMBER

NORTH SEA PATROLS

In November, SYDNEY and MELBOURNE joined the 2nd Light Cruiser Squadron at Rosyth, from where they patrolled in the North Sea. When working with the capital ships they operated with the 2nd Battlecruiser Squadron.

HMAS MELBOURNE in the North Sea. Note the aircraft forward of the bridge structure.

The main object of the patrols was to prevent minor enemy ships laying mines off the naval bases and trade ports. The ships suffered damage and casualties from appalling weather, particularly in winter Experimental work on submarine detection was carried out with a special type of paravane built to explode either on contact or by remote control.

1917

APRIL

SEAPLANE EMBARKED ON 'BRISBANE'

The first Australian-built cruiser BRISBANE sailed for the Mediterranean in December, 1916. Following an alarm that the raider WOLF was active in the Indian Ocean, BRISBANE was despatched to the area and arrived in Colombo in April, 1917, to join the Royal Navy seaplane carrier RAVEN II.

The latter embarked Short 184 seaplanes and a Sopwith 'Baby' Seaplane. To make the searching forces more effective, it was decided that RAVEN II patrol the Maldive Islands with the Short seaplanes, while BRISBANE would embark a Sopwith 'Baby.' A derrick was provided for loading and unloading the craft.

Although the Allied search for WOLF proved unsuccessful, BRISBANE'S aircraft made two flights daily for some weeks. The cruiser relinquished her aircraft in June upon being ordered back to Australia.

JUNE

TORPEDO BOAT DESTROYERS TO MEDITERRANEAN

During June and July, the six River class torpedo boat destroyers sailed for the Mediterranean. En route to Malta all six were deployed as convoy escorts, PARRAMATTA reporting the sinking of an enemy submarine. Following a training period the boats formed a new patrol to search for enemy warships on the eastern seaboard of the Adriatic Sea.

DECEMBER
FURTHER AIRCRAFT EXPERIMENTS

After the successful trials aboard BRISBANE, both SYDNEY and MELBOURNE acquired seaplanes which were launched from a specially built revolving platform above the gun turrets. SYDNEY's first successful launch took place on 8th December, 1917, MELBOURNE's during March, 1918. Both cruisers employed their Sopwith 'Camels' during action in the Heligoland Bight in June, 1918.

The battlecruiser AUSTRALIA was also fitted with an aircraft platform atop the starboard 12-inch turret and she launched a two-seat Sopwith on 4th April, 1918, and again on 14th May, the first occasions a two-seater had flown off a ship's gun turret.

1918
NOVEMBER
SURRENDER

Life aboard AUSTRALIA became extremely dull during the latter part of the war, although the tedium had been relieved in March and May, 1918, by the experiments in launching aircraft from her gun turret.

When the German Fleet was ordered to sail to the Firth of Forth to surrender, the entire Grand Fleet was drawn up in two lines to receive them. AUSTRALIA, at the head of her squadron, led the capital ships of the British port line; MELBOURNE and SYDNEY were with their squadron. As each German ship arrived it was placed under the charge of a Royal Navy ship. AUSTRALIA was given custody over HINDENBURG, MELBOURNE over the NURNBERG, and SYDNEY over the EMDEN.

NOVEMBER
RAN STRENGTH

Peak war personnel levels were attained in 1918, with 5,050 officers and men. By June, 1919, the number had risen to 5,250. These figures compared to 3,800 at the outbreak of war.

DECEMBER
HOMEWARD BOUND

In December, arrangements were finalised for the RAN ships to return to Australia. MELBOURNE, accompanied by KURUMBA, sailed for home in February, 1919, AUSTRALIA, SYDNEY, BRISBANE and the depot ship PLATYPUS in April.

The destroyers were directed back to Australia despite their involvement in a series of operations in the Black Sea in support of White Russian forces following the Armistice.

Fleet list

Type	Strength 11/1918	Lost 1914/18	To be Completed
Battlecruiser	1	–	–
Cruiser	5	–	1
Torpedo Boat Destroyer	6	–	–
Sloops	2	–	–
Submarines	–	2	–
Mine Warfare Ships	2	–	–
Patrol Craft	6	–	–
Examination Vessels	4	–	–
Colliers	1	–	1
Requisitioned Colliers	–	–	–
Depot Ships	2	–	–
Lighters	4	–	–
Oilers	1	–	–
Special Service Vessel	–	–	1
Tenders	3	1	–
Training Ships	2	–	–

HMAS AUSTRALIA, 1919
(Photo – Sydney Maritime Museum).

LIFE ON BOARD

Visit of Prime Minister Billy Hughes.

HMAS AUSTRALIA's coaling party. (Photo – H. Adlam).

Washing day.

Ship's Band.

The stoker's fire party.

Snow fight at Scapa Flow.

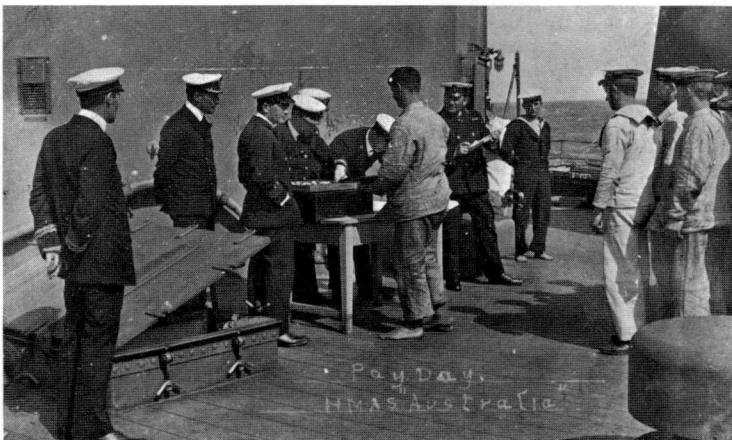

Pay day.

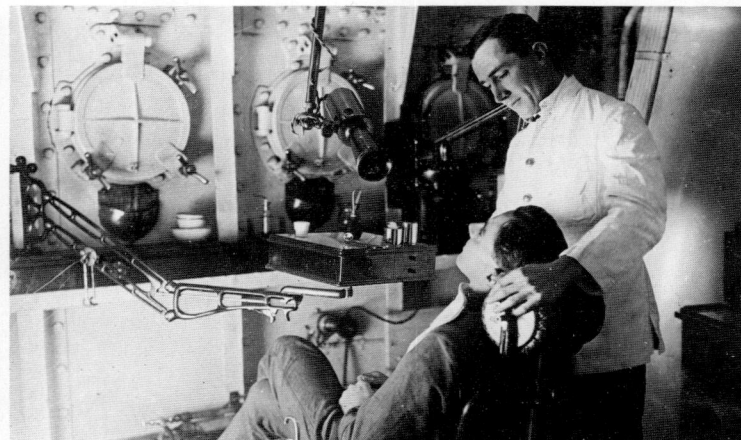

The flagship's dentist.

INDEFATIGABLE CLASS

Australia

AUSTRALIA developed from the earlier Invincible class of battlecruisers, still carried the same weak protection in a larger hull, thereby creating a larger target. Like the earlier trio, the ship was fitted with a main turret arrangement intended to provide the maximum broadside fire. The turrets were mounted fore and aft with the second pair 'en enchelon' amidships. To allow these turrets to cross fire, the superstructure was modified to allow each gun an arc of fire over the opposite beam of ten degrees. Six inch armour protected the deck and 7 inches on the main armament.

During the course of the Great War, the number of 4-inch guns was reduced. Initially two of the weapons were deleted and a 4-inch anti-aircraft mount was added atop the after superstructure to meet the new challenge from the air. A further 4-inch gun was also added at the stern.

Another modification made to the battlecruiser included the removal of the troublesome anti-torpedo netting. During December, 1917, trials were undertaken launching a 'Sopwith Pup' from the deck and in March/April, 1918, with a '1½ Strutter' from a specially-built platform on Q turret. On 22nd October, 1918, the ship operated two Sopwith 'Camels' from the two midship turrets.

Following four years of strenuous war service from the Pacific to the Atlantic, AUSTRALIA returned home to Sydney on 15th June, 1919. A highlight of her brief postwar service occurred in May, 1920, when she led the RAN fleet for review by the Prince of Wales in Port Phillip Bay. Later in 1920 she embarked an Avro 504k aircraft, stored aft at Q turret on the main deck.

AUSTRALIA was decommissioned on 12th December, 1921, and remained in reserve until April, 1924. On 12th of the month, the eleven year old flagship was ceremoniously scuttled off Sydney in 150 fathoms, 24 miles from Inner South Head.

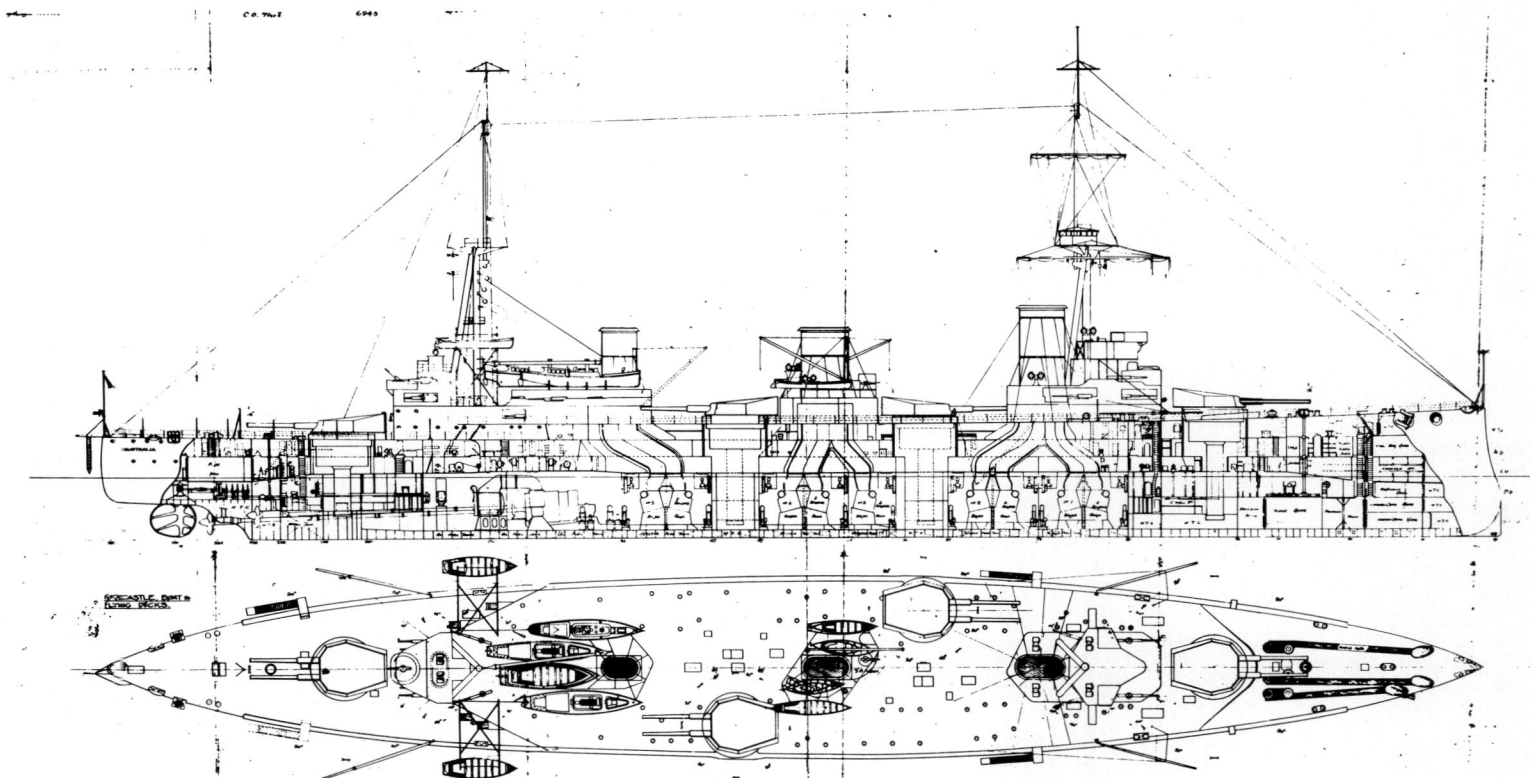

HMAS AUSTRALIA; general arrangement plans; (Naval Ship Design Section)

Displacement (tons): *Standard* 18,800 *Full Load* 21,300
Dimensions (feet): *Length* 590 *Beam* 80 *Draught* 30
Machinery: Parsons turbines, 4 shafts, 43,000 shp
Speed (knots): 25
Range (miles): 6,300 at 10 knots
Manning: 820
Armament: Eight 12-inch (4 × 2), Sixteen 4-inch (16 × 1), Four 3 pdr. (4 × 1), Five MG, Two 18-inch torpedo tubes (submerged) (2 × 1).

Ship	Pend No.	Builder	Cons. Time	Comp.	Fate
Australia	C6 (2/1915) O9 (1/1918) 81 (4/1918)	J. Brown	3 y	21/6/13	Scuttled 12/4/24

AUSTRALIA's forward 12-inch gun mounting being lowered into position during construction.

HMAS AUSTRALIA in Sydney Harbour.

HMAS AUSTRALIA in the Suez Canal. Note the single 4-inch gun and twin 36-inch searchlights above the 12-inch mounting. Two other 4-inch guns protrude just below the open mount.

Left – Detailed view of the main 12-inch guns and bridge super-structure. Seven 4-inch guns are also visible. Note the searchlights abreast the bridge.

Below – HMAS AUSTRALIA in Farm Cove, Sydney, just after the outbreak of war and taking aboard supplies.

Bottom – Her final voyage; AUSTRALIA is towed from Sydney to be ceremonially scuttled on 12th April 1924.

COLONIAL LIGHT CRUISER

Protector

Despite her age and lack of modern equipment PROTECTOR was still considered suitable for war service at late as 1914. During the following four years the ship operated as a parent ship to the submarines AE1 and AE2 and later used her 4 inch guns to good effect as port guard ship at Rabaul.

Following the destruction of the German cruiser EMDEN, PROTECTOR was ordered to the Cocos Islands to report on the wreck before assuming tender duties at Western Port in January, 1916. The old cruiser remained on these duties until 1st April 1921 when she was renamed CERBERUS. In 1924 she reverted to her original name and was laid up in June.

Eventually PROTECTOR was sold for £677.10s to Mr. J. Hill of Melbourne and in 1931 was resold to the Victorian Lighterage Company. Renamed SIDNEY she operated as a wool and coal lighter until requisitioned by the United States Army in July 1943. During her voyage to New Guinea in charge of Australia Army water transport personnel, she collided with a tug off Glad-

stone and broke adrift. To avoid her becoming a shipping hazard, the near eighty year old hull was beached ashore on Heron Island.

Displacement (tons): 920
Dimensions (feet): *Length* 180.6 *Beam* 30 *Draught* 12.6
Machinery: Two compound surface condensing engines, Twin screws, 1,500 hp
Speed (knots): 14
Range (miles): N/A
Manning: 90
Armament: Three 4 inch (3 × 1), Two 12 pdr. (2 × 1), Four 3 pdr (4 × 1).

Ship	Pend No.	Builder	Cons. Time	Comm.	Fate
Protector	–	W.M. Armstrong	–	19/6/84	Sold 1924

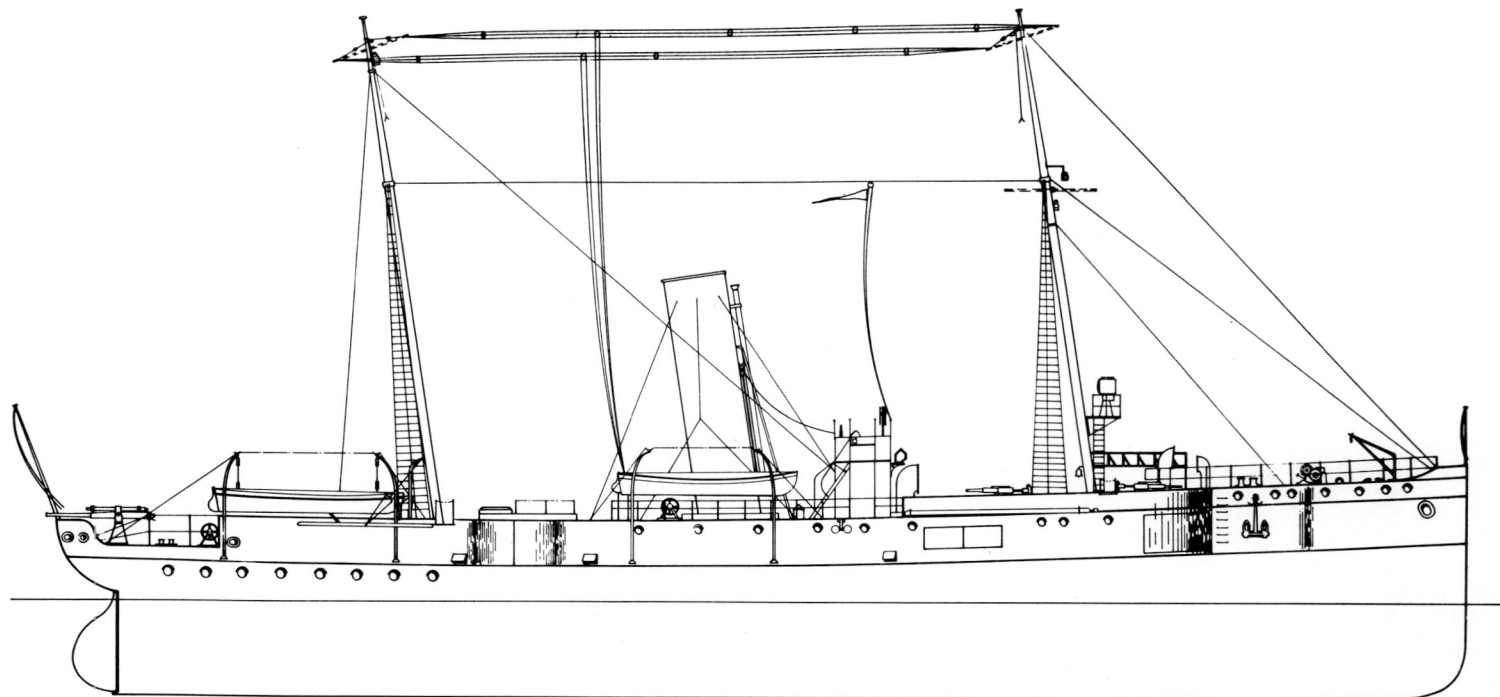

HMAS PROTECTOR, 1914; profile. (Naval Ship Design Section)

Top – HMCS PROTECTOR, as built. (Photo – S.A. State Library).

Above – HMAS PROTECTOR, 1920.

Left – HMAS PROTECTOR as she appeared in the Great War. The two forward 4-inch guns were removed for war duties.

CHALLENGER CLASS

Encounter

Upon completion, ENCOUNTER was rated as a second class protected cruiser, but in later years was given the light cruiser status. Her vital deck spaces and main guns were protected by three inch armour.

ENCOUNTER arrived in Australian waters in early 1906 to serve on station. On 1st July, 1912, she was loaned to and commissioned into the RAN as a sea-going training ship to undertake this duty until BRISBANE was completed. The ship served in the Great War as a combatant, initially in New Guinea, where she captured the German steamer ZAMBESI on 12th August, 1914. She subsequently served around Fiji, Borneo, Hong Kong and in the Indian Ocean.

The cruiser was presented outright to the RAN in December, 1919, but by this time she was operating as a training ship. During this period her two forward 6 inch guns sponsons on both sides were plated over. In the early 1920s, proposals were afoot to use her as a depot ship for the J class submarines. However, on 1st January, 1923, she was renamed PENGUIN, as a depot and receiving ship in Sydney and was not paid off until 15th August, 1929. Cockatoo Island stripped down the hull during 1930–31 and on 14th September, 1932, ENCOUNTER was sunk by naval gunfire off Sydney.

Displacement (tons): 5,880
Dimensions (feet): *Length* 372 *Beam* 56 *Draught* 20.8
Machinery: Triple expansion, twin screws, 13,000 IHP
Speed (knots): 21
Range (miles): N/A
Manning: 475
Armament: Eleven 6-inch (11 × 1), Nine 12 pdr. Six 3 pdr, Three MG, Two 18 inch torpedo tubes (2 × 1).

Ship	Pend. No.	Builder	Cons. Time	Comp.	Fate
Encounter	–	Devonport	4y 10m	21/11/05	Scuttled 14/9/32

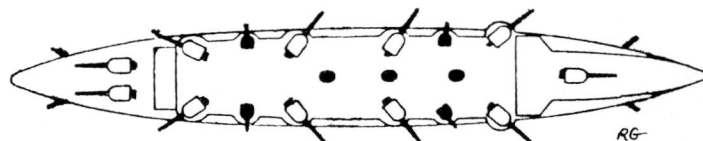

HMAS ENCOUNTER; armament plan 1914. (R. Gillett)

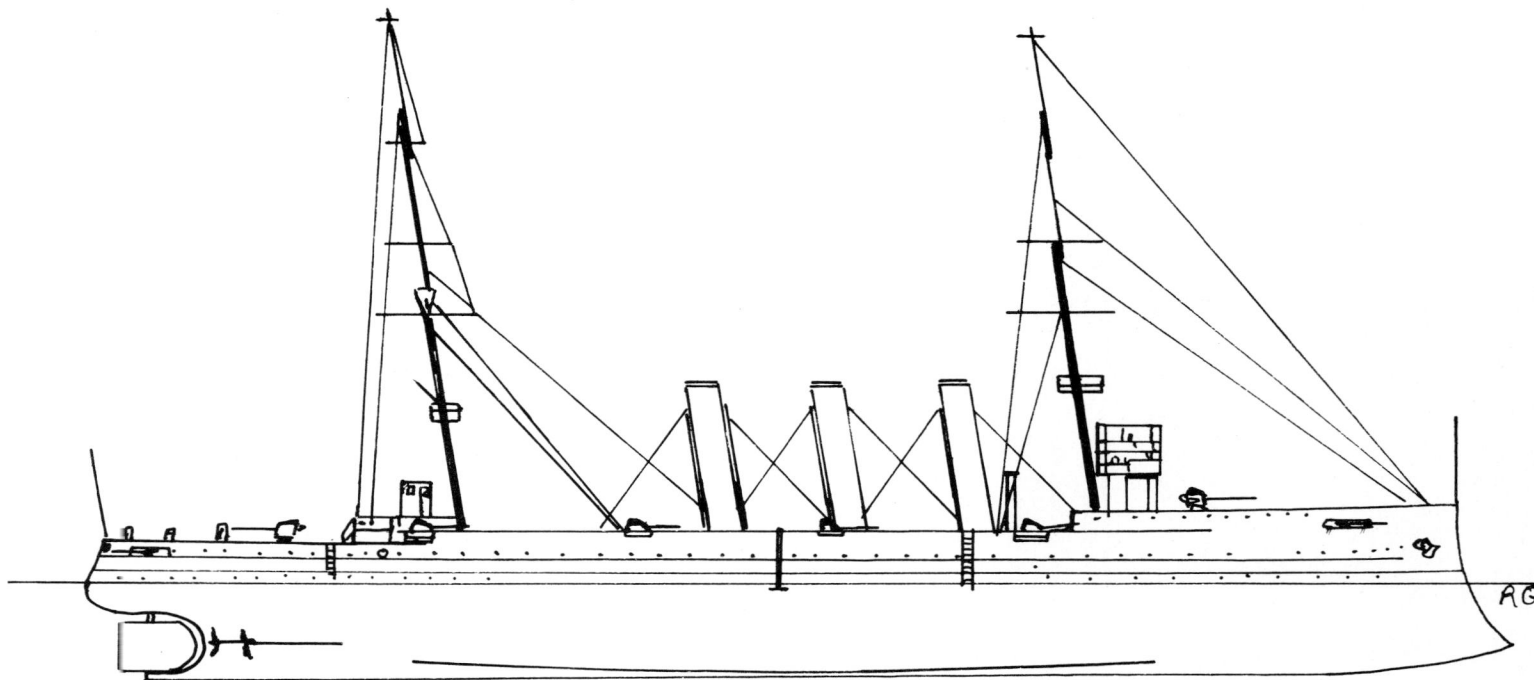

HMAS ENCOUNTER; profile. (R. Gillett)

Left – Onboard the captured SEEADLAR September, 1917, with HMAS ENCOUNTER in the background.

Below – HMAS ENCOUNTER.

Bottom – HMAS ENCOUNTER; two 6-inch guns are located on the poop and four on the port beam, (all trained forward). (Photo – Alexander Turnbull Library).

PELORUS CLASS

Pioneer, Psyche

Originally designated third class protected cruisers, PIONEER and PSYCHE served in the Royal Navy until March, 1915 and July, 1915 respectively. Both were then transferred to the RAN. PIONEER commissioned as an HMA Ship on 1st April, 1914 and PSYCHE on 1st July, 1915.

Both cruisers possessed an original design speed of 20 knots and carried two inch armour over the vital deck spaces. Although two 14 inch torpedoes were carried the tubes were not usually mounted and were racked up inside the quarterdeck.

During 1915 two of PSYCHE's 4 inch guns were removed to arm the sloop FANTOME. PIONEER lost four 3 pdr guns in 1916 and when laid up all armament was removed. By 1918 PSYCHE was armed with two 4.7 inch and two 3 pdr guns.

Despite their age, lack of speed and horrid living conditions PIONEER served in the Indian Ocean around German East Africa and Zanzibar and PSYCHE around Malaya, the Bay of Bengal and Hong Kong. PIONEER experienced more actual fighting and fired more rounds of ammunition than any other RAN ship in the Great War. Following her decommissioning on 7th November, 1916 the ship gave further service as an accommodation vessel at Garden Island until her sale in 1922.

On 20th November, 1917 PSYCHE was re-activated for patrol duties on the eastern seaboard but paid off again on 26th March, 1918. She was sold on 21st July, 1922 for use as a timber lighter.

PIONEER was towed to Cockatoo Island in May, 1923 to be broken up and on 18th February, 1931 her hull was finally scuttled off Sydney.

Displacement (tons): 2,135 (Psyche) 2,200 (Pioneer)
Dimensions (feet): *Length* 314 *Beam* 36.9 *Draught* 17
Machinery: Triple expansion, twin screws, 7,000 ihp
  Speed (knots): 16
  Range (miles): N/A
  Manning: 224
  Armament: Eight 4 inch (8 × 1), Eight 3 pdr (8 × 1), Three MG, Two 14 inch torpedo tubes (2 × 1).

Ships	Pend. No.	Builder	Cons. Time	Comp.	Fate
Pioneer	–	Chatham Dy	2y 11m	11/1900	Scuttled 2/31
Psyche	–	Devonport Dy	2y ?m	1900	Sold 7/22

PSYCHE. (Photo – S. Given).

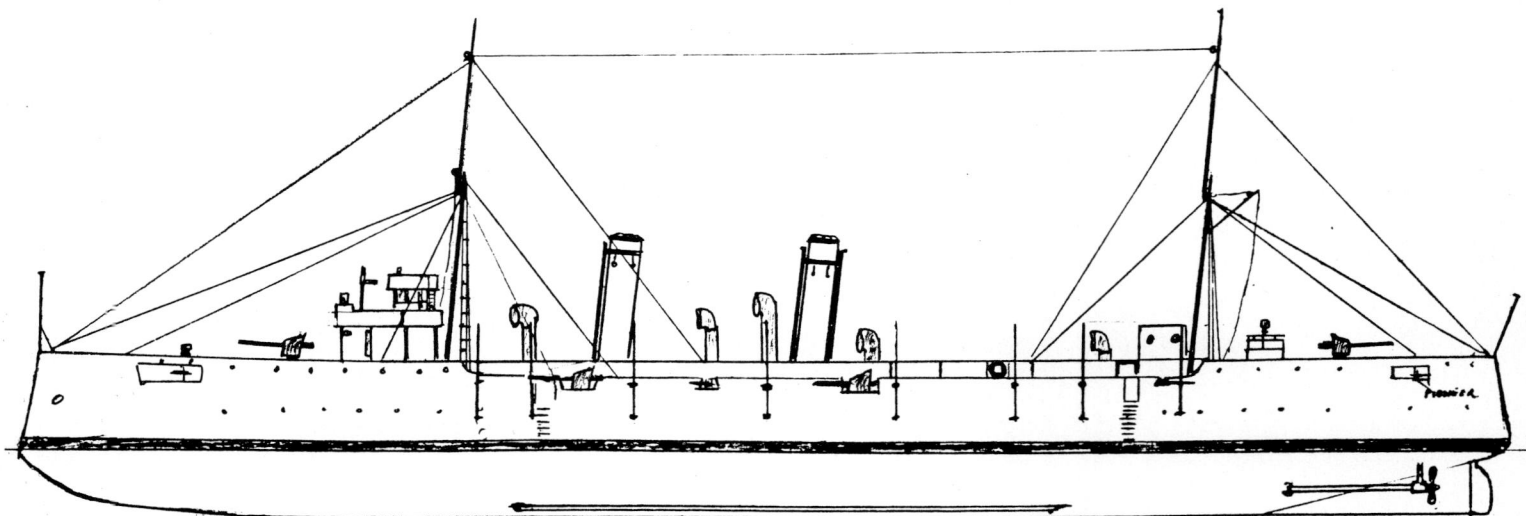

HMAS PIONEER; profile

Left – HMAS PSYCHE, 1915–17. (Photo – National Library).

Below – HMS PIONEER as a unit of the Royal Navy's Australia Station; one of the two 4-inch guns mounted on the fo'c'sle is visible below the bridge.

HMS. PIONEER

TOWN CLASS

Brisbane, Melbourne, Sydney

Between 1911 and 1913, the Royal Navy constructed three light cruisers of the Chatham type of the Town class, to counter the heavily armed cruisers of the German Fleet. The ships possessed an excellent turn of speed, enabling them to work with the fast fleet units, and had a radius of action sufficient for cruising. To fulfill RAN requirements for new cruiser tonnage, the Government decided upon two units of the Chatham type as opposed to a new untested design. A third ship, BRISBANE, was laid down on 25th January, 1913, the same day as HUON, the first totally built torpedo-boat destroyer erected in Australia.

Although the three Towns were armed with a submerged 21-inch torpedo tube, on each beam, it is doubtful whether they were used in any important action, as to use them the ship would be required to place itself broadside on and so create a larger target. All three experienced active service in the Great War, MELBOURNE and SYDNEY in the North Sea with the Grand Fleet, and BRISBANE in the Mediterranean.

Although the 6-inch guns could throw a 100 pound shell, their elevation was limited and as six were carried on the broadside, (three to port and three to starboard), only five guns could be fired during an action. For saluting purposes, four 3 pounder weapons were mounted. The same guns could also be used against small attacking craft.

During her Indian Ocean missions between April and June 1917 BRISBANE acquired the use of a Sopwith 'Baby' seaplane for scouting purposes. The tiny plane weighed a mere 1,715 pounds and had a wing span of 25.8 feet. The 'Baby' was stored on deck and hoisted onto the water for launching. MELBOURNE and SYDNEY also conducted aircraft tests, initially with Sopwith 'Pups' and later Sopwith 'Camels'. Specially-built aircraft platforms, were fitted above 'A' turret. Later in September, 1920, MELBOURNE received an Avro 504k, following successful trials aboard the battlecruiser AUSTRALIA.

The four years of war also witnessed the replacement of the original single masts (forward) with a new tripod variant, and the addition of more powerful search lights. Each ship boasted protective armour of three inches on the beams and two inches on deck.

In the late 1920s it was decided to remove MELBOURNE and SYDNEY from the active fleet. Both were sold for breaking up. In 1929 MELBOURNE proceeded to the United Kingdom while SYDNEY was scrapped locally by Cockatoo Island from

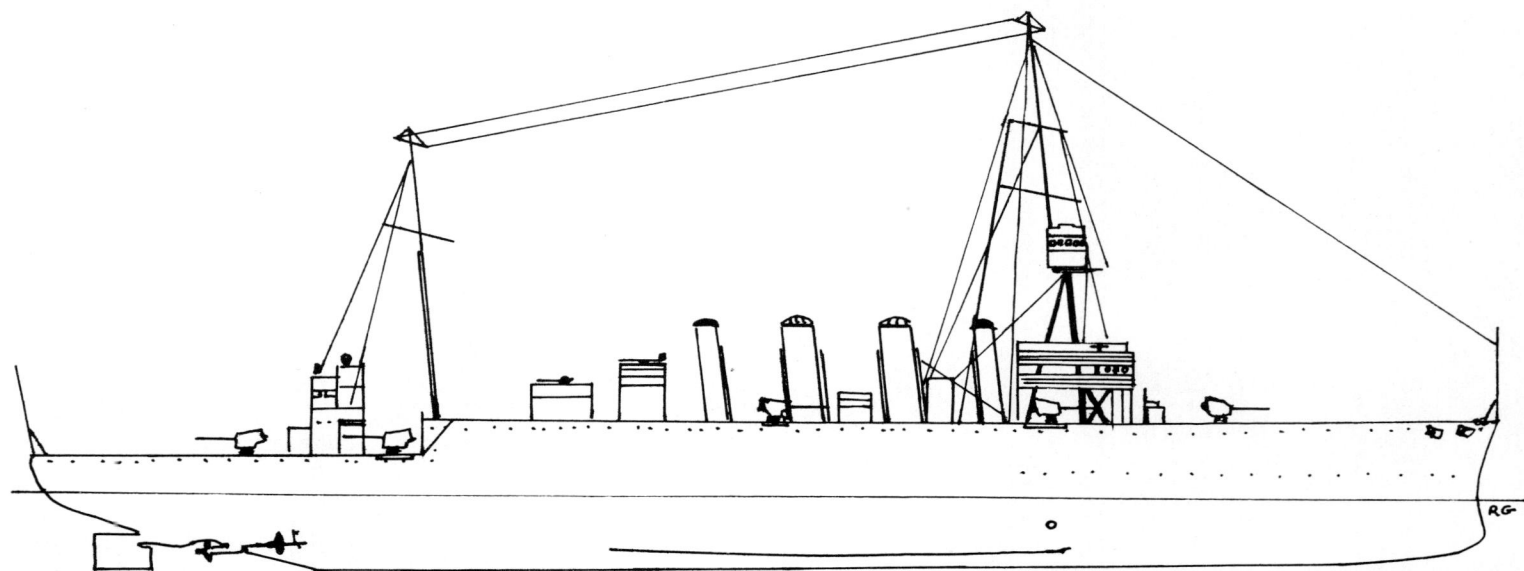

HMAS BRISBANE; profile and armament plan. (R. Gillett)

HMAS SYDNEY in Trinity Inlet, Cairns, August, 1914. The submarines AE 1 and AE 2 lie alongside. (Photo – Cairns Historical Society).

10th January, 1929. BRISBANE paid off the same year, but was retained in reserve as she was three years younger. Eventually she too was deleted, sailing for the United Kingdom on 15th Arpil, 1935 where she arrived on 24th September. BRISBANE was sold in June, 1936 and broken up.

Displacement (tons): 5,400
Dimensions (feet): *Length* (oa) 457 *Beam* 50 *Draught* 18
Machinery: Parsons, turbines, 4 screws, 22,000 i.h.p.
Speed (knots): $25\frac{1}{2}$
Range (miles): 4,000
Manning: 390
Armament: Eight 6-inch (8 × 1), One 3-inch AA (1 × 1) Ten MG, Two 21-inch torpedo tubes (2 × 1) 7 torpedoes carried.

Ship	Pend. No.	Builder	Cons. Time	Comm.	Fate
Brisbane	–	Cockatoo	3y 9m	30/10/16	Paid Off 1929
Melbourne	86 (1/1918) 93 (4/1918)	Cammell-Laird	1y 9m	18/1/13	Paid Off 23/4/28
Sydney	A1 (1/1918) 52 (4/1918)	London & Glasgow	2y 4m	6/13	Paid Off 8/5/28

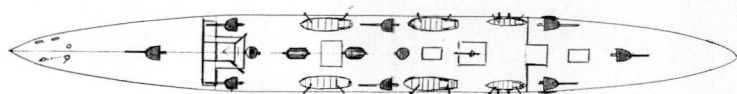

HMAS BRISBANE

Right – Overview of HMAS MELBOURNE's fo'c'sle deck; four of the 6-inch guns are visible, a searchlight is fitted on either side of the after funnel. Note that the second and third funnels are larger in diameter.

Below – HMAS MELBOURNE at Sydney in the 1920s; the two 3 pounder guns are mounted at the after end of the fo'c'sle deck and the searchlights carried between the funnels for war service have been removed. Only one searchlight is carried on the after superstructure and another on the port side bridge wing.

Above – Detailed view of HMAS SYDNEY's Sopwith 'Pup' on its revolving platform in December, 1917.

Left – HMAS SYDNEY in the North Sea, May, 1917; an aircraft platform has been erected before the bridge.

Left – HMAS MELBOURNE at Port Melbourne. (Photo – P. Williams).

Below – HMAS BRISBANE, July 1935.

Bottom – HMAS BRISBANE during the Great War; a 3-inch anti-aircraft gun is fitted behind the after stack; searchlights sited on the bridge wings amidships and abaft the mainmast atop the platform.

RIVER CLASS

Huon, Parramatta, Swan, Torrens, Warrego, Yarra

PARRAMATTA, Australia's first torpedo-boat destroyer cost £81,500 to construct. She and her sister YARRA were the first modern torpedo vessels locally owned and manned since the arrival of the first class boat COUNTESS OF HOPETOUN, built for the colony of Victoria by Yarrow in 1891. Both were ordered in 1909 as part of the new fleet of twelve ships. Until the arrival of the boats, all exercises and training had been undertaken in the 'COUNTESS', the smaller CHILDERS (63 tons), LONSDALE, NEPEAN, MOSQUITO and TB 191 (all 12½ tons).

PARRAMATTA and YARRA were soon joined by WARREGO, re-erected at Cockatoo Island. All were ready for war service from the outset and received orders to proceed to New Guinea for the the early phases of operations. On 11th September, 1914, WARREGO and YARRA gained the distinction of partici-pating in Australia's first naval action of the war, landing troops to over-run an enemy wireless station at Kabakaul in New Britain.

On the centre-line the six TBDs mounted three single 18-inch torpedo tubes. These could be trained outboard at most angles,

however to do so meant that numerous ventilators needed to be removed as well as a galley funnel. The 4-inch weapon was sited before the bridge on a bandstand, a single 12 pounder aft and 12 pounders on either beam.

Despite their lack of 'modern' equipment, the six units pro-vided useful service as reserve training ships at the principal ports from 1924 to 1928.

HUON was dismantled in 1929 and sunk by gunfire from AUSTRALIA and CANBERRA on 10th April, 1931; PARRA-MATTA was dismantled in October, 1929, sold and then foun-dered in the Hawkesbury River on 8th December, 1934; SWAN was dismantled in October, 1929, sold and then foundered in the Hawkesbury on 2nd March, 1934; TORRENS was sunk as a target by CANBERRA on 24th November, 1930; WARREGO was dismantled in October, 1929, but sank at Cockatoo Island on 22nd July, 1931, and YARRA was dismantled in October, 1929, and sunk on 22nd August, 1932.

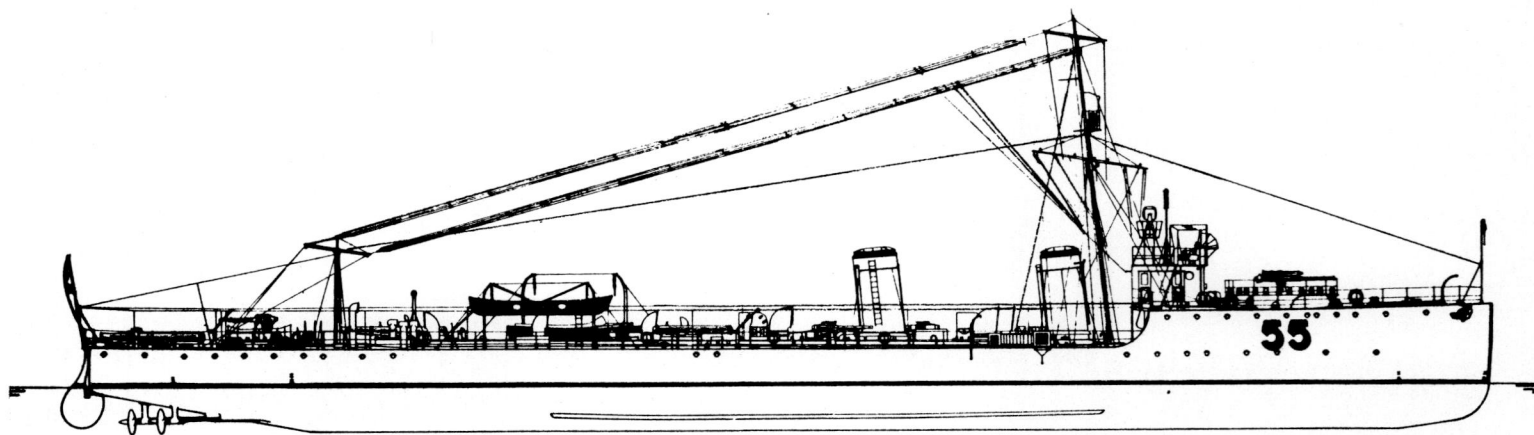

HMAS PARRAMATTA, 1916; profile. (P. Webb)

HMAS WARREGO in the Fitzroy Dock, Cockatoo Island, November, 1914.
TORRENS, still under construction, is behind. (Photo – Cockatoo Island
Dockyard)

Displacement (tons): 700
Dimensions (feet): *Length* (oa) 250 *Beam* 26.8 *Draught* 11
Machinery: Parsons turbines, 10,000 shp
Speed (knots): 28
Range (miles): 2,410 @ 15 knots
Manning: 66
Armament: One 4 inch (1 × 1), Three 12 pdr (3 × 1), Three
  Lewis, One MG, Three 18 inch torpedo tubes (3 × 1).

Ship	Pend. No.	Builder	Cons. Time	Comm.	Fate
Huon	50	Cockatoo	1y 10m	14/12/15	P.O. 7/6/28
Parramatta	55	Fairfield	1y 4m	10/9/10	P.O. 20/4/28
Swan	61	Cockatoo	1y 6m	16/8/16	P.O. 15/5/18
Torrens	67	Cockatoo	1y 5m	3/7/16	P.O. 1926
Warrego	70	Cockatoo	2y	1/6/12	P.O. 19/4/28
Yarra	79	Fairfield	1y 10m	10/9/10	P.O. 1919

Right – HMAS YARRA, late war. (Photo – P. Britz).

Middle right – HMAS YARRA returning to Sydney; several depth charges are mounted right aft, then a single 18-inch torpedo tube, a 12 pounder gun and further depth charges abreast the gun. (Photo – P. Britz).

Bottom right – HMAS HUON during the early 1920s

Bottom – HMAS TORRENS and the fleet oiler HMAS KURUMBA, post-war. J class submarines lie alongside.

Below – HMAS HUON, 4th February, 1915. (Photo – P. Williams).

Top – The single 4-inch gun of HMAS PARRA-MATTA mounted on a bandstand forward of the bridge; note the lack of a protective shield.

Left – Bridge deck of HMAS PARRAMATTA.

Far left – Overview of HMAS PARRAMATTA. A torpedo tube trained to starboard is visible above the funnel. (AWM J3201)

Above – HMAS SWAN, Malta, September, 1918. (Photo – P. Britz)

ESPIEGLE CLASS

Fantome

FANTOME was one of six steel screw sloops constructed for the Royal Navy between 1901 and 1904, but still retaining sailpower. She was schooner rigged but with square sails on the foremast.

Two of the original 4 inch guns were mounted on the forecastle, one on either beam, two amidships abreast the funnel and the final pair below the poop and the open bridge. During her Royal Navy service FANTOME operated as survey ship between 1907 and 1914.

At the time of transfer to the RAN (27th November 1914) FANTOME carried two 4 inch and four 12 pounder guns. Following operations in New Guinea she returned to Sydney on 21st February 1915 to pay off. However on 27th July she recommissioned, mounting an odd selection of guns from PSYCHE (2 × 4 inch), GAYUNDAH (1 × 12 pdr) and three 12 pdrs (from storage).

Despite her obsolete design, lack of effective armament and low speed, FANTOME gave extensive service in the Bay of Bengal, the Persian Gulf and around Malaya. Post-war she reverted to the survey role and after consideration for conversion to a depot ship in 1923 was paid off on 17th April 1924. After sale in January 1925 the sloop was converted to a hulk to carry limestone and was not broken up until 1956.

Displacement (tons): 1,070
Dimensions (feet): *Length* 185 *Beam* 33 *Draught* 11.3
Machinery: 2 screws, 1,400 ihp
Speed (knots): 13.25
Range (miles): 4,000 @ 10 knots
Manning: 150
Armament: Six 4 inch (6 × 1), Four 3 pdr (4 × 1), Three MGS (original).

Ship	Pend. No.	Builder	Cons. Time	Comm.	Fate
Fantome	–	Sheerness Dy	2y	27/11/14	Sold 30/1/25

HMS FANTOME as a survey ship at Cairns.

COLONIAL SLOOP (YACHT)

Una

One of the most unusual ships commissioned by the RAN during the Great War was KOMET, the former yacht of the Administrator of German New Guinea.

The ship was captured by crew members of the patrol vessel NUSA on 11th October 1914 as she lay at anchor. Australian personnel steamed the yacht to Sydney where she was modified to an armed sloop at Cockatoo Island. KOMET was renamed UNA on 17th November 1914 and proceeded to the Borneo region for patrol work.

Subsequent war service included an expedition to the New Hebrides. After paying off on 23rd August 1920, she was recommissioned as the official yacht for the inspection of the Australian fleet in Port Philip by HRH The Prince of Wales. She then became inactive.

UNA was sold on 6th January 1925 for work as a pilot vessel with the Port Melbourne Pilot Service. She was retired in 1953.

Displacement (tons): 1,438
Dimensions (feet): *Length* 210 *Beam* 31 *Draught* 15
Machinery: 1,350 hp
Speed (knots): 16
Range (miles): N/A
Manning: 114
Armament: Three 4 inch (3 × 1), Two 12 pdr (2 × 1).

Ship	Pend. No.	Builder	Cons. Time	Comm.	Fate
Una	–	Vulkan Vegesack, Germany	–	17/11/14	Sold 1/25

HMAS UNA, Melbourne, 1920.

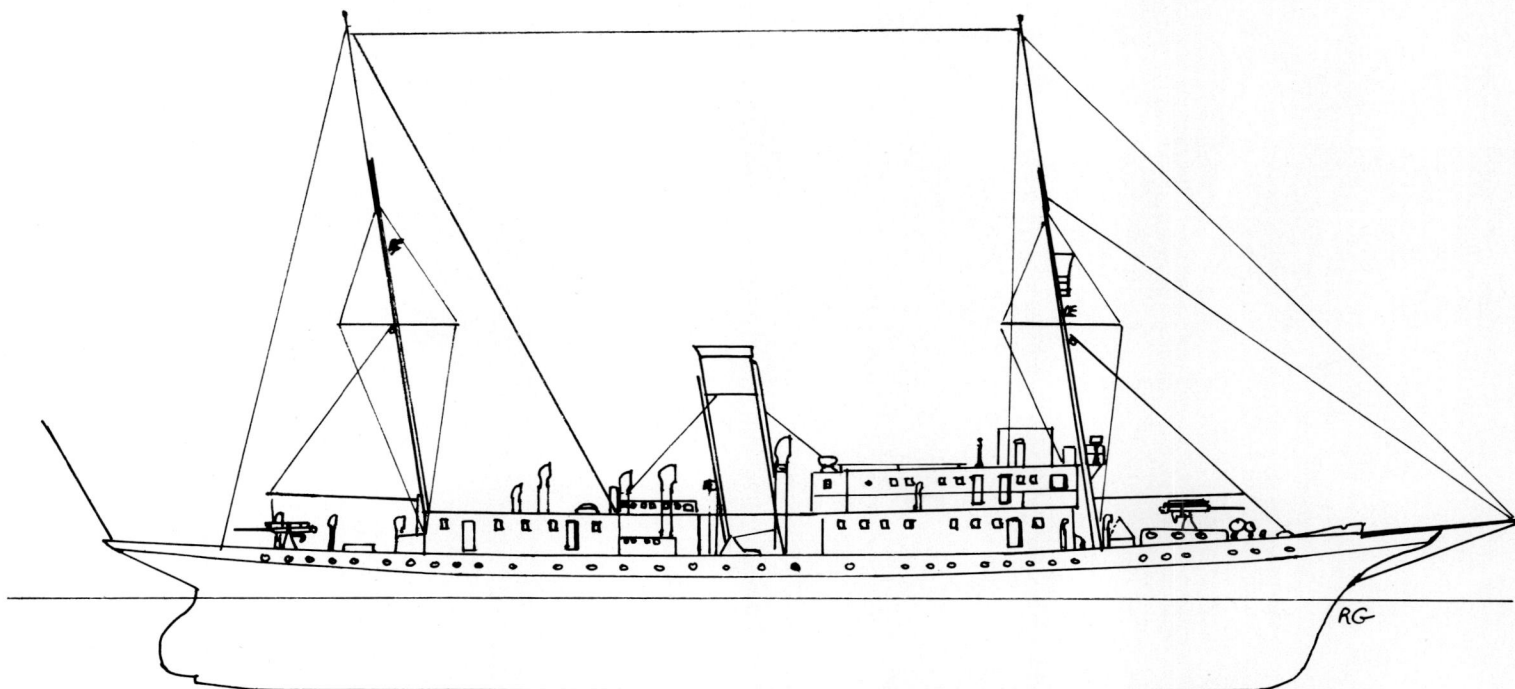

HMAS UNA; profile. (R. Gillett from plans courtesy of Cockatoo Dockyard)

HMAS UNA, immediately prior to conversion to a sloop (for war service); one 4-inch gun was mounted on the centreline forward and one on each side of the sloop abaft the superstructure. (Photo – Cockatoo Island Dockyard)

AUSTRALIAN E CLASS

AE1, AE2

Original pre-war plans had envisaged three C class submarines for the new fleet, but in 1913 only two of the improved E type were authorised. Both were classed as sea-going and carried the prefix 'A' for Australian.

AE1 and AE2 arrived in Sydney on 24th May, 1914, after making Australian landfall at Darwin on the 5th. Both were docked at Cockatoo Island to be prepared for operational service, and to repair defects shown up during the delivery voyage. Four torpedo tubes were fitted, one bow, one stern and two beam (one firing to port and the other to starboard). Because of restricted space aboard, only four spare torpedoes were carried atop the tubes, giving a maximum strike of eight. No gun armament was fitted.

The boats had limited underwater endurance. For surface running they could erect an enclosed control position atop the conning tower. Their diesel/electric propulsion, with twin screws, was the type used by all subsequent Royal Navy submarines.

Unfortunately, both boats were lost during the course of the war; AE1 without trace while on patrol near Cape Gazelle in New Guinea waters on 14th September, 1914, and AE2 after attacking Turkish naval units in the Sea of Marmora on 30th April, 1915.

Displacement (tons): *Surfaced* 725 *Submerged* 810
Dimensions (feet): *Length* (oa) 181 *Beam* 22.6 *Draught* 12.6
Machinery: Diesels (surfaced), electric motors (submerged), twin screws, 1600 h.p. (diesels), 840 h.p. (electric).
Speed (knots): 15 (surfaced), 10 (submerged)
Range (miles): 3,000 @ 10 knots (surfaced)
Manning: 34
Armament: Four 18-inch torpedo tubes (4 × 1).

Ship	Pend. No.	Builder	Cons. Time	Comm.	Fate
AE1	80, 1	Vickers Ltd.	–	28/2/14	Lost 14/9/14
AE2	81, 2	Vickers Ltd.	–	28/2/14	Sunk 30/4/15

Above – HMA Submarine AE 2. Note pendant number on bow and conning tower. (Photo – S. Given)
Left – HMA Submarine AE 1.

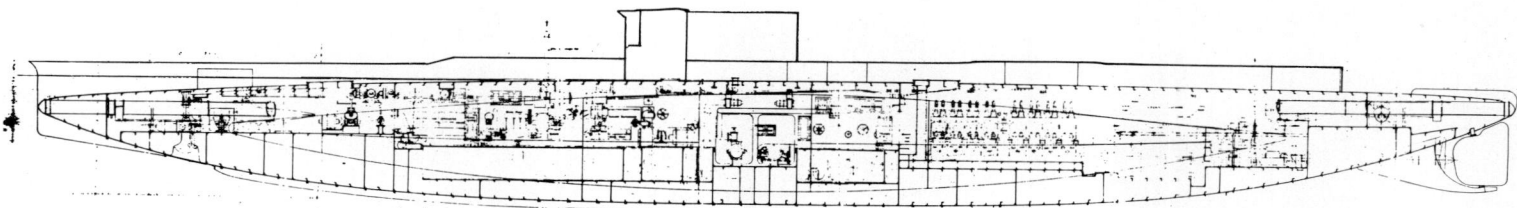

HMAS AE1; general armament drawing. (Naval Ship Design Section)

CASTLE CLASS

Brolga, Gunundaal, Koraaga

During the Great War 145 auxiliary minesweepers of the Castle class were constructed for war service with the Royal Navy. Another 20 were cancelled and 52 completed as fishing vessels. Three of the class were purchased by the New South Wales Government in 1915 and were requisitioned by the RAN in late 1917.

The three trawlers, engaged in minesweeping operations along the NSW and Victorian coasts, made sweeps for mines laid by the German raider WOLF. Throughout their commissions the trawlers were manned by the RAN Brigade.

KORAAGA was returned to the NSW Government in February 1918 and her sisters in the immediate post-war period. BROLGA was sold to a New Zealand concern in 1923 and in 1925 to the Coastal Trading Company Ltd of New South Wales. KORAAGA and GUNUNDAAL were both sold in 1923, the former to Cam and Sons. The latter passed through various owners before ending with Cam and Sons.

BROLGA was lost on 13th August 1926 after striking a reef off the Victorian coast, GUNUNDAAL met her end on 4th November 1929 at Cape Howe. KORAAGA grounded off Bass Point on 8th September, 1931, and sank the following day off the southern NSW township of Gerringong.

Similar Castle class trawlers, TR 19 and TR 20 built in Canada served in the RAN in the Second World War as GOOLGWAI and DURRAWEEN respectively.

Displacement (tons): 221 (gross)
Dimensions (feet): *Length*-117 (Brolga) 115 (Gunundaal and Koraaga)
Machinery: 57 hp
Speed (knots): N/A **Range (miles):** N/A **Manning:** N/A
Armament: Light calibre weapons.

Ship	Pend. No.	Builder	Cons. Time	Comm.	Fate
Brolga	–	Smiths	–	10/17	P.O. 1918
Gunundaal	–	Smiths	–	1917	P.O. 1918
Koraaga	–	Smiths	–	1917	P.O. 1918

The minesweeping trawler GUNUN-DAAL. (Photo – Dufty Collection)

AUXILIARY MINESWEEPERS –
Three Ships

Three auxiliary minesweepers (all built as tugs) gave useful service to the fleet. They were not retained for long periods and resumed their mercantile careers. CECIL RHODES was scrapped in the 1940s. CHAMPION sank after being laid up in the 1950s. JAMES PATERSON was not retired until 1966.

Name	Details	Status
Cecil Rhodes	*Tug* 160 gross 104 × 21.1 × 11.2 feet 77 nhp	Built 1894 Req. 1917
Champion	*Tug* 307 gross 135 × 24 feet 150 hp	Built 1895 Req. 1918 Req. 1919
James Paterson	*Tug* 247 tons 131.6 × 24 × 12.6 feet	Built 1902 RAN WWI

Above – JAMES PATERSON. (Photo – S. Given)

Left – CHAMPION in April, 1924. (Photo – R. Hart)

Top left – Auxiliary minesweeper CECIL RHODES. (Photo – R. Gillett collection)

COASTAL PATROL VESSEL

Gayundah

Originally constructed for the Queensland Marine Defence Force, GAYUNDAH and her sister ship PALUMA, were thirty years old when war began in 1914. While PALUMA was restricted to harbour training duties, GAYUNDAH was actively employed as a patrol vessel along the eastern seaboard until she paid off at Williamstown on 23rd August, 1918.

As built, the gunboat mounted an impressive armament comprising one 8-inch (1 × 1), one 6-inch (1 × 1), two Nordenfelts and two small guns. The 6-inch weapon was replaced by a 4.7-inch gun in 1899, as were the Nordenfelt machine guns by two 12 pdrs.

Following a refit at Cockatoo Island in 1914, when the forrard 8-inch gun was replaced, GAYUNDAH's armament comprised one 4.7-inch gun aft, supported by two 12 pdrs., one on each beam forward, one Maxim and two Nordenfelt machine guns. In July, 1915, a 12 pdr. was removed for installation in FANTOME.

Displacement (tons): 360
Dimensions (feet): *Length* 120 *Beam* 26 *Draught* 9.6
Machinery: Horizontal direct-acting compound engines, twin screws 400 h.p.
Speed (knots): 10.5
Range (miles): 2,100 @ 10 knots
Manning: 55
Armament: One 4.7-inch (1 × 1), Two 12 pdr. (2 × 1), One Maxim (1 × 1), Two Nordenfelts (2 × 1).

Ship	Pend. No.	Builder	Cons. Time	Comp.	Fate
Gayundah	–	Armstrong Mitchell	1y ?m	10/1884	Sold 1921

Above – HMAS GAYUNDAH; her original 8-inch gun (removed in 1914) is visible forward, a 1½-inch Nordenfelt is mounted atop the superstructure on both beams. (Photo – R. Gillett collection)

Left – HMAS GAYUNDAH, 8th January, 1914; the 4.7-inch gun mounted on the stern has been removed for refitting.

Below – Sending a diver down from HMAS GAYUNDAH. (Photo – R. Gillett collection)

FIRST CLASS TORPEDO BOAT

Countess of Hopetoun

COUNTESS OF HOPETOUN was the last 'built-for-the-purpose' warship constructed for the Victorian Colonial Navy. Like CHILDERS she voyaged to Melbourne under her own power (sail and steam). In 1914 she was one of only two torpedo boats effective during the period before PARRAMATTA and YARRA entered service.

During 1914–18 COUNTESS OF HOPETOUN was employed as a patrol boat & target tower within Port Phillip and later as a tender to the Williamstown Dockyard. By this time the original Nordenfelt guns had been removed, leaving only the twin revolving torpedo tubes amidships, the single fixed bow tube and four sets of torpedo dropping gear. Post-war she was laid up in reserve but in 1920 was brought forward for the visit of HRH The Prince of Wales.

Displacement (tons): 75
Dimensions (feet): *Length* 130 *Beam* 13.6 *Draught* 5.7
Machinery: Single screw, 1186 h.p.
Speed (knots): $19.\frac{1}{2}$
Range (miles): N/A
Manning: 19
Armament: Three 14 inch torpedo tubes, Four sets of dropping gear, small arms.

Ship	Pend. No.	Builder	Cons. Time	Comm.	Fate
Countess of Hopetoun	–	Yarrow	1y ?m	1892	Sold 4/24

HMAS COUNTESS OF HOPETOUN, 1919; the searchlight has been deleted and she is painted wartime naval grey; the single bow torpedo tube is visible.

FIRST CLASS TORPEDO BOAT

Childers

By the outbreak of the Great War, CHILDERS was no longer considered suitable for extended front-line service. Her hull had been afloat for more than thirty years spanning a career in the Victorian, Commonwealth and Royal Australian Navies.

    However the need for some form of patrol force within Port Phillip saw her return to use in 1914. Prior to her decommissioning on 27th April 1916 CHILDERS also served as a tender to the Williamstown Dockyard. After being beached ashore on Swan Island, the hull was sold for £20 in August 1918.

Displacement (tons): 63
Dimensions (feet): *Length* 118.2 *Beam* 12.6 *Draught* 5.9
Machinery: Single screw, 750 h.p.
Speed (knots): 19
Range (miles): 1,000 @ 11 knots
Manning: 12
Armament: One 14 inch torpedo tube (1 × 1), Four sets of dropping gear for 14 inch torpedoes, small arms.

Ship	Pend. No.	Builder	Cons. Time	Comm.	Fate
Childers	–	Thornycroft	1y ?m	1884	Sold 5/8/18

HMAS CHILDERS (Photo – P. Williams)

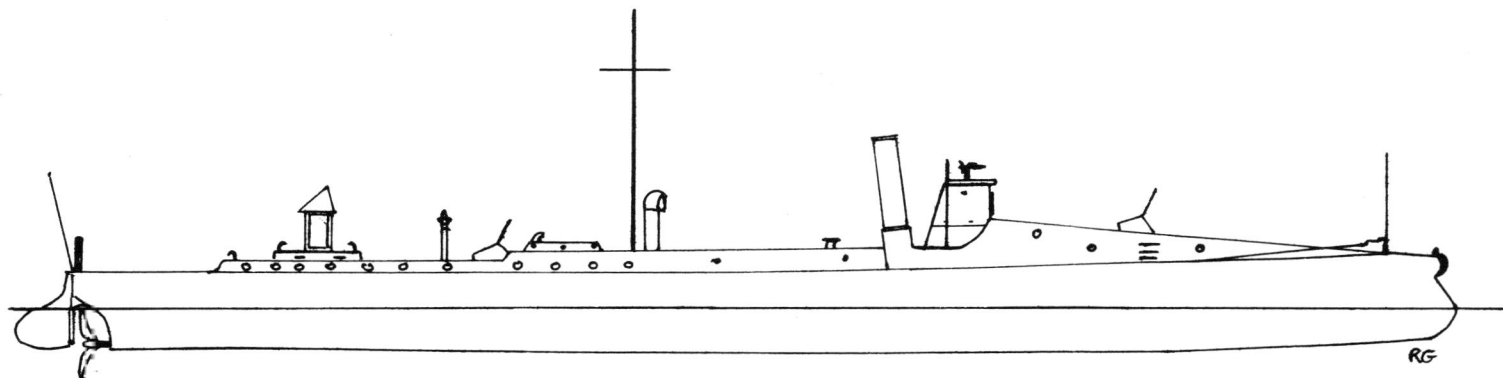

HMAS CHILDERS; profile, 1914. (R. Gillett)

Left – CHILDERS (left) and COUNTESS OF HOPE-
TOUN (right), both HMVS, during exercises in Port
Phillip, 1896. (Photo – P. Williams)

Below – HMCS CHILDERS in the early years of the
20th century. She is being controlled from an open
position immediately forward of the twin stacks.

SECOND CLASS TORPEDO BOATS

Lonsdale, Nepean

LONSDALE and NEPEAN were originally constructed for the colony of Victoria and arrived in Melbourne aboard the SS PORT DARWIN on 7th July, 1884. They were integrated into the Commonwealth Naval Forces in 1904 and into the RAN seven years later. They were never actively employed during the Great war.

Being of the same vintage as CHILDERS, but much smaller and without any significant sea-keeping qualities, LONSDALE and NEPEAN were beached ashore on Swan Island in July 1912 and then ordered for disposal by sale during July 1914. No buyers were found for the hulls.

LONSDALE and NEPEAN were eventually broken up at Fishermans Bend during 1929–30.

Displacement (tons): $12\frac{1}{2}$
Dimensions (feet): *Length* (oa) 67 *Beam* 7.6 *Draught* 3.2 aft
Machinery: Compound surface condensing, 150 ihp
Speed (knots): 17
Range (miles): N/A
Manning: 7
Armament: Two sets of dropping gear for 14 inch torpedoes. (original).

Ship	Pend. No.	Builder	Cons. Time	Comm.	Fate
Lonsdale	–	Thornycroft	–	1884	Hulked 1914
Nepean	–	Thornycroft	–	1884	Hulked 1914

HMCS LONSDALE, 1905; a 14-inch torpedo is carried in the torpedo-dropping gear amidships.

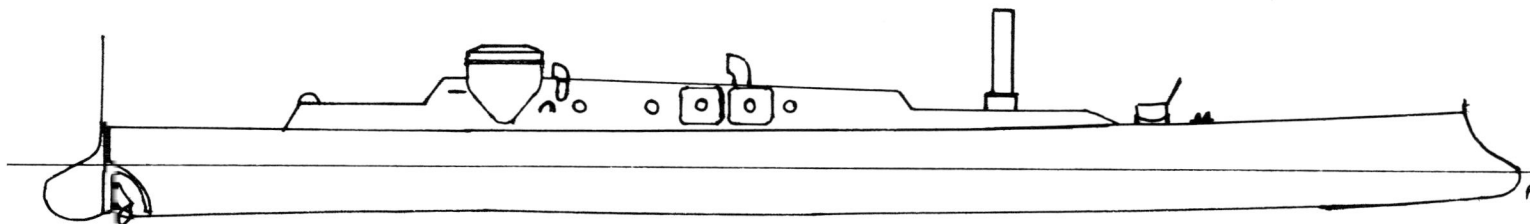

NEPEAN, profile, 1914, decommissioned with torpedoes and associated fittings removed. (R. Gillett)

PORT GUARDSHIP

Cerberus

Ship	Pend. No.	Builder	Cons Time	Comp.	Fate
Cerberus	–	Palmers	3y	9/70	Sold 23/4/24

Having completed more than forty years service when war broke out, CERBERUS was still considered of some use to the fleet and was employed as port guard ship in Port Phillip in addition to her depot ship responsibilities.

By 1914 the old monitor's four ten inch guns were inoperative and she carried only light defensive weapons. As originally designed, CERBERUS could be submerged by the flooding of several compartments, so that only the turret and breastwork remained above water level. Ventilators were provided fore and aft to ensure a free flow of air.

CERBERUS was also used as an explosives storeship and in 1921 commenced yet another phase of her long career as a depot ship for the J class submarines. She was renamed PLATYPUS (II) on 1st April 1921. The fifty-four year old ship was sold in April 1924 and stripped of all fittings. Two years later she was aquired for use as breakwater at Black Rock in Port Phillip and scuttled on 2nd September 1926. She still fullfils this duty.

Displacement (tons): 3,340
Dimensions (feet): *Length* 225 *Beam* 45 *Draught* 15.6
Machinery: Horizontal engines, twin screws, 1,370 i.h.p.
Speed (knots): $9\frac{1}{2}$
Range (miles): N/A
Manning: 96 (original)
Armament: Light guns.

HMVS CERBERUS in the Alfred Graving Dock, early in the monitor's career. (Photo – P. Williams)

HMAS CERBERUS; by the Great War her main 12-inch guns were considered unsuitable for action. For self-defence she was fitted with two small guns atop the flying bridge.

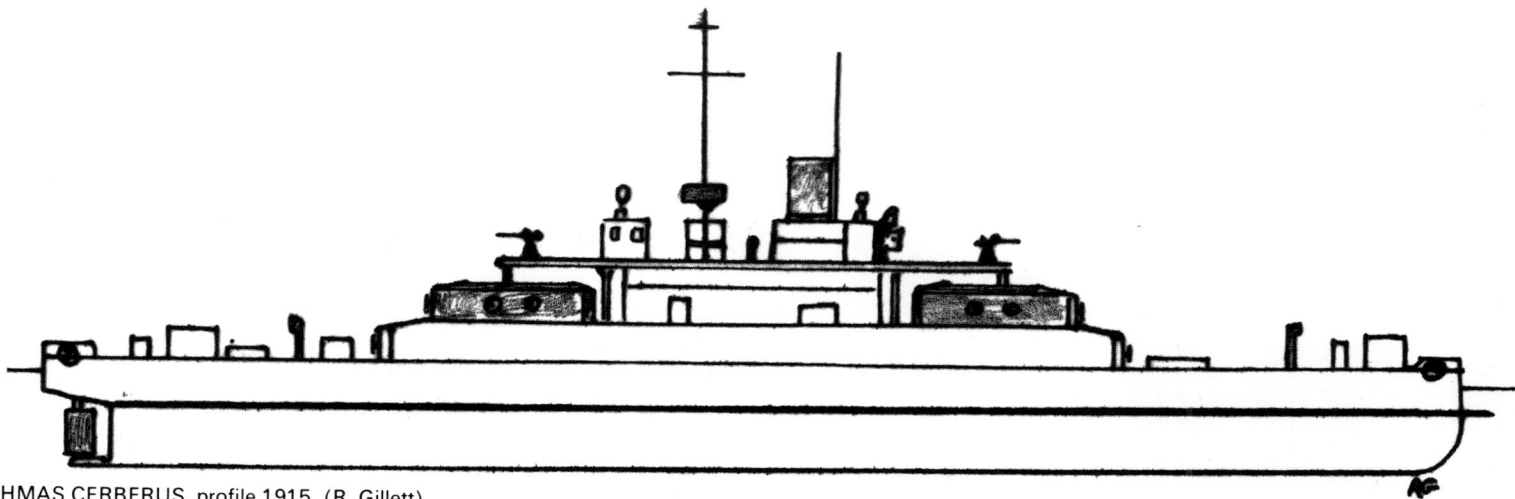

HMAS CERBERUS, profile 1915. (R. Gillett)

REQUISITIONED AND CAPTURED PATROL CRAFT
Seven Ships

When war commenced on 5th August 1914 only the captured NUSA and SUMATRA were initially employed as patrol craft. With the departure to the European theatre of the battlecruiser AUSTRALIA, modern cruisers and destroyers the situation soon changed and it was found necessary to requisition five more vessels to patrol in local and New Guinea waters.

Name	Details	Status
Alacrity	*Tug* 353 tons 145.6 × 27 feet	Built 1893 Purchased 1917 Paid Off 7/18 Sold 1925
Coogee	*Ferry* 762 tons 225 × 30 feet 12 knots 1 × 4.7 inch, 2 × 3 pdr.	Built 1887 Req. 3/18 Comm. 20/5/18 M/S 1/19 Ret. 2/19
Gannet	*Coaster* 208 tons 120 × 24.1 feet 420 h.p. = 10 knots 1 × 12 pdr.	Built – Req. – Comm. 25/7/18 Ret. –
Mourilyan	*Coaster* 1349 tons 220.7 × 36.2 × 18.9 feet 2330 h.p. = 11½ knots 1 × 4.7 inch, 2 × 12 pdr. Hotchkiss guns	Built 1908 Req. 24/4/18 Comm. 23/5/18 Paid Off 20/12/18 Ret. 8/1/19
Nusa	*Yacht* 64 tons 1 × 12 pdr.	Captured 14/9/14 Sold 1921
Sleuth	*Yacht* 108 tons 100 × 16.4 × 8.2 feet 160 h.p. = 10 knots 1 × 3 pdr.	Built 1901 Req. 1/17 Comm. 13/1/17 Tender 1918 Sold 19/2/20
Sumatra	*Steamer, ex German* 584 tons 1 × 12 pdr.	Captured 11/9/14

MOURILYAN

NUSA

HMAS SLEUTH: a 3 pounder gun is fitted forward.

HMAS SUMATRA, September, 1914, shortly after her capture. HMAS NUSA lies alongside (J3125),

REQUISITIONED EXAMINATION VESSELS
Four Ships

Name	Details	Status
Ajax	*Pilot Steamer* 344 tons 128.6 × 21 feet	Built 1875 RAN WWI Ret. 1918
Alvina	*Yacht* 194 tons 138.8 × 20.2 × 11.6 feet	Built 1887 RAN WWI Ret. 1918
Captain Cook	*Pilot Steamer* 396 tons 156 × 25 feet 12 knots	Built 1893 RAN WWI Ret. 1918 Army 1939 Paid Off 1945
Otter	*Tug* 271 tons 128.6 × 21.2 × 10.1 feet	Built 1884 Queensland Marine Defence Force 1887 Q. Govt. 1901 RAN WWI Ret. 1918 RAN 1939 Ret 1940

AJAX

CAPTAIN COOK.

OTTER

ARMED MERCHANT CRUISER
One Ship

'BERRIMA' was requisitioned from P. & O. Steam Navigation Co. and converted at Cockatoo Island to enable her to carry 1,500 men. She was used primarily to transport Australian troops to New Guinea and the islands. During December, 1914, and January, 1915, she towed the submarine AE2 across the Indian Ocean whilst part of the second ANZAC convoy to the Middle East. BERRIMA was torpedoed in the English Channel on 18th February, 1917, and beached ashore.

Name	Details	Status
Berrima	11,120 tons: IHP 9,000 = 14 knots: 4 × 4-inch	Built – Req. 8/1914 Comm. 8/1914 Paid Off 10/1914

The armed merchant cruiser HMAS BERRIMA.

Mallina (Photo – I. J. Farquhar)

COAL HULK

Hankow

HANKOW was purchased by the Navy in July 1913 to serve as coal hulk for fleet units at Garden Island. The vessel was originally built as the sailing ship CITY OF HANKOW. She was modified for naval service by the addition of derricks which could bring coal from her holds to the bunkers of ships alongside.

In 1923 the hulk was towed to Thursday Island by the collier BILOELA and served there until October 1927. On 11th November HANKOW arrived back in Sydney for a brief refit. On 26th February 1928 she was taken in tow by PLATYPUS and left for Thursday Island, arriving on 18th January 1929. In August 1932 she was removed to Darwin and sunk for target practice by ALBATROSS on 18th September.

HANKOW, 1921. An oil fuel lighter is moored in the foreground. (Photo – R. Gillett collection)

REQUISITIONED COLLIERS
Two Ships

After the outbreak of war with Germany, the RAN requisitioned two merchant ships for use as colliers in the early New Guinea campaigns.

Name	Details	Status
Koolonga	*Steamer*	Built Req. 6/8/14 Ret. 5/15
Mallina	*Steamer* 3213 tons	Built 1909 Req. 14/8/14 Ret. 1/2/15

SUBMARINE DEPOT SHIP

Platypus

Immediately prior to the Great War, PLATYPUS was ordered as a parent ship for the RAN's first submarines AE1 and AE2. As both boats were lost in the conflicts early stages and PLATYPUS was not completed until March 1917, it was decided to retain the ship in English waters as a submarine depot ship based at Campbeltown and Killybegs.

As part of the 'Gift Fleet' presented to the RAN in 1919 comprised six J class submarines PLATYPUS assumed her original role. The ship and six submarines sailed from Portsmouth on 8th April 1919 and arrived in Sydney on 15th July. Economic restrictions coupled with the unreliability of the J class saw all the class paid off by mid 1922.

PLATYPUS herself was paid off as a submarine depot ship on 12th July 1922 and recommissioned the next day as the fleet's destroyer depot and repair ship. In 1929 the ship reverted to the submarine-parent role following the acquisition of OXLEY and OTWAY. She recommissioned of 16th August 1929 as a submarine depot ship with the new name of PENGUIN.

On 10th May 1930 OXLEY and OTWAY were decommissioned and PENGUIN was re-designated a base ship, situated at Garden Island. She continued in this role until 26th February 1941 when recommissioned and renamed PLATYPUS. After initial service as a training ship she reached Darwin on 19th May 1941 to commence service as base ship. Following a refit at Williamstown from May to December 1943 she was detailed to New Guinea as a maintenance vessel and finally paid off on 13th May 1946.

While laid up PLATYPUS served as a headquarters ship for the reserve fleet and was not sold until February 1958.

Displacement (tons): 3,476
Dimensions (feet): *Length* 325 *Beam* 44 *Draught* 15.8
Machinery: Triple expansion engines, twin screws, 3,500 ihp
Speed (knots): 15½
Range (miles): N/A
Manning: 360
Armament: Not fitted.

Ship	Pend. No.	Builder	Cons. Time	Comp.	Fate
Platypus	C8 (1.18)	John Brown	2y 4m	2/3/17	Sold 20/2/58

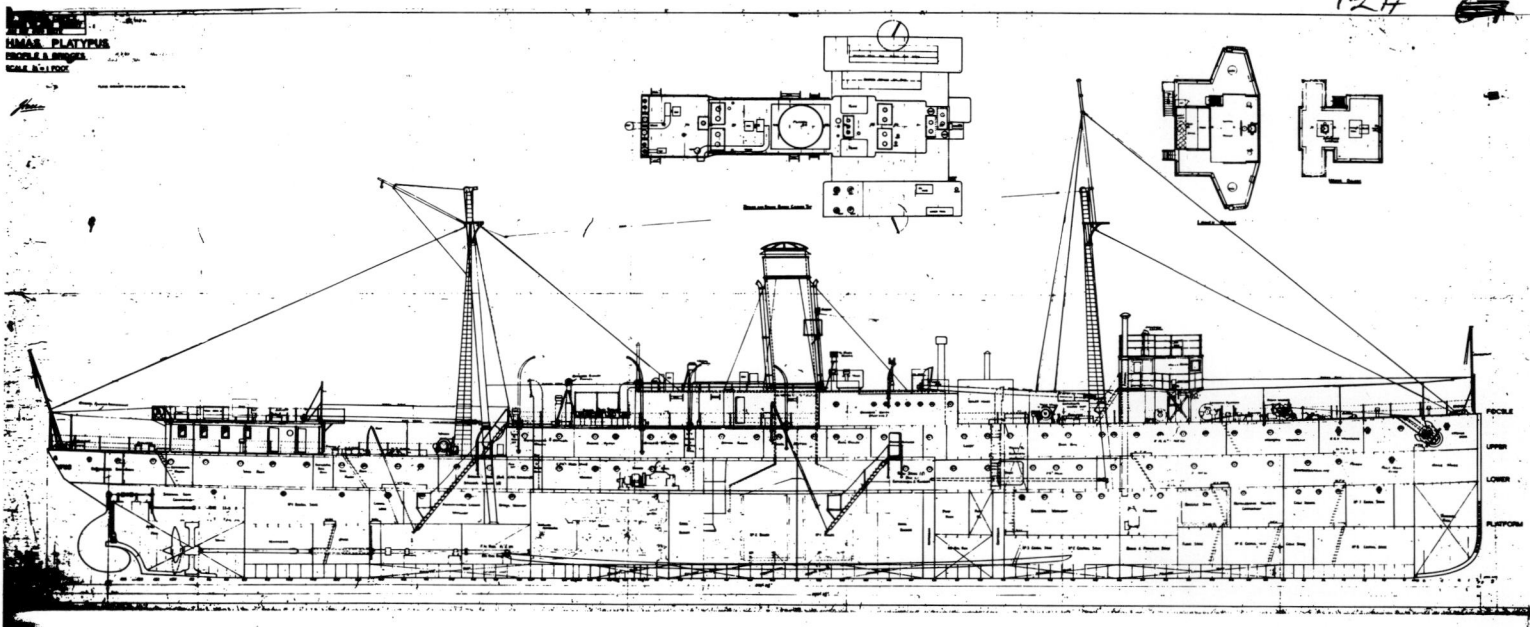

HMAS PLATYPUS; profile as designed (Naval Ship Design Section)

Right – HMAS PLATYPUS, July, 1919, in the Sutherland Dock, Cockatoo Island, during her post-delivery refit. She carries no armament. Note the tall masts.

Below – HMAS PLATYPUS in the mid-war period; masts have been reduced; no armament mounted. The training vessel KOORONGA is proceeding past the depot ship.

Bottom – HMAS PLATYPUS with J class submarines, HMAS ENCOUNTER (right) and HMAS MERLOURNE (left), 1919. (Photo – Sydney Maritime Museum)

STATIONARY DEPOT SHIP

Penguin

Originally a barque-rigged composite screw sloop of the Royal Navy Osprey class, PENGUIN was completed in August 1877 and re-engined at the Devonport dockyard after her first commission.

Between 1881 and 1886 she was laid up in reserve. Shortly after being recommissioned four machine and one light guns were added to her original armament. Following re-activation the sloop was ordered to the East Indies and in December 1889 was converted to a survey ship. For the next 16 years PENGUIN was active in Australian waters until paying off on 31st March 1907.

During 1908 she was converted to a stationary depot ship. Her main deck was roofed over and the ship moored on the south-western side of Garden Island.

PENGUIN was subsequently commissioned into the RAN on 1st July 1913 and continued to provide base-ship services until 1st January 1923 when she was paid off and sold. During the short service of AE1 and AE2 she acted as a rather inappropriate depot ship.

The 45 year old vessel was converted to a floating crane and operated in Sydney Harbour until 1960. She was subsequently burnt to the waterline in Kerosene Bay, Sydney.

Displacement (tons): 1,130
Dimensions (feet): *Length* 170 *Beam* 36 *Draught* 16.1
Machinery: Single screw, 666 ihp
Speed (knots): 9.87
Range (miles): N/A
Manning: Originally 140/150
Armament: Originally, Two 4.7 inch MLR, Four 64 pdr MLR.

Ship	Pend. No.	Builder	Cons. Time	Comm.	Fate
Penguin	–	Napier	2y ?m	1/7/13	Sold 1/23

Port quarter view of HMAS PENGUIN.

Stationary depot ship HMAS PENGUIN moored on Garden Island's southwest shore. The old Royal Navy sloop TORCH lies at anchor in reserve.

REQUISITIONED DEPOT SHIPS
Two Ships

Two auxiliaries were placed into service to support the two requisitioned colliers and other fleet units around New Guinea and Malaya.

Name	Details	Status
Esturia	*Oiler* 2143 tons	Built 1910 Req. 11/9/14 RN 1917 Ret. 3/8/17
Upolu	*Steamer* 1,141 tons 220 × 30 feet	Built 1891 Req. 8/1914 Ret. 9/12/14

HMAS ESTURIA and HMAS SWAN, 1917. (EN411)

REQUISITIONED HOSPITAL SHIP
One Ship

During the early part of the war the RAN requisitioned the ten year old GRANTALA from the Adelaide Steamship Company for conversion to a hospital ship. After only four months the red crosses were removed from GRANTALA's sides and the ship resumed her commercial career. GRANTALA was broken up in 1934.

Name	Details	Status
Grantala (YA8)	*Steamer* 3,655 tons 350 × 45 feet 14½ knots	Built 1904 Req. 7/8/14 Paid Off 22/12/14

OIL LIGHTERS
OFL Nos. 1, 2, 3, and 4

Four 500 ton oil fuel lighters were constructed locally for fleet duties. The craft were moored off Garden Island secured to bouys and required tugs for all harbour movements. Each lighter survived the war to serve again in the Second World War. OFL 4 remains in reserve, 1983.

Displacement (tons): 944 (full load)
Dimensions (feet): *Length* 156 *Beam* 30 *Draught* 9.25
Machinery: Dumb
Manning: 5/7
Armament: N/A

Oil Lighter No. 1 at Garden Island.

GRANTALA.

FLEET OILER

Kurumba

Although built for the RAN, KURUMBA served with the Royal Navy from the first months of 1917 to early 1919. She transferred to Australian control on 13th March 1919 and arrived in Sydney during July.

Like the collier BILOELA, KURUMBA was considered suitable for conversion to carry an operational detachment of two seaplanes but the scheme was dropped in 1923.

Up to June 1928, when she paid off into reserve, KURUMBA made 13 voyages to Borneo and or New Guinea. The oiler remained out of commission until the new war in 1939. She was eventually sold on 30th January 1948 but was not broken up until 1966.

Displacement (tons): 7,806
Dimensions (feet): *Length* 378 *Beam* 45.6 *Draught* 23.3
Machinery: Triple expansion, 2,300 hp
Speed (knots): 10
Range (miles): N/A
Manning: 65
Armament: One 4 inch, Two smaller.

Ship	Pend. No.	Builder	Cons. Time	Comp.	Fate
Kurumba	X36 (1.18)	Swan Hunter	1y 3m	7/12/16	Paid Off 6/28

KURUMBA. (Photo – H. Cliff)

REQUISITIONED SUPPLY SHIP
One Ship

A Union Steamship Company vessel, AORANGI was acquired in mid-1914 for service in New Guinea. To equip her for naval duties AORANGI was fitted out at Garden Island, the work being completed in August 1914. After naval service the ship was sold to the Admiralty on 13th July 1915 for duties as a storeship. However AORANGI was sunk as a blockship in Scapa Flow on 10th August 1915. In September 1920 she was refloated for use as a stores hulk at Malta and was finally broken up in 1925.

Name	Details	Status
Aorangi	*Steamer*	Built 1883
	4,268 gross	Req. 4/14
	389.1 × 46 feet	Ret. 3/5/15
	13 knots	

AORANGI.

HARBOUR TENDER

Gordon

GORDON was built for the Victorian Colonial Government as a turnabout torpedo launch but by 1914 was employed as a harbour tender and training boat. On 14th November 1914 she was rammed and sunk by a picket boat attached to Williamstown Dockyard. GORDON was raised, found unfit for any further service and broken up.

As a torpedo launch GORDON carried two 14 inch torpedoes in dropping gear and one four barrelled Nordenfelt machine gun.

Displacement (tons): 12
Dimensions (feet): *Length* 56 *Beam* 10 *Draught* 5
Machinery: Compound surface condensing, 150 ihp
Speed (knots): 14
Range (miles): N/A
Manning: 7
Armament: Removed.

Ship	Pend. No.	Builder	Cons. Time	Comm.	Fate
Gordon	–	J.S. White	–	4/86	Scrapped 1914

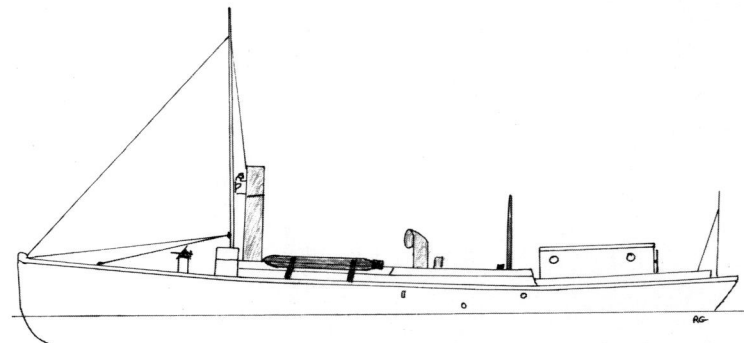

HMAS GORDON; profile showing original armament. (R. Gillett)

GORDON (left) with LONSDALE and NEPEAN, 1905.

COLLEGE TENDER

Franklin

The steam yacht FRANKLIN was originally constructed as the private pleasure craft, ADELE, in 1906. She was purchased from the estate of Henry Dutton of Kapunda, South Australia on 31st May 1915 and renamed for Sir John Franklin, a former Governor of Tasmania and naval officer.

In RAN service FRANKLIN initially served on tender duties to the Naval College, Jervis Bay and during May 1920 carried H.R.H., The Prince of Wales on a ceremonial review of the Australian Fleet.

FRANKLIN paid off on 18th September 1922 and was transferred to the Administrator for the Territory of New Guinea. In this new role she served until 1932 and was then laid up. The vessel was requisitioned as an examination vessel in the Second World War and operated from both Darwin and Sydney. During subsequent operations as a stores carrier she was wrecked off Port Kembla and became a total loss on the breakwater on 7th May 1943.

Displacement (tons): 350
Dimensions (feet): *Length* 145 *Beam* 22.4 *Draught* 9.1
Machinery: Triple expansion, single screw, 68 nhp.
Speed (knots): 12
Range (miles): N/A
Manning: N/A
Armament: Small arms.

Ship	Pend. No.	Builder	Cons. Time	Comm.	Fate
Franklin	–	Hawthorn & Co.	–	14/9/15	Deleted 1924

FRANKLIN, May 1920. (Photo – P. Williams)

WATER TENDER

Ripple

RIPPLE was acquired by the RAN during mid 1913, having been launched in 1904. She served with the fleet as water tender until after the Second World War. In 1949 RIPPLE was acquired by the Sydney Training Depot, Snapper Island for use as a training ship but was returned in 1951 and sold for breaking up.

Prior to her purchase fleet units were serviced by another water tender, built in Sydney and also named RIPPLE.

Displacement (tons): 390
Dimensions (feet): *Length* 120 *Beam* 21 *Draught* 9
Machinery: Triple expansion, 310 ihp
Speed (knots): 8
Range (miles): N/A
Manning: N/A
Armament: N/A.

Ship	Pend. No.	Builder	Cons. Time	Comm.	Fate
Ripple	–	Foster & Minty	–	1/7/13	Deleted 1947

RIPPLE, 1950. (Photo – L. Forsythe)

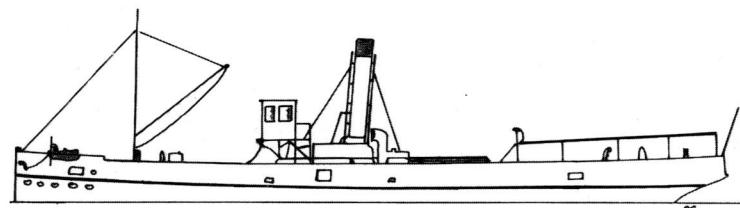

RIPPLE, profile, 1920. (R. Gillett)

DEPOT TENDER

Togo

TOGO was purchased for £7,500 by the RAN on 14th August 1916 from Broomby and Dent, Launceston, Tasmania where she had been employed as a passenger steamer.

Although envisaged for use as a tug in naval service she was instead employed on tender duties based at Flinders Naval Depot, Western Port.

In October 1917 she commenced minesweeping training for Brigade personnel in Victorian waters. In April 1918 she was renamed PHILLIP.

Displacement (tons): 153 (gross)
Dimensions (feet): *Length* 122 *Beam* 23
Machinery: Triple expansion, 46 nhp
Speed (knots): N/A
Range (miles) N/A
Manning: N/A
Armament: N/A

Ship	Pend. No.	Builder	Cons. Time	Comm.	Fate
Togo	–	–	–	8/16	Sold 1921

TOGO, 1906.

NAVAL TUG

Albert

The gunboat ALBERT, named after Prince Albert, consort of Queen Victoria operated with the Victorian Colonial Navy from completion to 1895 and with the Victorian Public Works Department until the Great War. She was then acquired by the RAN and taken to Cockatoo Island for conversion to a naval tug.

When she was stripped down to the main deck, work on the conversion was halted due to high costs and in September 1917 she was listed for disposal.

ALBERT was sold into private ownership and appears to have been purchased by a Sydney based oil company for use as a lighter.

Displacement (tons): 370
Dimensions (feet): *Length* (oa) 120 *Beam* 25 *Draught* 9.6
Machinery: Two direct acting compound steam engines, 400 ihp.
Speed (knots): 10
Range (miles): 2,100 @ 10 knots
Manning: 41
Armament: Nil

Ship	Pend. No.	Builder	Cons. Time	Comm.	Fate
Albert	—	Armstrong Mitchell	—	1/84	Sold 1917

ALBERT under conversion to a naval tug. (Photo – Cockatoo Island Dockyard)

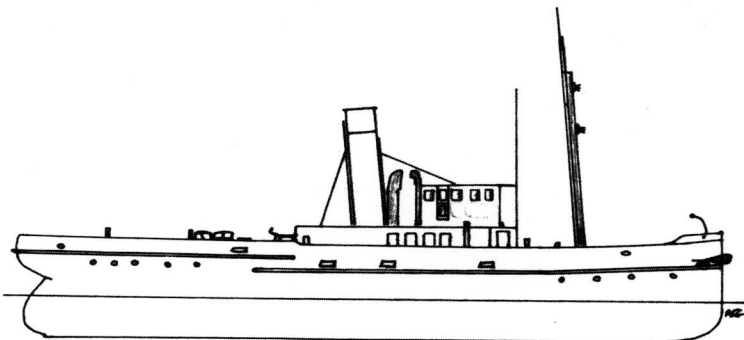

ALBERT; profile showing proposed appearance as naval tug. (R. Gillett from plans courtesy of Cockatoo Dockyard)

REQUISITIONED TUGS

Although taken over for mine warfare duties, the auxiliary minesweepers CECIL RHODES, CHAMPION and JAMES PATERSON performed minor towing assignments. Privately-owned tugs in the major ports were employed whenever necessary.

ALONGSIDE TRAINING VESSEL

Paluma

During 1914–16 the ex-Queensland colonial gunboat PALUMA was employed as a training ship at Williamstown. She did not proceed to sea at any time. In 1916 she was laid up in reserve until her sale in 1918 to the Victorian Ports and Harbours Department.

Under new ownership the ship was renamed RIP, received a new funnel, built up bows and derricks, and employed as a lighthouse tender and workship. In January 1949 RIP was removed from service and broken up during 1950–51.

PALUMA, originally built as a gunboat, was used as a survey ship in Northern Australian waters with the Royal Navy before reverting to the Queensland Marine Defence Force in 1895. She never mounted her intended main 8 inch gun but was instead fitted with two single 5 inch guns forward. The single 6 inch gun aft was replaced by a 4.7 inch gun in August 1905.

Displacement (tons): 360
Dimensions (feet): *Length* 120 *Beam* 26 *Draught* 9.6
Machinery: Horizontal direct action compound steam engines, twin screws, 400 hp.
Speed (knots): $10\frac{1}{2}$
Range (miles): 2,100 miles @ 10 knots
Manning: 49
Armament: Two 5 inch (2 × 1), One 4.7 inch (1 × 1), Two 12 pdr (2 × 1), Two MG (2 × 1)

Ship	Pend. No.	Builder	Cons. Time	Comm.	Fate
Paluma	–	Armstrong Mitchell	–	9/84	Sold 1918

HMCS PALUMA, 1910; two 6-inch guns are fitted on either side of the space intended for the 8-inch weapon.

BOYS TRAINING SHIP

Tingira

Built in Scotland as the clipper ship SOBROAN, TINGIRA was acquired by the RAN in 1911 for use as a boys' training ship. Her entire naval career was spent moored in Rose Bay or at Garden Island. She was paid off in June 1927.

TINGIRA was sold on 3rd November 1927, resold in 1935 and broken up in Sydney after 1940.

Displacement (tons): 2,131 (registered)
Dimensions (feet): *Length* 317 *Beam* 40 *Draught* 16
Machinery: N/A
Speed (knots): 16 (sails)
Range (miles): N/A
Manning: 65
Armament: Small arms.

HMAS TINGIRA.

Ship	Pend. No.	Builder	Cons. Time	Comm.	Fate
Tingira	—	Hall & Co.	—	25/4/12	Paid Off 30/6/27

Rope-work aboard the training ship.

The Mid-War Period
1919–1939

AT THE END OF THE GREAT WAR, the Royal Navy found itself with hundreds of unwanted, but still useful, warships. In an effort to modernise the RAN, it was decided to transfer four classes of ships to Australia to form the backbone of the peacetime fleet.

A total of 15 vessels, comprising a destroyer leader, five destroyers, three sloops and six submarines, were transferred between March and June, 1919. The first group, the three Flower class sloop minesweepers, reached Sydney on 8th June, 1919, followed by the J class submarines on 10th July. ANZAC and the five S class destroyers arrived in April, 1920.

Despite many grandiose plans for the 'gift fleet', it was soon found that the submarines were not a successful design and in late 1921 and early 1922, all except J7, (still under refit), were reduced to reserve. Financial restrictions also prevented the continuous operation of the ships. Only GERANIUM and MARGUERITE had commissions of any notable length, while MALLOW lingered on in reserve with only periodical active commissions.

The leader ANZAC was the most fortunate. This ship remained in full commission from 1920 to 1933, but her companions, the five S class destroyers were laid up in December, 1925, (STALWART), May, 1930, (SUCCESS), December, 1929,

Ten ships, comprising seven classes, of the RAN's mid-war fleet are represented in this 1921 view of the Garden Island Naval Dockyard. Two S class destroyers, including HMAS TATTOO are secured to buoys off Farm Cove; two J class submarines lie alongside the training ship/ex cruiser HMAS ENCOUNTER at the end of the island; the coal hulk, HANKOW, is secured to the cruiser wharf, with an oil lighter opposite; two Flower class corvettes, under charge of hired tugs, are being moved away from the Town class cruiser (below the sheerlegs). (Photo – R. Gillett collection)

(SWORDSMAN), January, 1928, (TASMANIA), and October, 1921, (TATTOO). The latter was brought forth from reserve in 1926, from August, 1931, to June, 1933, and again from October, 1933.

The special service vessel SUVA had the shortest commission of any ship in the RAN when she commissioned on 23rd June, 1919, to convey Admiral of the Fleet, Lord Jellicoe, and his staff on a tour of the Australian station. Although she paid off on 12th August, SUVA can still claim to have flown the flag of an Admiral of the Fleet longer than any other RAN ship.

New Construction

The improved Town or Birmingham class light cruiser ADELAIDE laid down for service in the Great War, was not fully commissioned until 1922. Her late completion meant that the ship was still considered suitable for retention up to 1939 and able to fight again in another war. BRISBANE, six years older, was unfortunately deleted in 1935. Had she been retained, the cruiser would have undoubtedly provided a valuable escort in coastal waters.

Despite the world economic depression the RAN received a number of new warships in the mid to late twenties. The two heavy cruisers AUSTRALIA and CANBERRA, delivered in 1928, were followed in 1929 by the submarines OTWAY and OXLEY and the locally constructed ALBATROSS. For survey work HMS SILVIO transferred from the Royal Navy to the RAN in 1925 and in 1933, five V and W class destroyers accompanied the leader STUART, as replacements for ANZAC and the S class destroyers.

New construction midway through the decade provided the light cruiser SYDNEY, followed by two sister ships PERTH and HOBART in 1938/39 and the first two sloops of the Grimsby class. But while new ships were entering service, other tonnage was being sent to the shipbreakers. The cruiser BRISBANE was sold in 1935, ANZAC and the five S class destroyers in 1936/37. The three Flower class sloops were scuttled off Sydney in 1935. Australia's

first 'aircraft carrier' ALBATROSS was transferred to the Royal Navy.

Thus during the period 1919–39, the RAN commissioned 33 new warships, but lost 34, already built or acquired mid war. By the outbreak of war in September, 1939, only 14 ships were available for active service.

The Fleet in June, 1919

Ships	Type	Entered Service	Status 1919
Australia	Battlecruiser	1913	Active
Protector	Light Cruiser	1884	Tender
Pioneer	Light Cruiser	1913	Reserve
Psyche	Light Cruiser	1915	Reserve
Encounter	Light Cruiser	1912	Training
Brisbane	Light Cruiser	1916	Active
Melbourne	Light Cruiser	1913	Active
Sydney	Light Cruiser	1913	Active
Huon	Torpedo Boat Destroyer	1915	Reserve
Parramatta	Torpedo Boat Destroyer	1910	Reserve
Swan	Torpedo Boat Destroyer	1916	Active
Torrens	Torpedo Boat Destroyer	1916	Active
Warrego	Torpedo Boat Destroyer	1912	Active
Yarra	Torpedo Boat Destroyer	1910	Reserve
Fantome	Sloop	1915	Reserve
UNA	Sloop	1914	Reserve
Gayundah	Patrol Boat	1884	Reserve
Countess of Hopetoun	Torpedo Boat	1891	Active
Cerberus	Base Ship	1870	Depot
Alacrity	Patrol Boat	1914	Reserve
Nusa	Patrol Boat	1914	Reserve
Sleuth	Patrol Boat	1917	Tender
Platypus	Depot Ship	1919	Active
Penguin	Depot Ship	1913	Depot
OFL 1-4	Lighters	1914	Active
Kurumba	Oiler	1916	Active
Franklin	Tender	1915	Active
Ripple	Tender	1913	Active
Togo	Tender	1916	Reserve
Tingira	Training Ship	1912	Active

Garden Island in 1922. HMAS PLATYPUS, the submarine depot ship, lies alongside with four J class submarines outboard; the Special Service Vessel SUVA and Town class cruiser HMAS SYDNEY are also pictured; HMAS J7, the second submarine off PLATYPUS could be distinguished from her sisters by her conning tower which was set further aft than that of the other boats.

THE FOLLOWING PHOTOGRAPHS illustrate some of the events, acquisitions or losses to affect the Australian Fleet in the mid-war period.

Following long and valuable careers in the Great War, PIONEER and PSYCHE were laid up at Garden Island and employed as accommodation vessels.

The former flagship and largest warship to serve in the RAN, the battlecruiser AUSTRALIA was towed from Sydney Harbour on 12th April, 1924 to be sent to the bottom in accordance with warship limitations imposed by the Washington Naval Conference of 1922. The first photograph shows the ship clearing Sydney Heads, her foremast and mainmast reduced and stripped of most fittings. The second shows the scuttling party boarding the ship to set the demolition charges.

Top – Australia's first aircraft carrier, ALBATROSS, under construction at Cockatoo Island in 1927. (Photo – Cockatoo Island Dockyard)

Above – The fleet's third generation of submarines were HMA Ships OTWAY and OXLEY, ordered in 1924 and completed three years later. Four additional boats were suggested to form a flotilla of six, but were not ordered due to financial and manpower shortages.

Left – One of the most active units up to 1928 was the auxiliary KURUMBA, depicted here in drydock at Cockatoo Island. Note the lack of any armament. (A2620)

Overview of Garden Island taken in 1927. HMAS TINGIRA is alongside the island on lower right of the photograph. Other ships visible include, (from top left) HMAS PENGUIN (ex ENCOUNTER), HMAS MORESBY, two Flower class sloops and a Town class cruiser w th HMAS ANZAC outboard.

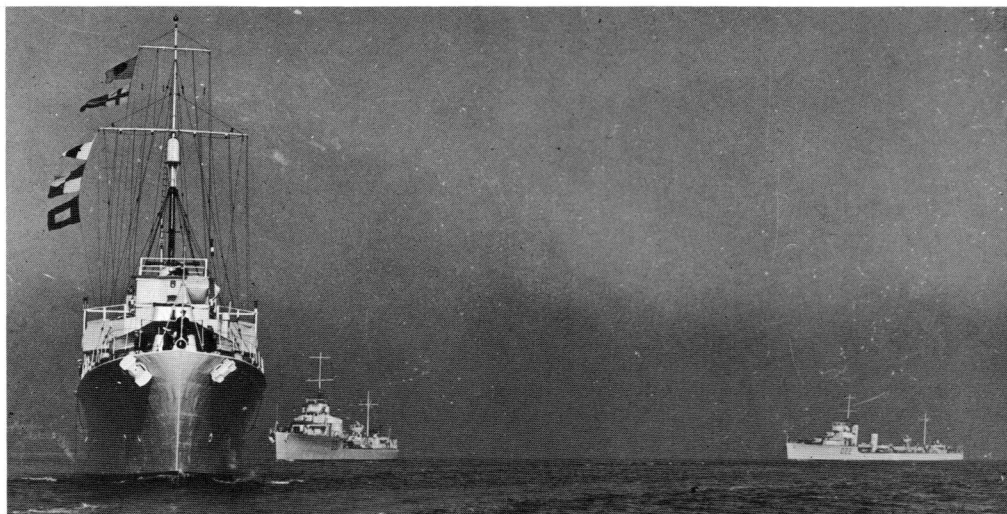

Below — HUON is sunk by naval gunfire on 10th April 1931, by HMA Ships AUSTRALIA and CANBERRA.

Bottom — HMAS AUSTRALIA, 1930s; the aircraft, crane and catapult have not yet been fitted; four single 4-inch guns (without shields) are carried abreast the after-funnel and catapult space; quadruple-torpedo tubes below the after-funnel; searchlights atop the aft superstructure; four 2 pounders abreast the fore and centre funnels.

Between 1933 and 1937, the RAN boasted eleven destroyer type ships, HMAS ANZAC, five S class, HMAS STUART and four V and W class Ships. The above photograph shows, (from left), two V and W class, a third V and W alongside HMAS MORESBY, HMAS PENGUIN (ex PLATYPUS) and BRISBANE (in reserve), two V and W class including HMAS VAMPIRE, ANZAC and an S class and a further two S class destroyers. The seaplane carrier is visible above MORESBY, with HMAS ADELIADE just to the left.

SEAPLANE CARRIER

Albatross

In June, 1924, the Government decided that two cruisers, (AUS-TRALIA and CANBERRA) and two ocean-going submarines, (OXLEY and OTWAY), would be constructed in Great Britain. It was agreed that the £1 million saved by not building the cruisers locally would be used to construct a seaplane tender, named ALBATROSS at Cockatoo Island Dockyard.

The June, 1925 decision specified that the vessel should have a maximum speed of not less than 21 knots and a cost not exceeding £1 million.

ALBATROSS featured a large protected hangar running almost half the length of the ship and divided into three bays. Three electric cranes were fitted to the flight deck, one to port and two to starboard. Provision was made for a catapult but the gear was not fitted until 1936 during her final years in Australian service. Workshops, cafeterias and amenity areas were situated around the hangar. Administration and accommodation spaces were located aft.

Four 4.7 inch 40 calibre Mk VIII QF AA guns were mounted, two aft on the centreline in X and Y positions, and one on each beam, forward of the cranes on the flight deck. The weapons were provided with a total of 600 HE, 280 Senu AP, 60 target smoke and 60 practice rounds. Thirty-six 250lb SAP, 72 100lb LC and 100 20lb bombs were stored in the bomb room for use by the aircraft.

The ship was laid down as No. 106 on 16th April, 1926. Although many parts of the carrier (steel plates and sections) were imported from the United Kingdom, the engines were built on Cockatoo Island. ALBATROSS, launched on 21st February, 1928, was the largest warship ever built in the country and commenced sea trials in November, having cost £1,187,881.

As originally designed ALBATROSS was to carry six Seagull III amphibians (ordered by the R.A.A.F. in 1925). A further three were to be held in reserve (purchased in 1929 at scrap value). In 1931 only four aircraft were embarked and during 1933 all were removed and the ship paid off.

In 1929 two 2 pdr. guns were added to the ship's armament.

ALBATROSS remained in reserve from 26th April, 1933, to 19th April, 1938, when she recommissioned for transfer to the

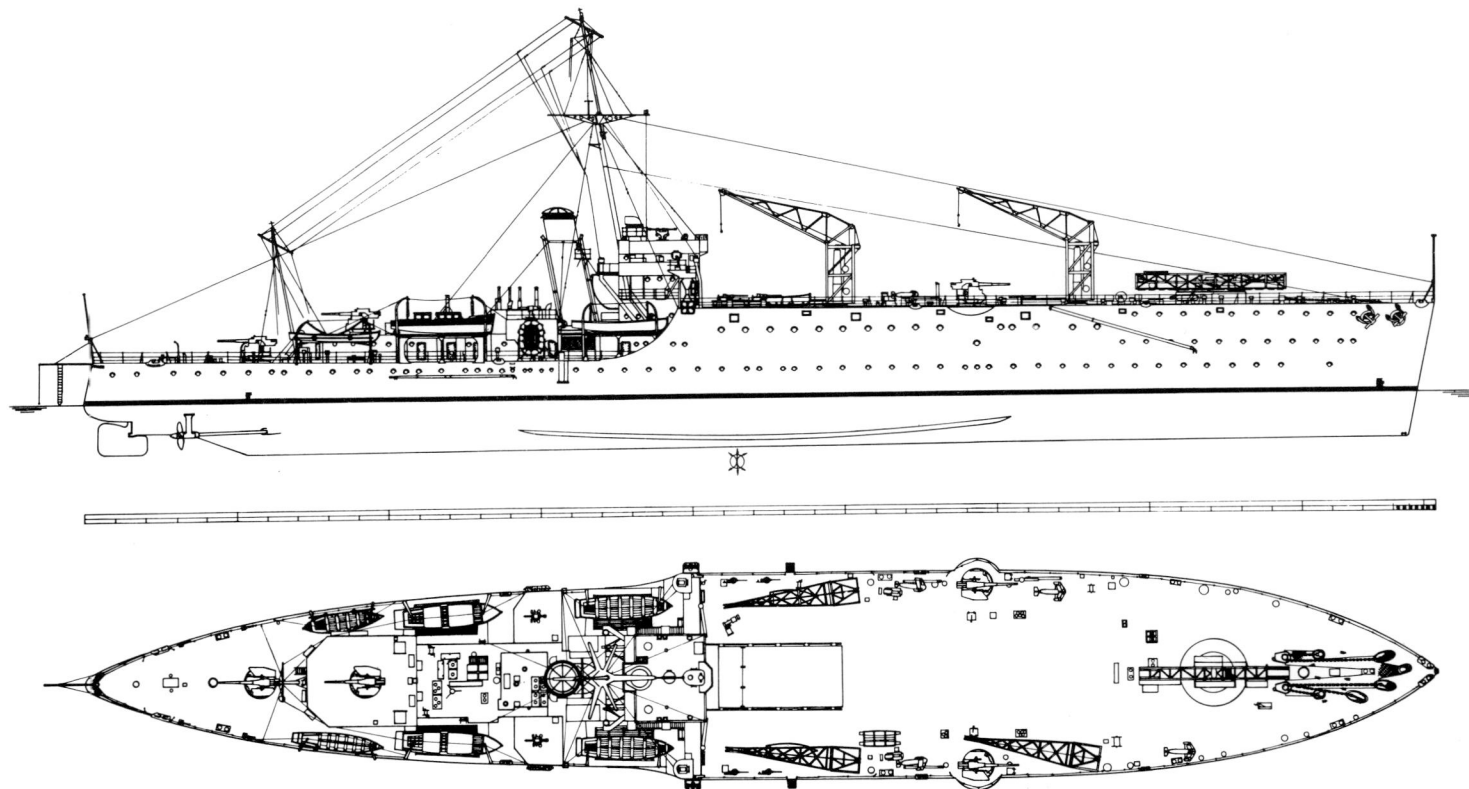

HMAS ALBATROSS, 1936; (P. Webb)

HMAS ALBATROSS; a Seagull III is being hoisted aboard.

Royal Navy as part payment (£266,500) for the cruiser HOBART (HMS APOLLO). The carrier sailed from Sydney on 11th July, and arrived in the U.K. to be manned by Royal Navy personnel. Not long after, she again paid off but was recommissioned in September, 1939, and embarked six Walrus aircraft for anti-submarine patrol work in the South Atlantic.

The ship was refitted in Mobile, U.S.A., from January to April, 1942, and thence operated on the east coast of Africa. Back at Devonport ALBATROSS was converted to a landing craft repair ship from April to May, 1944. Following service during the Normandy invasion she paid off to reserve in June, 1945, and on 8th August, 1945, was formally decommissioned.

ALBATROSS was sold in 1946 and in 1947 converted to a migrant ship, named HELLENIC PRINCE. The old carrier was eventually broken up in Hong Kong from 12th August, 1954.

Displacement (tons): *Standard* 4,800 Full load 6,000
Dimensions (feet): *Length* 433.7 *Beam* 77.9 (over sponsons) *Draught* 18.0 (max forward)
Machinery: 2 sets Parsons single reduction geared turbines, 2 shafts, 10,800 s.h.p. (max)
Speed (knots): 22.87 maximum
Range (miles): 12,150 @ 10 knots, 4,200 @ 22 knots
Manning: 342
Armament: Four 4.7 inch (4 × 1), Two 2 pdr (2 × 1), Four Vickers MGs, Ten .303 Lewis MGs (10 × 1), Ten .303 Lewis MGs (5 × 2), Six Seagull III amphibians (see notes).

Ship	Pend. No.	Builder	Cons. Time	Comm.	Fate
Albatross	D22 (WWII)	Cockatoo	2y 9m	23/1/29	RN 1938

Right – HMAS ALBATROSS at Port Melbourne. One of the ship's 4.7-inch guns is visible on the port side amidships. Three cranes for hoisting the seaplanes are also in place; the mounting for the aircraft catapult is vacant.

Below – ALBATROSS under construction. (Photo – Cockatoo Island Dockyard)

Bottom – HMAS ALBATROSS, late twenties; all four main guns are under cover and the three cranes are battened down.

Left – An unusual view of HMAS ALBATROSS showing her narrowing stern section; two 4.7-inch guns are on the centreline aft in X and Y positions; searchlights are carried on the bridge wings; a seaplane is parked on the main deck forward.

Below – Aboard the carrier looking towards the bridge.

Bottom – En route for England for transfer to the Royal Navy; note the catapult (fitted in 1936) and Seagull V seaplane secured on top; the two 2 pounder guns added in 1929 are visible on either side of the aircraft.

IMPROVED TOWN CLASS

Adelaide

ADELAIDE the oldest British-designed cruiser to participate in the Second World War, mounted the BL 6-inch Mk XIII as her main armament, a more capable weapon than was fitted to the three Town class ships. She was completely modernised prior to the outbreak of war. The work involved conversion to oil-burning, (as distinct from coal and oil), and the removal of the forefunnel, two 21-inch submerged torpedo tubes and the two forward gun mountings. Her original 3-inch anti-aircraft gun in 'X' position was replaced by a single 4-inch mounting and the two 3 pdr.

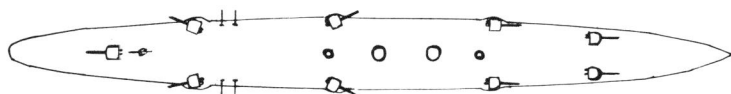

HMAS ADELAIDE; deck plans showing armament as built 1922,

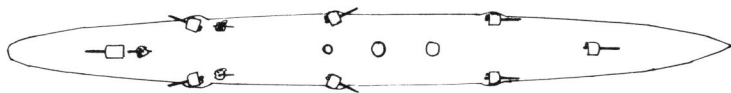

1939

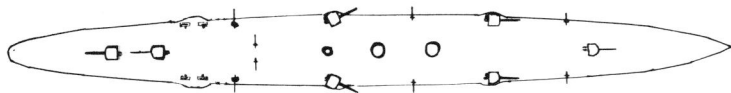

and 1945. (R. Gillett)

mountings on either beam by a single 4-inch mounting. The forward 6-inch gun was remounted on the centreline, immediately before the bridge.

During 1942–43 two more 6-inch guns were deleted from the waist and replaced by two sets of depth charge throwers. At the same time the 4-inch mounting in 'X' position was replaced by a 6-inch gun. Several 20mm mounts were also added amidships and abreast the bridge for short-range anti-aircraft defence. To provide increased protection, the main guns were fitted with new shields.

On 26th February, 1945, ADELAIDE paid off to reserve and was sold in 1947.

Displacement (tons): *Standard* 5,560 *Full Load* N/A
Dimensions (feet): *Length* (oa) 460.0 *Beam* 50.0 *Draught* 18.6
Machinery: Parsons turbines; twin screws; 25,000 s.h.p.
Speed (knots): $25\frac{1}{2}$
Range (miles): N/A
Manning: 470
Armanent: Nine 6-inch (9 × 1), One 3 inch (1 × 1), One 12 pdr (1 × 1), Four 3 pdr. (4 × 1), Ten smaller (20mm and MGs), Two 21 inch torpedo tubes.

Ship	Pend. No.	Builder	Cons. Time	Comm.	Fate
Adelaide	147	Cockatoo Island	7y 4m	5/8/22	Sold 21/3/47

Opposite – The light cruiser ADELAIDE under construction at Cockatoo Island, 1920; the tripod foremast is being fitted with a director tower and control top; the smaller mainmast is aft; mountings for the forward and broadside 6-inch guns are visible.

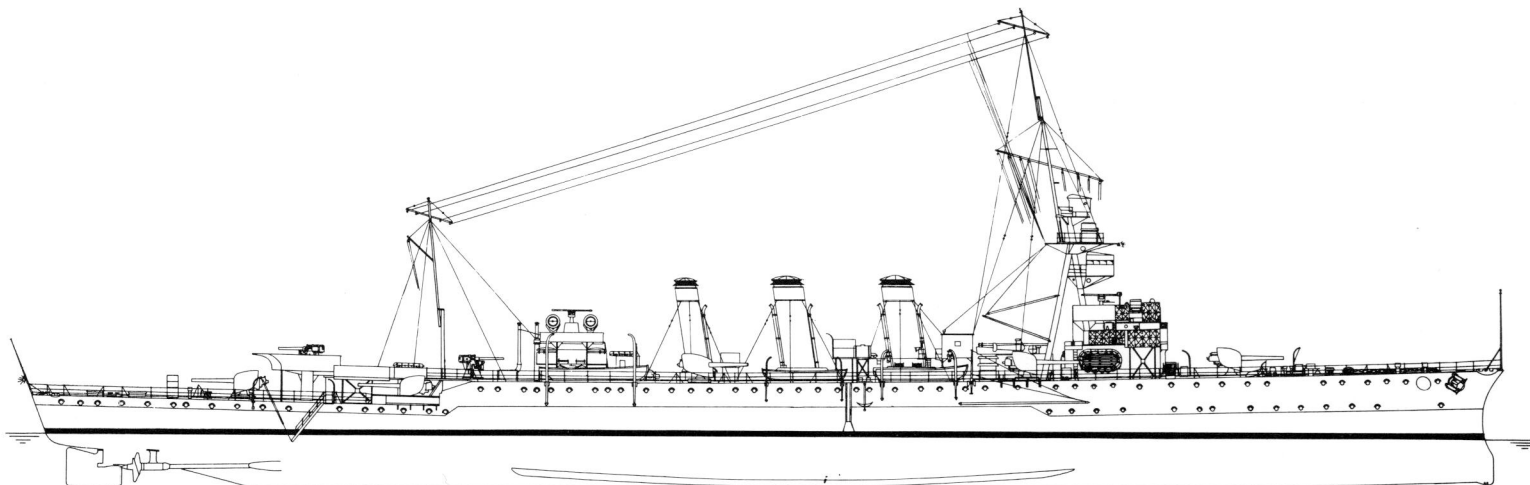

HMAS ADELAIDE; profile in March, 1939. (P. Webb)

HMAS ADELAIDE proceeds down harbour for working up trials following an extensive pre-war refit. The pilot boat CAPTAIN COOK, an examination vessel in the Great War, is behind the cruiser's mainmast.

Below – HMAS ADELAIDE, mid 1920s; two 6-inch guns are sited forward of the bridge, one on each beam; two searchlights amidships and abaft the fourth funnel; a wireless cabin is sited between the fore and second funnels and the control top and director tower are painted black.

Left – HMAS ADELAIDE, 1944, in her final operational appearance; completely camouflaged; tower erected forward of the forefunnel; 6-inch guns on waist replaced by depth charge throwers; 4-inch gun in X position replaced by 6-inch weapon; 20 mm mounts fitted abreast the bridge and amidships. Note the square-shaped shields fitted to the main 6-inch guns.

Below – HMAS ADELAIDE, May, 1941, showing modifications to the ship after modernisation; single 6-inch gun forward; gunnery control position altered on tripod foremast; fore funnel deleted; midship searchlights removed and single 4-inch anti-aircraft guns fitted abaft and abreast the mainmast (total 3).

COUNTY CLASS

Australia, Canberra

Ordered in 1924 as part of a five year naval construction programme. Six sister ships were also built for the Royal Navy. Prior
to the Second World War, AUSTRALIA was extensively modernised between April, 1938, and August, 1939. This work included
the substitution of four twin 4-inch Mk XVI guns for the original
single mounts. As built (and for war service), both AUSTRALIA
and CANBERRA were allowed 150 rounds per eight inch gun and
200 rounds per four inch gun. Each 2 pdr. was allotted 1,000
rounds.

AUSTRALIA was again refitted at Liverpool in late 1940
and her torpedo tubes removed in 1942. By late 1943, two quadruple 0.5 inch MGs had been deleted and seven single 20mm
mounts fitted. The latter were replaced by seven twin mounts
by early 1944. During 1945 eight single 40mm bofors were added,
all 20mm mountings and the twin 8-inch turret in X position
removed.

In early 1941, CANBERRA lost her four single pom-poms,
while two eight-barrelled pom-poms and 20mm mounts were
added. Two of the 20mm mounts were sited atop her B and X
8-inch turrets. CANBERRA was lost in August, 1942, and replaced by SHROPSHIRE.

Both cruisers were fitted with catapults, AUSTRALIA in
September, 1935, and CANBERRA in April, 1936. Until 1936
Seagull IIIs were embarked and subsequently Seagull Vs.
AUSTRALIA's aircraft and catapult were removed in October,
1944.

AUSTRALIA was refitted post-war and remained in commission until 31st August, 1954.

Displacement (tons): *Standard* 9,850 *Full Load* 13,630
Dimensions (feet): *Length* (oa) 630 *Beam* 68.4 *Draught* 21.8
Machinery: Brown Curtis geared turbines, 4 screws, 80,000 s.h.p.
Speed (knots): 31.5
Range (miles): 10,400 @ 11 knots
Manning: 848
Armament: Eight 8-inch (4 × 2), Four 4-inch (4 × 1), Four 2
pdr. pom-poms, Four 3 pdr., Four .303 Vickers, Eight .303
Lewis, Eight 21-inch torpedo tubes (2 × 4) (see notes). One
Seagull III amphibian.

Ship	Pend. No.	Builder	Cons. Time	Comm.	Fate
Australia	I84 D84 (1940)	John Brown & Co. Ltd.	2y 8m	24/4/28	Sold 25/1/55
Canberra	I33 D33 (1940)	ditto	2y 10m	9/7/28	Sunk 9/8/42

Opposite above – HMAS AUSTRALIA as commissioned and with tall funnels.

Opposite below – HMAS CANBERRA, July, 1928. Space is reserved for flying
operations, but no crane or catapult is fitted.

HMAS CANBERRA, March, 1941, profile. (P. Webb)

Right – AUSTRALIA prior to launching on 17th March, 1927. Propellor blades have yet to be fitted to the starboard outboard shaft.

Bottom – HMAS AUSTRALIA, 1930s; the aircraft, crane and catapult have not yet been fitted; four single 4-inch guns (without shields) are carried abreast the after-funnel and catapult space; quadruple-torpedo tubes below the after-funnel; searchlights atop the aft superstructure; four 2 pounders abreast the fore and centre funnels.

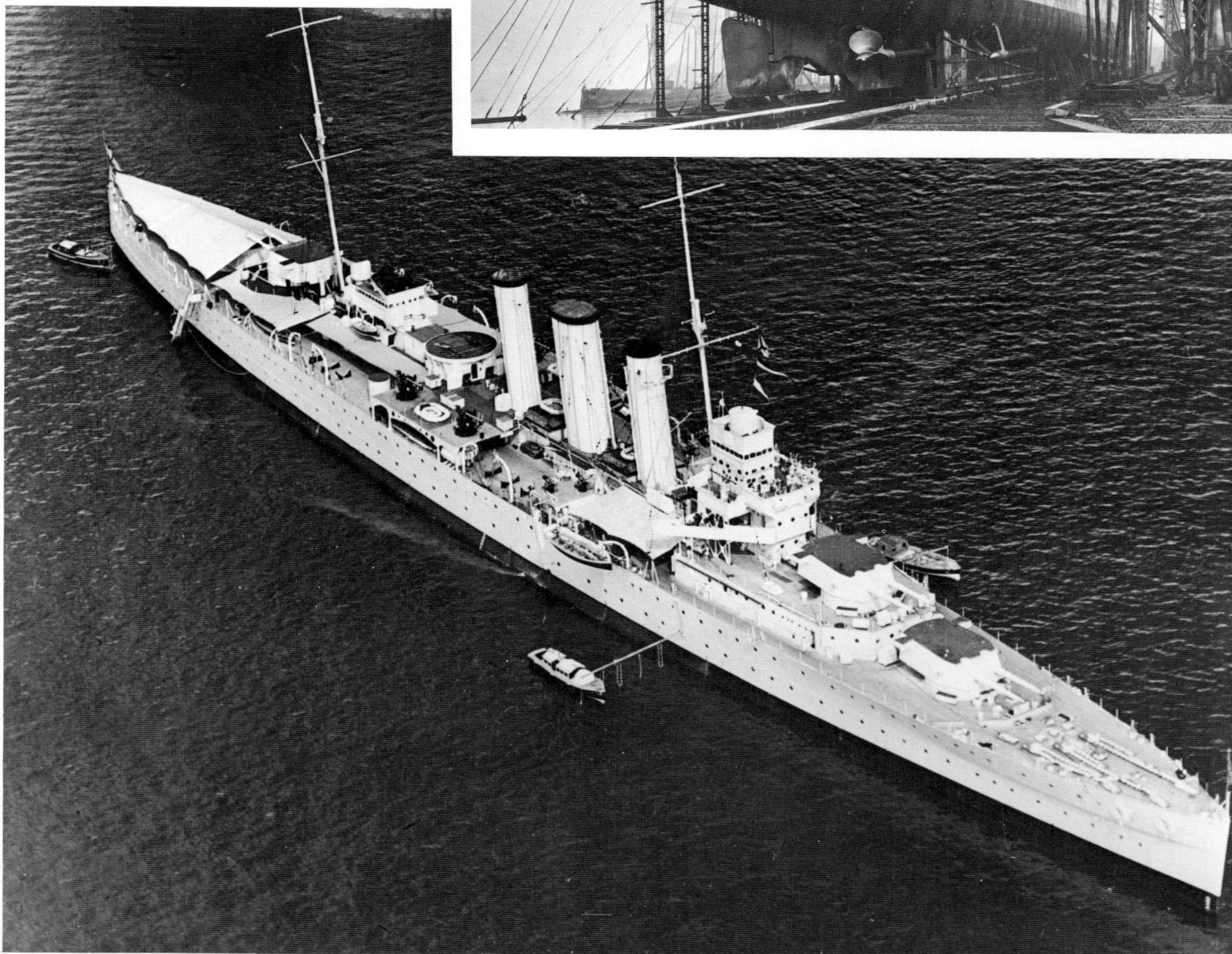

Left – HMAS AUSTRALIA, 19th October, 1939; four single 4-inch guns replaced by twins with shields and remounted on the upper deck; catapult and Seagull V carried; bridge modernised and rebuilt; two aircraft cranes fitted and gunnery control positions re-arranged.

Below – HMAS CANBERRA pre-war. The catapult and aircraft are in place; 4-inch single mounts are still retained.

Right – HMAS AUSTRALIA, 1941, displaying her wartime camouflage. A Seagull V is secured to the catapult.

Below – HMAS AUSTRALIA, 1945; twin 4-inch guns still carried on the higher deck; aircraft facilities removed; small calibre anti-aircraft gun atop B and X mounts; new radars fitted to fore and main masts; torpedo tubes deleted.

MODIFIED LEANDER

Hobart, Perth, Sydney

These cruisers were ordered by the Admiralty in 1933 for the Royal Navy. HOBART and PERTH were commissioned into the British fleet as HMS APOLLO and HMS AMPHION during January, 1936 and July, 1936, respectively. SYDNEY was commissioned as an RAN unit from the outset, although she was laid down as HMS PHAETON.

Each ship was fitted to carry a Seagull V amphibian, with the 53-foot revolving catapult sited between the funnels. Before transferring to the RAN, HOBART and PERTH were refitted and their four single 4-inch guns replaced by four twin mountings. The old 46-foot fixed catapults were also removed. The outbreak of war prevented SYDNEY being given a major refit and she retained the four single 4-inch mountings until her loss.

Between January and February, 1941, PERTH was armed with a quadruple pom-pom amidships, but this weapon was deleted the following July. Later she received 20mm mounts atop both 'B' and 'X' turrets.

HOBART underwent refit in Devonport in late 1942, when her catapult was removed and one single and five twin 20mm and two quadruple pom-poms were fitted. On 20th July, 1943, she suffered severe torpedo damage and in the ensuing refit (8/1943 to 1/1945), four twin 20mm mounts were removed and one single 20mm, five single 40mm bofors (Mk III) and three twin Hazemeyer bofors fitted. At the same time HOBART's four twin 4-inch mountings were repositioned, tripod masts fitted and the catapult structure deleted, (the catapult itself had been removed in June, 1941).

SYDNEY was lost on 19th November, 1941, following an action with the German raider KORMORAN and PERTH on 1st March, 1942, after fighting a powerful Japanese force in the Sunda Strait. HOBART survived the conflict and in December, 1947, was decommissioned and placed in reserve. In 1953 she was selected for conversion to a training ship, but although taken to Newcastle and work on her begun, the scheme was cancelled and she was returned to reserve and sold in February, 1962.

Displacement (tons): *Standard* 7,105 (Hobart) 6,980 (Perth) 6,830 (Sydney) *Full Load* 9,000
Dimensions (feet): *Length* (oa) 555.0 *Beam* 56.8 *Draught* 19.6
Machinery: Parsons geared turbines; four Admiralty 3 drum boilers; 4 screws; 72,000 s.h.p.
Speed (knots): 32.5
Range (miles): 7,000 @ 16 knots
Manning: 685
Armament: Eight 6-inch (4 × 2), Eight 4-inch (4 × 2) (except Sydney Four 4-inch (4 × 1)), Four 3 pdr., Three 4-barrell 0.5 inch MGs, Eight 21-inch torpedo tubes (2 × 4), One Seagull V amphibian (see notes).

Ship	Pend. No.	Builder	Cons. Time	Comm.	Fate
Hobart	I63 D63 (1940)	Devonport Dockyard	2y 5m	28/9/38	Sold 22/2/62
Perth	I29 D29 (1940)	Portsmouth Dockyard	3y 1m	29/6/39	Sunk 1/3/42
Sydney	I48 D48 (1940)	Swan Hunter	2y 2m	24/9/35	Sunk 19/11/41

HMAS SYDNEY; profile as completed with crane but no aircraft catapult. (R. Gillett)

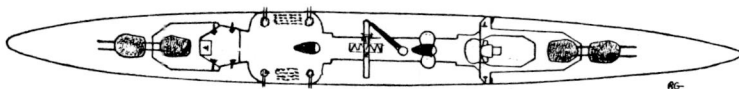

HMAS PERTH; plan showing original armament.

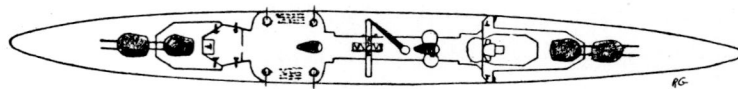

HMAS SYDNEY; plan showing original armament.

HMAS SYDNEY, Port Melbourne, 1938; searchlights are carried on the bridge adjacent to the fore-funnel and mainmast; HA control tower atop bridge; four-barrelled 0 5-inch MGs abreast the bridge; four single 4-inch guns (no shields) abreast after-funnel; Seagull V on catapult amidships; quad-torpedo tubes below 4-inch gun deck.

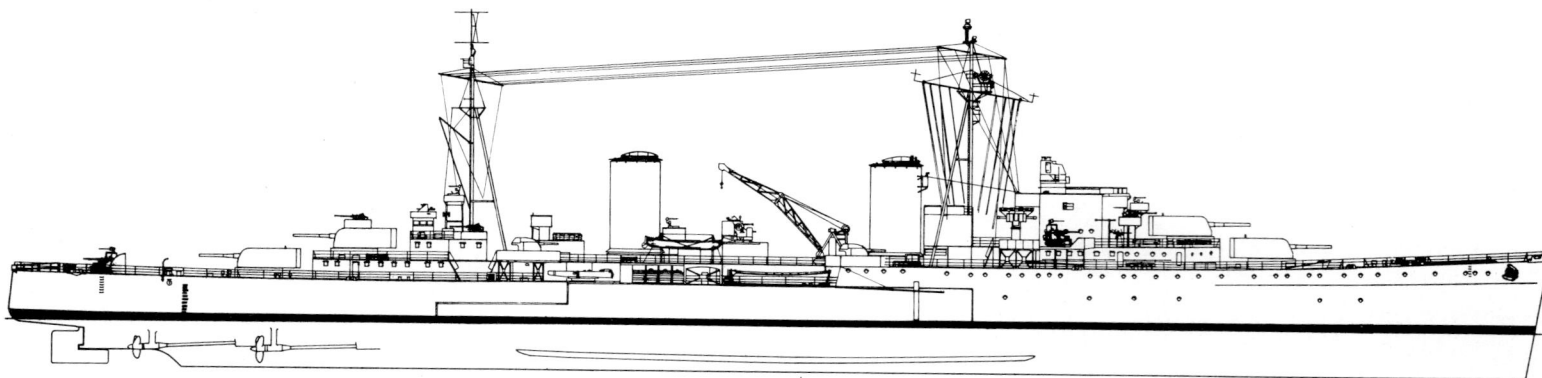

HMAS HOBART, April, 1945; profile. (P. Webb)

Above – HMAS PERTH in early 1942, not long before her loss. Note flaps on funnels; Seagull V and twin 4-inch mountings; light anti-aircraft guns atop B and X turrets.

Left – Launching a torpedo, HMAS SYDNEY.

Below left – Seagull V amphibian above HMAS SYDNEY.

Below – HMAS SYDNEY, May, 1941.

Right – HMAS HOBART, Chowder Bay, Sydney Harbour, 17th August, 1940.

Below – HMAS SYDNEY on return from her Mediterranean sea victories.

DESTROYER LEADER

Anzac

Ship	Pend. No.	Builder	Cons. Time	Comm.	Fate
Anzac	F61 (2/1917)	Denny	1y 2m	1920	Paid Off 30/7/33
	G60 (4/1917)				
	G50 (1/1918)				
	G70 (4/1918)				

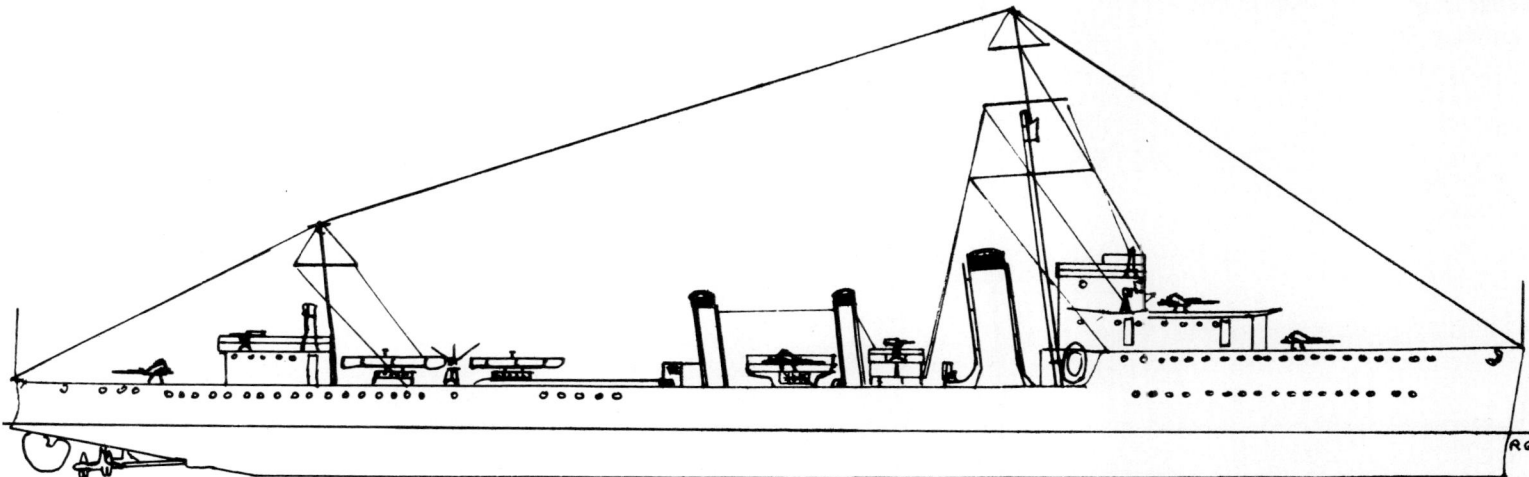

ANZAC was completed for the Royal Navy on 24th April, 1917, as a unit of the later Marksman class. She was the only three-funnelled destroyer to serve in the RAN and the first Australian warship to mount superfiring guns in A and B position before the bridge structure. Q gun was sited on a bandstand between the second and third funnels and Y mount on the quarterdeck. Pom-poms were carried on X deck (aft) and on a small platform abaft the larger funnel.

During her active service with the fleet, ANZAC exercised in eastern Australian waters, interspersed by three visits to New Britain and New Guinea.

She was sold on 8th August, 1935, and after being stripped down was sunk as a target on 7th May, 1936.

Displacement (tons): *Standard* 1,310 *Full load* 1,660
Dimensions (feet): *Length* (oa) 325 *Beam* 31.10 *Draught* 12.1
Machinery: Brown Curtiss turbines, 3 screws, 136,000 s.h.p.
Speed (knots): 34
Range (miles): 2,500 @ 15 knots
Manning: 122
Armament: Four 4-inch (4 × 1), Two 2 pdr. pom-pom (2 × 1), Four Lewis (4 × 1), Four 21-inch torpedo tubes (2 × 2).

Right – HMAS ANZAC, in the Alfred Graving Dock. A 2 pounder gun is mounted below the searchlight and a 4-inch gun on the poop. (Photo – P. William)

HMAS ANZAC; profile. (R. Gillett)

ADMIRALTY S CLASS

Stalwart, Success, Swordsman, Tasmania, Tattoo

The five S class destroyers were originally completed for the Royal Navy between January and April, 1919, but never served in the British Fleet. They were commissioned as HMA Ships from the outset. Like ANZAC, the ships spent their careers active on the eastern seaboard, but TASMANIA visited New Guinea in 1924.

Three 4-inch quick-firing guns were mounted; A mount on the foc'sle, Q mount amidships upon a bandstand and Y mount, right aft. The five S class were the first RAN destroyers to feature depth charge throwers, carried on both sides of the pom-pom platform. During their RAN service no alterations were made to the armament carried.

Although not worn out, the ships were gradually paid off after an average service life of only seven years. TATTOO was recommissioned on 5th October, 1933 for service as a training ship. In July, 1936 she was replaced by VAMPIRE. On 4th June, 1937, all five were sold for breaking up.

Displacement (tons): *Standard* 905 *Full load* 1,075
Dimensions (feet): *Length* (oa) 276 *Beam* 26.9 *Draught* 10.1
Machinery: Brown Curtiss all-geared turbines, 2 screws, 27,000 s.h.p.
Speed (knots): 36
Range (miles): 2,000 @ 15 knots
Manning: 90

Armament: Three 4-inch (3 × 1), One 2 pdr. pom-pom (1 × 1), Four Lewis (4 × 1), One Maxim, Four 21-inch torpedo tubes (2 × 2), Two DCTs.

Ship	Pend. No.	Builder	Cons. Time	Comm.	Fate
Stalwart	F4A (4/1919)	Swan Hunter	1y	27/1/20	Paid Off 1/12/25
	H14 (1920)				
Success	F1A (4/1919)	Doxford	1y ?m	27/1/20	Paid Off 21/5/30
	H02 (1920)				
Swords-man	F3A (3/1919)	Scotts	1y ?m	27/1/20	Paid Off 21/12/29
	H11 (1920)				
Tasmania	G97 (2/1919)	Beardmore	1y 1m	27/1/20	Paid Off 9/1/28
	H25 (1920)				
Tattoo	F2A (4/1919)	Beardmore	1y 3m	27/1/20	Paid Off 30/6/33
	H26 (1920)				

Opposite above – HMAS TASMANIA.

Opposite below – HMA Ships TATTOO, SUCCESS and SWORDSMAN, Sydney, 1920. Note the platforms mounting a single 4-inch gun between the stacks, torpedo tubes (two twin) and searchlight platforms.

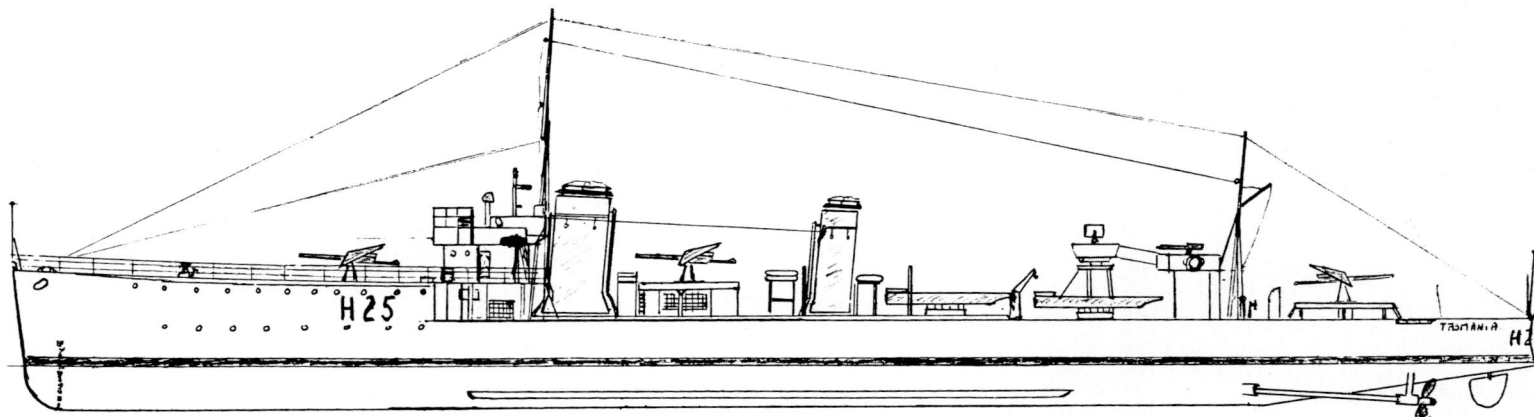

HMAS TASMANIA; profile. (H. Adlam)

Right – HMAS SUCCESS and HMAS TASMANIA (rear) in 1926). The torpedo tubes are trained in the attacking position. The crew member riding the tubes fired the weapons. (Photo – M. Macdonald).

Below – HMAS SWORDSMAN at speed. (Photo – M. MacDonald)

Bottom – HMAS TASMANIA, 1920; the shields to the bridge are in a lowered position.

HMAS SUCCESS; a 4-inch gun is mounted on a bandstand aft and immediately forward the 2 pounder pom-pom. (Photo – H. Cliff).

SCOTT CLASS

Stuart

Constructed for the Royal Navy as a flotilla leader, STUART was completed in December, 1918. Along with the four V and W class destroyers, she was transferred to the RAN in October, 1933. During the course of the war she underwent numerous armament changes, (see below).

HMAS STUART: deck plans showing armament outfit in 1933,

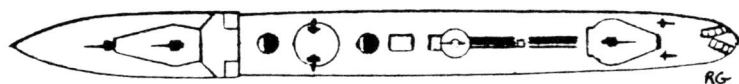

1941,

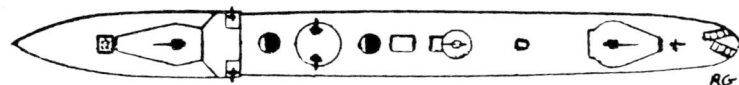

1942

1944. (R. Gillett)

In 1944 as a fast troop transport she was defensively armed against attacks by submarines and aircraft. STUART survived the war and paid off in February, 1946.

In her original RAN configuration STUART carried 120 rounds for each 4.7 inch gun, 100 rounds for the 3 inch and 500 rounds per pom-pom.

Displacement (tons): *Standard* 1,530 *Full Load* 2,053
Dimensions (feet): *Length* (oa) 332.6 *Beam* 31.9 *Draught* 12.3
Machinery: Brown-Curtis turbines; twin screws; 40,000 s.h.p.
Speed (knots): 36
Range (miles): 5,000 @ 15 knots
Manning: 185
Armament: *1939* – Five 4.7-inch (5 × 1), One 3-inch (1 × 1), Two 2 pdr. (2 × 4), Four Lewis, One Maxim, Six 21-inch torpedo (2 × 3). *1941* – Three 4.7-inch (3 × 1), One 3-inch (1 × 1), Two 2 pdr. (2 × 4), Five 20mm (5 × 1), One Breda gun, One .303 Vickers (1 × 1), Four .303 Lewis, Six 21-inch torpedo tubes (2 × 3), Two DCR, Two DCTs. *1942* – (Escort): Two 4.7-inch (2 × 1), Three 20mm (3 × 1), Two 2 pdr. (2 × 4), One 3-inch (1 × 1), One Hedgehog ahead-throwing weapon. *1944* – (Transport): One 4-inch (1 × 1), Seven 20mm (1 × 2, 5 × 1), Three 2 pdr. (3 × 4), One Hedgehog ahead-throwing weapon, DCs.

Ship	Pend. No.	Builder	Cons. Time	Comm.	Fate
Stuart	G46 (1919)	Hawthorn Leslie	1y 2m	11/10/33	Sold 3/2/47
	F20 (1919)				
	D00 (1920)				
	I00 (1940)				

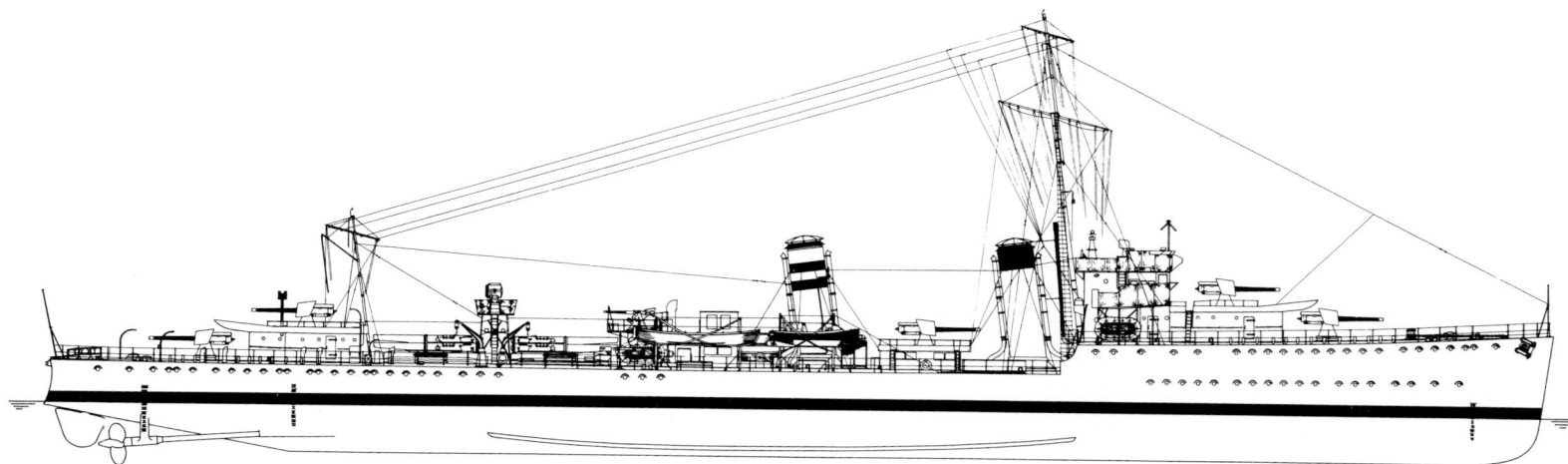

HMAS STUART; profile at the time of her transfer to the RAN, October, 1933. (P. Webb)

Above left – HMS STUART, 1927; five 4.7-inch guns in A, B, Q (on bandstand), X and Y positions; one 3-inch gun abaft the second funnel; two triple-torpedo tubes; searchlight between the tubes; and both foremast and mainmast. (Photo – P. Britz)

Above – HMAS STUART 1941; camouflaged for mediterranean service; after-funnel reduced; 'Q' and 'X' 4.7 inch mounts deleted for light a/a weapons; and mainmast removed.

Left – HMAS STUART, 1942, modified to escort destroyer; 'A' 4.7-inch gun replaced by hedge-hog mortar; radars fitted to foremast; 20mm Oerlikons added to bridge wings; 2 pounders between funnels; torpedoes deleted; 20mm Oerlikons added aft.

Below – HMAS STUART, seen port broadside 1942, as an escort destroyer. The mortar is visible forward. Two years later her armament was altered to fit her for duty as a fast transport.

V AND W CLASS

Vampire, Vendetta, Voyager, Waterhen

In October, 1933, VAMPIRE, VENDETTA, VOYAGER and WATERHEN were transferred to the RAN, (along with the leader STUART), as replacements for the smaller, yet younger, S class destroyers. VAMPIRE and VENDETTA were completed in late 1917, VOYAGER and WATERHEN in mid 1918. The four ships underwent numerous armament changes throughout their long careers. As built each 4-inch gun was allotted 120 rounds.

The four RAN ships comprised three types; VAMPIRE completed as a flotilla leader with two triple torpedo tubes and referred to as a V Leader; VENDETTA, based on the V Leader design, but with less cabin accommodation and two twin tubes; VOYAGER

and WATERHEN identical to the V class but with the triple torpedo tubes included when under construction. Between 1936 and 1938 VAMPIRE was employed as a training destroyer at Western Port, Victoria.

During World War II the after-set of 21-inch torpedo tubes was replaced, initially by a four-barrelled .5-inch Vickers machine gun and then by a single 12 pdr. HA gun in three ships and two 2 pdr. guns in VAMPIRE. To allow for the additional guns, a bandstand was fitted in the tube space. One 0.5-inch MG (1 × 4) was also added to each of the bridge wings on all ships except WATERHEN. All four mounted 0.5-inch MGs (1 × 4) aft of the

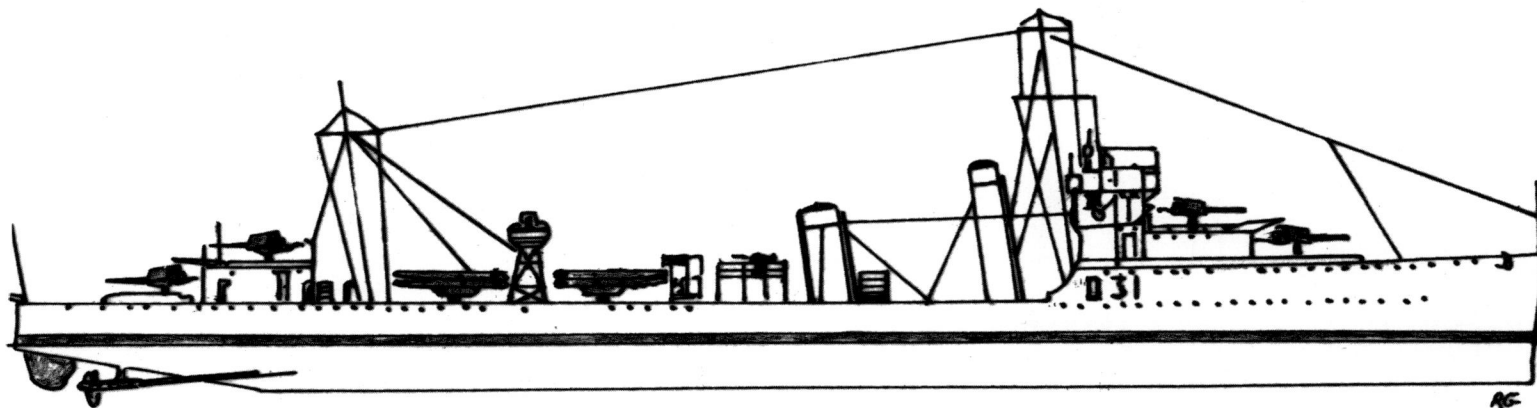

HMAS VOYAGER, 1939, profile. (R. Gillett)

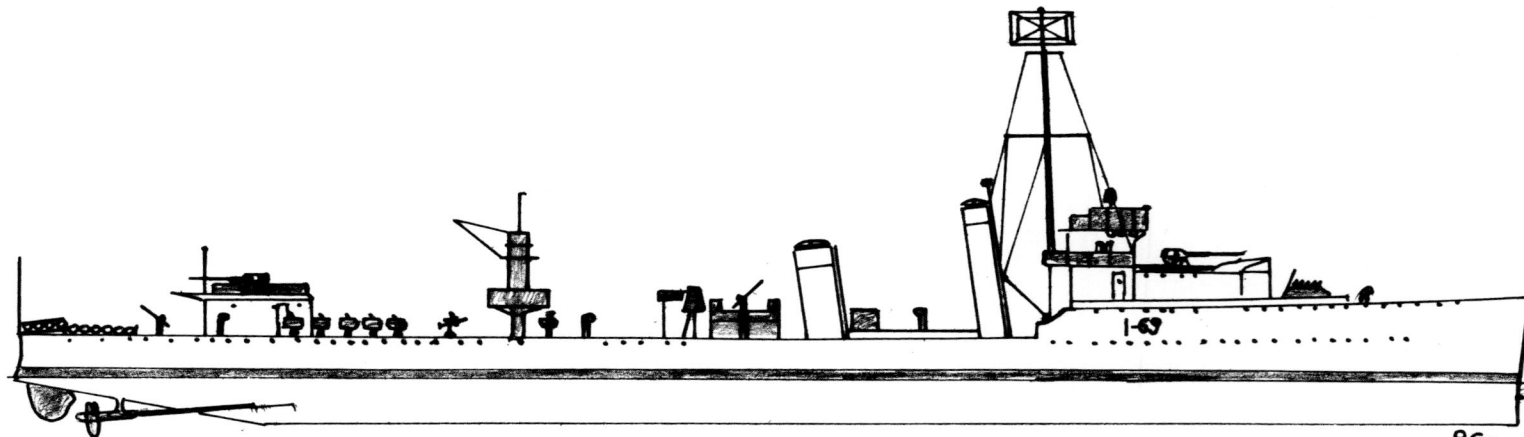

HMAS VENDETTA; profile showing armament as escort destroyer, 1945. (R. Gillett)

second funnel on the pom-pom platform (the weapon having been deleted). Fifty depth charges were normally carried.

During 1941 WATERHEN was lost while transporting troops on the 'Tobruk Ferry'. VAMPIRE was sunk by Japanese aircraft and VOYAGER was lost after grounding at Betano Bay, Timor. Unable to be refloated she was destroyed by her own crew.

VENDETTA, working as an escort, was armed with two 4-inch, two 2 pdr. pom-poms, four 20mm Oerlikons, three .303-inch Vickers and four .303-inch Lewis guns, plus 50 depth charges. On 27th November, 1945, she paid off and was sold for scrap.

Displacement (tons): *Standard* 1,188 (Vampire) 1,090 (Vendetta) 1,100 (Voyager & Waterhen) *Full Load* 1,470

Dimensions (feet): *Length* (oa) 312.1 *Beam* 29.6 *Draught* 9.8

Machinery: Brown-Curtis geared turbines (except Waterhen – Parsons geared turbines and Voyager – Yarrow geared turbines); twin screws; 27,000 s.h.p.

Speed (knots): 34

Range (miles): 3,500 @ 15 knots

Manning: 127

Armament: Four 4-inch (4 × 1), One 2 pdr. pom-pom (1 × 4), One .303 Vickers (1 × 4), Four .303 Lewis (2 × 2), Six 21-inch torpedo tubes (2 × 3), DCR.

Ship	Pend. No.	Builder	Cons. Time	Comm.	Fate
Vampire	F0A (1917)	J. Samuel White	11 m	11/10/33	Sunk 8/4/42
	G70 (1.18)				
	G50 (4.18)				
	D68 (1919)				
	I68 (1940)				
Vendetta	FA3 (1917)	Fairfield	11 m	11/10/33	Sold 20/3/46
	F29 (1.18)				
	D69 (1919)				
	I69 (1940)				
Voyager	G36 (6.18)	Alex Stephen	1y 1m	11/10/33	Lost 23/9/42
	D31 (1919)				
	I31 (1940)				
Waterhen	G28 (9.18)	Palmers	1y	11/10/33	Sunk 30/6/41
	D22 (1919)				
	I22 (1940)				

HMAS VAMPIRE, 1935. (Photo – P. Britz)

HMAS VENDETTA pre-war. (Photo – Ron Wright collection)

HMAS VOYAGER, 1930s. Note the 2 pounder pom-pom abaft the after-funnel. (Photo – P. Britz)

Right – HMAS VOYAGER at Alexandria, 1941. (Photo – R. Gillett collection)

Far right – HMAS WATERHEN, 1941; the after-set of tubes now occupied by 12 pounder gun; machine guns have replaced the pom-pom abaft the second funnel; mainmast deleted; foremast altered.

Below right – **HMAS VENDETTA** under tow for Singapore to Melbourne, March, 1942; machine guns are visible on the bridge wings.

Below – VOYAGER aground at Timor, September, 1942. (157242)

Bottom – HMAS VENDETTA in Jacquinot Bay, New Britain, 4th November 1944, as modified to an escort destroyer; 4-inch guns in 'B' and 'X' positions; 2 pounder pom-poms abaft the after-funnel and right aft; machine guns on the bridge wings and aft of the original searchlight platform; depth charges fitted on throwers abreast X mount and in rails at the stern. A hedgehog anti-submarine weapon is carried in 'A' position.

FLOWER CLASS MINESWEEPING SLOOPS

Geranium, Mallow, Marguerite

Originally laid down in mid-1915 and completed for the Royal Navy in 1916. The trio sailed to Australia in 1919 to clear mine-fields laid by the German raider WOLF. All paid off in Sydney on 18th October, 1919.

Known collectively as the Flower class, the two Arabis type (GERANIUM and MARGUERITE) and one Acacia type (MALLOW) sloops experienced only short mid-war careers. GERANIUM operated for eight years as a survey ship and MARGUERITE nine and a half on fleet and reservist duties. Although idle for most of her RAN career MALLOW was also employed training reservists. For a time MARGUERITE oper-ated as destroyer depot ship, but was found to be totally unsuitable in this role.

During 1924 GERANIUM was allotted a Fairy IIID sea-plane for survey operations. The plane was accommodated on a small ramp on the stern and later above the after superstructure.

After some years laid up in reserve GERANIUM was handed over to Cockatoo Island for dismantling on 10th June, 1932.

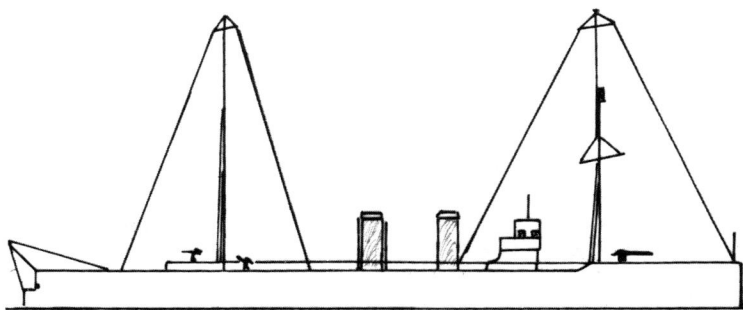

HMAS MALLOW; profile. (R. Gillett)

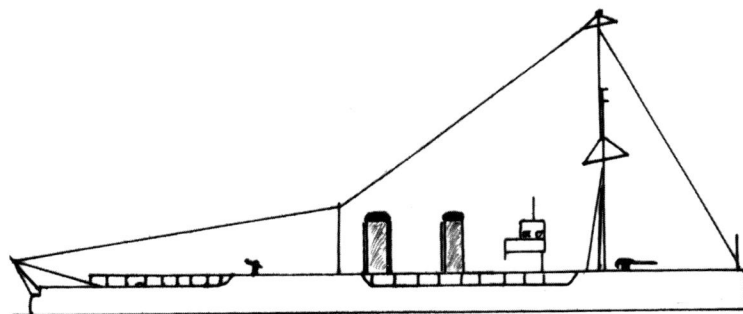

HMAS MARGUERITE; profile. (R. Gillett)

HMAS GERANIUM in the Fitzroy Dock, Cockatoo Island. Note the absence of gun forward and enlarged bridge wings. (Photo – S. Given)

MALLOW followed on 25th July and MARGUERITE in September. GERANIUM was sunk off SYDNEY on 24th April, 1935, MARGUERITE and MALLOW on 1st August, 1935.

Displacement (tons): 1,250 (Arabis class) 1,200 (Acacia class)
Dimensions (feet): *Length* 267.9 (262.6) *Beam* 33.6 (33) *Draught* 11.9 (11.3)
Machinery: Triple expansion, single screw, 2,000 s.h.p.
Speed (knots): $16\frac{1}{2}$
Range (miles): 2,000 to 2,050 @ 15 knots
Manning: 80 to 90
Armament: One 4.7 (1 × 1), Two 3 pdr. (2 × 1) – GERANIUM
One 4-inch (1 × 1), One 3 pdr. (1 × 1) – MALLOW
One 4-inch (1 × 1), Two 3 pdr. (2 × 1) – MARGUERITE.

HMAS GERANIUM.

Ship	Pend. No.	Builder	Cons. Time	Comm.	Fate
Geranium	T56 (1.16) T37 (1.18)	Greenock	7m	1919	Paid Off 11/11/27
Mallow	M68 (2.15) T27 (9.15) T59 (1.18)	Barclay Curle	–	1919	Paid Off 20/11/25
Marguerite	T51 (1.16) T60 (1.18)	Dunlop	5m	1919	Paid Off 23/7/29

HMAS GERANIUM as a survey ship; guns deleted; deckhouse abaft mainmast; minesweeping davits removed.

Top – HMAS MARGUERITE as a minesweeper, June, 1920; one 4.7-inch gun forward; two 3 pounder guns aft; minesweeping gallows at stern.

Left – HMAS MALLOW as a minesweeper. Note searchlights on bridge-wings and absence of guns.

Above – Scuttling of GERANIUM, 24th April, 1935.

GRIMSBY CLASS (1935–36)

Swan, Yarra

Ordered in 1934 and constructed to the same design as the Royal Navy's Grimsby class. Although primarily intended as escorts both sloops could operate as minesweepers. In 1939 SWAN became the leader of the 20th Minesweeping Flotilla which comprised ORARA, DOOMBA and her sister ship YARRA.

During 1942, SWAN received a 40mm Bofors and six 20mm Oerlikon guns and had her three single 4-inch guns replaced by two twin 4-inch mountings. One of the 40mm Bofors was sited in 'B' position and the twin 4-inch weapons in 'A' and 'X' positions. She was also armed with one Vickers and two Lewis machine guns and embarked 40 depth charges.

YARRA was lost on 4th March, 1942, when the convoy she was escorting was attacked by three cruisers and four destroyers of the Imperial Japanese Navy.

SWAN paid off in 1948, but recommissioned as a cadet training ship on 10th February, 1956. She paid off for the final time on 21st September, 1964, and was broken up in Sydney during 1965–66.

Displacement (tons): *Standard* 1,060 *Full Load* 1,500
Dimensions (feet): *Length* (oa) 266.3 *Beam* 36.0 *Draught* 10.0

Machinery: Parsons geared turbines; two Admiralty 3 drum boilers; 2 screws; 2,000 s.h.p.
Speed (knots): $16\frac{1}{2}$
Range (miles): 9,000 @ 10 knots
Manning: 160
Armament: Three 4-inch (3 × 1), Four 3 pdr. (4 × 1), One .05-inch MG (1 × 1), Two DCTs, Two DCCs (see notes).

Ship	Pend. No.	Builder	Cons. Time	Comm.	Fate
Swan	L74 (1939) U74 (1940)	Cockatoo	1y 7m	21/1/37	Sold 5/4/64
Yarra	L77 (1939) U77 (1940)	Cockatoo	1y 8m	21/1/36	Sunk 4/3/42

HMAS YARRA on trials, January, 1936.

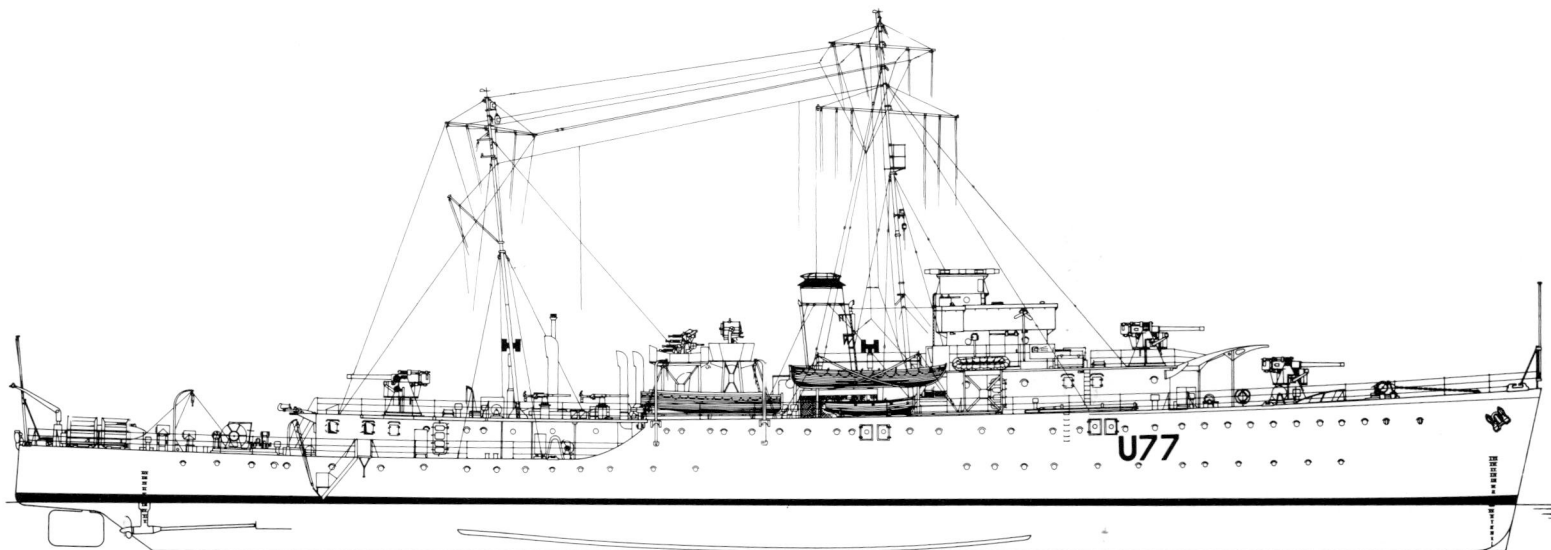

HMAS YARRA, September, 1940; profile. (P. Webb)

Left – HMAS SWAN, 1936,; there 4-inch guns in 'A', 'B' and 'X' positions; machine gun (four barrelled) mounted on bandstand behind the searchlight and funnel; four 3 pounders adjacent to bandstand; depth charges aft with minesweeping gear.

Below – HMAS YARRA, 1941.

J CLASS
J1, J2, J3, J4, J5, and J7

Ship	Pend. No.	Builder	Cons. Time	Comm.	Fate
J1	–	Portsmouth	–	1919	Sold 2/1924
J2	–	Portsmouth	–	1919	Sold 2/1924
J3	–	Pembroke	–	1919	Sold 1/1926
J4	–	Pembroke	–	1919	Sold 2/1924
J5	–	Devonport	–	1919	Sold 2/1924
J7	–	Devonport	–	1919	Sold 11/1929

All six J class were transferred to the RAN on 25th March, 1919. J7 differed from the other boats, having been laid down as a unit of the K class and featuring a remodelled conning tower which was set further aft. During Royal Navy service the class served in the 11th Flotilla at Blyth, for duties with the Grand Fleet. The Js were intended to submerge and attack an enemy on sight. In the RAN their two beam tubes and the original 3-inch anti-aircraft guns were removed.

Despite their youth all boats were found to be in poor condition and were refitted immediately after arriving in Sydney. A base was established in Geelong, Victoria, but in August, 1921, three units were laid up, followed by two more in May 1922 and the last one in June 1922.

J1, J2, J4 and J5 were sold in February, 1924, J3 in January, 1926, and J7 in November, 1929. The first four were all scuttled. J3 and J7 ended their days as breakwaters in Port Phillip.

Displacement (tons): *Surfaced* 1,210 *Submerged* 1,820 (J7 – 1,760 submerged)
Dimensions (feet): *Length* 274.9 *Beam* 23 *Draught* 14
Machinery: Vickers solid injection diesel engines
Speed (knots): *Surfaced* $19\frac{1}{2}$; *Submerged* $9\frac{1}{2}$
Range (miles): 5,000 @ 12 knots
Manning: 44
Armament: Six 18-inch torpedo tubes (4 bow & 2 beam) One 3-inch (1 × 1).

Wardroom, J class.

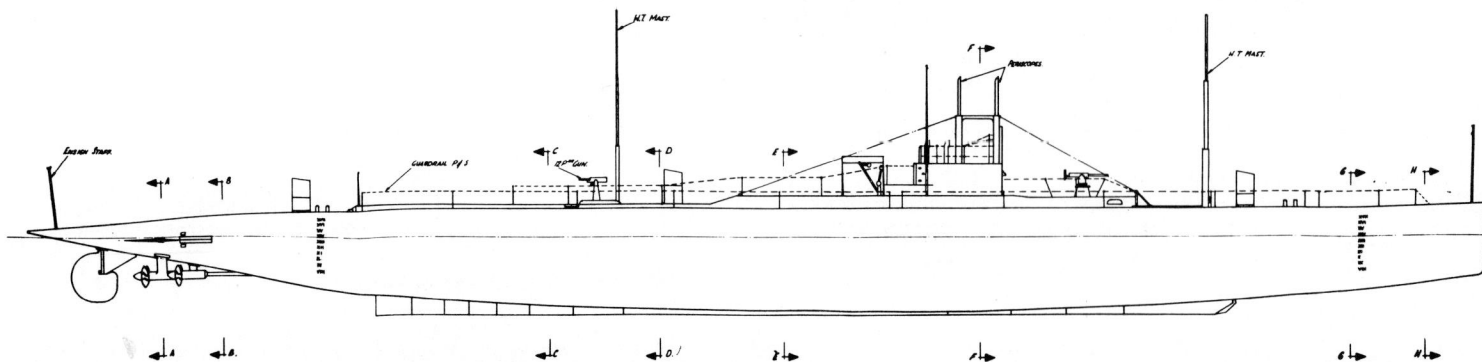

J class submarine; profile. (Naval Ship Design Section)

HMAS J2. (Photo – P. Britz)

Four J class boats alongside HMAS ENCOUNTER. (Photo Sydney Martime Meseum)

Right – Forward torpedo room, J. class.
Below – Two units of the J class at Flinders Naval Depot.
Bottom – HMAS J7. Note the disappearing gun in the raised position before the conning tower.

HMA Submarines, J Class.

OBERON CLASS SUBMARINES

Otway, Oxley

Ship	Pend. No.	Builder	Cons. Time	Comm.	Fate
Otway	–	Vickers	2y 3m	15/6/27	RN 4/1931
Oxley	–	Vickers	2y 1m	15/4/27	RN 4/1931

The RAN's third generation of submarines OTWAY and OXLEY were ordered on 27th June, 1924, together with the two County class heavy cruisers. Seven sister boats were also ordered for the Royal Navy and completed between 1926–28. Plans for four additional RAN units never advanced beyond the initial stages.

OTWAY and OXLEY left Portsmouth in February, 1928, and en route to Australia suffered damage to their engine room columns from heavy seas in the Bay of Biscay. Repairs were effected in Malta from February to November, 1928. The pair finally arrived in Sydney on 14th February, 1929, but due to the economic problems of the depression era were laid up and eventually transferred to the Royal Navy on 10th April, 1931.

OXLEY was sunk on 10th September, 1939, after a collision with the British submarine TRITON off Norway. OTWAY survived the Second World War to be sold for scrapping on 24th August, 1945.

Displacement (tons): *Surfaced* 1,354 *Submerged* 1,835
Dimensions (feet): *Length* 275 *Beam* 27.9 *Draught* 13.3
Machinery: 2 shaft diesel electric, 2,950 s.h.p. surface, 1,350 b.h.p. submerged
Speed (knots): *Submerged* 9 *Surfaced* $15\frac{1}{2}$
Range (miles): 8,500 @ 10 knots surfaced
Manning: 54
Armament: Eight 21-inch torpedo tubes (6 bow 2 stern), One 4-inch (1 × 1), Two MGs (2 × 1).

HMS OTWAY, June, 1935. After war service with the Royal Navy OTWAY was hulked and later broken up. (Photo – Wright & Logan)

A stern view of HMAS OXLEY, Jervis Bay, 1929. (Photo – M. MacDonald)

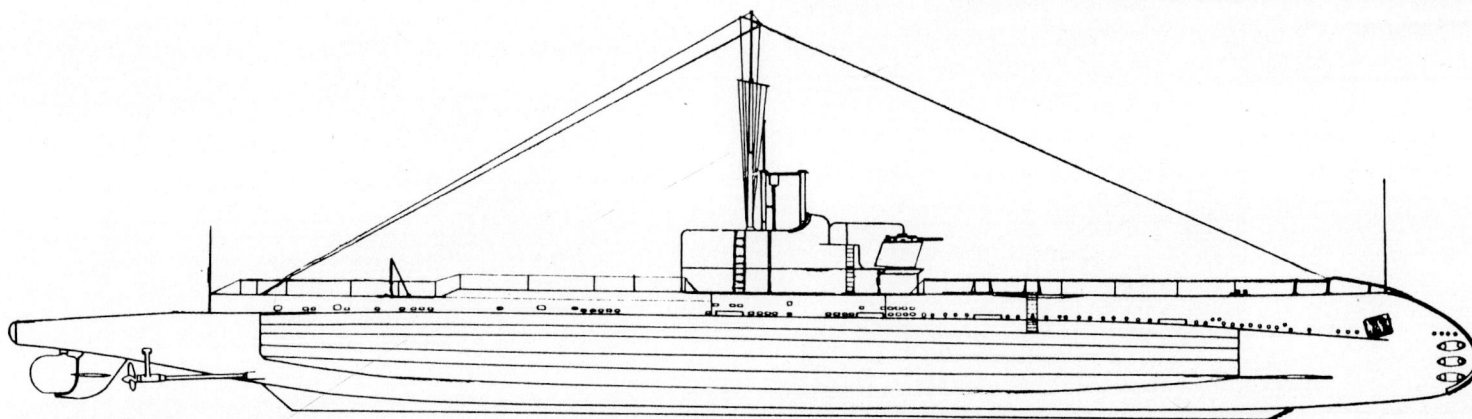

HMAS OTWAY; profile 1929. (R. Gillett)

NET CLASS

Kookaburra

The RAN's first boom defence vessel, KOOKABURRA, was ordered in 1937 and constructed to the design of the British Net class. Her armament outfit was later altered to one 12 pdr., two .303-inch Vickers and two Maxim guns. The 3-inch gun (later 12 pdr.) was mounted abaft the funnel, atop the deckhouse.

To allow sufficient room for handling boom defence gear, the superstructure was set well back from the bow. Heavy wooden planking gave added protection to the bows. Protruding horns and the rounded stern, were designed to work with the boom wires and kedge anchors.

When lifting gear at the bow, it was soon found that KOOKABURRA rose by the stern. The problem was alleviated in the three ship Bar class by the addition of 18 tons boiler water as ballast and an increase in displacement.

KOOKABURRA was laid up in 1958.

Displacement (tons): *Standard* 533
Dimensions (feet): *Length* (oa) 135.0 *Beam* 26.6 *Draught* 10.3
Machinery: Triple expansion, single screw, 450 h.p.
Speed (knots): $9\frac{1}{2}$
Range (miles): N/A
Manning: 32
Armament: One 3-inch (1 × 1), Two .303 Vickers, Two Maxim (2 × 1).

Ship	Pend. No.	Builder	Cons. Time	Comm.	Fate
Kookaburra	P15 (1939) Z15 (1940)	Cockatoo	10m	28/2/39	Sold 8/1965

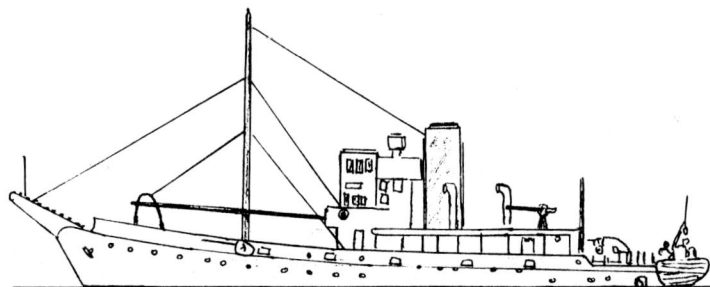
HMAS KOOKABURRA, shortly after commissioning; a large searchlight is mounted above and behind her high bridge superstructure.

HMAS KOOKABURRA, 1939; the single 3-inch gun (trained forward) is mounted aft. (Photo – P. Britz)

HMAS KOOKABURRA; profile 1939. (R. Gillett)

FLEET COLLIER

Biloela

Completed too late for war service, BILOELA served as a fleet collier from 1920 to 1927. During her short career in the RAN the ship made several voyages to New Guinea and the New Herbrides until the disposal of the squadrons coal-burning cruisers and destroyers necessitated her decommissioning on 14th November, 1927.

During the early 1920s plans were formulated for BILOELA's conversion to a seaplane carrier embarking twelve aircraft, but a long with a similiar plan for KURUMBA the scheme was dropped, as it would divert the ships from their principal task of fleet support. The planned armament of two 4-inch guns was never mounted.

After sale in March, 1931 (for £14,500) BILOELA was renamed WOLLERT (1932), IVANHOE (1937), then YOH SING and finally CREE. She was sunk on 21st November, 1940 by an enemy submarine.

Displacement (tons): 9,390
Dimensions (feet): *Length* 382.1 *Beam* 54 *Draught* 22.2
Machinery: Triple expansion, single screw, 2,300 h.p.
Speed (knots): 11
Range (miles): 5,000 @ 10 knots
Manning: 70
Armament: Nil.

Ship	Pend. No.	Builder	Cons. Time	Comp.	Fate
Biloela	–	Cockatoo	1y 8m	5/7/20	Sold 3/31

HMAS BILOELA.

BILOELA, 10th April, 1919. (Photo – S. Given)

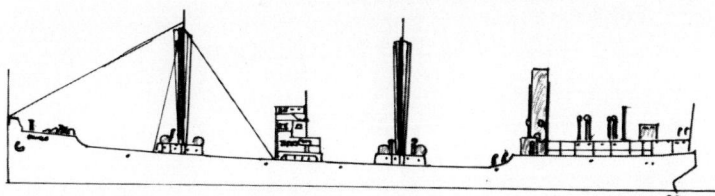
BILOELA; profile. (R. Gillett)

HMAS BILOELA, 1929. (Photo – NSW Government Printer)

DEPOT SHIP

Penguin

Originally constructed for the Royal Navy, ENCOUNTER, (PENGUIN) was presented to the RAN in 1912 for use as a seagoing training ship. After service in the Great War as a combatant she reverted to the training role and in 1923 was converted to an accommodation and depot ship with all armament removed and renamed PENGUIN.

The ship was paid off in 1929 and stripped of all fittings. The hull was scuttled off Sydney on 14th September 1932.

Displacement (tons): 5,880
Dimensions (feet): *Length* (oa) 376 *Beam* 56 *Draught* 21.3.

Ship	Pend. No.	Builder	Cons. Time	Comp.	Fate
Penguin	–	Devonport	4y 11m	11/1905	Scuttled 14/9/32

HMAS PENGUIN (ex ENCOUNTER) as a depot and accommodation ship, Garden Island; all armament save two small weapons abaft the mainmast have been deleted.

COAL LIGHTER

Mombah

Employed in Sydney Harbour to 1929 then sold to Melbourne Harbour Trust in May, 1930.

Requisitioned by RAN on 25th March, 1944, for service at Darwin then Morotai. Paid off to reserve 6th July, 1946, and sold February, 1948.

During 1944–45 fitted with small self-defence weapons.

Displacement (tons): 3,440 gross
Dimensions (feet): *Length* 315, *Beam* 50, *Draught* 23
Machinery: None
Armament: Small calibre.

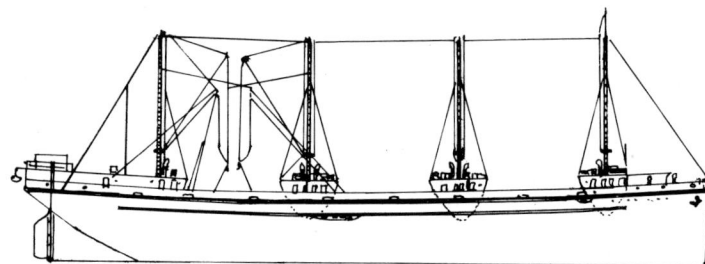

MOMBAH; profile and plan as fitted (Cockatoo Dockyard)

REQUISITIONED SPECIAL SERVICE VESSEL
One Ship

The nine year old SUVA was taken up for war service as an armed boarding steamer by the Royal Navy prior to her RAN service. She was eventually scrapped in 1947.

Name	Details	Status
Suva	*Steamer* 2,229 gross 300.3 × 41.1 × 19.7 feet 414 hp = 14 knots 2 × 3 pdr	Built 1906 Req. (RN) 15/7/15 Comm. (RAN) 23/6/19 Paid Off 12/8/19 Ret. 8/19

HMAS SUVA, July, 1919; a montage showing the official visit of Admiral Viscount Jellicoe to Cairns, Queensland.

SURVEY SHIP

Moresby

'MORESBY' was acquired by the RAN in June, 1925, for survey operations. During 1940 she served as an anti-submarine training vessel before resuming survey duties. The outbreak of war with Japan necessitated her reversion to the escort/anti-submarine role.

Survey work was recommenced in December, 1943, and included assignments in the Darwin and Bathurst Island regions. One of her final surveys was carried out during November, 1945, in Yampi Sound. MORESBY paid off on 14th March, 1946.

Displacement (tons): *Standard* 1,320
Dimensions (feet): *Length* (oa) 276.6 *Beam* 35.0 *Draught* 12.0
Machinery: Inverted 4 cylinder triple expansion engines, 2,500 h.p.
Speed (knots): 17
Range (miles): N/A
Manning: 140
Armament: One 3 pdr. (1 × 1)

Ship	Pend. No.	Builder	Cons. Time	Comm.	Fate
Moresby	T05 (9.18) J54 (WWII)	Barclay Curle	6m	20/6/25	Sold 3/2/47

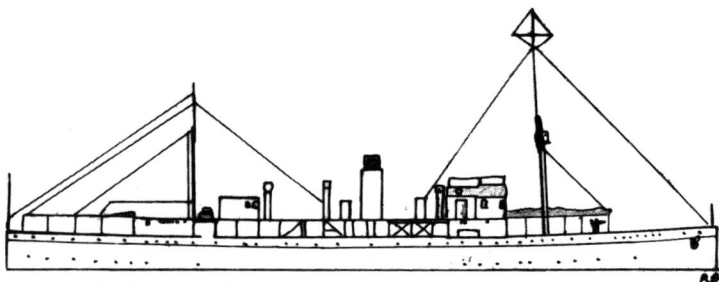
HMAS MORESBY in Sydney Harbour.

HMA Ships GERANIUM and MORESBY (right) in Cairns, Queensland.

HMAS MORESBY: profile. (R. Gillett)

HMAS MORESBY in heavy seas, 1928. (Photo – Naval Photographic Club)

HARBOUR TUG

Wattle

WATTLE served as a naval dockyard tug in Sydney Harbour from 15th February, 1934, until placed in reserve in 1969. On 4th August, 1971, she was sold to the Lady Hopetoun and Port Jackson, Marine Steam Museum Ltd. and was removed from naval moorings on 14th August. She was subsequently purchased by the Victorian Steamship Association in 1979 and is now located in Port Phillip.

Displacement (tons): *Standard* 120
Dimensions (feet): *Length* (oa) 80.8 *Beam* 17.6 *Draught* 9.3
Machinery: 300 i.h.p.
Speed (knots): 10
Range (miles): N/A **Manning:** 4

Ship	Pend. No.	Builder	Comp.	Fate
Wattle	–	Cockatoo Island	15/2/34	Museum vessel 1971

Dockyard tug WATTLE: the cruisers AUSTRALIA and ADELAIDE lie alongside the sherlegs. One of the small RAN harbour workboats is secured above the tug's bow. (Photo – R. Gillett Collection)

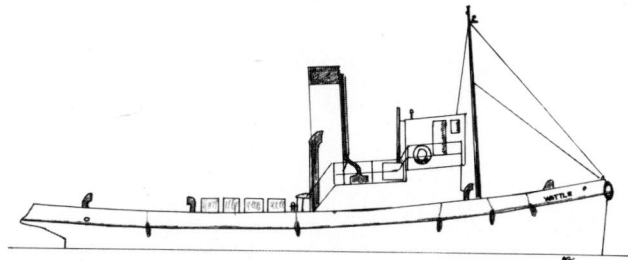

WATTLE; profile. (R. Gillett)

TRAINING SHIP

Kooronga

Constructed as a small tug, KOORONGA was renamed CERBERUS II on 6th June, 1924, and operated as a tender to Flinders Naval Depot, Western Port, Victoria. During the Second World War, while carrying the name KOORONGA, she provided training for RANR ratings.

Note: During the mid-war period both TATTOO and VAMPIRE were employed as training ships/tenders at Western Port, Victoria.

Displacement (tons): *Standard* 60
Dimensions (feet): *Length* (oa) 70.0 *Beam* 14.0 *Draught* 4.2
Machinery: Allen diesel, 126 b.h.p.
Speed (knots): 9
Manning: N/A **Armament:** Nil.

The training boat KOORONGA during the 1920s.

Ship	Pend. No:	Builder	Comp.	Fate
Kooronga	–	Williamstown	1917	Sold 1948

The Second World War 1939–1945

AUSTRALIA'S LARGEST WARSHIPS throughout the Second World War were her three heavy and four light cruisers. Of these seven warships, only ADELAIDE, with its design pre-dating World War One, could be termed obsolete. During the course of the conflict she remained in Australian and Pacific waters, primarily to show the flag. At the same time her armament was considerably altered to meet the increased threat from aircraft and submarines.

Despite more than twenty years afloat, ADELAIDE was at some periods the lone Australian naval presence in coastal waters of any public relations value. During September and October, 1940, she was despatched to New Caledonia on a flag-showing mission when it was feared that Vichy forces might be contemplating an overthrow of the pro-allied government. ADELAIDE proved herself ideal for convoy escort duties, and for shore bombardments from her updated 6-inch guns. She was camouflaged later in the year.

The two largest cruisers, AUSTRALIA and CANBERRA, were products of the Washington Naval Conference, which set maximum tonnages for all warships. The opportunity was taken pre-war to completely overhaul AUSTRALIA, but with the outbreak of hostilities it was not possible to modernise her sister ship.

AUSTRALIA saw extensive service throughout the war years and represented the RAN in the Mediterranean, at Dakar and in the Pacific at the Coral Sea, Leyte Gulf and Lingayen Gulf battles. CANBERRA, enjoyed a less spectacular career and seldom fired her main and secondary armament. One exception

Aboard HMAS AUSTRALIA, January, 1945, with ARUNTA alongside.

was during March, 1941, when she intercepted the German supply ship COBURG and the oil tanker KETTY BROVIG. CANBERRA opened fire with her 8-inch guns on COBURG, which was then scuttled by her crew. KETTY BROVIG was also abandoned and sunk. On 9th August, 1942, CANBERRA was attacked by Japanese cruisers. She received damage to her boiler rooms, bridge and 4-inch gun deck. When she began to list to starboard, her crew were transferred to other allied ships. USS SELFRIDGE and USS ELLET, nearby American destroyers, hastened the end of the sinking ship with the use of gunfire and torpedoes.

The three light cruisers, HOBART, PERTH and SYDNEY were the most modern units available at the outbreak of war in September, 1939. All were originally laid down for the Royal Navy in 1933 as modified versions of the original five ship Leander class ordered in the late 1920s, and completed from 1933 to 1935. SYDNEY was the first to be completed, although the last to be ordered. As designed, each of the three cruisers was to carry a weapon supply of 200 rounds per 6-inch gun, 200 rounds per 4-inch gun and 2,500 rounds per 0.5-inch barrel. These figures varied for war service as did those of the heavy cruisers of the County class.

In June, 1943, HMS SHROPSHIRE was commissioned as an Australian ship to replace CANBERRA, lost in action. SHROP-SHIRE was originally constructed as a member of the four-vessel London type of County class cruisers and could be distinguished from AUSTRALIA by the absence of torpedo bulges and her modified bridge structure.

Destroyers

Five destroyers, the leader STUART and the four V and W class, were active at the outbreak of World War Two. These ships had been transferred to the RAN in 1933 and were all aged between 21 and 22 years. They replaced the five S class destroyers which were younger than the V and W boats. Despite the age difference, the S boats were all sold for scrap in 1937 and subsequently scuttled off Sydney.

The V and W classes were highly regarded as destroyers. They carried a more powerful and better arranged armament than the S boats. During the course of the war the four destroyers underwent many armament changes. Only VENDETTA survived the conflict, but as an escort destroyer.

The flotilla leader, STUART, like VENDETTA, remained in commission throughout the conflict and was converted to an escort destroyer, and finally a fast transport. During the changes of role, her armament was significantly altered and by 1944, when she was classed as a transport, it comprised only one 4-inch gun, seven 20mm Oerlikons, some pom-poms, a Hedgehog and depth charges.

After paying off in February, 1946, STUART was sold in 1947. She lay at a buoy in a state of decay in Berrys Bay, Sydney, until her bare hull, cut down to the waterline, was towed up-harbour to Homebush Bay and allowed to settle in the mud.

The RAN's most powerful destroyers between 1939 and 1945 were the three locally-built Tribal class. The ships were originally intended for convoy escort duties. As a result, they carried a smaller torpedo outfit for a heavier gun armament. ARUNTA and WARRAMUNGA enjoyed active war careers, operating with both RAN and USN fleet units. BATAAN was not completed until 1945.

To bolster the RAN's destroyer force, five N class were loaned from 1940 for the duration. Despite being Australian-manned, the five vessels formed the 7th Flotilla, Royal Navy, and were maintained by the British Admiralty. Eventually the four surviving ships were returned and replaced by the less satisfactory Q class. In 1942 two of these, QUIBERON and QUICKMATCH, commissioned as HMA Ships.

Eventually QUIBERON and QUICKMATCH, with their three sister ships, QUADRANT, QUALITY and QUEEN-BOROUGH were permanently transferred to Australian control.

Sloops and Frigates

The four Grimsby class sloops of the RAN, were constructed in two sub-groups, to the British design of the mid-1930s. The class gave additional consideration to convoy escort work and were armed with 4-inch 45-calibre quick-firing guns. During the course of the war both PARRAMATTA and YARRA were lost.

Although numerous Bathurst class AMSs were entering service, the requirement for a large escort vessel, but smaller than a fleet destroyer, was still evident. To fill the gap, orders were placed with local shipyards for the construction of a modified version of the British River class vessel. Being smaller and cheaper to build, six of the class were completed in time for operations against the Japanese. With the exception of BARCOO, the wartime frigates were produced by non-naval yards, who were capable of constructing these uncomplicated ships of war.

The period between January, 1942, and late 1943, saw the height of Japanese naval activity. The submarine menace forced the decision to re-arm the survey ship MORESBY as an anti-submarine vessel. MORESBY had originally been built for this purpose for the Royal Navy in the Great War, but had operated only in the survey role with the RAN. After re-arming, MORESBY was despatched to patrol the southern and eastern coastal waters and in April, 1943, depth-charged a suspected enemy submarine. Late in 1943 she reverted to survey activities. During her time as an escort MORESBY carried 70 rounds for her 4-inch gun, 60 rounds for the 12 pdr. and 41 depth charges.

HMAS AUSTRALIA leading HMAS ADELAIDE. (Photo – S. Given).

Australian Minesweepers (Corvettes)

Three of the fifty-six corvettes commissioned by the RAN, were lost on active service, 1942–44. Originally twenty units were constructed for the Royal Navy but were retained by the RAN.

Mine Warfare Ships

All 37 vessels used for mine-laying and sweeping roles during the Second World War were modified merchant ships, requisitioned from the private trade. Only DOOMBA, with her naval origins, displayed a warship hull. She was one of only five auxiliary minesweepers to carry a 4-inch gun. The others were ORARA, MEDEA, MERCEDES and TONGKOL. All the auxiliary minesweepers were fitted with the usual outfit of four depth charges, DOOMBA was again the exception. She carried fifty.

The minesweepers not purchased were chartered from local companies. DURRAWEEN cost £121.19s per month, TOLGA, £105 per month. Of the 35 vessels taken up for war sweeping duties GOORANGAI, PATRICIA CAM and TERKA were lost. Others subsequently operated in the roles of minefield tender (BERMAGUI), boom defence vessels (BERYL II, GUNBAR and MARY CAM), stores carriers (BIRCHGROVE PARK, BOMBO, COOLEBAR, PATRICIA CAM and TERKA), anti-submarine vessel (DOOMBA), training vessel (ORARA) and general purpose vessel (SAMUEL BENBOW).

The RAN's principal minelayer, BUNGAREE, laid over 18,000 mines along the Australian coast. One of these mines sank the minesweeping corvette WARRNAMBOOL off Queensland on 13th September, 1947. BUNGAREE was supported by the controlled minelayer ATREUS, which operated from Melbourne.

Two minefield tenders were also active. URALBA served from Brisbane and later in New Guinea waters.

The first minesweeping group was formed on 13th November 1939 and comprised the sloops YARRA and SWAN and the auxiliaries DOOMBA and ORARA. Groups were later based at Sydney (Group 50), Melbourne (54) Hobart (60), Port Adelaide (63), Fremantle (66), Darwin (70), Brisbane (74) and Newcastle (77).

Patrol Craft

The patrol force was comprised of built-for-the-purpose and re-quisitioned craft. The latter included anti-submarine and channel patrol boats, examination vessels and the secretive Services Reconaissance Department craft. Additional support was available from the Naval Auxiliary Patrol, which manned hundreds of small launches in the larger ports.

The most useful patrol craft were the Fairmile B and Harbour Defence Motor Launches, of which 35 and 28 were commissioned. The larger Fairmile Bs were seaworthy craft and carried a significant armament. Two were lost in late 1944. The smaller HDML, like the Fairmile Bs, were based around Australia and in New Guinea.

All the auxiliary patrol craft, except ABRAHAM CRIJNS-SEN, were requisitioned from the private trade. The 525 ton ABRAHAM CRIJNSSEN, originally constructed as a minesweeper for the Royal Netherlands Navy, escaped to Fremantle on 20th March, 1942, after the fall of the Netherlands East Indies. She was commissioned for anti-submarine work and also served as a tender for Dutch submarines in local waters.

Shortly after the declaration of war in September, 1939, an examination service was established at the main ports in Australia and New Guinea, with more than 30 ships carrying out enforcement of harbour defences. Every vessel entering the port was required to stop for inspection while shore batteries covered the procedure. Most of the examination vessels were unarmed, others mounted only small calibre weapons. ADELE, which operated from September, 1939, to May, 1943, originally served with the RAN as a tender to the Naval College Jervis Bay, from 1915 to September, 1922. She and FAURO CHIEF were both lost during their period of service as examination vessels.

Twenty-five craft were operated by the Services Reconnaissance Department, a division of the Allied Intelligence Bureau. The vessels undertook commando, reconnaissance and secret missions; the KRAIT escapade being an example of the latter, when the tiny 68 gross ton vessel destroyed two and damaged five Japanese ships in the occupied Singapore Harbour.

A Naval Auxiliary Patrol was formed in 1941. Most of the boats were armed with machine guns and depth charges. Many were commissioned, including some which were ordered to New Guinea and other war zones. Apart from the normal patrol and harbour work, the commissioned boats also served as air-sea rescue, stores and channel patrol boats. Over 340 boats saw service, 148 as full time boats, including 87 commissioned as HMA ships. One hundred and twenty-three full-time boats were active in January 1943.

Boom Defence

Four specialist and 29 auxiliary boom defence vessels saw service in the Second World War. The former comprised one Net and three Bar class, all of which were constructed at the Cockatoo Island Dockyard.

Boom defence was effected by the use of a system of nets held together by steel rings and supported by floats. The vessel's boom gallow, which projected over the bow, was used to lower and reclaim the nets which were strategically placed across harbour or port entrances to keep out enemy submarines. A gate was opened and closed by the boom gate vessel to allow the entry of friendly vessels.

The auxiliary boom defence vessels were an odd assortment

of former ferries and lighters, schooners and launches. Despite their shape, size or lack of speed, all of them rendered useful service. KINCHELA, the former lighter was so slow her crew unofficially re-christened her 'Deadslow', while KOOMPARTOO became known as the 'African Queen'.

Support

At the outbreak of war in September, 1939, the RAN had only a handful of support ships, including PLATYPUS, KURUMBA, MORESBY, RIPPLE and KOORONGA, plus some lighters. The need for all types of support vessels resulted in the requisitioning of craft ranging in size from launches to coasters, and the implementation of a new construction programme, to fulfill specific needs. Numerous built-for-the-purpose lighters and launches were completed by the close of 1945.

The majority of requisitioned vessels were paid off and returned to their pre-war owners during the period 1945 to 1947. Even new construction was prematurely sold, simply because there was no need for large numbers in peacetime. Fifteen steel motor lighters were ordered, but only 11 completed for naval service. The remaining four began their careers flying the red ensign as merchant vessels. Local yards also produced small craft for the Royal Navy; 12 additional MSLs were built for the Admiralty.

Apart from the vessels mentioned, other craft, such as the 45 foot tow boats, were completed for naval service, but, after victory, were transferred to other navies or to the RAAF or to Australian Army water transport squadrons. Many Second World War built support craft remained on the fleet list and operated up to the early 1980s.

To facilitate production during 1939 to 1945, all three Australian armed services took delivery of identical craft; steel lighters, tow boats and torpedo recovery boats being prime examples.

Ten support vessels were lost during the war. WAREE was lost in 1946 on her return from naval duties.

Change of Roles

During the course of the war, many ships were converted to, or assumed, new roles to satisfy the changing requirements of the fleet. The following table lists these ships with their previous service in the RAN noted in brackets.

Air Sea Rescue
COONGOOLA (Patrol)

Boom Defence Vessel
BERYL II (MWS)
BUNGAREE (MWS)
COONGOOLA (Patrol)
GUNBAR (MWS)
MARY CAM (MWS)
GIPPSLAND (MWS)
KURU (Patrol)
LARRAKIA (Patrol)
VIGILANT (Patrol)

Examination Vessel
LARRAKIA (Patrol)
MIRAMAR II (Patrol)
VIGILANT (Patrol)
WARRAWEE (MWS)

General Purpose Vessel
SAMUEL BENBOW (MWS)

Patrol
DOOMBA (MWS)
HEROS (Towing)
ST. GILES (Towing)

Repair
PING WO (Stores)
SAN MICHELE (Patrol)

Stores
BARETO (Examination)

BINGIRA (Patrol)
BIRCHGROVE PARK (MWS)
BOMBO (MWS)
BUNGAREE (MWS)
COOLEBAR (MWS)
FALIE (Examination)
GERARD (Examination)
PATRICIA CAM (MWS)
SOUTHERN CROSS (Examination)
TERKA (MWS)
URALBA (MWS)
WHANG PU (Repair)
WILCANNIA (Patrol)

Survey
BUNGAREE (MWS)
LAURABADA (Patrol)
SAMUEL BENBOW (MWS)
VIGILANT (Patrol)

Tender
BERMAGUI (MWS)
BINGERA (Patrol)
BIRCHGROVE PARK (MWS)
KING BAY (Examination)

Training
BINGERA (Patrol)
ORARA (MWS)

ROMOLO after her encounter with HMAS MANO-ORA in June, 1940.

1939

SEPTEMBER

STATE OF THE FLEET

In September, 1939, the Royal Australian Navy was only a small force which comprised fourteen warships and five principal support vessels. Two additional sloops were under construction at Cockatoo Island in Sydney and the oldest cruiser, ADELAIDE, had recently completed an extensive refit.

The nucleus and pride of the Australian Squadron was the cruiser force. In addition to its two heavy cruisers AUSTRALIA and CANBERRA, and ADELAIDE which dated from 1922, the RAN possessed three modern light cruisers, PERTH, SYDNEY and HOBART. PERTH, commissioned into the Royal Australian Navy while in Britain and yet to reach Australia, was retained on the West Indies Station at the Admiralty's request on the outbreak of War.

The destroyer force comprised five ships, all veterans of the Great War. Led by the flotilla leader, STUART, the force comprised the four 'V' and 'W' class ships, VAMPIRE, VENDETTA, VOYAGER and WATERHEN. Of the sloops, only SWAN and YARRA were available for active duties, and the new boom-defence vessel, KOOKABURRA was only just completing trials after commissioning in February, 1939.

One of the more immediate requirements for the navy on warfooting was escort and minesweeping vessels. To help bridge the gap until new construction, in the form of the Bathurst class 'maid of all work' minesweepers could be commissioned, the RAN turned to the merchant marine and began to requisition commission and sometimes purchase, privately-owned ships. They

Fleet strength – September, 1939

Ships	Class	Type	Max. Speed (kts)	Age (Years)	Principal Armament
Australia	County	Heavy Cruiser	$31\frac{1}{2}$	11	Eight 8-inch, Eight 4-inch, Eight 21-inch TT
Canberra	County	Heavy Cruiser	$31\frac{1}{2}$	11	Eight 8-inch Four 4-inch Eight 21-inch TT
Hobart	Leander	Light Cruiser	$32\frac{1}{2}$	3	Eight 6-inch Eight 4-inch Eight 21-inch TT
Perth	Leander	Light Cruiser	$32\frac{1}{2}$	3	-ditto-
Sydney	Leander	Light Cruiser	$32\frac{1}{2}$	4	Eight 6-inch Four 4-inch Eight 21-inch TT
Adelaide	Town	Light Cruiser	$25\frac{1}{2}$	17	Eight 6-inch Three 4-inch
Stuart	Scott	Flotilla Leader	$36\frac{1}{2}$	21	Five 4.7-inch One 3-inch Six 21-inch TT
Vampire	V	Destroyer	34	22	Four 4-inch Six 21-inch TT
Vendetta	V	Destroyer	34	21	-ditto-
Voyager	V	Destroyer	34	21	-ditto-
Waterhen	W	Destroyer	34	21	-ditto-
Swan	Grimsby	Escort Sloop	$16\frac{1}{2}$	2	Three 4-inch
Yarra	Grimsby	Escort Sloop	$16\frac{1}{2}$	3	-ditto-
Kookaburra	Net	Boom Defence vessel	$9\frac{1}{2}$	1	One 3 inch

fully illustrated by the requisitioning of the Brisbane passenger ferry DOOMBA. Like many other boats she had been constructed as a warship for service in the Great War, later converted to mercantile post-1919 and then reconverted for another war. DOOMBA, was in fact the first vessel taken up for duties as an auxiliary minesweeper.

Apart from the locally requisitioned vessels, additional ships were obtained from four other sources.

a) Constructed locally
b) The Royal Navy,
c) Requisitions from foreign concerns
d) Captured during the course of the war.

A total of sixty-seven major craft, including three destroyers, six frigates, two sloops and 56 minesweepers were constructed locally, in addition hundreds of minor warships and support craft were laid down and completed. During the course of the war, the heavy cruiser SHROPSHIRE and seven destroyers were transferred from the Royal Navy.

HMAS OLIVE CAM, 6th October, 1939; one of the first auxiliary warships to be taken up for war service.

ranged from small launches and trawlers to coasters and passenger ships to the size of MANOORA (10,900 tons).

The small number of specialist warships available for active service was, in no small measure due to the decisions made in the mid to late 1930s. With little regard for the global situation, the Government of the day ordered the disposal of the destroyer leader ANZAC, five 'S' class destroyers and three Flower class sloops. As a result, the fleet was now commissioning antiquated merchant ships, some more than forty years old, to fulfill duties the warships could have easily performed without major modification.

The RAN's requisitioned fleet of coasters, trawlers and small boats were to perform a myriad of duties in the six years of conflict. The irony of the situation was

HMAS GOORANGAI, lost in November, 1940.

The Admiralty requisitioned MORE-TON BAY, ARAWA and KANIMBLA, three passengers liners which were in port in Sydney for conversion to armed merchant cruisers. All were hurriedly stripped of their peacetime fittings and armed with 6-inch guns as the main armament, with 3-inch guns for defence against aircraft attack.

To assist the fleet the Australian Naval Board decided to increase the number of patrolling cruisers by requisitioning and commissioning the coastal liners MANOORA and WESTRALIA, as armed merchant cruisers. The trawlers and other vessels requisitioned for minesweeping duties were divided into groups and positioned around the Australian coastline.

OCTOBER

DESTROYERS SAIL NORTH

In October the Commonwealth approved an Admiralty request that the Fleet's destroyers sail to Singapore for anti-submarine training, and furthermore offered the use of a 6-inch gun cruiser for overseas duties. Accordingly on 13th October the cruiser HOBART sailed from Sydney, followed the next morning by the destroyers STUART, VENDETTA and WATER-HEN. VAMPIRE and VOYAGER left Fremantle for Singapore direct. While the ships were at sea the Admiralty signalled a request that the flotilla be sent to augment the Mediterranean command. Despite misgivings about the lack of anti-submarine units left to safeguard the coasts, the Commonwealth agreed. On 13th November, the five destroyers slipped out of Singapore for the long voyage to the Mediterranean. The vessels again met up with each other at Malta on Christmas Eve, 1939.

1940

MAY

NEW CONSTRUCTION, FLEET DEPLOYMENTS

By May the Cabinet in Australia had accelerated war measures and had announced that the RAN would man ten local defence vessels being built by Australian shipyards for the Royal Navy. The vessels, designed in Australia with Admiralty assistance, were designated Bathurst Class Minesweepers – or AMS Vessels. Before the end of the war, fifty six of these vessels would be constructed in Australia for service as escort ships and minesweepers and for anti-submarine duties from the Pacific to the Persian Gulf and in the Atlantic Ocean.

The Cabinet also decided to raise and train almost 1,800 men for overseas service. This was the maximum number which Flinders Naval Depot could handle over the following year. Equally far-reaching was the decision to offer the heavy cruisers AUSTRALIA, (then at the Cape of Good Hope after escorting a convoy carrying the AIF), and CANBERRA to serve under the Admiralty. HOBART, having spent several months on convoy and patrol duty around the Gulf of Aden and in Colombo, was at her moorings in Aden where on 22nd May, 1940, she was joined by SYDNEY, originally detailed for service with her sister ship in the Red Sea but now under orders to join the Mediterranean Fleet.

JUNE

HOME WATERS, 'MANOORA' SINKS 'ROMOLO'

After Italy's entry into the war, Australia was required to account for Italian shipping in home waters. The Italian liner REMO was seized at Fremantle, but her sister ship ROMOLO, despite all efforts to delay her departure, sailed from Brisbane for Yokohama on 5th June. MANOORA, her Adelaide Steamship Company colours not yet replaced by wartime camouflage, was despatched from her anchorage at Hervey Bay to shadow the ship. However the contact was lost during the night and the search discontinued.

When news of Italy's belligerence arrived the ships were 160 miles apart, so the order was rescinded. As luck would have it a British steamer reported sighting a vessel trying to camouflage herself at a position south-east of San Cristobal. MANOORA sailed north and on 12th June sighted the Italian vessel, being scuttled by her own crew. After picking up the passengers and crew MANOORA fired seven rounds of gunfire into the sinking ship.

JUNE
WAR WITH ITALY

Following the outbreak of war with Italy, Allied responsibility for naval affairs in the Mediterranean was divided on a geographical basis: the west under the care of the French fleet, and the east entrusted to the British fleet based at Alexandria, aided by a small but powerful French squadron.

By June, 1940, the British Fleet was alone, following the withdrawal of the French units. First contact with Italian forces at sea occurred on 28th June while steaming in general cover of a Malta convoy. The 7th Cruiser Squadron, including SYDNEY, was informed of the presence of three enemy destroyers. The British force altered course to intercept them. In a short action before nightfall, the Italian destroyer ESPERO was hit; SYDNEY being detailed to sink her.

BARTOLOMEO COLLEONI.

JULY
MEDITERRANEAN SEA BATTLES

The Mediterranean Fleet proceeded to sea again on 7th July. The next day both a submarine and a flying boat reported the presence of a large Italian fleet, including two battleships, evidently escorting a Benghazi-bound convoy. On 9th July the two fleets sighted each other. SYDNEY and the cruisers in the van of the fleet came under heavy fire until the battleship WARSPITE could reach the scene. STUART joined the destroyers in a counter-attack after the first hour of battle. However the Battle of Calabria was inconclusive; the enemy deciding to disengage and head for home, losing a destroyer during the withdrawal.

On 17th July, SYDNEY was ordered to support the destroyers ILEX, HERO and HASTY, in anti-submarine operations north of Crete, and to attack Italian ships in the Gulf of Athens. At the same time the cruisers GIOVANNI DELLE BANDE NERE and BARTOLOMEO COLLEONI sailed from Tripoli for the island Leros in the Aegean. At 0720 on 19th July, the two cruisers were sighted by the British destroyers. HYPERION made a wireless report and led the destroyers on a north-easterly course to engage the enemy until SYDNEY could reach the scene.

Captain Collins, commanding SYDNEY, had decided to stay in support of the destroyers longer than anticipated and, now was only forty miles away. Altering course and increasing speed to 30 knots, SYDNEY was kept well in the picture through a stream of messages from the accompanying destroyers.

The enemy cruisers concentrated their gunfire on the destroyers, while trying to evade torpedo attacks. No hits were registered on the British warships. At 0820 SYDNEY sighted the enemy and hoisted her battle ensigns; nine minutes later at a distance of 19,000 yards, the Australian cruiser opened fire.

The RAN cruiser rushed to the southward, on the port beam of the Italian vessels. Unable to discern the strength and number of the new attacker, the Italians turned south and made smoke. The engagement now became a running battle with HAVOCK joining the other destroyers and making torpedo attacks on the fleeing cruisers. SYDNEY altered course periodically to give her main guns enhanced arcs of fire – changing targets as each enemy cruiser emerged briefly through the smoke.

SYDNEY's gunfire proved the most effective. At 0835 she scored a hit on BANDE NERE's forward funnel.

COLLEONI had by now received shell-hits in the forecastle and boiler rooms and at 0925 was seen to be stopped in the water, smothered in gunfire. The Italian Admiral turned to see if he could help the COLLEONI, but then continued on a south-westerly course, with SYNDEY in pursuit. At 0933 Captain Collins ordered the destroyer HYPERION to sink COLLEONI by torpedo. SYDNEY had by now scored a second hit on BANDE NERE, but found the range opening. By 1022 SYDNEY could no longer see the fall of her own shot and with ten rounds of shell left in her forward turret, abandoned the chase to return to Alexandria.

Although no enemy ships appeared, SYDNEY was attacked by aircraft. Her arrival at the base was delayed when she turned back to aid the damaged HAVOCK, laden with prisoners. SYDNEY with three of the destroyers entered Alexandria on the morning of the 20th to a rousing welcome, being cheered by every ship's company from the harbour boom to her berth two miles up-stream. Loudest in the cheering were the Australian destroyers decorated with no less than seven national flags.

After the Battle of Calabria and the action off Cape Spada, the Italian Navy was more cautious in ordering forays into the Aegean. Following the latter action, the Royal Navy was ordered to no longer endanger their ships by stopping to rescue enemy survivors.

In the following months SYDNEY's operations were many and varied; destroying an enemy tanker in the Aegean in company with NEPTUNE, searching in the Gulf of Athens, participating in the bombardment of Bomba and Bardia, on this occasion with STUART and WATERHEN, and, in September, 1940, disguised as an Italian cruiser, bombarded the airstrip on the island of Scarpanto.

HMAS SYDNEY returning to Alexandria in July, 1940.

APRIL
THE RED SEA

The eve of Italy's declaration of war found HOBART on patrol duties based on Colombo and from April at Aden in the Red Sea where she was joined by the new sloop PARRAMATTA on 30th July, 1940. Before long both ships were employed with RN units in ferrying supplies to the British force holding Somaliland. By 15th August, the British position there was untenable. HOBART received orders to supervise the removal of the last of the garrison and to render the main port, Berbera, inoperable to the advancing Italian forces. In the glare of exploding oil dumps, the crew organised the rescue of wounded troops and refugees and found time to make more tangible contributions to aid the British rear-guard. The Walrus aircraft was catapulted on a reconnaissance mission over the desert and three volunteers took the ship's Hotchkiss gun to join the gunners holding the Tug Argan Gap. When HOBART left Berbera after bombarding the town, the gun crew were still fighting ashore. All were eventually captured. However they were released by British forces eight months later during the offensive in Eritrea.

AUGUST
VETERAN CRUISER IN PACIFIC

During August, 1940, ADELAIDE, proceeded from her base at Fremantle for refitting in Sydney, but was soon involved in a delicate political operation. New Caledonia was under the control of French officials, following the orders of the Vichy government, despite the fact the majority of inhabitants wished to rally to the banner of free France. The light cruiser was ordered to take a Gaullist leader to the island, arriving off Noumea on 19th September. Ultimately a coup was successful in overturning the government. ADELAIDE remained in the region for another three weeks to strengthen the new regime. Despite threats of retaliation, the entire episode was resolved without Australian casualties.

SEPTEMBER

YARRA JOINS RED SEA FORCE

Despite control of the western coast of the Red Sea, the Italians made no immediate moves against the British, apart from heavy air raids on Aden. The two Australian ships of the force were joined by the sloop YARRA on 18th September. On the night of 20–21 October, YARRA scored a hit on one of two Italian destroyers which had slipped out of Massawa to attack the convoy she was escorting.

HMAS YARRA.

STUART SINKS 'GONDAR'

During this period STUART also scored a notable victory. Limping home to Alexandria on the night of 29th September with a burst steampipe suffered during a voyage to Malta, the destroyer leader detected a submerged Italian submarine. STUART immediately went to action stations and dropped depth charges. She continued the hunt throughout the night. A Sunderland flying boat from Alexandria arrived and blew the submarine GONDAR to the surface. Faced by aerial attack and shellfire from STUART, the Italians scuttled their boat. STUART returned to Alexandria with the Italian survivors. After undergoing repairs the ship left for Malta where she was refitted.

'AUSTRALIA' AT DAKAR

While HOBART, PARRAMATTA and YARRA were experiencing the heat of the Red Sea, AUSTRALIA patrolled with the British Home Fleet in Arctic waters. During August one cruise took her as far north as Bear Island, another to the coast of Norway. On 2nd September, 1940, she sailed to north-west Africa to join the large British force dispatched to neutralise – and hopefully, win to the Allied cause – the

French naval base at Dakar, which was seen as a threat to British supply lines in mid-Atlantic.

Prime Minister Churchill's decision that the French fleet must not fall into the hands of Hitler, had been underlined by the bombardment of Oran by a British squadron in July, and the disarming of the French force at Alexandria. When news of the sailing of the British and Free French force to Dakar reached France, three Gloire class cruisers were dispatched to that port.

On 19th September, AUSTRALIA sighted the three cruisers off Dakar and began shadowing them. On assurance that they were heading for Casablanca, AUSTRALIA signalled 'Bon Voyage' and let them pass.

On 23rd September the British warships gathered off Dakar. Free French emissaries tried to go ashore to reach the French authorities, but were fired upon. Gunfire from shore defences gave evidence that the Vichy Commander was not sympathetic to General de Gaulle. When two French destroyers attempted to break out, AUSTRALIA was able to force them back into harbour.

In the afternoon of the following day the destroyer L'AUDACIEUX attempted to enter the port. AUSTRALIA and two RN destroyers were ordered to intercept. The

cruiser's fourth salvo set the French ship aflame but AUSTRALIA refrained from further shelling so that lives might be saved before the ship sank.

The abortive invasion continued on 24th and the British ships and shore defences exchanged heavy gunfire. AUSTRALIA suffered two hits on 25th, but no casualties. Her only loss was the Walrus and its crew of three, brought down amid the confusion of British anti-aircraft fire. With the battleship RESOLUTION torpedoed by a French submarine, and warships and troopships coming under increasingly violent attack, the hapless expedition left the scene on 26th September with nothing achieved.

During the late months of the year AUSTRALIA served on convoy duties to Gibraltar and the West African coast before sailing to Liverpool for a refit.

OCTOBER

MINEFIELDS

During late 1940 the German raider ATLANTIS was active in the Indian Ocean, while her sister ship PINGUIN, cruised off the southern and eastern Australian coasts, laying minefields off Sydney, Newcastle and Hobart. The smaller PASSAT mined the waters around the Banks Strait, Cape Otway and Wilson's Promontory.

On 7th November, the merchant ship CAMBRIDGE, bound from Melbourne to Sydney, was sunk and a day later the CITY OF RAYVILLE off Cape Otway. Following these loses, SWAN and YARRA and a flotilla of minesweepers commenced the tedious job of sweeping the area clear of all danger.

NOVEMBER

NEW TONNAGE

In November, 1940, the RAN received the first of five new N class destroyers with the commissioning of NAPIER. She was followed in early 1941 by NESTOR and NIZAM, NORMAN in September and finally NEPAL in May, 1942. NAPIER and NIZAM commenced service as convoy escorts in the North Atlantic, NESTOR in the Arctic and NORMAN also in the North Atlantic. On 15th Decem-

ber, 1941, NESTOR engaged and sank the German submarine U127.

DECEMBER

FIRST CORVETTE COMMISSIONED

BATHURST, first of fifty-six Australian minesweepers, was commissioned for service on 6th December, having been constructed at Cockatoo Island.

1941

JANUARY

SCRAP IRON FLOTILLA

In the Mediterranean Australian presence now consisted of VAMPIRE, VENDETTA, VOYAGER, WATERHEN and Force 'W', including the British monitor

TERROR, gunboats LADYBIRD and APHIS and a number of minesweepers and anti-submarine trawlers. Their job was to undertake bombardments and night offensive patrols and to safeguard supply ships and water carriers essential to the campaign.

Plans for the capture of Bardia were made and supported by the RAN force. In January, STUART re-entered service after her Maltese overhal. The force, back in action again, sailed from Alexandria on 11th January as screen to the battleship BARHAM and the aircraft carrier EAGLE, bound for an operation in the Aegean. STUART, VAMPIRE and VOYAGER supported the 6th Australian Division in the capture of Tobruk on 21st and 22nd January.

MARCH

BATTLE OF MATAPAN

During March the Italian Fleet emerged for battle. The Italian force included 8-inch gun cruisers as well as light cruisers and destroyers. Sighted by the British cruiser screen, including PERTH, the Italians decided to make smoke and head for the British. The Italians pressed home their speed advantage over the cruisers and straddled them with heavy and sustained gunfire. Forced to come to the rescue to save the cruisers, aircraft from the carrier FORMIDABLE were launched, thereby disclosing the presence of the carrier and consequently of the main fleet. Now fully alerted the Italians broke off action and sailed to the north-west, shadowed by the cruisers they had been chasing. A further strike was begun from FORMIDABLE and a hit scored. The cruisers were ordered to keep in touch with the enemy and if possible to send in destroyers for a torpedo attack. The Royal Navy commander

The first Australian-built minesweeping 'corvette', BATHURST, on trials and flying the Red Ensign. (Photo P. Britz)

decided on a night attack. The resultant battle of Matapan, fought over the 28th and 29th March, saw the end of any challenge to the supremacy of the Royal Navy in the Mediterranean by the Italian Fleet.

After five minutes of action the Italians had been beaten. The destroyers, including STUART, were ordered to finish off the cruisers. With the main Italian force well away, withdrawal was ordered. The next day the fleet returned to rescue survivors where the Italian cruisers had sunk.

APRIL

GREECE EVACUATIONS

On 17th April Yugoslavia capitulated to the Nazis, and Greece surrendered several days later. Withdrawal from Greece was the only choice for the British forces. Evacuation commenced on 24th April. PERTH was despatched to assist in the evacuation from Rafti, while STUART and VOYAGER joined the convoy going to Megara. VOYAGER escorted a convoy bound for Alexandria. Both STUART and PERTH were in the evacuation force at Nauplia. Final embarkations were on 29th April. PERTH, the cruiser PHOEBE, and nine destroyers were allocated to Kalamata, but on arrival found that the Germans had arrived. The operation was abandoned.

MAY

CRETE

With the evacuation of the Greek mainland completed, the island of Crete was strengthened to withstand an expected German attack.

The battle for the island commenced on 20th May, with German airborne attacks on British-held airfields. A seaborne invasion force was halted by the Navy, but German air attacks took a heavy toll of the vessels convoying supplies. By 26th May,

when NIZAM managed to reach Suda Bay with reinforcements, the allied force had lost through sinking or damage, two battleships, a carrier, six cruisers and eight destroyers. The following day it was decided to evacuate the forces from Crete – an exercise that could only be carried out by the fleet. PERTH was damaged by a bomb. NAPIER and NIZAM saw the operation through to its conclusion on 1st June.

IRAQ AND SYRIA

YARRA meanwhile was in the Persian Gulf. The Government of Iraq had been overthrown by a pro-German coup d'état and British troops were sent directly from Karachi to Basra to deal with the situation. YARRA formed part of the escort which was under the command of the C.-in-C. East Indies, who was flying his flag in the New Zealand cruiser LEANDER.

As expected, Iraq took a dim view of British troops landed and when more arrived declared war on Britain. By 31st May the war was over and British forces were occupying all important points in the country.

YARRA served in support of the land forces in the Shatt-el Arab River region. Possession of Syria now became of importance to Britain. Germany had already established a foothold in Syria, in efforts to support Iraq. The campaigning was ideal for naval co-operation with STUART, NIZAM and PERTH participating in the action.

The campaign was short and sharp with bombardment the main preoccupation, PERTH being accidentally bombed by Allied aircraft. The forces returned to Alexandria in July.

THE TOBRUK FERRY, 'WATERHEN' LOST

The forward British fortress of Tobruk

now became vital to the position in the Middle East. The sea was the sole means of supplying it and the port of Mersa Matruh.

The main fleet destroyer duties now devolved on ships of the 'N' class and the 'V' and 'W' class destroyers were used for the shuttle service between Alexandria and Mersa Matruh. The vessels lasted as long as their engines allowed. In all the destroyers made a total of 139 runs in and out of Tobruk. VAMPIRE sailed from Alexandria on 28th May, bound for a refit in Singapore, following considerable machinery trouble.

The four remaining Australian destroyers kept up the run to Tobruk from May to June/July, 1941. VENDETTA held the record number of thirty-nine passages. The sloop PARRAMATTA, which had joined the Australian ships in June after forty unbroken weeks in the Red Sea, also participated in the run to Mersa Matruh. On 24/25th June she survived an onslaught from nearly fifty dive-bombers, which had claimed HMS AUCKLAND. PARRAMATTA, with help from WATERHEN and VENDETTA, was able to save many of AUCKLAND's crew and the troops she was carrying.

Several days later the RAN suffered its first naval loss of the war. On 29th June, WATERHEN, in company with DEFENDER, was attacked by dive-bombers off Solum. The old ship was crippled and the following day sank. Her crew were rescued by the British destroyer.

The Australian destroyers were feeling the strains of twelve months continuous service. On 13th July, VOYAGER arrived in Alexandria on only one engine and eleven days later sailed for home. STUART, the famous flotilla leader, made her final run at the end of July and on 22nd August left Alexandria. Of the 'Scrap Iron Flotilla' only VENDETTA remained. She finally left in October, 1941, bound for Singapore.

HMA Ships LISMORE (J145) and MARYBOROUGH at Tripoli, July, 1943.

JUNE
CORVETTES TO RED SEA

BATHURST and LISMORE, the first Australian minesweepers to be built under the wartime building programme, arrived for service with the Red Sea Force in June, 1941. After carrying out a series of survey sweeps of convoy anchorages in the Red Sea, both vessels proceeded to Alexandria to join the Mediterranean Fleet, but were returned as unsuitable, owing to their lack of anti-aircraft armament. They were subsequently employed off the coast of French Somaliland until they went to the Far East in December, 1941.

AUGUST
'YARRA' AND 'KANIMBLA' JOIN FORCES IN PERSIAN GULF

A force of British and Indian vessels which included KANIMBLA and the sloop YARRA was scratched together. On the night of 25th August, YARRA pressed onto Khorramshahr, sinking the Persian sloop BABR with gunfire and later, under fire from the river bank, boarded and secured two gunboats. Earlier KANIMBLA had reached her destination, Bandar Shapur, and occupied it quickly, although the cruiser had to make brief use of her guns. On 27th August, Persia bowed to the inevitable. The Persian Gulf was now secure.

NOVEMBER
'PARRAMATTA' LOST

On 18th November, 1941, the long-awaited but ill-fated British offensive in the Western Desert began. The same day YARRA and her sister ship PARRAMATTA departed on convoy escort duty to Tobruk.

To provide ammunition for the Tobruk garrison, PARRAMATTA left for the port with two other vessels on 25th November. The group was shadowed by a German U-Boat and in the early hours of 27th November, north-east of Tobruk, PARRAMATTA was struck amidships by a torpedo fired from 1,500 yards. Within a few minutes PARRAMATTA rolled to starboard and went under. Only twenty-four ratings from her crew of 160 survived.

'SYDNEY' SUNK

Before the close of 1941 the RAN would suffer the loss of the light cruiser SYDNEY. After arriving in her name-port in February, 1941, SYDNEY had undergone refit and in November sailed for Fremantle for convoy/escort duties. On 11th November she set out from Fremantle to act as escort for the troopship ZEALANDIA to Sunda Strait where the trooper was handed over to two other cruisers and SYDNEY returned alone to Fremantle.

The German raider KORMORAN which had begun operations in the South Atlantic, had captured one and sunk seven other vessels, before sailing into the Indian Ocean in May, 1941. On 19th November, 150 miles south-west of Carnarvon, Western Australia, her lookout sighted smoke. At the time she was disguised as the STRAAT MALAKKA, a Dutch ship of remarkably similar size and appearance. The smoke soon resolved itself into the cruiser SYDNEY. Recognising this, KORMORAN, turned away.

SYDNEY, some ten miles distant, signalled to the merchant ship to identify herself. The German raised signal flags for the STRAAT MALAKKA and radioed QQQ, the Allied signal for the approach of a suspicious vessel. At about 1715 the two ships were sailing on a parallel course, about a mile apart. SYDNEY asked for the four-letter secret code and the raider, unable to answer, had no alternative but to fight. The Dutch colours came down

KORMORAN.

and were replaced by the German war flag.

Shortly after opening fire, KORMORAN scored hits on the Australian cruiser's bridge and director tower. SYDNEY, responded with a full salvo which went right over the raider. KORMORAN had the range and scored further hits on the fourth and fifth salvoes. Even though badly alight SYDNEY replied with local control, scoring hits on her enemy amidships and in the engine room. After eight or nine salvoes the German fired two torpedoes, one hitting the Australian cruiser under the

forward two turrets. SYDNEY was now dead in the water with only occasional fire coming from small guns.

KORMORAN turned away to port in order to destroy the enemy, but her engines gave out at the crucial moment. Four torpedoes from SYDNEY passed close astern while KORMORAN launched a third torpedo which missed. The range was now about six miles and, in view of the damage sustained, the Germans decided to abandon ship. Explosive charges were laid and set off. Fire quickly reached the 220 mines

in her stern section. KORMORAN blew apart and sank within two or three minutes.

SYDNEY was last seen ablaze at 2200. Later the German crew discovered that their adversary had not reached harbour. SYDNEY sank with all hands and except a single life raft, nothing was ever found of her. The 315 men from the raider survived the action and became prisoners of war in Australia.

DECEMBER
WAR IN THE PACIFIC

On 7th December, 1941, war broke out in the Pacific region, when the Empire of Japan attacked the widely dispersed points of Pearl Harbour, Hong Kong, the Phillipines, Guam and Wake Island.

Australia's reaction was immediate. The

Fleet dispositions – December, 1941

Ships	Type	Location	Transferred from European Theatre if Applicable
Australia	Cruiser	South Altantic/ Sydney	11/1941
Canberra	Cruiser	Refit – Sydney	
Hobart	Cruiser	Mediterranean	12/1941
Perth	Cruiser	Australian Station	
Adelaide	Cruiser	Australian Station	
Kanimbla	Armed M.C.	Indian Ocean	
Manoora	Armed M.C.	Netherlands East Indies	
Westralia	Armed M.C.	Netherlands East Indies	
Stuart	Leader	Refit – Melbourne	4/1942
Vampire	Destroyer	Singapore	
Vendetta	Destroyer	Refit – Singapore/ Melbourne/Sydney	12/1942
Voyager	Destroyer	Refit – Sydney	3/1942
Napier	Destroyer	Mediterranean	1/1942
Nestor	Destroyer	Mediterranean	1/1942
Nizam	Destroyer	Mediterranean	1/1942
Norman	Destroyer	Great Britain	1/1942
Swan	Sloop	New Guinea	

Ships	Type	Location	Transferred from European Theatre if Applicable
Warrego	Sloop	Darwin	
Yarra	Sloop	Mediterranean	12/1941
Ballarat	A.M.S.	Netherlands East Indies	
Bathurst	A.M.S.	Red Sea	
Bendigo	A.M.S.	Singapore	
Burnie	A.M.S.	Singapore	
Deloraine	A.M.S.	Sydney	
Goulburn	A.M.S.	Singapore	
Lismore	A.M.S.	Red Sea	
Lithgow	A.M.S.	Sydney	
Maryborough	A.M.S.	Singapore	
Mildura	A.M.S.	Australia	
Toowoomba	A.M.S.	Australia	
Townsville	A.M.S.	Australia	
Warrnambool	A.M.S.	S.E. Australia	
Wollongong	A.M.S.	S.E. Australia	
Kookaburra	B.D.V.	Darwin	
Kangaroo	B.D.V.	Darwin	
Karangi	B.D.V.	Sydney	
Koala	B.D.V.	Darwin	

The first Japanese air-raid on Darwin. HMAS KATOOMBA lies in the floating dock, SS ZEALANDIA burning and hospital ship MANUNDA.

Advisory War Council recommended that HOBART be returned to the Australian Station. The three 'N' class destroyers were also to be released for duty in the Far East. NORMAN, the fourth ship of the 'N' class to be completed, spent a period with the British Fleet in Russian waters before joining her sisters at Colombo in the Far East.

Britain made the gesture of strengthening the naval force based at Singapore. The new battleship PRINCE OF WALES and the veteran battlecruiser REPULSE sailed out post-haste. The Japanese soon launched a lightning attack down the Malayan Peninsula and were well on the way to capturing Singapore. With complete mastery of the air, Japanese forces sighted the two British capital ships on 10th December and immediately set upon them with wave after wave of unopposed torpedo bombers. PRINCE OF WALES and REPULSE both sank with heavy loss of life. VAMPIRE, which had been in the company of the two ships, rescued 225 survivors.

1942
JANUARY
REINFORCEMENTS

The last convoy for Singapore was escorted by the sloop YARRA. The ships were attacked many times during the voyage and the liners, FELIX ROUSSEL and EMPRESS OF ASIA were set on fire. The former managed to extinguish her fires but the EMPRESS could not. YARRA fought off the attackers and went in close to the burning liner to take off troops. BENDIGO and WOLLONGONG assisted in the rescue work. Singapore fell on 15th February.

FEBRUARY
AUSTRALIAN MAINLAND ATTACKED

On 19th February, Darwin was attacked by Japanese carrier-based planes in an attempt to eliminate its use as an American base.

The rapid advances of the Japanese made it prudent to withdraw women and children from the areas in their path. Evacuation commenced in New Guinea, Papua and Darwin. The veteran cruiser ADELAIDE escorted three Dutch merchant ships to Portuguese Timor with reinforcements. The Portuguese protested and sent a troop ship from East Africa for the province's defence and the Dutch were withdrawn. PERTH and EXETER, together with the destroyers ELECTRA, JUPITER and ENCOUNTER, were instructed to join the Dutch force in the Netherlands East Indies.

BATTLE OF THE SUNDA STRAIT

On 28th February, 1942, PERTH and the American cruiser HOUSTON departed Tanjong Priok for Tjilatjap via the Sunda Strait. PERTH had received reports of an enemy convoy of ten transports, escorted by cruisers and destroyers, fifty miles north-east of Batavia, but did not anticipate encountering the enemy during the voyage. Followed by HOUSTON she steamed at 22 knots along the northern coast of Java and arrived in Bantam Bay prior to entering the Sunda Strait when, at 2306 on 28th February, a Japanese destroyer was sighted. The two Allied cruisers had in fact encountered the entire Japanese invasion fleet.

Fifty transports, six cruisers and ten destroyers were either at anchor in the bay or in close proximity. PERTH opened fire with her front turrets and swung in a five mile wide circle; a manouevre immediately followed by HOUSTON. At 2326 PERTH suffered a hit on her forward funnel and at 0005 was struck by the first of two torpedoes. An hour later she had expended all her ammunition. Four Japanese ships had been destroyed in the action.

Being so badly hit orders were given to abandon PERTH and, after being struck by two more torpedoes, she went down.

Twenty minutes later HOUSTON was also sunk, taking with her 600 of the crew. Only 320 of PERTH's 680 crew were picked out of the water by the Japanese, and of these 105 ratings were to die while prisoners of war.

In Bandung, the Commander of the Allied Naval Forces, informed the British and American commanders that the Governor-General of the Netherlands East Indies had dissolved the naval command. The British Admiral withdrew his force to India, and the American Admiral to Australia. The Australians withdrew from Batavia and went overland to Tjilatjap. With the position deteriorating by the hour ships were ordered to avoid the port and make direct for Fremantle or Colombo. Two convoys arrived off the port and were sent on, one to Colombo and the other, escorted by YARRA, made for Fremantle. The Japanese, already south of Tjilatjap, attacked the ships as they tried to reach safe waters.

MARCH

'YARRA' AND CONVOY SUNK

BURNIE sailed on 2nd March, 1942, after BENDIGO had left. She reached Fremantle and safety, as did her four sisters GOULBURN, TOOWOOMBA, BALLARAT and MARYBOROUGH, all of which had formed the Sunda Strait patrol. YARRA, remaining behind to guard a convoy of three ships which were incapable of more than nine knots speed, was spotted on 2nd March by Japanese aircraft. At sunrise on 4th March YARRA's lookout sighted three enemy heavy cruisers and two destroyers on the horizon. YARRA proceeded to lay smoke and placed herself between the enemy ships and the scattering convoy. By 0800 the Japanese had destroyed all four ships –

YARRA was the last to go, ablaze and circled by enemy destroyers.

Only 34 of her crew survived the action and on 9th March when the Netherlands submarine KII found them, only 13 remained alive.

APRIL

'VAMPIRE' LOST

On 4th April, a large enemy force was reported 360 miles south-east of Ceylon and steering north-west. The Royal Navy's main force sailed to intercept the Japanese, but failed to make contact. The Japanese then attacked Trincomalee on 9th April. HERMES, VAMPIRE and five smaller ships which had left harbour, attempted to return when all was quiet but were sighted by a reconnaissance aircraft from the Japanese battleship HARUNA. The small force was attacked by dive bombers before help could be sent from shore. HERMES was the first ship lost. VAMPIRE was soon straddled by four bombs in quick succession. These sealed her fate and after further hits her back broke. Survivors were rescued by boats from the nearby hospital ship VITA.

MAY

BATTLE OF THE CORAL SEA

On 7th May, 1942, a sequence of actions known as the Battle of the Coral Sea commenced. At dawn Japanese carrier-based aircraft sank two American vessels. Shortly afterward, US aircraft sighted the enemy carrier SHOHO and sank her. This forced the Japanese Admiral to order his main invasion fleet from its objective, Port Moresby.

On 8th May, came the climax of the battle: aircraft from the two carrier groups finally found their prey. The US carrier LEXINGTON was crippled. One of the two remaining Japanese carriers was so

badly damaged by American air attack that all Japanese forces were finally ordered back to Rabaul.

It was later claimed that the victory of the Coral Sea was 'The Battle That Saved Australia'.

MIDGET SUBMARINES IN SYDNEY

On 30th May, 1942, a Japanese aircraft carried out reconnaissance of the Sydney area. On the next night a force of three midget submarines attempted to penetrate the defences of the harbour where the cruisers CANBERRA, ADELAIDE, KANIMBLA and WESTRALIA, the minesweepers WHYALLA, GEELONG and BOMBAY, USS CHICAGO, the Dutch submarine K9 and the depot ship KUTTABUL were at anchor. One midget was caught in the anti-torpedo net near the west boom gate, and the second was sighted outside the Heads and damaged by depth charges dropped by YANDRA. The third penetrated the defences and fired two torpedoes at CHICAGO. One passed below the cruiser and exploded under KUTTABUL, sinking the old ferry. The second torpedo failed to explode and ran aground on Garden Island.

While the cruiser CHICAGO was proceeding down harbour a submarine was located on its way in. As many ships as possible weighed anchor and kept on the move. The submarine was attacked and her crew killed. The damaged boat was later salvaged.

After some activity on the eastern Australian coast the Japanese submarines were withdrawn in June, 1942.

JUNE

'NESTOR' LOST

The four completed 'N' class destroyers were ordered to the Indian Ocean in January, 1942, but NESTOR and NAPIER

Remains of the Japanese midget-submarine No. 14, looking aft and showing the effects of the demolition charges.

BERRA, HOBART, the US cruisers SALT LAKE CITY and CHICAGO and three destroyers, sailed from Brisbane to link up with a US amphibious force. Twelve days later the ships met up with an even larger fleet of transports guarded by three US aircraft carriers.

AUGUST

'CANBERRA' SUNK AT SAVO ISLAND

At dawn on 7th August, the first waves of US Marines landed at Guadalcanal and Tulagi, and soon secured the sites. The Japanese reaction was immediate. Hastily organising a surface strike force of seven cruisers and a destroyer, they began to attack the Allied force without delay. It was a bold decision as it involved steaming in broad daylight down the length of 'The Slot' between the Solomons.

Incredibly, the sole sighting of the approaching enemy force – by an RAAF Catalina – was not passed on to Allied leaders. The Americans had split their forces into three groups. Two were guarding

subsequently returned to the Mediterranean in June to work with the Malta convoys.

NESTOR constantly attacked from the air was eventually lost on 16th June, after being straddled by two bombs on the 15th. Taken in tow the destroyer sank deeper in the water. As she was causing danger to the destroyer JAVELIN attempting to tow the cripple to safety, JAVELIN was ordered to sink NESTOR after collecting her crew.

JULY

WORKING WITH THE AMERICANS

On 14th July, 1942, Task Force 44, made up of the flagship AUSTRALIA, CAN-

HMAS NESTOR, being depth charged by HMS JAVELIN on 16th June, 1942.

HMAS CANBERRA, sinking off Savo Island, 9th August, 1942.

the channels on either side of Savo Island. AUSTRALIA in company with CANBERRA, CHICAGO and two destroyers, patrolled the southern channel, while the northern channel was guarded by the US cruisers VINCENNES, ASTORIA and QUINCY, and two destroyers.

Shortly after midnight on 9th August the Japanese reached Savo Island and at 0136 began firing on the unsuspecting cruisers CANBERRA and CHICAGO. At 0143 an American destroyer, with the Allied ships brilliantly silhouetted by flares, frantically signalled: 'Warning. Warning. Strange ships entering harbour!'

CANBERRA had been caught while steaming slowly at twelve knots in a state of 'modified second degree of readiness'; half her crew were asleep, her aircraft bombed-up but defuelled, armament and damage control parties closed-up, her guns empty and trained fore-and-aft. The Australian cruiser was struck by twenty-four shells in two minutes. With both engine-rooms hit, her power and lighting gone and fires blazing amidships and between decks, she listed to starboard.

While CHICAGO was pursuing a lone enemy destroyer, the Japanese force destroyed the three American cruisers. In thirty-two minutes of gunfire and torpedo attacks the Japanese force had destroyed four Allied warships and inflicted 1,270 casualties, including thirty-five killed. At 0240 the Japanese force regrouped and headed for Rabaul.

It was decided the stricken CANBERRA had to be sunk. In total 263 rounds of 5-inch shells and four torpedoes were poured into her hull by Allied ships and on 9th August, 1942, she slipped beneath the sea.

A Board of Inquiry was convened in Sydney within weeks of the action. The Board found that CANBERRA was not in a proper state of readiness, but judged the crew's behaviour 'satisfactory'.

'ARUNTA' COMMENCES OPERATIONS

On 26th August the long-expected Japanese invasion of Port Moresby came nearer. Nauru and Ocean Island were occupied within the next few days. The new Tribal class destroyer ARUNTA, escorting the troop transport TASMAN, was at Milne Bay and both vessels were ordered to Port Moresby, where ARUNTA, the only naval vessel present, could provide anti-submarine protection for ships in the port.

Later while escorting the transport MALAITA to Cairns, ARUNTA recorded an asdic contact believed to be an enemy submarine. She attacked with depth charges and oil was sighted in the spot for some days. Later it was verified that ARUNTA had sunk the Japanese submarine RO33.

Also in the Port Moresby region were the sloop SWAN and minesweeper CASTLEMAINE, both escorting a convoy of small ship reinforcements. Allied Intelligence revealed that the Japanese were planning large-scale reinforcements. Task Force 44

was sent to Milne Bay to counter the move. The force was without HOBART and the destroyer American PATTERSON, which were undergoing repairs so the South Pacific destroyers HENLEY and HELM were temporarily attached in their place.

Convoys to the area were more or less constantly escorted by ARUNTA, STUART, BALLARAT and BENDIGO.

SEPTEMBER

'N' CLASS AT MADAGASCAR

In September, 1942, NAPIER, NIZAM and NORMAN accompanied the aircraft carrier FORMIDABLE, cruisers BIRMINGHAM and MAURITIUS, fast minelayer MANXMAN, battleship WARSPITE, and five other destroyers, on an operation designed to bring the pro-Vichy island of Madagascar under the control of the Allies. Force A sailed for Kilindini in two sections and was joined there by NEPAL. The former RAN seaplane carrier ALBATROSS was also in the force.

N class destroyers at Durban, 1942. From left HMA Ships NIZAM, NORMAN and NEPAL.

The ships encountered little opposition – the threat of bombardment was enough to secure most landing points. Several Vichy merchant ships were rounded up and NIZAM proceeded south to refit at Simonstown, after which she joined the South Atlantic force based at Capetown. The remaining ships of the flotilla spent the next two or three months escorting convoys between Kilindini and Durban. In 1943 the 'N's' were joined by the 'Q' class destroyers QUICKMATCH, QUIBERON (both Australian manned), and QUALITY, attached to the South Atlantic Station.

'VOYAGER' AGROUND

During September, VOYAGER sailed from Darwin to take re-inforcements to Timor to relieve stranded Australian and Dutch troops who were carrying on a very successful guerilla war. While disembarking the fresh troops at Betano Bay, VOYAGER went aground. All attempts to save the ship failed and her crew were picked up by WARRNAMBOOL and KALGOORLIE.

OCTOBER

NEW PATROL CRAFT

HDML 1074 was commissioned on 7th October, for anti-submarine and patrol duties. No. 1074 was imported from England, the first of 28 similar harbour defence launches, which were to provide extremely useful service around Australia and New Guinea.

1943

JANUARY

FIRST FAIRMILE B JOINS FLEET

New Years day witnessed the commissioning of the first locally-built Fairmile B Motor Launch, No. 814, from the Halvorsen yard in Sydney. Thirty-four would be commissioned by April, 1944.

TASK FORCES RESTRUCTURED

The first two months of the new year witnessed the defeat of the Japanese forces in Papua and on Guadalcanal. The US naval forces in the south-west Pacific were re-organised to become the Seventh Fleet. The combined Australian-American Task Force 44, under Rear-Admiral Crutchley, was re-titled Task Force 74. By early 1943, the tactical position had altered so that landing ships were of greater value to the combined Australian-US forces than were Armed Merchant Cruisers. KANIMBLA, MANOORA and WESTRALIA were subsequently paid off for conversion to Landing Ships Infantry. The trio remained under Australian control with KANIMBLA being commissioned into the RAN for the first time.

The Task Force now comprised AUSTRALIA, HOBART, WARRAMUNGA, ARUNTA and the American LAMSON. At the end of June the force sailed back to the Coral Sea.

The 8-inch gun heavy cruiser SHROPSHIRE was commissioned into the RAN at Chatham on 20th April, 1943, to replace the lost CANBERRA.

Task Force 74 was offered for service to the US Third Fleet but ARUNTA, WARRAMUNGA and LAMSON remained with the Seventh Fleet. Within two days HOBART was torpedoed. The crippled ship returned to Espiritu Santo, where temporary repairs were made. She was subsequently escorted back to Sydney by WARRAMUNGA and ARUNTA for permanent repairs and did not re-enter service until early 1945. By September SHROPSHIRE had been refitted and joined Task Force 74 at Brisbane at the close of October, 1943.

SEPTEMBER

SRD MISSION TO SINGAPORE

Before leaving 1943, mention should be made of the lone voyage of KRAIT, an SRD craft operated in the service of the Allied Intelligence Bureau by a volunteer crew. This former Japanese ship was used in the attack on enemy ships in Singapore harbour by limpet mines.

The Commando volunteers were landed near the port, after which KRAIT hid for some fourteen days – no mean feat in itself. The company was successfully picked up after a raid in which seven Japanese merchant ships were sunk or badly damaged.

Task Force 74, now in New Britain, comprised the cruisers AUSTRALIA, SHROPSHIRE, NASHVILLE and the destroyers WARRAMUNGA, ARUNTA, HELM and RALPH TALBOT. The force resumed the bombardment role, the destroyers first at Gasmata. Next to be attacked were the Arawe Islands. WESTRALIA, freshly converted to her new status as a landing ship participated in this landing.

SHIPS REDEPLOYED

In August, 1943, Lord Louis Mountbatten was appointed Supreme Commander of Allied Forces in south-east Asia. Part of his job was to plan major amphibious operations for 1944, using a battle fleet based on Ceylon. The Eastern Fleet, accordingly returned to Colombo. Under the new plan all six destroyers of the 'N' and 'Q' classes were based at Colombo, as were the

Moving north to the attack aboard the SRD craft KRAIT, between Exmouth Gulf and Lombok Strait.

Bathurst class minesweepers formerly in use in the Mediterranean.

NOVEMBER

NEW FRIGATE COMMISSIONS

The first frigate to ever join the RAN commissioned on 18th November, when GASCOYNE entered service. By VJ Day five sister ships had been completed. Two more followed in subsequent months.

1944

FURTHER ADVANCES

Task Force 74 spent the first two months of 1944 refitting. The force then supported the landings in the Admiralty Islands. After these operations, Task Force 74 was rejoined by AUSTRALIA, which had com-

HMAS GASCOYNE, December, 1943, after commissioning, at anchor in Farm Cove.

pleted her refit. The flag was transferred to the heavy cruiser on 21st April.

German U-boat activity in the Indian Ocean dwindled due to inability to re-arm their submarines with torpedoes. Those remaining were ordered to use their weapons up and then return to Germany. On 11th February, LAUNCESTON, IPSWICH and the Indian JUMNA, sank the Japanese submarine RO 110 with depth charges about twenty miles off Vizagapatam.

In April, 1944, US forces attacked Hollandia. All three Australian landing ships were employed, WESTRALIA at Cape Cretin and KANIMBLA and MANOORA at Goodenough Island. At the same time a diversionary attack in the general area of Sumatra, the Andaman and Nicobar Islands was carried out by the Eastern Fleet, which included the Australian destroyers NAPIER, NEPAL, NIZAM and QUIBERON. Pacific landings were made in May with Admiral Crutchley still in command. Task Force 74 bombarded mainland targets at Sawar and Sarmi.

SEPTEMBER

THE BATTLE OF LEYTE GULF

The Japanese were preparing for another naval battle and sent the two giant battleships YAMATO and MUSASHI, the light cruiser NOSHIRO, and six destroyers to reinforce their position on Biak. Task Force 74 now based on Seeadler harbour in the Admiralty group bombarded Noemfoot Island.

The force sailed from Seeadler Harbour and provided gun support at Aitape until the end of July. The Japanese attempt to recapture Aitape ended in failure. The stage was being set for the last, and possibly greatest, battle – the Battle of Leyte Gulf, in which Task Force 74, with the three LSIs was present.

By 1st September the ships that had been sent south to Sydney to refit ready for Leyte and the Battle of the Philippines

HMAS WESTRALIA, October, 1944.

were back at their anchorages. Task Force 74 was reorganised as part of Task Force 75, the whole fleet becoming the close-support and covering force for the landing on the islands of Morotai, KANIMBLA and MANOORA were among the landing ships in attendance. AUSTRALIA and SHROPSHIRE bombarded the landing areas and Morotai fell to the Allies without a struggle.

The assault on the Philippines at Leyte was under the overall command of General MacArthur. The naval side of the operation was undertaken by the Seventh Fleet aid.

Each allied force possessed its own surface air cover, fire support, bombardment, minesweeping and supply groups. Task force 78 was subdivided into three sections. The third known as the Panaon Attack Group included the three LSIs KANIMBLA, MANOORA and WESTRALIA. Close cover for all three areas of the Northern Attack Force was provided by Task Force 77 (renumbered TF 75), which included AUSTRALIA and SHROPSHIRE, as well as the destroyers ARUNTA and WARRAMUNGA.

An important part of the plan was the destruction of the major part of the enemy fleet. The invasion fleet reached Leyte without incident. As the time for battle approached, the British Eastern Fleet carried out a diversion designed to give the impression that a landing was imminent on the Nicobar Islands. Two Australian destroyers present were QUIBERON, in the destroyer screen for the battlecruiser RENOWN, and NORMAN, part of a bombardment group headed by the heavy cruiser LONDON.

Preparations for the Leyte invasion were undertaken by GASCOYNE in Leyte Gulf. Minesweepers had cleared the area of mines on 17th October, leaving GASCOYNE and an American minesweeper to buoy the channel and shoals. Fire-support battleships entered the gulf the same evening and opened fire on the beaches on the 19th. On 20th October the Panaon Attack Group landed, the troops and cargo being discharged without enemy interference.

During the battle two ships of the support group were put out of action. HONOLULU by a torpedo from a Japanese torpedo bomber, and AUSTRALIA by a Japanese dive bomber. The majority of AUSTRALIA's bridge and control personnel were killed or injured and the whole bridge areas was severely damaged by exploding cannon shells and petrol fires. The ship was now useless as a fighting ship as her radar and director control tower were out of action.

AUSTRALIA was ordered to join the damaged HONOLULU in the southern Transport Area, with WARRAMUNGA acting as screen. AUSTRALIA and WAR-

RAMUNGA made for Manus where the wounded were landed for hospital treatment. From there the two ships sailed to Espiritu Santo where repairs were undertaken. AUSTRALIA was ready to rejoin the task force by 28th November.

In the meantime SHROPSHIRE and ARUNTA stood by for calls for fire support and patrolled the transport area at night.

NOVEMBER
BRITISH PACIFIC FLEET/ ESTABLISHED

In November, the British Pacific Fleet was formed under the command of Admiral Sir Bruce Fraser. The ships remaining in the Indian Ocean formed the East Indies Station. In December Admiral Fraser transferred his flag to the battleship HOWE and left Ceylon for Fremantle with a screen of four destroyers. The main body of the fleet followed in February, 1945. The fleet comprised the battleship KING GEORGE V, carriers INDOMITABLE, ILLUSTRIOUS, INDEFATIGABLE, VICTORIOUS and FORMIDABLE, cruisers SWIFTSURE, CEYLON, ARGONAUT, BLACK PRINCE, ACHILLES, GAMBIA, NEWFOUNDLAND and UGANDA. Destroyers which included QUIBERON and QUICKMATCH comprised the 4th Flotilla, 25th Flotilla and 27th Flotilla. The 'N' class destroyers were attached to the Pacific Fleet, but were used in support of the campaign in Burma.

1945

JANUARY
LINGAYEN

Following the action at Leyte Gulf, the Australian ships withdrew to Manus where they prepared for the invasion of Luzon. The Seventh Fleet was given the task of protecting the landings in the north of the island in the undefended area of Lingayen Gulf. By 5th January, AUSTRALIA and the two Tribal destroyers were at Lingayen.

The first Australian ship to suffer damage during operations was ARUNTA, near-missed by a kamikaze. Despite having her steering gear damaged and hull holed in several places, she still managed to remain in action. On 6th January AUSTRALIA and SHROPSHIRE joined forces to bombard the east side of the gulf. The latter was near-missed on a number of occasions. Later the same day, when the bombardment force was withdrawing, AUSTRALIA suffered another suicide plane attack. Again damage was heavy and many vital personnel were killed or injured. Except for a special bombardment firing, there were now only sufficient crews to man one 4-inch mounting each side.

AUSTRALIA was still able to serve in a reduced role and with SHROPSHIRE was allocated a counter-battery role. On 8th January, AUSTRALIA was struck by two more kamikazes. Both planes hit the water short of the cruiser and skidded into her side, one blowing a fourteen-foot hole in the port side. WESTRALIA was near-missed and showered by splinters at the stern. During the main landings AUSTRALIA was damaged by a kamikaze attack. The enemy plane hit a strut of the foremast and swung into the fore-funnel cutting off the top third. There were no casualties on this occasion.

On 9th January, AUSTRALIA and ARUNTA were directed to report, with other damaged ships, to a fast returning convoy to Leyte. On arrival there AUSTRALIA was repaired and ordered to

Units of the British Pacific Fleet in Wooloomooloo, November, 1944. The former RAN training/target vessel BURRA BRA (left) is being moored with the assistance of a tug. (Photo – R. Gillett Collection)

Manus on her way back to Australia for refit.

Much of the Seventh Fleet now joined the Pacific Fleet for the attack on Iwo Jima. SHROPSHIRE together with ARUNTA and WARRAMUNGA, were part of the force ordered to remain at Lingayen as a covering defence force. WARREGO and GASCOYNE were used for buoy-laying throughout the campaign.

On 16th January, the ships proceeded up Manila Bay to bombard the beaches at Corregidor.

HMAS AUSTRALIA at Lingayen, January, 1945. A Tribal class destroyer lies alongside. Note the damage to the cruiser's funnels and her severe list.

MARCH

'HOBART' RETURNS TO SERVICE

On 1st March, the Australian warships sailed for Manus. SHROPSHIRE and ARUNTA proceeded on to Sydney for refits and were replaced in the south-west Pacific by HOBART, now back in fighting trim after being torpedoed in the Solomons campaign in July, 1943. HOBART and WARRAMUNGA sailed for Leyte to take part in the Cebu operation. The task force bombarded the landing area. The landing was made on 26th March.

MAY

NAZI SURRENDER, TARAKAN

During May the three 'N' class destroyers formed part of the screen for Task Force 57, and spent most of their time with the logistic support group. On 8th May the unconditional surrender of Germany was announced.

Meanwhile the Australian warships with the British Fleet at Okinawa were providing the covering force for landings at Tarakan, Borneo. The LSIs MANOORA and WESTRALIA, with HOBART, WARRAMUNGA and four frigates, BURDEKIN, BARCOO, HAWKESBURY and LACHLAN, the latter acting as a hydrographic vessel, took part in the operation.

A landing was made on 1st May with Task Force 74 carrying out bombardments. The Japanese retreated and HOBART and WARRAMUNGA were released for other duties at Hollandia. By 23rd June resistance was over and Tarakan was in Allied control. Australian forces were gradually working their way through New Guinea and were pressing on with an invasion of Wewak. Preliminary bombardments were made by HOBART, WARRAMUNGA and ARUNTA, while SWAN, COLAC and DUBBO gave the necessary gunfire support cover.

MAY

CORVETTE HIT

COLAC left Wewak for Madang and then sailed on to Torokina on the island of Bougainville. The vessel was ordered to halt the transfer of Japanese troops from Choiseul Island to Bougainville. She was badly damaged by gunfire from Japanese shore-based guns and had to be towed to Finschhafen. SWAN then towed her to Sydney for repairs.

JUNE

LANDLINGS AT BRUNEI

An operation similar to the one at Tarakan was carried out at Brunei Bay. Fire support was given by Task Force 74, the preliminary bombardments taking place on 8th June to cover LACHLAN which was serving as the buoy layer and close inshore reconnaissance vessel. The landing itself was made on 10th June. For the Brunei Bay operation, KANIMBLA joined WESTRALIA and MANOORA. After little or no opposition the three LSIs, HOBART and ARUNTA left the area on 11th June. The cruiser and destroyer rendezvoued with the flagship, SHROPSHIRE, and returned to Brunei Bay to take over the task fire support from the Americans. On 26th June the force sailed from Brunei to take up position ready for the invasion of Balikpapan.

JULY

THE LAST AMPHIBIOUS LANDING

Balikpapan, the last amphibious assault of World War II, was carried out on 1st July, 1945. SHROPSHIRE led HOBART and six other Australian ships in the combined force used for the invasion. No naval resistance was experienced and little air activity, largely due to the naval and air bombardments prior to the landings. After bombardments on 9th July the task force left the area and was not required for any further action.

SHROPSHIRE reached Manila on 19th

July, where she was joined by WAR-RAMUNGA. The ships sailed with the rest of the task force, including the new Tribal class destroyer BATAAN, to rendezvous with Task Force 74 at Subic Bay. In the meantime ARUNTA had proceeded to Sydney for refitting.

For operations against the Japanese homeland, the 'N' class destroyers were attached to the Fleet Train, while QUIB-ERON and QUICKMATCH formed part of the screen for the British aircraft carriers FORMIDABLE, VICTORIOUS and IM-PLACABLE sailing for Manus.

AUGUST
SURRENDER

Plans proceeded for the actual invasion of Japan. However, on 6th August an American bomber dropped the first atomic bomb on Hiroshima; a second was dropped three days later on Nagasaki. Japan surrendered

on 15th August.

Australian ships present in Tokyo Bay for the official surrender of the Japanese on 2nd September included SHROP-SHIRE, HOBART, BATAAN, WAR-RAMUNGA, IPSWICH, BALLARAT and CESSNOCK. With the main British Fleet were NAPIER and NIZAM.

SEPTEMBER
RAN STRENGTH

By now the Australian fleet comprised more than 366 vessels, including 79 major ships.

The six years of war had cost the navy 2,170 officers and men. Peak manpower strength, including WRANS and nursing sisters, was reached on 30th June, 1945, when 39,650 were serving in the force.

After the surrender HOBART and WARRAMUNGA left Japan for Sydney for refit; SHROPSHIRE and BATAAN

left in November. The two destroyers called at ports in Japan to pick up prisoners of war from Japanese prison camps. At Sendai BATAAN picked up survivors from the crew of the cruiser PERTH.

With the surrender, the south-west Pacific Command ceased to exist, and command of the Navy reverted to the Australian Naval Board. This was a somewhat precipitate decision in view of the fact that the re-occupation of Allied territory would involve combined operations on a fairly large scale. Australian minesweepers formed part of a squadron ordered to Hong Kong.

At Rabaul the official surrender took place on HMS GLORY, a light fleet carrier. Japanese representatives were taken out to the ship to discuss the terms in the destroyer VENDETTA. The surrender of Bougainville was taken onboard DIA-MANTINA, Balikpapan on BURDEKIN, Timor on MORESBY and Nauru, and Ocean Island, also on DIAMANTINA.

Fleet list

Type	Strength September 1945	Lost 1939–45	To be completed
Cruiser	4	3	–
Destroyer	11	4	–
Sloop	2	2	–
Frigate	6	–	6
Aust Minesweeper	53	3	–
Infantry Landing Ship	3	–	–
Mine Warfare Ship	33	3	–
Fairmile B	33	2	–
HDML	28	–	–
Requisitioned Patrol Craft	18	–	–
Examination Vesseel	14	2	–
SRD	14	–	–
BDV	4	–	–
Requisitioned BDV	13	–	–
ASR	20	–	2
Combined Operations	3	1	–
GPV	11	–	11
120′ Lighter	2	–	9
85′ Lighter	8	–	–
OFL	8	–	4
Requisitioned Lighter	6	4	–
Lugger	10	1	–

Type	Strength September 1945	Lost 1939–45	To be completed
Oiler	1	–	–
Requisitioned Oiler	2	–	–
Repair Ship	1	–	–
Requisitioned Repair Ship	2	–	–
Requisitioned Ammunition/Stores	5	1	–
Survey	3	–	–
Requisitioned Survey	6	–	–
TRB	2	–	–
TRV	3	–	–
Tugs	3	–	–
Towboat	5	–	7
Requisition Tug	6	–	–
Training Ship	1	–	–
Requisitioned Training Ship	2	–	–
Miscellaneous Requisitioned Support Craft	10	3	–
Requisitioned Launch/ Motor Boat	10	–	–

COUNTY CLASS

Shropshire

SHROPSHIRE, originally built for the Royal Navy, was completed on 12th September, 1929. In the early part of the Second World War she operated in the Atlantic and Indian Oceans.

During early 1941, she was fitted with two 8-barrelled pom poms at Simonstown. Later, at Chatham between October, 1941, and February, 1942, her refit included replacing the single 4-inch mountings with four twin, plus seven single 20mm mountings. In late 1942 three additional single 20mm were added.

Following the loss of CANBERRA, SHROPSHIRE was offered to the RAN in September, 1942, transferring on 25th June, 1943. Prior to her transfer SHROPSHIRE was again refitted and the following changes affected; two quadruple 0.5 inch MGs removed, four single 20mm removed, seven twin 20mm fitted. At the same time her aircraft arrangements were deleted.

In 1945 her torpedo tubes were removed and all 20mm mountings were replaced by 11 single 40mm Bofors. SHROPSHIRE paid off in 1949 and remained in reserve until sold.

HMS SHROPSHIRE, 1940, firing a full port-broadside from her 8-inch main armament. In Royal Navy service the cruiser carried four twin 8-inch guns in A, B, X and Y positions; single 2 pounder pom-poms on each beam abreast the fore and centre stacks; two single 4-inch guns on each beam amidships; quadruple 21-inch torpedo tubes below the 4-inch weapons and two 3 pounder guns (port and starboard) abreast the mainmast. (Photo – P. Britz)

HMAS SHROPSHIRE, December, 1945; profile. (P. Webb)

Displacement (tons): *Standard* 9,830 *Full Load* 14,540
Dimensions (feet): *Length* (oa) 633.0 *Beam* 66.0 *Draught* 22.6
Machinery: Parsons geared turbines; 4 screws; 80,000 s.h.p.
Speed (knots): 32
Range (miles): 12,800 @ 12 knots
Manning: 820
Armament: Eight 8-inch (4 × 2), Eight 4-inch (4 × 2), Twelve 40mm (12 × 1), Two 2 pdr. (2 × 1), Eight 21-inch torpedo tubes (2 × 4).

Ship	Pend. No.	Builder	Cons. Time	Comm.	Fate
Shropshire	73 (Royal Navy)	WM. Beard-more & Co.	3y 7m	20/4/43	Sold 16/7/54

HMAS SHROPSHIRE in 1945. (Photo P. Britz)

HMAS SHROPSHIRE, 1943; she carries wartime camouflage; twin 4-inch guns have replaced the single mounts; tripod mainmast has replaced the original structure and aircraft facilites have been removed.

ARMED MERCHANT CRUISERS
Two Ships

To accompany the fleet on early missions, and for convoy escort duties, two Australian coastal passenger ships, MANOORA and WESTRALIA, were requisitioned and fitted out as armed merchant cruisers. Both ships were provided with seven 6-inch and two 3-inch anti-aircraft guns, plus one Walrus amphibian. Another three ships, KANIMBLA, ARAWA and MORETON BAY, were also requisitioned, but operated as HM Ships. The threat from enemy warships and raiders had lessened by 1942 and in the ensuing year KANIMBLA, MANOORA and WESTRALIA were taken in hand for conversion to infantry landing ships, KANIMBLA commissioning as an HMA Ship for the first time.

KANIMBLA as a coastal passenger ship.

HMAS KANIMBLA.

Name	Details	Status
Manoora **(F48)**	*Steamship* 10,856 gross tons 480 × 91 × 24 feet 8,200 b.h.p. = 16½ kts 7 × 6-inch, 2 × 3-inch 6 × 20mm, 4 Lewis, 2 DCTs, 1 Walrus Amphibian	Built 1935 Req. 14/10/39 AMC 12/12/39 PO 28/9/42 LSI 2/2/43 PO 6/12/47 Ret. 31/8/49
Westralia **(F95)**	*Steamship* 8,108 gross tons 445 × 60.3 × 22.7 feet 6,750 b.h.p. = 15½ kts 7 × 6-inch, 2 × 3-inch 10 × 20mm, 4 × .303 Lewis, 2 DCTs, 1 Walrus Amphibian	Built 1929 Req. 2/11/39 AMC 17/1/40 PO 12/1942 LSI 31/5/43 PO 19/9/49 Ret. 27/3/51

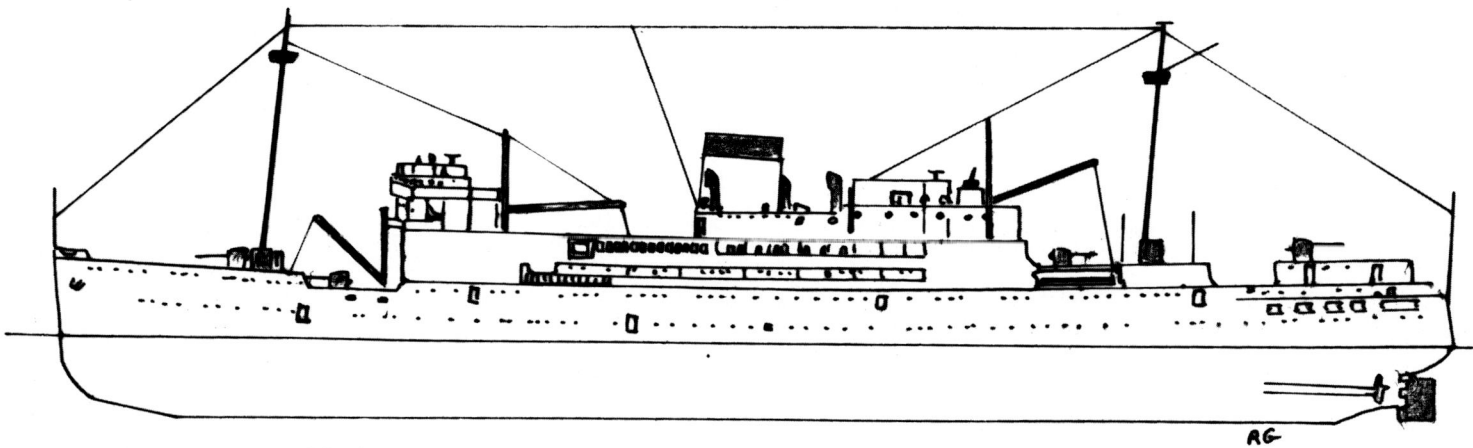

HMAS MANOORA: profile. (R. Gillett)

Left – HMAS WESTRALIA; the 6-inch guns mounted forward are protected by shields, while the 6-inch gun aft on the poop deck is an open mount. Other open mounts are carried on the top deck (at the after end of the superstructure) and immediately below on the main deck.

Below – HMAS WESTRALIA in Sydney Harbour. The tug HMAS HEROS lies in Chowder Bay.

TRIBAL CLASS

Arunta, Bataan, Warramunga

HMAS WARRAMUNGA, during trials off the NSW coast, 4th January 1943.

HMAS WARRAMUNGA, 1942; profile. (P. Webb)

The RAN Tribals were based on the British class but mounted the twin 4-inch gun in 'X' position in lieu of the fourth 4.7-inch mount in the Royal Navy ships.

Originally eight Tribal class destroyers were to be built in Australian shipyards. The three units completed were powerful ships able to reach 36 knots and were intended to relieve cruisers on convoy escort work.

By the close of war in 1945, ARUNTA and WARRA-MUNGA had lost their six 20mm guns for six 40mm Bofors in single mountings and four 2 pounder pom-poms.

BATAAN and WARRAMUNGA served with the United Nations Forces during the Korean War and in the 1950s ARUNTA and WARRAMUNGA were converted to anti-submarine destroyers.

BATAAN and WARRAMUNGA were scrapped after being sold. ARUNTA was lost at sea on 13th February, 1969, en route to the ship breakers.

Displacement (tons): *Standard 1,927 Full Load 2,700*
Dimensions (feet): *Length* (oa) 377.6 *Beam* 36.6 *Draught* 15.6 (max)
Machinery: Parsons geared turbines; twin screws; 44,000 s.h.p.
Speed (knots): 36
Range (miles): 5,700 @ 15 knots
Manning: 261
Armament: Arunta and Warramunga: Six 4.7-inch (3 × 2), Two 4-inch (1 × 2), One 2 pdr. pom-pom (1 × 4), Six 20mm (6 × 1), Four 21-inch torpedo tubes (1 × 4), Two DCTs. Bataan: Six 4.7-inch (3 × 2), Two 4-inch (1 × 2), One 2 pdr. pom-pom (1 × 4), Six 40mm (6 × 1), Four 21-inch torpedo tubes (1 × 4), Two DCTs.

Ship	Pend. No.	Builder	Cons. Time	Comm.	Fate
Arunta	I30 (1942) D5 (1943) I30 (1945)	Cockatoo	2y 5m	30/4/42	Sold 1/11/68
Bataan	D9 (1945)	Cockatoo	3y 4m	26/6/45	Sold 1958
Warramunga	I44 (1942) D10 (1943) I44 (1945)	Cockatoo	2y 9m	23/11/42	Sold 15/2/63

HMAS ARUNTA, 1942, as built, with original armament; note the searchlight before the mainmast.

HMAS WARRAMUNGA, 1947; 40mm Bofors and 2 pounder pom-poms have replaced the 20mm Oerlikons on the bridge wings, between the funnels and forward of the 4-inch mount; the mainmast has been deleted.

HMAS ARUNTA, 1942.

HMAS ARUNTA, 1945.

N CLASS

Napier, Nepal, Nestor, Nizam, Norman

Five N class destroyers were transferred on their completion to the RAN. Although Australian-manned and commissioned, they remained the property of the Royal Navy. Three other N class were built. Two were operated by the Netherlands and one by Poland.

NAPIER had a larger deck-house aft for additional accommodation and served as the flotilla leader.

During the war 20mm mountings were added to each ship and the 0.5-inch MGs deleted. The after set of torpedo tubes could be replaced by a 4-inch gun and eventually all five ships lost the tubes to provide increased anti-surface and anti-air capabilities. The 2 pdr. pom-pom was sited abaft the funnel. Later 40mm Bofors replaced the 20mm Oerlikons.

NESTOR, the only RAN N class to be lost, was damaged by enemy aircraft near Crete on 15th June, 1942, and despite a valiant

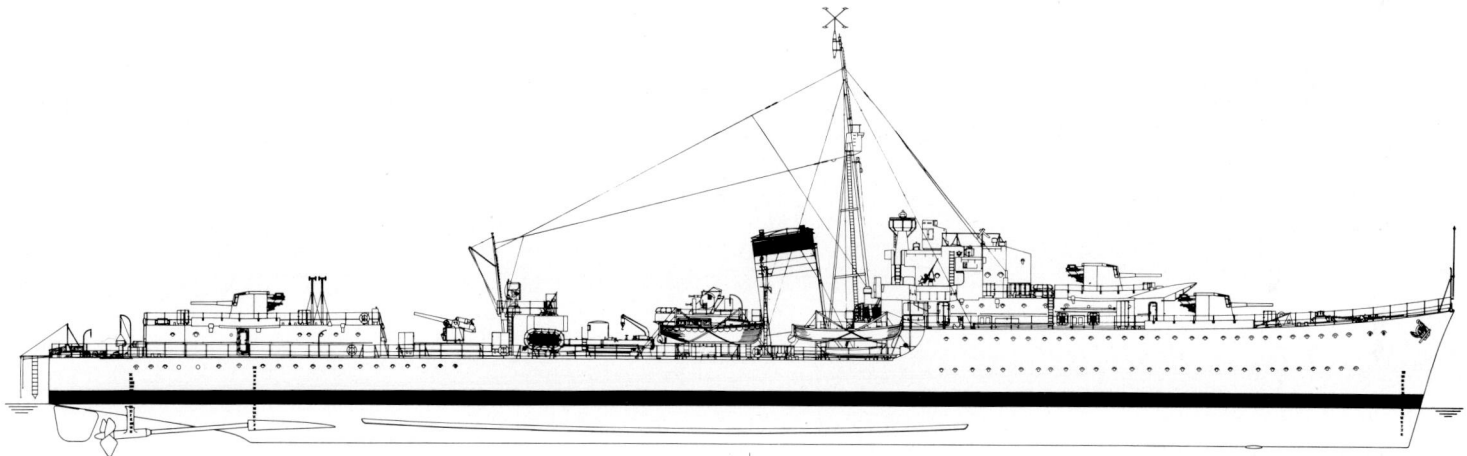

HMAS NAPIER, June, 1942; profile. (P. Webb)

HMAS NIZAM; profile. (R. Gillett)

HMAS NAPIER, November, 1940; a 4-inch anti-aircraft gun is carried instead of the second torpedo mounting.

effort by HMS JAVELIN to tow the destroyer to safety, sank the ensueing morning.

After the war, the four surviving ships reverted to the Royal Navy, and their crews transferred to the Q class destroyers QUADRANT, QUALITY and QUEENBOROUGH.

Displacement (tons): *Standard* 1,760 *Full Load* 2,550
Dimensions (feet): *Length* (oa) 356.6 *Beam* 35.8 *Draught* 16.4 (max)
Machinery: Parsons geared turbines; two Admiralty 3 drum boilers; twin screws; 40,000 s.h.p.
Speed (knots): 36
Range (miles): N/A
Manning: 226
Armament: Six 4.7-inch (3 × 2), One 2 pdr. pom-pom (1 × 4), Four 20mm (4 × 1), Four 0.5-inch MGs (2 × 1), Ten 21-inch torpedo tubes (2 × 5), Two DCTs.

Ship	Pend. No.	Builder	Cons. Time	Comm.	Fate
Napier	G97 (1940) D13 (1945)	Fairfield	1y 4m	28/11/40	Paid Off 10/1945 and reverted to RN
Nepal	G25 (1942) D14 (1945)	Thornycroft	2y 6m	1/5/42	-ditto-
Nestor	G02 (1941)	Fairfield	–	3/2/41	Sunk 16/6/42
Nizam	G38 (1941) D15 (1945)	John Brown	1y 5m	8/1/41	Paid Off 10/1945 and reverted to RN
Norman	G49 (1941) D16 (1945)	Thornycroft	2y 1m	15/9/41	-ditto-

HMA Ships NAPIER (left), NEPAL and NIZAM, 1945.

HMAS NEPAL during a hurricane in the Indian Ocean, March, 1943. (Photo M. Macdonald)

HMAS NIZAM. Note the 40mm Bofors in place of the torpedo tubes.

HMAS NESTOR: note the pom-pom mount abaft the single funnel.

Q CLASS

Quiberon, Quickmatch

Eight Q class destroyers were completed, two were transferred to the RAN upon completion (QUIBERON and QUICKMATCH), two RN units were lost, one transferred to the RNN and three commissioned with the RN. In October and November, 1945, the last trio were transferred to the RAN and commissioned as HMA Ships QUADRANT, QUALITY and QUEENBOROUGH.

As with the N class the after set of torpedo tubes was interchangeable with a 4-inch mounting. Four 40mm Bofors replaced four 20mm weapons on the searchlight platform. The 2 pdr. pompom was mounted abaft the funnel. The two Q class had stowage for 250 rounds per 4.7-inch gun, 1,800 rounds for the 2 pdr. gun and 2,400 rounds per 20mm gun.

With the exception of QUALITY, all ships were converted to fast anti-submarine frigates in the 1950s.

Displacement (tons): *Standard* 1,705 *Full Load* 2,500
Dimensions (feet): *Length* (oa) 358.9 *Beam* 35.9 *Draught* 13.3
Machinery: Parsons geared turbines; two Admiralty 3 drum boilers; twin screws; 40,000 s.h.p.
Speed (knots): 34
Range (miles): 4,680 @ 20 knots
Manning: 220
Armament: Four 4.7-inch (4 × 1), One 2 pdr. pom-pom (1 × 4), Six 20mm (6 × 1), Eight 21-inch torpedo tubes (2 × 4), Four DCTs, DCRs (70 depth charges).

Ship	Pend. No.	Builder	Cons. Time	Comm.	Fate
Quiberon	G81 (1942) D20 (1945)	J. Samuel White	1y 8m	6/7/42	Sold 15/2/72
Quickmatch	G92 (1942) D21 (1945)	J. Samuel White	1y 7m	14/9/42	Sold 1972

HMAS QUIBERON with original armament during 1943.

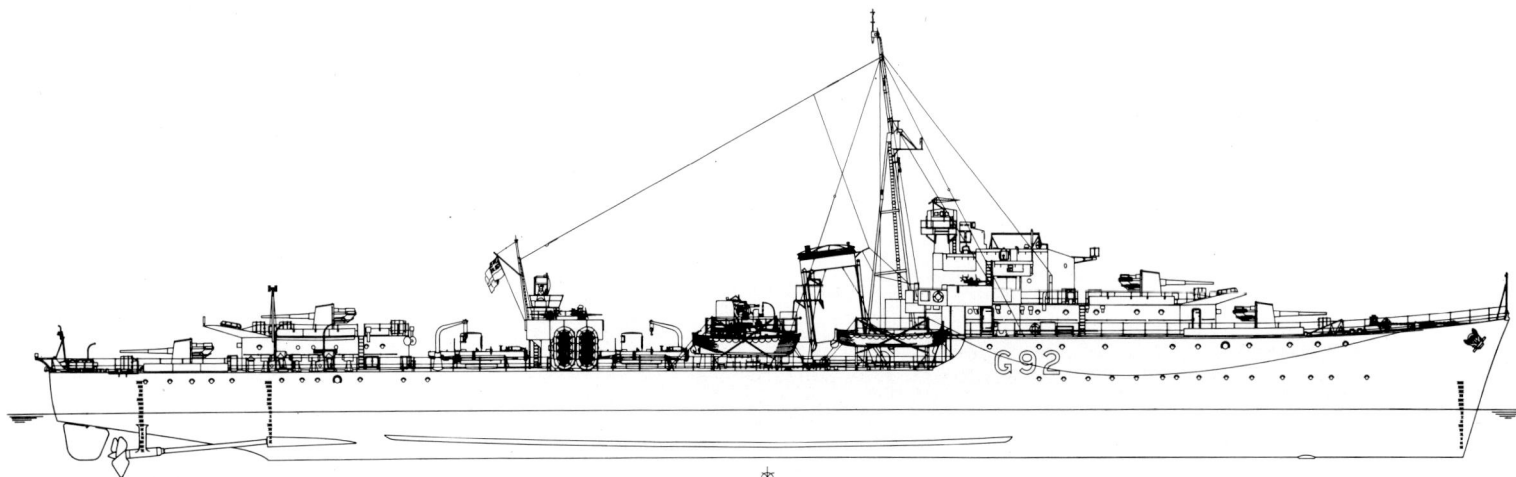

HMAS QUICKMATCH, September, 1942; profile. (P. Webb)

HMAS QUIBERON (Photo J. Mortimer)

HMAS QUICKMATCH, 1944; 40mm Bofors have replaced 20mm Oerlikons on the searchlight platform amidships; space for the after-set of torpedo tubes is vacant and a jeep is carried in lieu of the 4-inch gun.

GRIMSBY CLASS (1939–40)

Parramatta, Warrego

PARRAMATTA and WARREGO, modified versions of SWAN and YARRA were ordered in 1938. PARRAMATTA's armament was augmented in 1941 with the addition of two 20mm Oerlikons and later her single 4-inch mounting aft was replaced by a twin.

Like SWAN, WARREGO received a 40mm Bofors and six 20mm Oerklikon guns to bolster her defence against aircraft. The single 4-inch gun aft was replaced by a twin mounting and the four-barrelled 0.5 inch machine gun by the single 40mm Bofors. Forty depth charges, one Vickers and two Lewis machine guns were also carried.

PARRAMATTA was sunk in the Mediterranean by the German submarine U559 on 27th November, 1941. WARREGO operated in the survey role post-war and paid off on 8th August, 1963. She and SWAN were scrapped in Sydney during 1965–66.

HMAS PARRAMATTA: depth charges are carried aft; searchlight on platform amidships.

Displacement (tons): *Standard* 1,060 *Full Load* 1,575
Dimensions (feet): *Length (oa)* 266.3 *Beam* 36.0 *Draught* 10.1
Machinery: Parsons geared turbines, two Admiralty 3 drum boilers; twin screws;
Speed (knots): 16.5
Range: N/A
Manning: 160
Armament: Three 4-inch (1 × 2, 1 × 1), One 0.5-inch MG (1 × 1), Four DCTs, Two DCCs, (see notes).

Ship	Pend. No.	Builder	Cons. Time	Comm.	Fate
Parramatta	L44 (1940) U44 (1940)	Cockatoo	1y 5m	8/4/40	Sunk 27/11/41
Warrego	U73 (1940)	Cockatoo	1y 3m	22/8/40	Sold 4/1965

Above – HMAS WARREGO: searchlights carried on bridge wings and
20mm Oerlikons on the deck abreast
the superstructure.

Left – HMAS WARREGO, Cockatoo
Island, 1943; 20mm mounts are carried before the bridge and on the
bridge wings.

Right – HMAS PARRAMATTA arriving Fremantle, 1940; the four-barrelled machine gun is mounted in B position. (Photo – S. Sanderson)

Below – HMAS WARREGO, 1945; a tripod mast has replaced the original structure; single 40mm gun in B position; twin 4-inch gun aft. (Photo – P. Britz)

Bottom – HMA Ships STUART, WARREGO and NAMBUCCA.

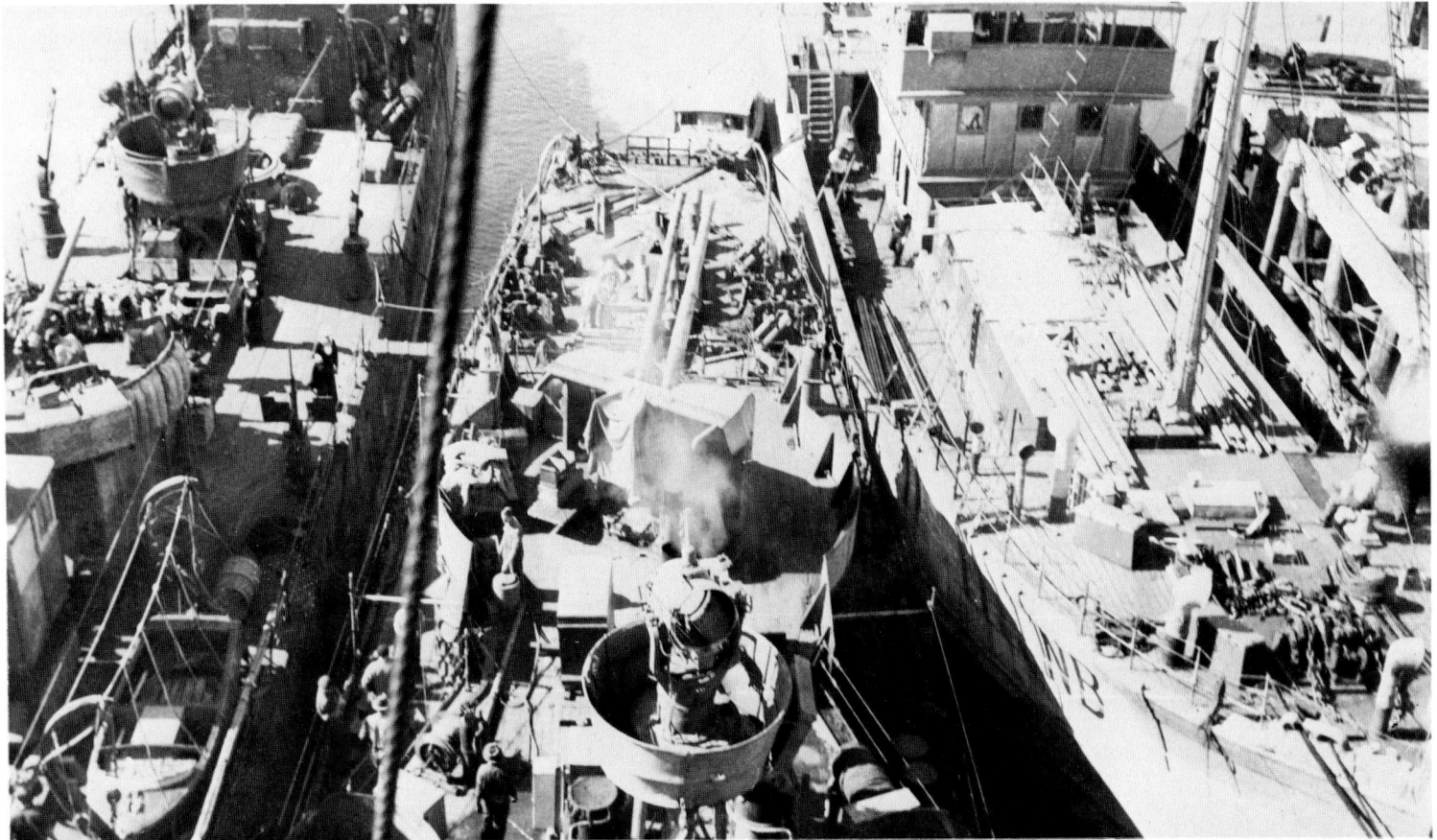

24 CLASS ANTI-SUBMARINE ESCORT VESSEL

Moresby

Ship	Pend. No.	Builder	Cons. Time	Comm.	Fate
Moresby	J54 (WWII)	Barclay	6m	20/6/25	Sold 2/1947

'MORESBY' was originally built for the Royal Navy as HMS SILVIO, one of 24 sloops designed for the anti-submarine role. During 1922–25 she was one of four of the class to be converted to a survey ship. She transferred to the RAN in 1925, but paid off in 1927.

MORESBY recommissioned in 1933. In 1940 she began operations as an anti-submarine training vessel, but resumed surveying in December, 1941. Shortly later, in January, 1942, she was re-armed as an escort, serving until November, 1943. MORESBY paid off on 13th March, 1946, and was sold on 3rd February, 1947, to be broken up.

Displacement (tons): *Standard* 1,320
Dimensions (feet): *Length (oa)* 276.6 *Beam* 35.0 *Draught* 12.0
Machinery: One 4 cylinder triple expansion engine; single screw; 2,500 s.h.p.
Speed (knots): 17
Range (miles): *N/A*
Manning: 141
Armament: One 4-inch (1 × 1), One 12 pdr. (1 × 1), Two .303 Vickers MGs, Two .303 Lewis MGs, Two DCTs, Two DC Rs.

HMAS MORESBY armed as an anti-submarine escort; the single 4 inch gun is mounted forward, two single depth charge throwers and depth-charge racks aft.

HMAS MORESBY and HMAS BUNGAREE (in background); MORESBY carries a single 4-inch gun aft with the two depth charge throwers and racks below, on the main deck.

RIVER CLASS

Barcoo, Burdekin, Diamantina, Gascoyne, Hawkesbury, Lachlan

Of the twelve River class frigates originally planned, eight were eventually completed, six of which experienced war service in the Pacific and New Guinea regions. Two, BARWON and MAC-QUARIE, were commissioned in January, 1946, and December, 1945, respectively.

The remaining four modified frigates, known as the Bay class were laid down during 1943, but not completed until 1946. A further ten Bay class were cancelled in April, 1944.

The six Rivers which saw war service were designed primarily as escort vessels and for this role were well armed. Several were fitted with the Hedgehog ahead-throwing anti-submarine weapon (in A position), which contained twenty-four 35lb bombs on spigates which were fired over the bow, up to 200 yards ahead.

The River class dated from April, 1941, with the requirement for a warship for Australian trade defence, a design featuring both anti-aircraft and anti-submarine capabilities. War experience since 1939 dictated an endurance of 5,000 miles at 10 knots, with a maximum speed of $20\frac{1}{2}$ knots.

Following additional orders for the River and Bay class ships no further orders were placed for Bathurst class minesweepers. The frigates were considered ideal for convoy work, with their superior endurance and speed. Original plans announced in early 1942, called for an armament comprising two 4-inch, two 2 pounder and two 20mm guns, plus eight DCTs. Later it was

HMAS MACQUARIE in Sydney Harhour; a 40mm Bofors is carried before the bridge.

decided to fit eight 20mm single mounts (in lieu of the 2 pounders and 20mm), 1 hedgehog and reduce to four DCTs.

Not long after entering service, BARCOO, BURDEKIN, GASCOYNE and HAWKESBURY were rearmed with two twin Oerlikons (replacing four single mounts) and two 40mm mounts (replacing two single 20mm guns). Two single .303 Bren guns and two single Vickers machine guns were removed from the quarter-deck.

BARCOO was converted to a survey ship post war and paid off on 19th December, 1963; BURDEKIN paid off on 18th April, 1946, and remained laid up until her sale in 1961; DIAMANTINA was decommissioned on 9th August, 1946, was converted to an oceanographic research ship in 1959 and paid off in 1981; GAS-COYNE paid off in April, 1946, recommissioned on 8th June, 1959, for oceanographic duties and paid off on 2nd February, 1966; HAWKESBURY paid off in late 1945, recommissioned in May, 1952, and paid off on 14th February, 1955; LACHLAN paid off in 1948 transferred to the RNZN in May, 1949 and was sold outright in 1962.

Displacement (tons): *Standard* 1,420 (Lachlan) 1,477 (Barcoo) 1,489 (Gascoyne)

Dimensions (feet): *Length* (oa) 301 *Beam* 36.6 *Draught* 12

Machinery: Two triple expansion engines, two Admiralty 3 drum boilers, twin screws, 5,500 i.h.p.

Speed (knots): 20

Range (miles): N/A

Manning: 140

Armament: Two 4-inch (2 × 1), Eight 20mm (8 × 1) 4 × .303-Vickers MGs (4 × 1), 4 × .303 Bren guns (4 × 2), One Hedgehog, DCs. (armament varied on individual ships).

Ship	Pend. No.	Builder	Cons. Time	Comm.	Fate
Barcoo	K375 (1944)	Cockatoo	1y 3m	17/1/44	Sold 15/2/72
Burdekin	K376 (1944)	Walkers	2y 5m	27/6/44	Sold 9/1961
Diamantina	K377 (1945)	Walkers	2y	27/4/45	Museum Ship 1981
Gascoyne	K354 (1943)	Morts	1y 4m	18/11/43	Sold 9/1971
Hawkesbury	K363 (1944)	Morts	1y 11m	5/7/44	Sold 15/2/72
Lachlan	K364 (1945)	Morts	1y 10m	14/2/45	RNZN Base Ship 1978.

HMAS BARCOO, 27th March, 1944, showing original armament including a hedgehog ahead-throwing weapon and a single 4-inch gun in 'A' and 'B' positions respectively; a 20mm Oerlikon on each bridge wing and four amidships (2 on each beam); single 4-inch gun in 'X' position; single 20mm in 'Y' position; depth charge throwers and rails right aft.

HMAS GASCOYNE in Sydney.

HMAS GASCOYNE at Balikpapan, Borneo, 2nd September, 1945; a 40mm Bofors is sited between the forward 4-inch gun and bridge and two more aft on either side of the after-4-inch gun; 20mm Oerlikons are carried abreast the bridge superstrucure and amidships; two small guns are also mounted on either side of the hedgehog. (114802).

BATHURST CLASS
Fifty-six Ships

Sixty Bathurst class minesweepers were constructed. The work was shared by eight Australian shipyards. Four were built for India, 36 for the RAN and 20 for the British Admiralty. The latter, however, were commissioned as RAN warships and manned by Australian naval personnel.

The Bathurst class minesweepers were the RAN's 'maids of all work', performing such tasks as convoy escort, anti-submarine patrol, search and rescue, evacuation and shore bombardment. For these missions each ship had a sufficient endurance to allow them to patrol the long Australian coastline and around New Guinea. The class were generally referred to as corvettes, although the official designation was AMS or Australian Minesweeper.

Three were lost during World War Two. ARMIDALE was attacked and sunk by Japanese warplanes on 1st December, 1942; WALLAROO and GEELONG were lost in collision. Post war WARRNAMBOOL was sunk on 13th September 1947, during minesweeping operations off the north Queensland coast.

The ammunition stowage space of each Bathurst was about 280 rounds for the main gun, 2,500 rounds for the smaller calibre weapons and up to 60 depth charges. The ships were also capable of transporting 300 troops in an emergency, 400 troops ship-to-shore or 100 men over a period of four days.

Of the twenty Admiralty vessels surviving at the end of hostilities in 1945, five were purchased by the Turkish Navy and

HMAS TOOWOOMBA being launched at Walkers on 26th March, 1941. (J. Strazcek)

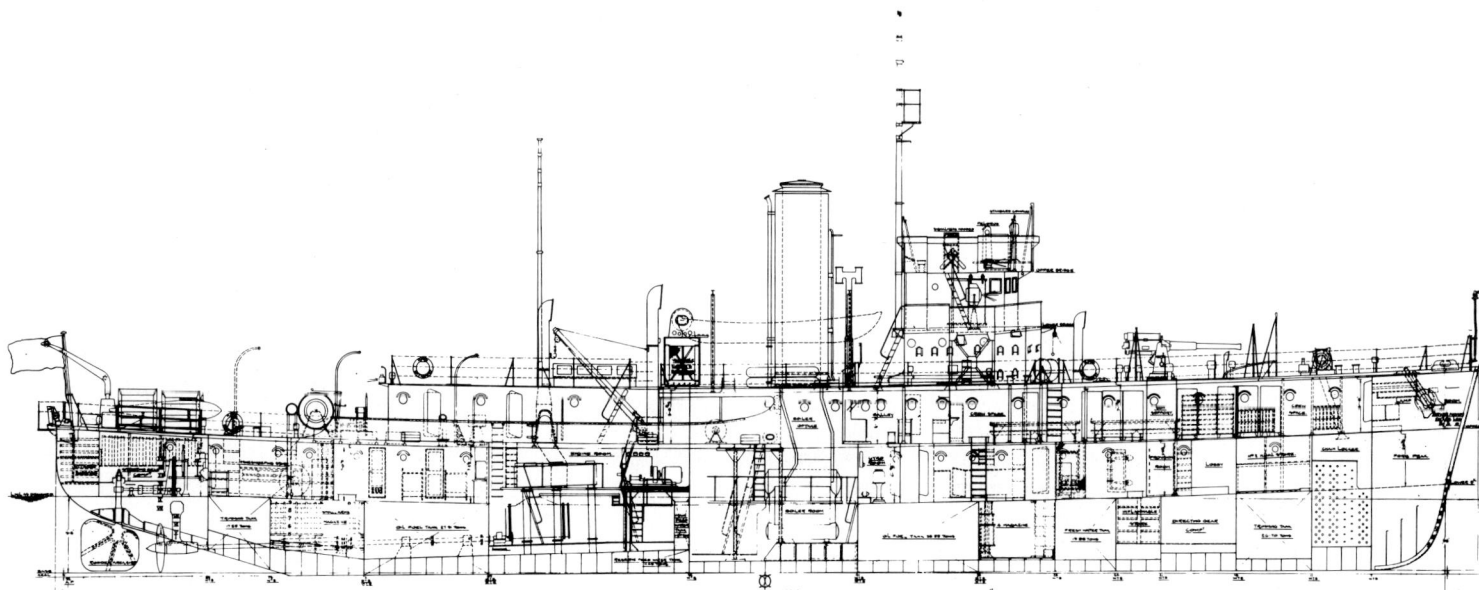

HMAS BATHURST profile as designed (Cockatoo Dockyard)

eight transferred to the Royal Netherlands Navy. Four of the Netherlands vessels were subsequently given to Indonesia.

By 1983 only BENDIGO (in service with the Peoples Republic of China), CASTLEMAINE (museum ship), COLAC (tank cleaning vessel), GLADSTONE (a refugee vessel) and WHYALLA (maintenance vessel with Victorian Ports & Harbours Dept.) still survived.

Displacement (tons): *Standard* 815
Dimensions (feet): *Length* (oa) 186.0 *Beam* 31.0 *Draught* 8.6
Machinery: Triple expansion; two boilers; twin screws; 1,750 i.h.p. (1st group) 2,000 i.h.p. (2nd group)
Speed (knots): 15.5
Range (miles): 2,640 @ 10 knots
Manning: 70 (approximate)
Armament: Typically: One 4-inch (1 × 1), or One 12 pdr. (1 × 1), Two 20mm (2 × 1), DCTs, 20 to 60 DCs, One 40mm (1 × 1) later added to some units.

HMA Ships BUNBURY (right) and TOWNSVILLE at Morotai, 2nd June, 1945. (109368).

BENDIGO flying a Red Ensign, on acceptance trials, May, 1941. Most of the armament is still to be fitted. (Photo – P. Britz)

HMAS ARARAT (125070)

HMAS DELORAINE

HMAS HORSHAM: a single 4-inch gun is fitted before the bridge and three single Oerlikons one on each bridge-wing and another abaft the mainmast. (Photo – S. Given)

HMAS KIAMA, 1943, port-broadside view; a single 4-inch gun is carried forward; three 20mm Oerlikons; two depth-charge throwers and four depth-charge chutes.

Ship	I.H.P.	Pend. No.	Builder	Cons. Time	Comm.	Fate
Ararat	2,000	K34	Evans Deakin	11m	16/6/43	Sold 1/1961
Armidale	2,000	J240	Morts	9m	11/6/42	Sunk 1/12/42
Ballarat	1,750	J184 B236 (1945)	Williamstown	1y 4m	30/8/41	Sold 7/1947
Bathurst	1,750	J158	Cockatoo	10m	6/12/40	Sold 6/1948
Benalla	2,000	J323	Williamstown	1y 1m	27/4/43	Sold 2/1958
Bendigo	1,750	J187 B237 (1944)	Cockatoo	8m	10/5/41	Sold 5/1947
Bowen	2,000	J285	Walkers	9m	9/11/42	Sold 5/1956
Broome	2,000	J191	Evans Deakin	1y 2m	29/7/42	Turkey 1946
Bunbury	2,000	J241	Evans Deakin	1y 2m	3/1/42	Sold 1/1961
Bundaberg	2,000	J231	Evans Deakin	1y 3m	12/9/42	Sold 3/1961
Burnie	1,750	J198 B238 (1944)	Morts	10m	15/4/41	RNN 7/1946
Cairns	1,750	J183 B239 (1945)	Walkers	1y 2m	11/5/42	RNN 1/1946
Castlemaine	2,000	J244	Williamstown	1y 4m	17/6/42	Museum Ship 9/1973
Cessnock	2,000	J175 J240 (1945)	Cockatoo	9m	26/1/42	Sold 4/1947
Colac	2,000	J242	Morts	9m	6/1/42	Tank cleaning vessel 1962.
Cootamundra	2,000	J316	Poole & Steel	1y 1m	30/4/43	Sold 3/1962
Cowra	2,000	J351	Poole & Steel	1y 2m	8/10/43	Sold 1/1961
Deloraine	2,000	J232	Morts	8m	23/11/41	Sold 8/1956
Dubbo	2,000	J251	Morts	9m	31/7/42	Sold 2/1958
Echuca	2,000	J252	Williamstown	1y 7m	7/9/42	RNZN 5/1952
Fremantle	2,000	J246	Evans Deakin	1y 1m	24/3/43	Sold 1/1961
Gawler	1,750	J188 B241 (1945)	B.H.P.	1y 7m	14/8/42	Turkey 1946
Geelong	1,750	J201	Williamstown	1y 3m	16/1/42	Sunk 18/10/44

Ship	I.H.P.	Pend. No.	Builder	Cons. Time	Comm.	Fate
Geraldton	2,000	J128 B242 (1944)	Poole & Steel	1y 5m	6/4/42	Turkey 1946
Gladstone	2,000	J324	Walkers	1y 6m	22/3/43	Sold 6/1956
Glenelg	2,000	J236	Cockatoo	8m	16/11/42	Sold 5/1957
Goulburn	1,750	J167 B243 (1944)	Cockatoo	1y 6m	28/2/41	Sold 10/1947
Gympie	2,000	J238	Evans Deakin	1y 3m	4/11/42	Sold 1/1961
Horsham	2,000	J235	Williamstown	1y 5m	18/11/42	Sold 8/1956
Inverell	2,000	J233	Morts	9m	17/9/42	RNZN 4/1952
Ipswich	2,000	J186 B244 (1944)	Evans Deakin	1y 3m	13/6/42	RNN 1946
Junee	2,000	J362	Poole & Steel	1y 2m	11/4/44	Sold 6/1958
Kalgoorlie	1,750	J192 B245 (1944)	B.H.P.	1y 8m	7/4/42	RNN 1946
Kapunda	2,000	J218	Poole & Steel	1y 2m	21/10/42	Sold 1/1961
Katoomba	1,750	J204	Poole & Steel	3m	17/12/40	Sold 5/1957
Kiama	2,000	J353	Evans Deakin	1y 2m	26/1/44	RNZN 5/1952
Latrobe	2,000	J234	Morts	10m	6/11/42	Sold 5/1956
Launceston	2,000	J179 B246 (1944)	Evans Deakin	1y 4m	9/4/42	Turkey 1946
Lismore	1,750	J145 B247 (1944)	Morts	11m	24/1/41	RNN 1946
Lithgow	1,750	J206	Morts	9m	14/6/41	Sold 8/1956
Maryborough	1,750	J195 B248 (1944)	Walkers	1y 2m	12/6/41	Sold 5/1947
Mildura	1,750	J207	Morts	10m	23/7/41	Sold 9/1965
Parkes	2,000	J361	Evans Deakin	1y 2m	25/5/44	Sold 5/1957
Pirie	2,000	J189 B249 (1944)	B.H.P.	1y 5m	10/10/42	Turkey 1946
Rockhampton	1,750	J203	Walkers	1y 7m	21/6/42	Sold 1/1961
Shepparton	1,750	J248	Williamstown	1y 3m	1/2/43	Sold 2/1958

HMAS MILDURA.

HMAS ROCKHAMPTON. Oerlikons are carried on the bridge wings and aft. Photo taken 2nd June 1945.

HMAS STRAHAN.

HMAS TOWNSVILLE.

TOOWOOMBA, prior to commissioning and flying the red ensign. No armament has yet been fitted.

Ship	I.H.P.	Pend. No.	Builder	Cons. Time	Comm.	Fate
Stawell	2,000	J348	Williamstown	1y 2m	7/8/43	RNZN 5/1952
Strahan	2,000	J363	State Dockyard	1y 4m	14/3/44	Sold 1/1961
Tamworth	2,000	J181 B250 (1944)	Walkers	1y	8/8/42	RNN 1946
Toowoomba	1,750	J157 B251 (1944)	Walkers	1y 2m	9/10/41	RNN 1946
Townsville	1,750	J205	Evans Deakin	1y 1m	19/12/41	Sold 9/1956

BATHURST CLASS ARMAMENT DETAILS – EARLY 1943

Ship	4-inch QF MK XVI	4-inch BL MK IX	12 pdr. MKIX	12 pdr. MK V	20mm Oerlikon	0.5-inch MK IV M.G.	0.5-inch Colt M.G.	.303-inch Vickers MG	.303-inch Lewis M.G.	MGs	DCTs	DCCs	OTHER	DCs
Ararat	–	1	–	–	3	–	–	–	–	–	–	–	–	–
Armidale	1	–	–	–	–	3	–	–	–	–	2	2	–	14
Ballarat	–	1	–	–	1	–	–	2	3	–	–	4	–	41
Bathurst	–	1	–	–	1	–	–	–	–	2	2	4	–	41
Benalla	1	–	–	–	3	–	–	–	–	–	–	–	–	–
Bendigo	–	1	–	–	3	–	–	2	2	–	2	4	–	41
Bowen	–	–	1	–	2	–	–	–	–	–	–	–	–	–
Broome	–	–	1	–	3	2	–	2	2	–	–	2	–	20
Bunbury	–	–	1	–	–	–	3	–	–	2	2	4	–	40
Bundaberg	1	–	–	–	3	–	3	–	–	2	2	4	–	20
Burnie	–	1	–	–	3	2	–	–	–	2	2	4	–	41
Cairns	–	–	1	–	–	2	–	–	–	2	2	4	–	20
Castlemaine	–	1	–	–	3	–	–	–	–	2	2	2	–	20
Cessnock	–	1	–	–	4	2	–	–	–	–	2	4	–	21
Colac	–	–	–	1	3	–	2	2	2	–	2	4	–	21
Cootamundra	1	–	–	–	–	–	–	–	–	–	–	–	–	–
Cowra	–	1	–	–	–	–	–	–	–	–	–	–	–	–
Deloraine	–	–	–	1	2	–	3	3	–	–	2	3	–	21
Dubbo	1	–	–	–	3	–	3	–	–	–	2	4	–	20
Echuca	–	1	–	–	3	–	3	–	2	–	–	2	–	20
Fremantle	1	–	–	–	–	3	–	–	–	2	2	4	–	40
Gawler	–	–	1	–	1	2	–	–	–	2	–	4	–	20
Geelong	–	1	–	–	3	–	3	–	–	–	2	4	–	41
Geraldton	–	–	1	–	2	2	–	–	–	2	–	2	–	20
Gladstone	1	–	–	–	3	–	–	–	–	–	–	–	–	–
Glenelg	–	–	1	–	–	–	3	–	–	2	2	4	–	40
Goulburn	–	1	–	–	3	–	–	2	2	–	2	4	–	41
Gympie	–	–	1	–	–	3	–	–	–	2	2	2	–	20
Horsham	1	–	–	–	3	–	3	–	2	–	2	4	–	40
Inverell	1	–	–	–	–	–	3	–	–	2	2	2	–	20
Ipswich	–	–	1	–	4	2	–	–	–	2	2	4	–	20
Junee	1	–	–	–	3	–	–	–	–	–	2	–	–	–
Kalgoorlie	–	1	–	–	3	–	–	2	–	–	2	4	–	40
Kapunda	1	–	–	–	–	–	3	–	–	2	2	2	–	20
Katoomba	–	–	1	–	3	–	3	3	2	–	2	4	–	41
Kiama	1	–	–	–	3	–	–	–	–	–	2	4	–	41
Latrobe	1	–	–	–	–	–	3	–	–	2	2	2	–	20
Launceston	–	–	1	–	1	2	–	–	–	2	2	2	–	21
Lismore	–	1	–	1	2	–	–	2	–	–	2	4	–	41
Lithgow	1	–	–	–	3	–	3	3	–	–	2	4	–	41
Maryborough	–	1	–	–	1	–	–	–	–	2	2	4	–	41
Mildura	–	1	–	–	3	–	3	–	–	–	2	4	–	41
Parkes	–	–	–	–	3	–	–	–	–	–	–	–	–	–
Pirie	–	–	1	–	3	–	–	–	–	2	2	2	–	20
Rockhampton	1	–	–	–	3	–	3	–	–	–	2	2	–	41
Shepparton	1	–	–	–	–	–	3	–	–	2	2	4	–	40
Stawell	–	1	1	–	2	–	–	–	–	–	–	–	–	–
Strahan	–	1	–	–	3	–	–	–	–	–	2	4	–	40
Tamworth	–	–	1	–	1	2	–	–	–	2	2	2	–	14
Toowoomba	–	1	–	–	2	–	–	–	–	–	2	2	–	41
Townsville	1	–	–	–	3	–	3	–	–	–	2	4	–	41
Wagga	1	–	–	–	3	–	–	–	–	–	–	–	–	–
Wallaroo	1	–	–	–	3	–	–	2	–	–	2	4	–	20
Warrnambool	–	1	–	–	3	–	–	–	–	–	2	–	–	–
Whyalla	–	1	–	–	3	–	3	–	–	–	2	4	–	41
Wollongong	–	–	1	–	2	2	–	–	2	–	2	2	–	21

NOTE: Vessels shown without full armament were in the main still under construction.

Ship	I.H.P.	Pend. No.	Builder	Cons. Time	Comm.	Fate
Wagga	2,000	J315	Morts	9m	18/12/42	Sold 3/1962
Wallaroo	2,000	J222	Poole & Steel	1y 3m	15/7/42	Sunk 11/6/43
Warrnambool	1,750	J202	Morts	10m	23/9/41	Sunk 13/9/47
Whyalla	1,750	J153 B252 (1944)	B.H.P.	1y 5m	8/1/42	Sold 2/1947
Wollongong	2,000	J172 B253 (1944)	Cockatoo	9m	23/10/41	RNN 1946

HMAS WHYALLA, 1944; a single 40mm Bofors has replaced the 20mm weapon abaft the mainmast; depth-charges have been replaced by minesweeping gear; she carries the British Pacific Fleet pendant number B252. (Photo – S. Given)

End of the line; Bathurst class AMSs awaiting disposal in Sydney. (Photo – R. Hart).

HMAS GEELONG, 1942; profile. (P. Webb)

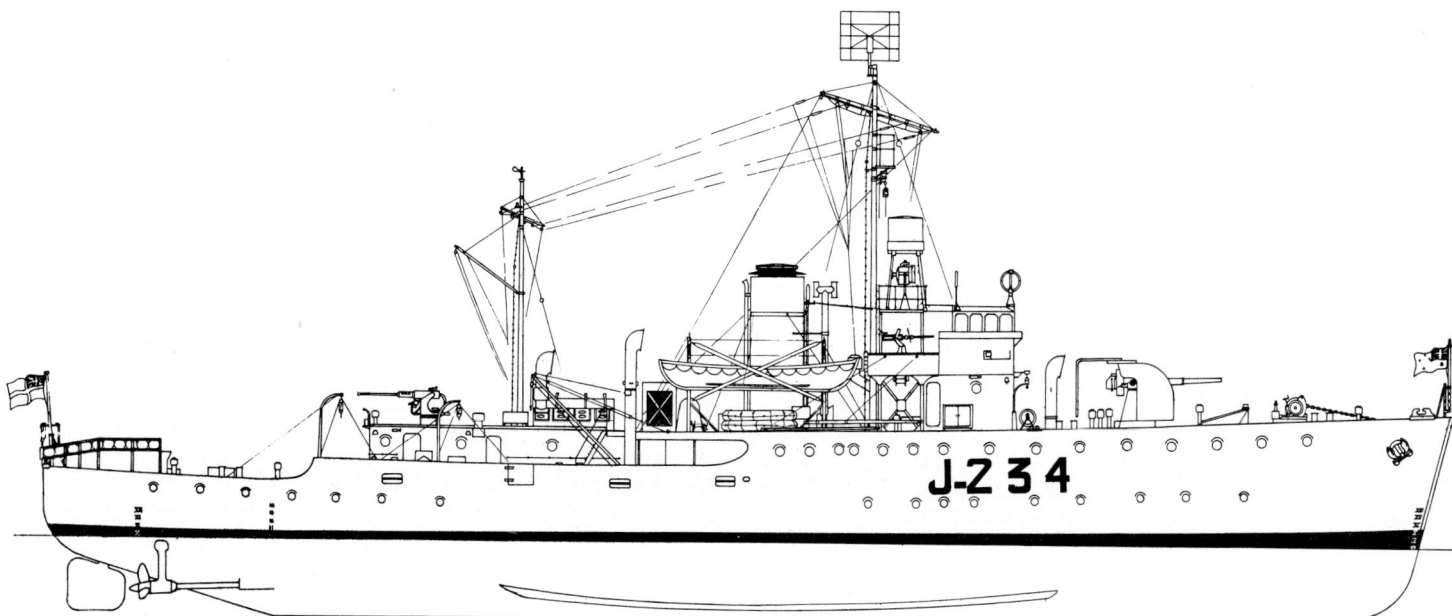

J-Z34

HMAS LATROBE, July, 1945; profile. (P. Webb)

INFANTRY LANDING SHIPS (LSI)
Three Ships

During 1943 one Royal Navy and two RAN AMCs were converted to LSIs for amphibious operations in the Pacific region. The trio were equipped to transport up to 1,250 troops each and carried from 18 to 24 landing craft. The latter were held in davits and lowered from port and starboard into the water. With their change of role the LSIs were defensively re-armed to allow additional space for the storage of the new equipment.

Name	Details	Status
Kanimbla (C78)	*Steamship* 11,000 gross tons 468.8 × 66.3 × 24.4 feet 19 knots 1 × 4-inch, 2 × 3-inch 2 × 2 pdr., 12 × 20mm 4 × .303 Vickers 24 Bren guns 1,280 troops, 22 LCVPs 2 LCMs	Built 1935 Req. 5/9/39 RN 6/10/39 LSI 1/6/43 Paid Off 25/3/49 Returned 13/12/50
Manoora (C77)	*Steamship* 10,856 gross tons 480 × 91 × 24 feet 8,200 b.h.p. = 15.7 kts 1 × 6-inch, 2 × 3-inch 8 × 20mm 1,250 troops, 17 LCVPs 2 LCMs 1 Walrus Amphibian	Built 1935 Req. 11/10/39 AMC 12/12/39 Paid Off 28/9/42 LSI 2/2/43 Paid Off 6/12/47 Returned 31/8/49
Westralia (C61)	*Steamship* 8,108 gross tons 445 × 60 × 22.7 feet 6,750 b.h.p. = 15½ knots 1 × 6-inch, 2 × 3-inch 12 × 20mm 1,250 troops, 16 LCVPs LCMs, 1 Walrus Amphibian	Built 1929 Req. 2/11/39 AMC 17/1/40 Paid Off 12/1942 LSI 31/5/43 Paid Off 19/9/46 Returned 27/3/51

Top right – HMAS MANOORA in Simpson Harbour, 10th September, 1945, carrying troops for the occupation of Rabaul. (117054)

Right – HMAS KANIMBLA. Unlike WESTRALIA, she mounted her 6-inch gun on deck right-aft. (89890).

Right – HMAS WESTRALIA 1946, prior to her paying-off; two single 3-inch guns are carried on the bandstand forward; 20mm Oerlikons on the bridge wings. Some of the ship's landing craft lie at her bow, (W7 and W3). (Photo – S. Given)

Below – HMAS WESTRALIA, 27th February, 1944; note the lone 6-inch weapon on bandstand aft. Landing craft are on davits on each beam and abaft the superstructure.

Bottom – HMAS MANOORA's landing barge M25 being lowered into the waters of Simpson Harbour, 10th September, 1945. (96264)

AUXILIARY MINELAYER
One Ship

CONTROLLED MINELAYER
One Ship

Name	Details	Status
Bungaree **(M29)**	*Steamer* 3,155 gross tons 369 × 48.6 × 22.3 feet 2,500 h.p. = 11 knots 2 × 4-inch, 1 × 12 pdr. 2 × 40mm, 8 × 20mm 6 MGs, 423 mines	Built 1937 Req. 10/1940 Comm. 9/6/41 Survey Ship 1/1944 Stores Ship 8/1944 Paid Off 7/8/46 Returned 5/11/47

Name	Details	Status
Atreus	4 × 20mm	

HMAS BUNGAREE, 13th March, 1943; the 4-inch guns forward and right-aft and the 12 pounder gun in 'X' position are all partially enclosed; 20mm Oerlikons are mounted abreast the foremast on the bridge wings, forward of the mainmast (amidships) and on each beam of the fore-mast and after mast.

HMAS BUNGAREE, Neutral Bay, Sydney Harbour, 1944; mines were launched from two special rails visible in the stern section; topside the ship is armed with a 4-inch gun and a 12 pounder in 'X' position. Note the depth charges below the 4-inch gun.

AUXILIARY MINESWEEPERS
Thirty-five Ships

After the outbreak of war in September, 1939, 35 vessels were eventually acquired for conversion to auxiliary minesweepers. Twenty-nine of these were in service when Japan struck on 7th December, 1941, and 11 at V.J. Day. Eight more were serving in other capacities.

HMAS ALFIE CAM; a single 12 pounder gun is mounted forward and two Oerlikons are carried on the bridge wings.

HMAS BOMBO; single 12 pounder with shield (forward) and two Oerlikons abreast the foremast. Note the searchlight just visible atop the bridge.

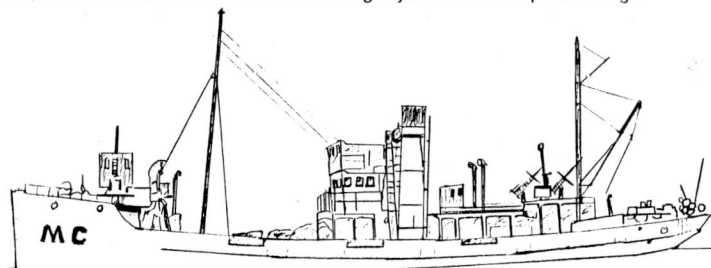

HMAS MARY CAM, 1942; profile. (R. Gillett)

Name	Details	Status
Alfie Cam (FY97)	*Trawler* 282 gross tons 128.5 × 23.5 × 12.6 feet 9½ knots 1 × 12 pdr., 1 × .303 Vickers, 4 DCs	Built 1920 Req. 22/6/40 Comm. 22/7/40 Purchased 29/6/43 Paid Off 6/7/44 Sold 27/9/44
Allenwood (FY18)	*Coaster* 398 gross tons 147 × 35 × 8.2 feet 8½ knots 1 × 12 pdr., 1 × .303 Vickers, 2 DCCs	Built 1920 Req. 29/7/41 Comm. 16/9/41 Paid Off 31/10/44 Returned 1/10/46
Bermagui (FY81)	*Coaster* 402 gross tons 144 × 32.1 × 8.2 feet 400 h.p. = 10 knots 1 × 12 pdr., 1 × .303 Vickers, 4 DCs	Built 1912 Req. 30/10/39 Comm. 11/12/39 Minefield Tender 4/1/44 Paid Off 23/11/45 Returned 22/7/46
Beryl II (FY71)	*Trawler* 248 gross tons 121.9 × 22.1 × 12.2 feet 9 knots 1 × 12 pdr., 1 × .303 Vickers, 4 DCs	Built 1914 Req. 7/9/39 Comm. 9/10/39 BDV 12/1943 Paid Off 13/12/45 Returned 24/5/46
Birchgrove Park (FY15)	*Collier* 640 gross tons 153.4 × 34.1 × 11.8 feet 10 knots 1 × 12 pdr., 2 × .303 Vickers 2 × 20mm, 4 DCs	Built 1930 Req. 9/5/41 Comm. 22/8/41 Stores Carrier 1942 Paid Off 19/4/45 Tender 25/7/45 Paid Off 12/1945 Returned 1946
Bombo (FY12)	*Coaster* 540 gross tons 154.3 × 30.1 × 13.6 feet 100 n.h.p. = 9½ knots 1 × 12 pdr., 1 × .303 Vickers, 4 DCs	Built 1930 Req. 22/2/41 Comm. 28/5/41 Stores Carrier 5/1944 Paid Off 25/2/46 Returned 25/7/47
Bonthorpe (FY85)	*Trawler* 273 gross tons 125.5 × 23.5 × 13.5 feet 10 knots 1 × 12 pdr., 1 × .303 Vickers, 4 DCs	Built 1917 Req. 27/11/39 Comm. 5/2/40 Purch. 30/6/44 Paid Off 17/2/45 Sold 1948
Coolebar (J25) (FY84)	*Coaster* 479 gross tons 150.3 × 30 × 8.8 feet 8 knots 1 × 12 pdr. 1 × .303 Vickers 4 DCs	Built 1911 Req. 20/10/39 Comm. 18/12/39 Stores Carrier 1943 Paid Off 1/6/45 Purch. 7/12/45 Sold 17/7/46

Name	Details	Status
Coombar (FY08)	*Coaster* 581 gross tons 166 × 30 × 11.4 feet 10 knots 1 × 12 pdr., 1 × .303 Vickers, 4 DCs	Built 1912 Req. 30/1/41 Comm. 30/4/41 Paid Off 26/10/45 Returned 19/7/46
Doomba (ex HMS Wexford (N01) (J01 – 1941)	*Ferry* 800 tons (disp.) 231 × 28.6 × 8.1 feet 2,200 h.p. = 16 knots 1 × 4-inch, 2 × .303 Lewis, 1 × 20mm 50 DCs	Built 1919 Req. 3/9/39 Comm. 25/9/39 A/S Vessel 6/1942 Paid Off 13/3/46 Sold 3/2/47
Durraween (FY93)	*Trawler* 271 gross tons 125.7 × 23.5 × 15.6 feet 62 h.p. = 9 knots 1 × 12 pdr., 1 × .303 Vickers, 4 DCs	Built 1918 Req. 22/6/40 Comm. 29/7/40 Paid Off 1/11/45 Returned 25/10/46
Goolgwai (FY75)	*Trawler* 271 gross tons 125.7 × 23.5 × 12.7 feet 9½ knots 1 × 12 pdr., 1 × .303 Vickers, 4 DCs	Built 1919 Req. 13/9/39 Comm. 6/10/39 Paid Off 29/10/45 Returned 17/6/47
Goonambee (FY 94)	*Trawler* 222 gross tons 117 × 22.1 × 11 feet 78 h.p. = 9½ knots 1 × 12 pdr., 1 × .303 Vickers, 4 DCs	Built 1919 Req. 28/6/40 Comm. 9/8/40 Purchased 29/6/43 Paid Off 21/6/44 Sold 4/10/44
Goorangai (FY74)	*Trawler* 223 gross tons 117 × 22.1 × 11 feet 78 h.p. = 9½ knots 1 × 12 pdr.	Built 1919 Req. 8/9/39 Comm. 9/10/39 Lost 20/11/40
Gunbar (FY98)	*Coaster* 480 gross tons 150 × 30 × 8.7 feet 10 knots 1 × 12 pdr., 1 × .303 Vickers, 4 DCs	Built 1911 Req. 30/9/40 Comm. 18/12/40 Paid Off 30/6/43 BDV 21/10/43 Paid Off 3/12/45 Purchased 1946 Sold 25/7/46
Kianga (FY19)	*Coaster* 338 gross tons 135.6 × 32 × 8.2 feet 9 knots 1 × 12 pdr., 1 × .303 Vickers, 4 DCs	Built 1922 Req. 28/7/41 Paid Off 17/1/46 Returned 17/10/46

HMAS DOOMBA at Port Melbourne, 1941; single 4-inch gun before the bridge and searchlight platform amidships. (Photo – R. Wright Collection)

HMAS GOONAMBEE.

HMAS KOROWA, Williamstown. Another auxiliary minesweeper is in the background being refitted.

HMAS MARY CAM, a requisitioned trawler converted to auxiliary mine-sweeper.

HMAS ORARA; 4-inch gun mounted before the foremast.

Name	Details		Status
Korowa (FY79)	*Trawler* 324 gross tons 138.3 × 23.7 × 12.7 feet 87 h.p. = 11 knots 1 × 12 pdr., 1 × .303 Vickers, 4 DCs		Built 1920 Req. 14/9/39 Comm. 6/10/39 Paid Off 6/9/45
Marrawah (–)	*Coaster* 472 gross tons 165 × 28.1 × 11.5 feet 10 knots 1 × 12 pdr.		Built 1910 Req. 3/9/41 Comm. (temp.) 3/9/41 Comm. 9/12/41 USN 12/2/43 RAN 28/8/45 Returned 23/6/46
Mary Cam (FY48)	*Trawler* 202 gross tons 115.8 × 22.2 × 12.1 feet 57 h.p. = 9 knots 1 × 12 pdr., 2 × 20mm MGs, DCs		Built 1918 Req. 4/5/42 Comm. 5/10/42 Purchased 29/6/44 BDV 1944 M/S 1945 Paid Off 14/11/45 Sold 3/4/46
Medea (FY32)	*Steamer* 778 gross tons 195.7 × 31.6 × 12.4 feet 9 knots 1 × 4-inch, 2 × 20mm MGs		Built 1912 Req. (RN) 11/1939 Comm. (RAN) 6/7/42 Paid Off 23/5/45 Returned 5/1945
Mercedes (FY34)	*Steamer* 793 gross tons 195.7 × 31.6 × 12.4 feet 9 knots 1 × 4-inch, 2 × 20mm MGs		Built 1912 Req. (RN) 11/1939 Comm. (RAN) 6/7/42 Paid Off 23/5/45 Returned 5/1945
Nambucca (–)	*Coaster* 498 gross tons 161 × 34.6 × 8.4 feet 10 knots 1 × 12 pdr., 1 × .303 Vickers, 4 DCs		Built 1936 Req. 7/11/39 Comm. 10/1/40 USN (as YGDS) 19/4/43 Written Off 30/12/45
Narani (FY07)	*Coaster* 381 gross tons 148.6 × 33.2 × 8.7 feet 8 knots 1 × 12 pdr., 1 × .303 Vickers, 4 DCs		Built 1914 Req. 5/12/40 Comm. 11/6/41 Paid Off 22/8/44 Returned 10/7/46
Olive Cam (FY76)	*Trawler* 281 gross tons 128.5 × 23.5 × 12.6 feet $9\frac{1}{2}$ knots 1 × 12 pdr., 1 × .303 Vickers, 2 × 20mm 4 DCs		Built 1920 Req. 18/9/39 Comm. 6/10/39 Purchased 29/6/43 Paid Off 14/11/45 Returned 24/4/46

Name	Details	Status
Orara (J130)	*Coaster* 1,297 gross tons 240.3 × 33.9 × 19.9 feet 16 knots 1 × 4-inch, 2 × .303 Lewis, 4 DCs	Built 1907 Req. 12/9/39 Comm. 9/10/39 Mobile Escort Training Vessel 11/1943 Paid Off 14/5/45 Sold 28/6/46
Paterson (FY10)	*Coaster* 446 gross tons 148.8 × 32.7 × 11.3 feet $8\frac{1}{2}$ knots 1 × 12 pdr., 2 × .303 Vickers, 4 DCs	Built 1920 Req. 21/12/40 Comm. 1/5/41 Paid Off 26/11/45 Returned 1/5/46
Patricia Cam (–)	*Fishing vessel* 301 gross tons 120.9 × 30.3 × 6.4 feet 160 h.p. = 8 knots 1 × 20mm, 2 × .303 Vickers, 1 × Browning	Built 1940 Req. 9/2/42 Comm. 3/3/42 Stores Carrier 1942 Sunk 22/1/43
Samuel Benbow (FY95)	*Trawler* 122 gross tons 115.5 × 22.1 × 12.1 feet 9 knots 1 × 12 pdr., 1 × .303 Vickers, 4 DCs	Built 1918 Req. 4/8/40 Comm. 5/9/40 Purchased 29/6/43 GPV 9/1944 Survey vessel 1945 Paid Off 1/11/45 Sold 24/5/46
Tambar (J141) (Z83)	*Coaster* 456 gross tons 145.2 × 30.1 × 8.7 feet 550 h.p.	Built 1912 Req. 18/10/39 Comm. 7/11/39 Paid Off 14/7/42 Recomm. 31/7/44 Paid Off 7/1945 Returned 11/7/45
Terka (FY99)	*Coaster* 420 gross tons 147.8 × 26.6 feet $9\frac{1}{2}$ knots 1 × 12 pdr., 1 × .303 Vickers, 4 DCs	Built 1925 Req. 12/1940 Comm. 31/1/41 Stores Carrier 7/1942 Water Carrier 12/1942 Stores Carrier 1/1943 Lost 26/3/44
Tolga (FY00)	*Coaster* 418 gross tons 147.8 × 26.6 × 9.2 feet $9\frac{1}{2}$ knots 1 × 12 pdr., 1 × .303 Vickers, 4 DCs	Built 1925 Req. 1/11/40 Comm. 30/12/40 Paid Off 3/3/46 Purchased 1/4/46 Scuttled 30/4/46
Tongkol (FY72) (J137)	*Trawler* 292 gross tons 125 × 24 × 13.8 feet $10\frac{1}{2}$ knots 1 × 4-inch, 1 × .303 Vickers, 4 DCs	Built 1926 Req. 7/9/39 Comm. 4/10/39 Purchased 7/11/43 Paid Off 1/6/44 Sold 20/9/44

HMAS PATERSON, Williamstown. An uncompleted AMS lies in the background.

HMAS TONGKOL; 4-inch gun forward; machine guns not mounted whilst in port; four depth charges aft, Brisbane 15th March, 1944.

Left – **HMAS WARRAWEE** in Port Phillip.

Right – UKI under conversion to an auxiliary minesweeper.

Name	Details	Status
Toorie (FY01)	*Coaster* 414 gross tons 151.6 × 27.8 × 9.6 feet 83 h.p. = 10 knots 1 × 12 pdr., 1 × .303 Vickers, 4 DCs	Built 1925 Req. 13/11/40 Comm. 14/1/41 Paid Off 1/1/43 Returned 28/1/43
Uki (FY80)	*Coaster* 545 gross tons 161 × 34.6 × 8.4 feet 70 h.p. = 9 knots 1 × 12 pdr., 1 × .303 Vickers, 4 DCs	Built 1923 Req. 3/11/39 Comm. 11/12/39 Paid Off 24/12/42 USN 25/3/43 RAN 29/9/44 Returned 27/10/44
Warrawee (FY16)	*Coaster* 423 gross tons 155.8 × 27.1 × 10.1 feet 1 × 12 pdr., 1 × .303 Vickers, MGs, 4 DCs	Built 1909 Exam. Vessel 4/9/39 Returned 20/9/39 Req. 12/5/41 Comm. 24/9/41 Paid Off 24/9/45 Returned 15/10/46

Detailed view of two trawlers taken up for duties as auxiliary minesweepers. Both units carry an outfit of depth charges in two rails and a depth charge thrower adjacent on each beam. (133603).

MINEFIELD TENDERS
2 Ships

Name	Details	Status
Gippsland (FY38)	*Steamer* 143 gross tons 113 × 22.9 feet 41 h.p. = $11\frac{1}{2}$ knots 2 × .303 Vickers	Built 1908 Req. 24/6/42 Comm. 18/9/42 Purchased 16/7/43 BDV 1944 Paid Off 26/5/44 Sold 11/1946
Uralba (FY33)	*Steamer* 603 gross tons 154.10 × 37 feet 8 knots 1 × 4-inch, 1 × 20mm	Built 1942 Req. 13/7/42 Comm. 23/11/42 Armament Carrier 1944 Paid Off 20/8/46 Returned 24/7/47

URALBA during her brief mercantile career with the North Coast Steam Navigation Company. (Photo – S. Given)

FAIRMILE B MOTOR LAUNCHES
ML Nos 424–431, 801–827

Thirty-five Fairmile B Motor Launches were ordered during 1943 for the hunting of enemy submarines, and if required, for convoy escort work and stationary patrols. Twenty launches were prefabricated in the United Kingdom for re-erection at the Green Point Naval Shipyard. The planned armament for the RAN Fairmile Bs originally included one 2 pdr. Mk XIV 9 cwt. gun, one 20mm Oerlikon gun, one 4-barrell .303 Vickers on a Mk I mount, two Lewis .303 single mountings, one Y gun, plus 14 depth charges from chutes and release gears. Two single shoulder shooting stripped Lewis .303 machine guns, three rifles and 24 grenades were also to be carried.

During the period of hostilities a wide variety of weapons armed the launches. Most vessels received a single 40mm Bofors and 0.5-inch Browning machine guns (singles), port and starboard while two 20mm guns were carried in lieu of the original smaller machine guns.

On 13th August, 1944, ML 430 was lost in collision with ML 819 in New Guinea waters. ML 827 capsized and sank on 20th November 1944 when under tow by CAMBRIAN SALVOR off New Britain. There were no casualties.

All RAN Fairmiles could operate on either one or two engines. For anti-submarine work ASDIC was fitted to many units. By August, 1949, the surviving 33 launches had been disposed of. Many still survive as private launches or ferries.

Displacement (tons): *Standard* 75
Dimensions (feet): *Length* (oa) 112.0 *Beam* 17.10 *Draught* 5.4
Machinery: Two Hall Scott Defender petrol engines, each 650 h.p.; twin screws
Speed (knots): 20
Range (miles): 840 @ 12 knots
Manning: 16
Armament: One 2 pdr (1 × 1), One 20mm (1 × 1), Two .303 Vickers, Two .303 Lewis, Two DCTs, Fourteen DCs.

Pend. No.	Builder	Cons. Time	Comm.	Fate
ML 424	Green Point	4m	28/1/43	Sold 8/1947
ML 425	Green Point	4m	6/2/43	Sold 8/1947
ML 426	Green Point	4m	5/3/43	Sold 7/1947
ML 427	Green Point	3m	15/3/43	Sold 8/1947
ML 428	Green Point	4m	31/3/43	Sold 8/1947
ML 429	Green Point	4m	15/4/43	Sold 8/1947
ML 430	Green Point	5m	6/5/43	Lost 13/8/44
ML 431	Green Point	4m	14/5/43	Sold 8/1947
ML 801	Green Point	3m	29/5/43	Sold 9/1947
ML 802	Green Point	4m	15/6/43	Sold 12/1947
ML 803	Green Point	4m	3/7/43	Sold 12/1947
ML 804	Green Point	4m	15/7/43	Sold 8/1947
ML 805	Green Point	4m	3/8/43	Sold 1/1948
ML 806	Green Point	5m	8/9/43	Sold 12/1947
ML 807	Green Point	4m	13/9/43	Sold 11/1947
ML 808	Green Point	4m	23/9/43	Sold 12/1947
ML 809	Green Point	4m	8/10/43	Sold 8/1947
ML 810	Green Point	4m	25/10/43	Sold 1/1948
ML 811	Green Point	4m	5/11/43	Sold 8/1947
ML 812	Green Point	4m	4/12/43	Sold 11/1947
ML 813	Halvorsen	8m	16/11/42	Sold 8/1947
ML 814	Halvorsen	8m	1/1/43	Sold 8/1947
ML 815	N. Wright	8m	11/1/43	Sold 11/1947
ML 816	N. Wright	1y	2/6/43	Sold 8/1949
ML 817	Halvorsen	6m	16/2/43	Sold 11/1947
ML 818	Halvorsen	8m	29/3/43	Sold 8/1947
ML 819	Halvorsen	9m	10/5/43	Sold 8/1947
ML 820	Halvorsen	5m	21/6/43	Sold 8/1947
ML 821	Halvorsen	5m	27/7/43	Sold 8/1947
ML 822	Halvorsen	5m	30/8/43	Sold 1/1948
ML 823	Halvorsen	5m	30/9/43	Sold 10/1947
ML 824	Halvorsen	5m	18/11/43	Sold 11/1947
ML 825	Halvorsen	4m	1/2/44	Sold 1/1948
ML 826	N. Wright	1y	1/1/44	Sold 11/1947
ML 827	N. Wright	1y	19/4/44	Lost 20/11/44

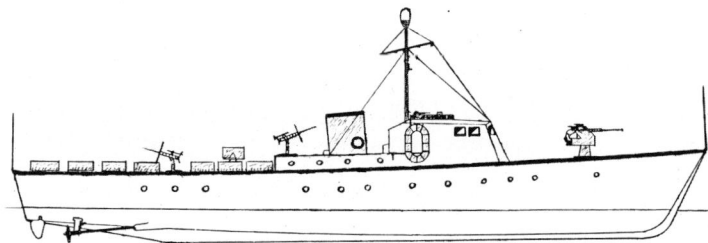

Fairmile B Motor Launch; profile. (R. Gillett)

ML 815; the 2 pounder pom-pom forward is trained to starboard as are the machine guns and single 20mm Oerlikon; six depth charges are carried on deck and another in a thrower.

ML 808.

ML 823, Sydney Harbour.

HARBOUR DEFENCE MOTOR LAUNCHES
HDML Nos 1074, 1129, 1161, 1321–1329, 1338–1343, 1346–1347 & 1352–1359

To perform the routine, but necessary, anti-submarine patrols and harbour defence, British designed HDMLs were acquired between 1942 and 1944. The 28 boats provided either stationary, endless-chain or line-abreast patrols. Nine units, 1321 to 1329 were originally constructed in Australia. The three British boats were supplied by the Admiralty and erected in the U.K. From the USA came 16 more. The British trio had previously served with the Royal Navy. All British and American built HDMLs were transported to Australia as deck cargo. Two additional HDMLs, Nos. 1344 and 1345, were not commissioned and were placed in reserve on 26th October, 1945.

Each HDML was designed for an armament comprising one 2 pdr. Mk XIV 9 cwt. gun, two twin .303 Lewis machine guns with twin mounting shields, 10 depth charges and two shoulder shooting stripped .303 Lewis machine guns.

No HDMLs were lost during the Second World War. The majority reduced to reserve post war, although four were allotted to the Royal Navy and transferred to the Phillipines Navy in 1958. Nos. 1338, 1339, 1341, 1342, 1343, 1346, 1347 and 1353 to 1359 may have been returned to the United States Navy, since they were acquired under the US lend-lease arrangements. Nos. 1340 and 1352, although reported as sold in 1948, could have also reverted to the USN.

Displacement (tons): *Standard* 58 (9 Aust. built); 50 (3 British built); 48 (16 US Built)

Dimensions (feet): *Length* (oa) 80.3 (Aust.); 72.0 (British); 72.0 (US) *Beam* 16.2 (Aust.); 15.6 (British); 15.6 (US) *Draught* 9.3 (Aust.); 8.8 (British); 9.0 (US)

Machinery: Two Buda diesels, 390 h.p. (Aust); Two Gardner petrol engines, 390 h.p. (British); Two Hercules diesels (US) All twin screws

Speed (knots): 11 or 12

Range (miles): 3,000 @ 9 knots

Manning: 12

Armament: Two 20mm (2 × 1), Two .303 Vickers, Eight DCs.

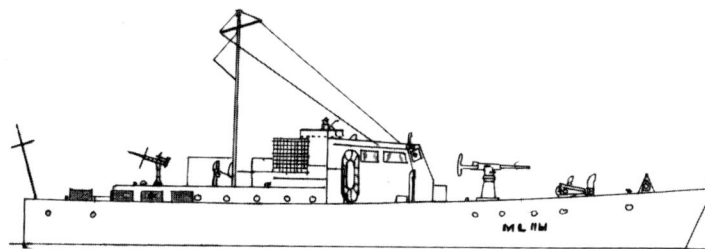

80 foot version; profile. (Naval Ship Design Section)

ML 1322; single 2 pounder forward and 20mm Oerlikon aft; no depth charges.

Pend. No.	Builder	Cons. Time	Comm.	Fate
HDML 1074	L. Robinson	–	7/10/42	Sold 1/1948
HDML 1129	Thornycrofts	–	7/11/42	Sold 12/1947
HDML 1161	Sittinghouse	–	9/1/43	Sold 12/1947
HDML 1321	Purdon	3m	11/11/43	Sold 8/1971
HDML 1322	Purdon	1y 2m	17/1/44	Wrecked 5/8/52
HDML 1323	MacFarlane	1y 3m	21/1/44	RN 1950
HDML 1324	MacFarlane	1y 7m	12/6/44	Laid up 1982
HDML 1325	E. Jack	1y 3m	4/11/43	Extant
HDML 1326	E. Jack	1y	19/1/44	RN 1950
HDML 1327	Purdon	1y 1m	29/5/44	Sold 1958
HDML 1328	MacFarlane	1y	16/1/45	RN 1950
HDML 1329	E. Jack	7m	14/6/44	RN 1950
HDML 1338	C. P. Leek	–	31/5/44	Paid Off 1946
HDML 1339	C. P. Leek	–	15/6/44	Paid Off 1946
HDML 1340	L. S. Thorson	–	12/5/44	Sold 1948
HDML 1341	L. S. Thorson	–	1/12/44	Paid Off 1946
HDML 1342	L. S. Thorson	–	24/7/44	Paid Off 1946
HDML 1343	L. S. Thorson	–	3/10/44	Paid Off 1946
HDML 1346	Truscott	–	6/1/45	Paid Off 1945
HDML 1347	Truscott	–	1/1/45	Paid Off 1946
HDML 1352	Freeport	–	12/5/44	Sold 1948
HDML 1353	Freeport	–	18/10/44	Paid Off 1946
HDML 1354	Freeport	–	11/12/44	Paid Off 1946
HDML 1355	Freeport	–	11/12/44	Paid Off 1946
HDML 1356	Elscot	–	20/12/44	Paid Off 1946
HDML 1357	Elscot	–	4/11/44	Paid Off 1946
HDML 1358	Elscot	–	21/10/44	Paid Off 1946
HDML 1359	Elscot	–	22/9/44	Paid Off 1946

ML 1322; a single 2 pounder pom-pom is mounted before the bridge. (69563)

ML 1129; 20mm Oerlikon before the bridge and Vickers .303 machine-gun aft.

REQUISITIONED PATROL CRAFT
Thirty-seven Ships

Between 3rd September 1939 and 9th July 1943, 37 vessels were acquired for the patrol force. No losses were incurred but nine were allotted new roles.

HMAS ABRAHAM CRIJNSSEN, December, 1942; the 3-inch gun is carried aft with 20mm guns immediately forward of the bridge and 3-inch gun.

HMAS BINGIRA, 1940.

Name	Details	Status
Abraham Crijnssen (FY55)	*Minesweeper* 525 tons 184.4 × 25.7 × 7 feet 1,690 h.p. = 15 knots 1 × 3-inch, 4 × 12.7mm 2 × 20mm, 1 MG	Built 1936–37 (RNN) RAN 9/1942 Comm. 28/9/42 Returned 5/5/43
Avocet	–	Req. 22/5/41 Returned 16/12/41
Bingera (FY88)	*Coaster* 922 gross tons 200.2 × 34.1 × 9 feet 12 knots 1 × 4-inch, 1 × 2 pdr. 2 × .303 Vickers 2 DCTs	Built 1935 Req. 2/12/39 Comm. 5/2/40 Training Vessel 1940 Stores Carrier 9/1944 Lighthouse Service Vessel 3/1946 Paid Off 12/8/46 Returned 13/12/46
Checoma	$6\frac{1}{2}$ tons 30.7 × 9.6 feet 55 h.p. = 8 knots	Built 1942 Req. 10/2/43 USN 6/1943 Purchased 6/8/43 Sold 11/6/46
Chinampa	60 tons 80 h.p. = $7\frac{1}{2}$ knots 1 × .303 Vickers 2 rifles	Built 1938 Req. 18/2/42 Comm. 1/3/42 Purchased 1/10/42 Sold 2/1946
Coongoola (Q18)	34 gross tons 60 × 15.6 × 5.8 feet 7 knots 1 × .303 MG 1 × 0.5-inch MG	Built – Req. 4/8/41 Comm. 4/8/41 BDV/ASR 12/1941 Purchased 3/1943 Paid Off 20/12/45 Sold 16/3/46

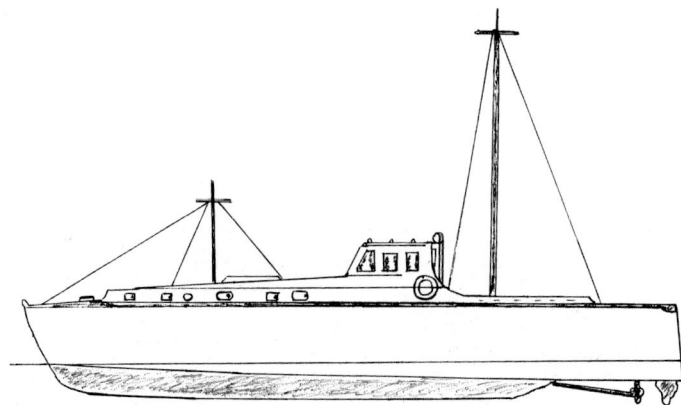

HMAS KYBRA, 1942; profile. (R. Gillett)

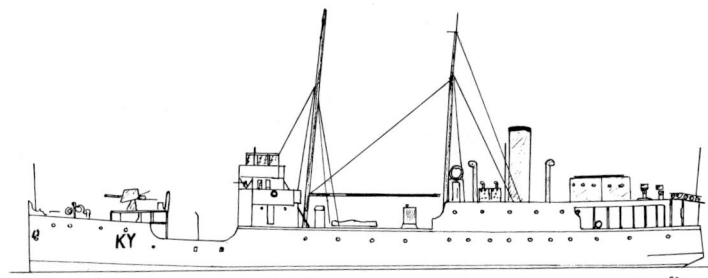

HMAS LARRAKIA, 1941; profile. (R. Gillett)

Name	Details	Status
Cygnet	–	–
Cygnus **(Q34)**	30 gross tons 54 × 14.6 × 3.9 feet 12½ knots 1 × .303 Vickers 2 rifles, 2 DCCs 4 DCs	Built – Req. 15/9/41 Purchased 11/6/42 Comm. 17/12/42
Fay C **(Q53)**	68 × 17 × 10 feet	Built 1941 Req. 9/6/42 Comm. 18/8/42 Purchased 13/3/44 Sold 1946
John Hardy **(Q70)**	61 gross tons 65 × 15.4 feet 120 h.p.	Built 1937 Req. 9/7/43 Purchased 13/4/44 Sold 2/1946
Kuru **(Q83)**	*Motor vessel* 55 gross tons 76.2 × 13.6 × 4.9 feet 270 h.p. = 13 knots 2 × 20mm, 1 × .303 Vicker, 1 × .303 Lewis 2 DCCs	Built 1938 Req. 1941 Comm. 8/12/41 Paid Off 22/10/43
Kybra **(FY90)**	*Coaster* 858 gross tons 204.2 × 31.1 × 11.10 feet 233 n.h.p. = 10½ knots 1 × 4-inch, 1 × 2 pdr. MGs, 2 DCTs	Built 1926 Req. 8/7/40 Comm. 30/9/40 Paid Off 23/11/45 Returned 25/3/46
Larrakia **(Q81)**	*Search & rescue vessel* 12 tons 45 × 10 × 3.3 feet 23 knots MGs	Built 1936 Exam. Vessel 14/10/39 Returned 12/11/39 Comm. 9/12/41 BDV – Sold 3/4/46
Laurabada **(FY64)**	*Yacht* 150 tons 100 × 25 × 10 feet 10 knots 2 × .303 Vickers	Built 1924 Req. 23/7/42 Comm. 23/7/42 Survey Vessel 1943 Paid Off 21/6/45 Army 21/6/45
Lucy Star **(Q71)**	–	Built – Req. 5/6/42 Comm. 18/2/43 Purchased 31/5/44
Lysander **(Q91)**	65½ gross tons 70 × 16 × 7 feet 2 × .303 Vickers	Built 1937 Comm. 2/1942
Magnetic	45.3 × 11.9 × 4.3 feet 40 h.p.	Built 1926 Sold 10/1947

HMAS KYBRA 12th April, 1943, showing her original armament; 4-inch gun forward, machine guns on bridge wings, 2 pounder (on bandstand) aft, and depth charges.

HMAS LARRAKIA, channel patrol-vessel, at Darwin, May, 1941.

HMAS LAURABADA at Port Moresby, 12th April, 1942, arriving from New Britain with 156 evacuees. Note Vickers machine guns abreast the foremast. (69370).

Name	Details	Status
Mako **(Q16)**	68 tons 50.4 × 12.3 × 4 feet 9 knots 1 × .303 Vickers 2 DCCs	Built 1914 Purchased 27/5/41 Comm. 4/10/41 Trans. to AIB
Marlean	30 gross tons 70 × 15 feet 11 knots 2 × .303 Vickers 2 DCCs	Built – Req. 17/9/41 Comm. 30/12/41 Purchased 22/6/42
Mars	–	–
Melinga	536 gross tons 154.1 × 34.6 feet	Built 1928 Chartered 3/11/42 Returned 19/6/42
Milga	66 × 15.7 × 6 feet 1 × .303 Vickers	Built 1918 Sold 16/3/46
Miramar II **(Q50)**	*Ferry* 82 gross tons 75 × 16 × 6 feet 12 knots 2 × .303 Vickers 4 DCCs	Built 1934 Exam. Vessel 4/9/39 Returned 17/11/39 Req. 26/5/41 Comm. 19/8/41 Purchased 15/12/42 Sold 12/1945
Miro **(Q42)**	*Ketch* 27 gross tons 57.6 × 15.6 × 7.6 feet 40 h.p. 1 × .303 Vickers 1 DCC	Built 1912 Req. 17/12/40 Purchased 12/1940 Sold 16/3/46
Moreton	–	Built – Purchased 4/1940
Moruya **(Q17)**	20 gross tons 47 × 12.3 × 5 feet $8\frac{1}{2}$ knots 1 × .303 Vickers 2 DCCs	Built – Comm. 4/10/41
Nepean **(Q36)**	76 × 16 × 5 feet 60 h.p. 1 × .303 Vickers	Built 1925 Req. 25/2/42 Comm. 31/7/42 Purchased 31/8/42 Sold 1945
Picton	38 × 13.8 × 4.8 feet	Built – Sold 1947
Pollyanna	30 tons 56.1 × 12.6 × 6.1 feet $12\frac{1}{2}$ knots 1 × .303 Vickers 2 DCCs	Built 1927
Prominent	–	Built – Req. 1/2/42

Name	Details	Status
San Michelle **(Q54)**	58.4 × 16.2 × 9.9 feet	Built 1939 Comm. 3/9/42 Purchased 8/3/43 Radar MV 1/1945 Sold 16/7/46
Shepherdness	2 DCCs	–
Vigilant **(FY06)** **(Q80)**	*Motor vessel* 106 gross tons 102 × 16.4 feet 640 h.p. = 13.5 knots 1 × .303 Vickers 2 × .303 Lewis, 2 DCCs	Built 1938 Req. 10/1940 Comm. 12/11/40 Exam. Vessel 5/1941 BDV 1/1943 Survey Vessel 6/1943 Paid Off 13/9/45 Sold 14/10/46
Westwind **(Q31)**	65 gross tons 78 × 16 × 9 feet 100 h.p. = 8 knots 1 × .303 Vickers 2 DCCs	Built 1914 Comm. 25/5/42 Purchased 5/8/42 Sold 3/1945
Wilcannia **(FY92)**	*Coaster* 1,049 gross tons 216.4 × 36.7 × 12.9 feet 12 knots 1 × 4-inch, 1 × 2 pdr. 3 × .303 Vickers 2 DCTs	Built 1934 Req. 28/6/40 Comm. 2/9/40 Stores Ship 7/1944 Paid Off 7/2/47 Returned 4/7/49
Winbah **(Q55)**	45 gross tons 62 × 15 feet 11 knots 2 × .303 Vickers 4 DCCs	Built 1936 Req. 22/9/41 Comm. 23/12/41 Purchased 25/7/42 Tender 1/1945
Yandra **(FY91)**	*Coaster* 990 gross tons 218 × 35.2 × 12.9 feet 1,025 b.h.p. = 12 knots 1 × 4-inch, 1 × .303 Vickers, 1 × .303 Maxim 1 × 2 pdr., 2 DCTs 2 DCRs	Built 1928 Req. 27/6/40 Comm. 22/9/40 Paid Off 25/3/46 Returned 7/1946

HMAS WILCANNIA, 1943; note 20mm mounts on bandstands abreast the bridge, searchlights on bridge-wings, 2 pounder aft, and depth charges on throwers (main deck) and right aft (rails).

VIGILANT, Cairns, 1938. (Photo – Cairns Historical Society)

VIGILANT, Sydney, 1938. (Photo – G. Haultain)

SNAKE CLASS SRD CRAFT

Black Snake, Diamond Snake, Grass Snake, River Snake, Sea Snake, Tiger Snake

Ship	Builder	Launched	Comm.	Army	Fate
Black Snake	J.J. Savage & Sons, Williamstown	1944	30/12/44	–	PO 3/11/45
Diamond Snake	-ditto-	17/5/45	23/7/45	1945	PO 19/10/45
Grass Snake	Millars Bunnings Shipbuilding Co., Fremantle	1944	24/2/45	–	PO 6/12/45
River Snake	-ditto-	1944	17/2/45	–	PO 3/11/45
Sea Snake	J.J. Savage & Sons, Williamstown	18/1/45	31/3/45	–	PO 6/12/45
Tiger Snake	-ditto-	6/44	22/8/45	–	PO 3/11/45

These craft were constructed in Melbourne and Fremantle under the auspices of the Commonwealth Small Craft Programme. Four trawlers in advanced stages of construction by J.J. Savage were transferred to S.R.D. on 27th March, 1944. One additional unit, CORAL SNAKE, was cancelled on 23rd August, 1945.

The Services Reconnaissance Department was formed in January, 1944, with headquarters in Melbourne. At this time S.R.D. operated KRAIT, a former Japanese fishing vessel, and ALATNA, a 62 foot sea ambulance launch originally built for the Australian Army.

All S.R.D. boats were designed to operate behind enemy lines in the western and south-west Pacific areas.

Displacement (tons): *Gross* 80 (78 Tiger Snake)
Dimensions (feet): *Length* (oa) 66 (70 Tiger Snake) *Beam* 17 (15 Tiger Snake) *Draught* 7.6 (7.6 Tiger Snake)
Machinery: Gray marine 64 YTL diesel, single screw, 300 h.p., sails could be employed (Sea Snake – Hercules diesel)
Speed (knots): 10 ($9\frac{1}{2}$ – Tiger Snake)
Range (miles): 500
Manning: 9
Armament: Two 20mm, MGs.

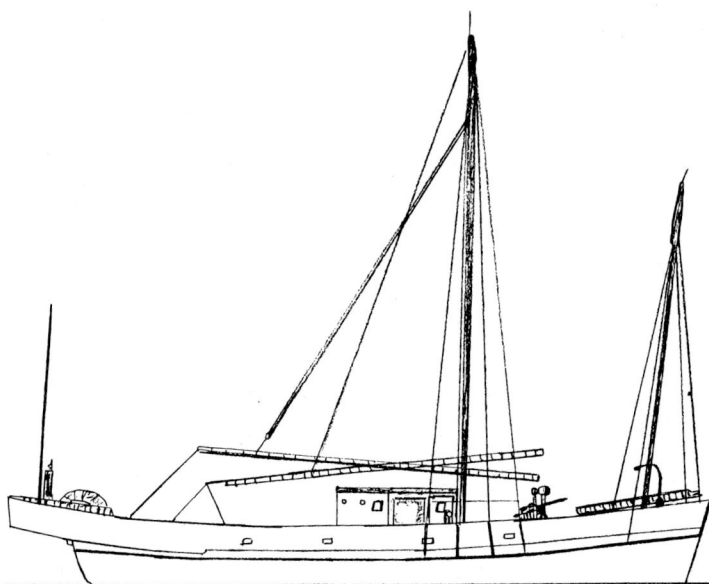

HMAS DIAMOND SNAKE, 1945; profile. (R. Gillett)

HMAS GRASS SNAKE shortly after commissioning.

Top – HMAS TIGER SNAKE, Marudi, Borneo, 20th July, 1945.

Above – HMAS BLACK SNAKE, 19th April, 1945.

Left – The SRD craft, HMAS TIGER SNAKE, with members of D Company 2/17 Infantry Battalion, sailing the Baram River, New Guinea, on 14th July, 1945. (112082)

300-TON WOODEN MOTOR VESSELS

Anaconda, Mother Snake

ANNACONDA and MOTHER SNAKE were formerly Army operated as AV 1369 (LAGUNTA) and AV 1354 (MURCHISON) respectively. ANACONDA reverted to Army control on 8th December, 1945, and was returned to Australia in 1946.

During the last year of the war, ANACONDA was employed as a workshop and headquarters vessel; MOTHER SNAKE served as a mothership to other SRD craft in Borneo and the Moluccas. Handed over to BBCAU in 1945.

A third vessel, AV 1358, GREENOUGH, was launched on 15th July, 1945, at Fremantle. Although fitted out for SRD operations she did not enter service.

Displacement (tons): *Gross* 316
Dimensions (feet): *Length (oa)* 125.0 *Beam* 24.0 *Draught* 12.6
Machinery: Two sets of diesels, 300 or 320 h.p.
Speed (knots): 9
Range (miles): N/A
Manning: 14 (Mother Snake 19)
Armament: One 20mm, MGs (Anaconda) One 40mm, Two 20mm (Mother Snake).

Ship	Builder	Launched	Comp.	Comm.	Fate
Anaconda	Australain Shipbuilding Annex, Tasmania	4/10/44	1945	23/5/45	Paid Off 8/12/45
Mother Snake	Australian Shipbuilding Board, WA	5/12/44	1945	30/6/45	Paid Off 3/11/45

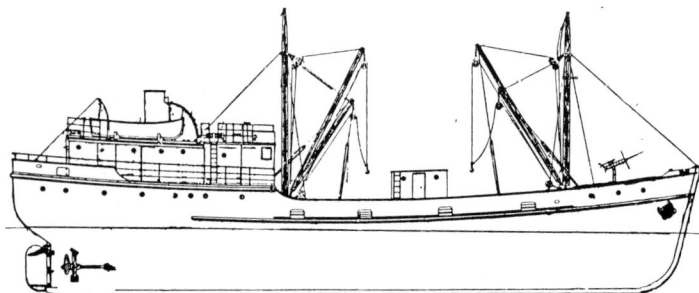

HMAS MOTHER SNAKE in New Gurnea waters with RIVER SNAKE and TIGER SNAKE alongside (Photo – P. Armstrong)

HMAS MOTHER SNAKE (Photo – P. Armstrong)

HMAS MOTHER SNAKE; profile. (R. Gillett)

62 FOOT SRD CRAFT

Alatna, Karina, Misima, Nyanie

All originally constructed for Australian Army as 62 foot fast supply vessels. ALATNA and MISIMA served with water transport units, while KARINA and NYANIE appear to have joined the RAN from completion.

All employed as tenders to 'junk' style Snake class SRD craft.

NYANIE was returned to Army control after paying off, while ALATNA was lost on 1st January, 1946, after being rammed by the SS MARINE RUNNER. Both KARINA and MISIMA were transferred to the British Borneo Civil Adminstration Unit.

Displacement (tons): 28
Dimensions (feet): *Length* 62, *Beam* 14.6, *Draught* 3
Machinery: 275 h.p.
Speed: 20 knots
Armament Machine guns

ALATNA as AM 1475, 1943.

Ship	Pend. No.	Builder	Cons. Time	Comm.	Fate
Alatna	AM 1475 FY 24	—	—	2.2.44	Lost 1.1.46
Karina	—	—	—	27.11.44	P.O. 2.11.45
Misima	AM 2829	—	—	2.8.45	P.O. 12.10.45
Nyanie	—	—	—	6.7.45	P.O. 24.12.45

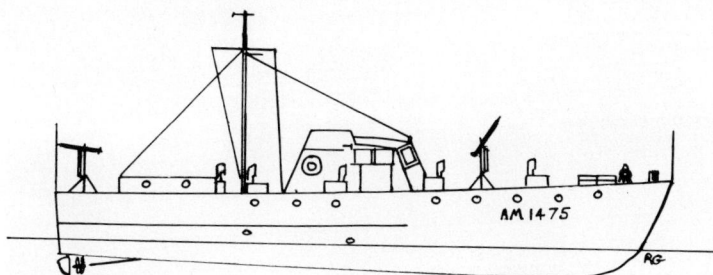

HMAS ALATNA, 1945; profile. (R. Gillett)

OTHER S.R.D. CRAFT
Five Ships

Name	Details	Status
Eduardo (MFV 2045)	*Trawler* 1 × 40 mm, 3 × 20 mm	Built – Comm. 3/1945 RN 10/1945
Heather	*Lugger* MGs	Built 1939 Req. 18/2/42 SRD 1944 Sold 11/1945
Krait	*Trawler* 68 gross tons 70.8 × 14.3 feet 8½ knots	Built – Captured 12/1941 Comm. 5/4/44 Paid Off 2/11/45 Museum Vessel 1963
Swallow	*Lugger* Used for training	Built – SRD 3/1945
Taipan	*Junk* 107 gross tons 81 feet long 275 h.p.	Built – Captured 8/1944 Army 1/1945 SRD 14/8/45 Paid Off 17/10/45 Sold 11/6/46

Note: Two additional craft, MAMBA and TARNEIT were not required for war service.

MINOR SRD CRAFT
8 Army Launches/Workboats

Name	Details	States
AM 1495	*Launch* 38 feet long	SRD 3/1945 PO 3/11/45
AM 1629	*Workboat* 40 feet long	SRD 3/1945 PO 3/11/45
AM 1830	*Workboat* 40 feet long	SRD 12/1944 PO 3/11/45
AM 1983	*Workboat* 40 feet long	SRD 6/1945 PO 3/11/45
AM 1985	*Workboat* 40 feet long	SRD 6/1945 PO 3/11/45
AM 2003	*Workboat* 40 feet long	SRD 1945 RAN 9/1945 PO 3/11/45
AM 2004	*Workboat* 40 feet long	SRD 1945 RAN 9/1945 PO 3/11/45
AM 2409	*Launch* 38 feet long	SRD 1945 RAN 9/1945 PO 3/11/49

KRAIT.

REQUISITIONED EXAMINATION VESSELS
Thirty-six Ships

Former merchant and privately owned vessels were taken over from late 1939 to form a viable examination service. Many were also used as patrol craft or as pilot boats for the port authorities.

ADELE laid up in Sydney prior to the Second World War. During the Great War, and after, she operated as a tender. (Photo – J. Mortimer)

BIRUBI, 17th April, 1958. (Photo – Maritime Services Board)

Name	Details	Status
Adele (KY89)	*Yacht* 288 gross tons 145 × 22.4 × 9.10 feet 68 h.p. = 12 knots 2 × .303 Vickers	Built 1906 Req. 18/9/39 Comm. 20/10/39 Lost 7/5/43
Akuna	*Yacht* 970 gross tons 210 × 31 × 15 feet 1,350 h.p. = 16 knots small arms	Built 1911 Req. 2/9/39 Returned 24/4/41 Req. 28/4/43 Returned 29/9/43
Arcadia (Q24) (FY56)	29 tons 48.6 × 13.6 × 6.9 feet 1 × .303 Vickers	Built – Req. 26/9/41 Purchased 4/11/42
Bareto	49.9 × 12.6 × 4.6 feet 50 h.p.	Built – Req. 2/11/39 Stores Carrier 31/1/40 Purchased 5/2/40 Sold 12/1945
Birubi	*Pilot Steamer* 427 gross tons 148 × 26 × 12.6 feet 650 i.h.p. = 11½ knots	Built 1927 Req. 3/9/39 Returned 31/7/43
Captain Cook	*Pilot Steamer* 524 gross tons 165.8 × 26.7 × 16 feet 800 i.h.p. = 12 knots	Built 1939 Req. 2/9/39 Returned 13/10/40
Ellan (FY57)	*Trawler* 40 gross tons 61 × 15.6 × 9.6 feet 105 h.p.	Built 1942 Req. 20/3/43 Comm. 20/8/43 Purchased 8/12/43 Paid Off 11/3/46 Sold 1946

CAPTAIN COOK. (Photo – Maritime Services Board)

HMAS JOHN OXLEY: a 20mm Oerlikon and machine gun are mounted aft.

KING BAY.

HMAS PALUMA at Townsville, 1942, during service with the Allied Intelligence Bureau.

Name	Details	Status
Emerald	–	Built – Req. 4/9/39 Returned 17/10/40
Factus	–	Built – Sold 1946
Falie **(FY02)**	*Ketch* 215 gross tons 109.7 × 21.9 × 9.9 feet	Built 1919 Req. 17/7/40 Comm. 4/10/40 Store Carrier 8/1943 Paid Off 1946
Fauro Chief **(Also ASR)** **(FY51)**	*Ketch* $19\frac{1}{2}$ gross tons 65 × 16 × 6.6 feet 35 h.p. = 8 knots 1 × .303 Vickers	Built – Commandeered 4/8/42 Comm. 4/9/42 Lost 5/1945
Gerard **(FY62)**	*Schooner* 194 gross tons 112.2 × 24.8 × 8.5 feet 187 h.p. = $8\frac{1}{2}$ knots 1 × 12 pdr., 1 × 20mm 2 × .303 Vickers	Built 1921 Req. 5/4/41 Comm. 1/7/41 Stores Carrier 7/1943 Paid Off 8/4/46 Returned 24/7/47
John Oxley **(FY65)**	*Pilot Steamer* 544 gross tons 161 × 32.1 feet 12 knots 1 × 20mm, MGs	Built 1927 Req. 28/1/43 Comm. 28/1/43 Paid Off 1/2/46
King Bay **(FY96)**	*Schooner* 237 gross tons 105.7 × 27.3 × 8.6 feet 47 n.h.p. = 8 knots 1 × .303 Vickers	Built 1938 Req. 8/7/40 Comm. 15/8/40 Paid Off 12/11/43 Tender 15/11/43 Paid Off 16/2/44 Army (AV708) 17/2/44 RAN 21/2/46 Returned 13/9/46
Kooraka	–	Built – Req. 2/9/39 Returned 22/11/39
Kyeema	–	Built – Req. 4/10/39 Returned 21/3/41
Larrakia	*Search & rescue vessel* 12 tons 45 × 10 × 3.3 feet 23 knots MGs	Built 1936 Req. 14/10/39 Returned 12/11/39 Comm. 9/12/41 Sold 3/4/46
Marana	*Steamer* 108 gross tons 97.6 × 21 feet	Built 1908 Req. 4/9/39 Returned 10/6/42

Name	Details	Status
Matthew Flinders (FY66)	*Steamer* 450 gross tons 160.3 × 28.1 feet 1 × 20mm, 2 MGs	Built 1914 Req. 23/1/43 Comm. 23/1/43 Paid Off 23/7/46 Returned 29/7/46
Miramar II	*Ferry* 82 gross tons 75 × 16 × 6 feet 12 knots 2 × .303 Vickers, 4 DCCs	Built 1934 Req. 4/9/39 Returned 17/11/39 Req. 26/5/41 Comm. 19/8/41 Purchased 15/12/42 Sold 12/1945
Mongana	–	Built – Req. 2/9/39 Returned 6/8/40
Norseman	–	Built – Req. 2/1941
Otter	*Tug* 271 gross tons 128.6 × 21.2 × 10.1 feet 12 knots	Built 1884 Req. 2/9/39 Returned 20/12/40
Paluma (Q93)	*Motor boat* 45 gross tons 66 × 14 × 5 feet 120 b.h.p = 11 knots 1 × .303 Vickers, 2 DCCs	Built 1941 Req. 11/9/41 Comm. 1/1942 Purchased 1/6/42 AIB 1942 Paid Off 9/12/45 Sold 27/5/46
Panawina	–	Built – Req. 3/9/39 Returned 31/1/40
Penguin	–	Built – Req. 20/12/39 Purchased 23/7/40
Premier	15 tons 46 × 14.4 feet 42 h.p. = 7 knots	Built – Req. 5/4/41 Returned 23/12/43
Seabird (521)	*Launch* 10½ gross tons 37 × 11 feet 75 h.p. 1 × MG	Built 1924 Req. 31/5/43 Purchased 27/6/44 Sold 8/1945
Sea Witch	–	Built – Req. 2/9/39 Returned 6/12/43
Sir Wallace Bruce	–	Built – Req. 2/9/39 Returned 6/10/43

Name	Details	Status
Southern Cross (FY17)	*Yacht* 298 gross tons 120 × 28.5 feet 120 h.p. = 9 knots 2 × .303 Vickers 1 × 0.5-inch Browning	Built 1933 Req. 29/3/41 Comm. 18/6/41 Stores Carrier 1941 Paid Off 1946 Returned 1946
Stradbroke	104 gross tons 80.2 × 18.8 × 8.9 feet 1 × .303 Vickers	–

LARRAKIA, 1936. (Photo – G. Haultain)

HMAS SEA BIRD in New Guinea waters. She carries the NAP pendant number 521.

Name	Details	Status
Venture	–	Built – Req. 24/11/39 Returned 26/11/39 Req. 4/12/39 Returned 5/12/39
Violet	–	Built – Req. 12/11/39 Returned 20/11/39 Req. 25/2/40 Returned 27/2/40
Wongala (FY78)	*Steamer* 424 gross tons 149 × 29.2 × 14.3 feet 1 × 12 pdr. 1 × .303 Vickers	Built 1919 Req. 1939 Comm. 14/7/40 Paid Off 19/7/44 Recomm. 17/11/47 Paid Off 6/1948 Sold 1951
Woolomai	35 × 10 feet 20 knots	Built 1937 Purchased 2/11/42 Sold 12/3/46

HMAS WONGALA, at Port Adelaide, 29th December, 1943; the 12 pounder gun is forward and Vickers machine gun and depth charges aft.

NAVAL AUXILIARY PATROL

The organisation that later developed into the Naval Auxiliary Patrol was the Volunteer Coastal Patrol. This force was founded on 28th March, 1938, by Captain Blackwood, RN (retired).

For the first nine months of World War II, the Patrol, though not granted recognition by any of the services or Governments in Australia, was considered especially by the Military (Eastern Command) a useful adjunct to their service. On occasions it co-operated with Military authorities in testing Beach Defence Schemes, on Coastal Reconnaisance work, Military Survey work, etc.

In June, 1940, when Italy declared war on the British Empire, the New South Wales police, who had been entrusted with the job of the security of Sydney Harbour, approached the VCP for assistance. The request resulted in official recognition, of the Patrol by the NSW State Government.

During 1941, when relations with Japan became strained, a number of Victorian yachtsmen decided it was time Port Phillip Bay had a Patrol and under the guidance of a Sydney member, set about forming one. The immediate aim was a patrol of two flotillas, each consisting of 32 boats. With the entry of Japan into the war, other yacht clubs realised their responsibilities and encouraged members to join. The number of boats in the Victorian pool exceeded 100 by August, 1942. Patrol boats were all former pleasure yachts and motor boats, and ranged in size from 60 foot auxiliary yachts to 20 foot open motor boats. On 25th June, 1941, the formation of the Naval Auxiliary Patrol was officially approved.

The Naval Board Minute III, dated 12th June, 1941, approved of the formation of the Naval Auxiliary Patrol in principle. The minute also stated that the object of the organisation was to provide an Auxiliary Patrol to utilise the resources of private owners of yachts, launches, fishing vessels and other types of suitable vessels at various points around the coastline of Australia for defence purposes. The Department of the Navy would bear the cost of any alterations or special equipment and fit vessels for the performance of special duties. Generally speaking, costs allowable were to be limited to the provision of fuel and lubricating oil consumed on duty. Cost of refit of engines and other equipment were expressly excluded.

In April, 1942, the Naval Auxiliary Patrol was transferred to the RANVR and was thereafter known as the RANVR (P).

As time passed a number of boats of the NAP were transferred to other duties and the number of personnel and boats in the Patrol naturally decreased, although the efficiency of the organisation was still maintained.

NAP boats were armed with rifles, revolvers, hand grenades, machine guns and depth charges of various sizes.

From June, 1944, onwards, the NAP was reduced to a minimum. A number of boats were used for Air Sea Rescue and Channel Patrol purposes, while the personnel were transferred to other duties. Many of the boats bought by the Navy for NAP duties were re-sold as being no longer required for naval purposes.

During August, all security patrols were abolished and the services of voluntary NAP personnel were only used to fill vacancies in the crews of night duty NAP boats caused by sickness.

The most famous action in which NAP vessels participated was on the night of 31st May, 1942, when LAURIANA, SEA MIST, STEADY HOUR and YARROMA attacked Japanese midget submarines loose within Port Jackson. With the scaling down of the service, most boats returned to private ownership. Many vessels survive today as pleasure boats.

BETTY TOO, a part-time boat based on the Brisbane River.

ACTIVITIES OF NAP OCTOBER, 1942

State	Strength Mobed & Unmobed	Number of Vessels	Duty Miles	Ship Hours	Crew Hours
Queensland	415	38	3,101	699	3,104
New South Wales	1,295	211	16,044	7,682	29,964
Tasmania	292	130	1,920	399	816
Victoria	341	117	6,002	1,500	7,021
South Australia	423	61	664	431	1,976
Western Australia	419	105	32,516	14,902	59,825
Totals	3,185	662	60,247	25,613	102,706

NAP VESSELS – POSITION AS AT 9TH MARCH, 1944

State	Establishment	Vessels Available for Local Duties	CPB's Proposed to man with NAP	Total
New South Wales	43	21 (inc 4 in reserve)	4	25
Queensland	30	24 (inc 4 in reserve)	6	30
Victoria	7	5	–	5
South Australia	15	7 (inc 2 in reserve)	1	8
Tasmania	7	5	2	7
Western Australia	24	24	–	24
Totals	126	86	13	99

The part time boat VAGRANT in Brisbane with OENONE (504) in the background.

COMMISSIONED VESSELS
87 Ships

Many of the following craft were designated channel patrol vessels.

HMAS LEILANI

HMAS PINAFORE, Western Australia.

Aeolus	Lady Madge	Reverie
Allambie	Lancelin	Riawe
Allura	Lauriana	Rondelle
Altair	Leeuwin	Sagittas (Q22)
Amohine II	Leilani (Q11)	Sea Mist (Q10)
Arista	Lolita (Q14)	Seeka
Avalon	Lorne	Shark
Avonita	Margaret	Siesta
Borough Belle	Marietta	Silver Cloud (Q52)
Bundarra	Marina	Sirocco (Q21)
Corsair	Marlean (Q20)	Spinaway
Dawn II	Marlin	Steady Hour (Q12)
Edelweiss	Martindale (Q33)	Stella Maris
Egeria (Tasma)	Melton Lass	Stingray
Esmaralda (Q15)	Mischief II	Sundowner
Flying Cloud	Miss Gladys	Swordfish II
Flying Foam	Miss Swan	Sylph II
Gladmore	Nereus (Q19)	Tangalooma
Gloria	Nitipa	Tasma (Q23)
Grelka (Q26)	Nokomis I (Q27)	Toomeree (Q65)
(Q32)		
Halcyon	Nordecia	Topsy A
Hermoine III	Nyroca I	Viking
Hiawatha	Para	Vlaming
Hoona	Pedare	Waimarie
Hurrica	Pedoro	Winnilya
Iolanthe	Peter Pan	Wongalere
James Innes	Pinafore	Yarroma (Q51)
Kazembe	Pioneer	Zanana
Koorine	Radical	NOTE – In addition there
Kweena		were 61 full time craft and numerous part-time vessels.

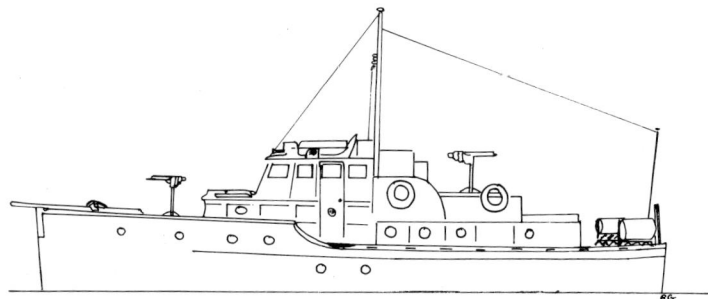

HMAS ESMERALDA; profile. (R. Gillett)

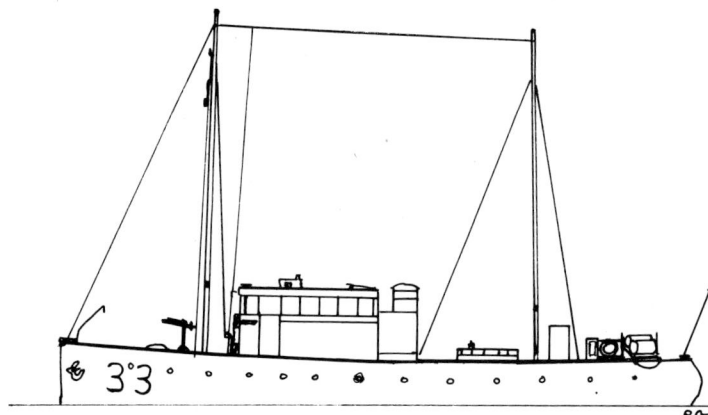

HMAS MARTINDALE; profile. (R. Gillett)

LAURIANA, Jacquinot Bay, 21st November, 1944, (under RAAF control as a rescue launch).

HMAS SIROCCO, Port Phillip.

HMAS MARLEAN, Sydney, 15th February, 1944, while operating as a channel patrol vessel.

BAR CLASS

Kangaroo, Karangi, Koala

To provide a realistic boom defence vessel force, three improved Bar class BDVs were ordered in 1939 and 1940 to assist the lone KOOKABURRA. The three Bar class displaced over 300 tons greater than the earlier vessel, were 40 foot longer and had the bridge superstructure sited further forward. This extra weight overcame the problem of KOOKABURRA which tended to come down to the buoy when laying a boom defence.

The Bars and KOOKABURRA were ordered to Darwin during 1940/41 to establish a workable boom defence for that port. All were in harbour during the Japanese air attack on 19th February, 1942.

The original 12 pdr. QF gun was later replaced by a HA/LA variant and was mounted abaft the funnel.

All three served in the post-war fleet, the last, KOALA, remaining in reserve until 1969.

Displacement (tons): *Standard* 768 *Full Load* 971
Dimensions (feet): *Length* (oa) 178.3 *Beam* 32.6 *Draught* 11.3
Machinery: Triple expansion; single screw; 850 i.h.p.
Speed (knots): 11
Range (miles): N/A
Maining: 32
Armament: One 12 pdr. (1 × 1), Two .303 Vickers, Two smaller.

Ship	Pend. No.	Builder	Cons. Time	Comm.	Fate
Kangaroo	P80 Z80 (1940)	Cockatoo	10m	27/9/40	Sold 28/8/61
Karangi	P282 Z216 (1942)	Cockatoo	10m	23/12/41	Sold 17/8/65
Koala	P69 Z69 (1942)	Cockatoo	7m	7/2/40	Sold 24/6/69

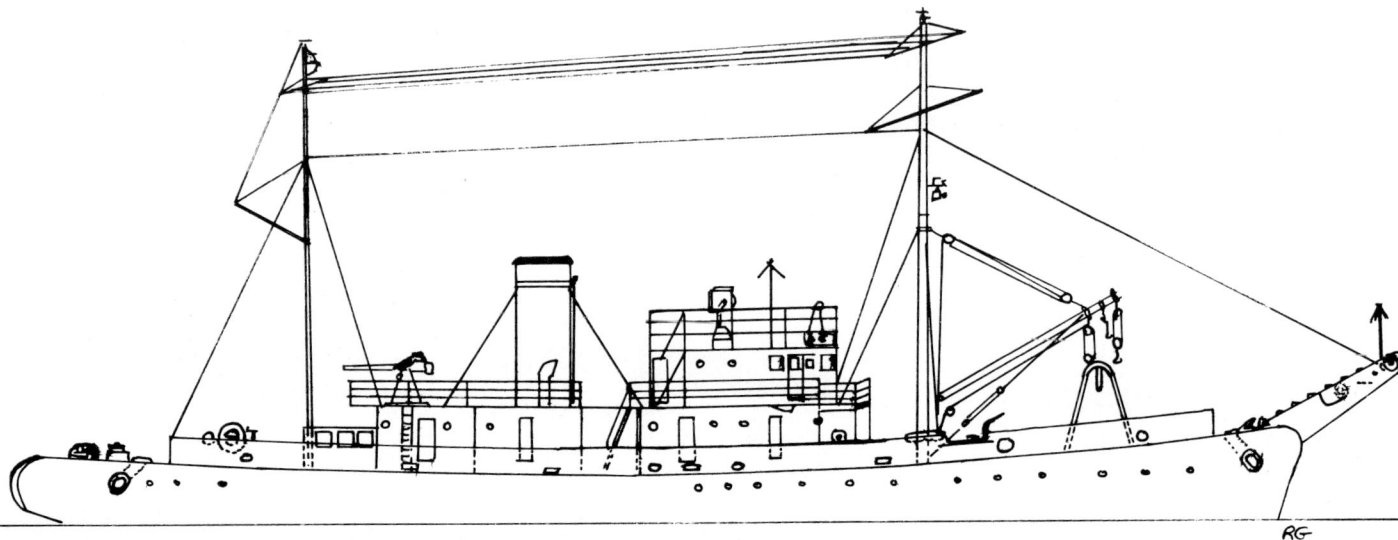

HMAS KOALA, 1940; profile. (Cockatoo Dockyard)

HMAS KOALA. (Photo – P. Britz)

HMAS KANGAROO.

HMAS KARANGI laying a boom defence at the entrance to Darwin Harbour; note the single 12 pounder gun abaft the funnel.

AUXILIARY BOOM DEFENCE VESSELS
Twenty-three Ships

A wide selection of craft were taken over as auxiliary boom defence craft as the four specialist ships could not satisfy all requirements around Australia.

Name	Details	Status
Bat	*Motor boat* 22 × 8.3 × 3.6 feet 10 h.p.	Built – Purchased 2/1943 Sold 1947
Bay Ferry	*Ferry* 11 gross tons 50 × 11.6 × 6 feet 45 h.p.	Built 1925 Req. 20/1/44 Purchased 12/7/44 Sold 6/4/46
Bdi	–	Built – Req. 1/4/41
Boyd	*Lugger*	Built – Transferred 11/8/42
Donna Matilda	(See Kakapo)	–
Kakapo	52 × 14 feet	Built – Req. 5/8/42 Purchased – Sold 7/1945
Kara Kara (Z221)	*Ferry* 525 gross tons 199 × 38.4 feet 13 knots 1 × 12 pdr., 2 × .303 Vickers, 2 others	Built 1926 Req. 27/2/41 Comm. 14/10/41 Purchased 7/11/41 Sold 1972

Name	Details	Status
Kiara (Q82)	50 × 13 × 3 feet 14 knots 1 × .303 Vickers 2 DCs	Built 1938 Req. 21/2/41 Comm. 25/5/41 Purchased 8/1941 Sold 7/1945
Kim	49 × 12.6 × 6 feet 15 h.p.	Built 1908 Req. 18/2/42 Purchased 8/8/44 Sold 1/1945
Kinchela (Z06) (Z96)	*Lighter* 370 gross tons 145 × 31 feet 9 knots 0.5-inch MGs	Built 1914 Req. 3/3/42 Comm. 28/8/42 Paid Off 18/12/45 Purchased 16/5/46 Sold 17/7/46
Kindur	–	Built – Req. 8/1943 (8 days) Req. 4/1944 (1 day)
Koompartoo (Z256)	*Ferry* 448 gross tons 191 × 38.3 × 13.8 feet 113 h.p. = 12½ knots 2 × 20mm, 4 × .303 Vickers	Built 1922 Req. 18/6/42 Comm. 23/12/42 Paid Off 1945 Sold 8/6/62
Kuramia (FY46)	*Ferry* 335 gross tons 156.5 × 33.2 × 12 feet 12 knots MGs	Built 1913 Req. 20/2/42 Comm. 30/6/42 Purchased 15/6/43 Paid Off 3/12/45 Scuttled 10/10/53
Lanikai (Z253)	*Schooner* 150 gross tons 87 × 29 feet 150 h.p. = 6 knots 2 × .303 Vickers	Built 1914 USN 5/12/41 RAN 9/12/42 USN 21/1/46
Magu	*USN Net & Boom Unit*	Built – Req. 27/7/43 Sold 1946
Maitland ex Moonglo	*Launch*	Built – Loaned 3/9/42

KARA KARA, as built, 1926.

HMAS KINCHELA, the slowest ship in the fleet; note the searchlight and machine guns on the bridge.

Name	Details	Status
Mina	*Lugger* 18 gross tons 51 × 13.6 × 6 feet	Built – Req. 18/2/42 Transferred 11/10/43 Sold 3/1947
Nicol Bay	–	–
Otter	*Trawler* 45 gross tons 55 × 14.10 × 6.3 feet 60 h.p.	Built 1942 Purchased 11/11/43 Diving Boat 1945 Sold 1968
Patricia	*Lugger* 49 × 12.10 feet	Built 1911 Req. 20/2/42 Purchased 28/7/43 Sold 10/11/45

Name	Details	Status
Royce	41 × 13.6 × 3.3 feet 24 h.p.	Built 1919 Req. 27/7/42 Purchased 19/2/43 Sold 6/1946
The Mist	–	Built – Req. 2/7/43 Purchased 28/3/44
Three Cheers (FY05)	58 × 15.6 feet	Built – Req. 25/11/42 Purchased 12/11/43 Comm. 20/10/44 Sold 3/7/46

63 FOOT AIR-SEA RESCUE VESSELS
Twenty Ships

The original ASR design was based upon an American anti-submarine vessel modified to satisfy rescue requirements. The Australian boats were extremely useful craft and gained distinction in patrol work during the war.

The primary mission of the ASR was the rescue of downed airmen, all boats being equipped with a sick bay aft. Most craft served in northern Australian or New Guinea waters, although AIR MIST was stationed at Newcastle, NSW.

During December, 1945, AIR MIST was wrecked 30 miles north of Newcastle near Morna Point when under tow of GERALDTON.

A proposal to transfer 15 ASRs to the RAAF was announced in 1946, but it was not until 1949 that 13 were transferred. AIR VIEW remains in service with the RAAF. Following the Second World War, the remaining RAN vessels were redesignated search and rescue vessels.

Ship	Pend. No.	Builder	Comm.	Fate
Air Bird	915	Harbour Boat	28/3/45	RAAF 1949
Air Chief	918	Fellows & Stewart	12/8/44	Sold 7/1966
Air Clan	922	Harbour Boat	11/12/44	RAAF 1949
Air Cloud	924	Harbour Boat	20/10/44	RAAF 1949
Air Faith	902	South Coast	8/2/45	RAAF 1949 Returned 1965 Sold 1968
Air Foam	912	South Coast	20/9/44	–
Air Guide	913	Fellows & Stewart	20/10/44	RAAF 1949 Returned 1965 Target 1971/72
Air Hope	908	South Coast	13/2/45	RAAF 1949
Air Master	919	Fellows & Stewart	31/8/44	Target 1968
Air Mercy	925	Fellows & Stewart	28/2/45	–
Air Mist	917	Fellows & Stewart	20/9/44	Wrecked 12/1945
Air Rest	921	Harbour Boat	20/9/44	RAAF 1950
Air Sailor	926	Fellows & Stewart	8/11/44	RAAF 1949
Air Save	920	Fellows & Stewart	20/9/44	RAAF 1949 Returned 1962 Sold 6/1968
Air Sense	914	Harbour Boat	1/3/45	RAAF 1949
Air Speed	910	Fellows & Stewart	28/2/45	–
Air Spray	911	Harbour Boat	13/2/45	RAAF 1949 Returned 1965 Sold 1969
Air Trail	916	Fellows & Stewart	8/2/45	Target 1968
Air View	923	Fellows & Stewart	20/11/45	RAAF 1949
Air Watch	927	Harbour Boat	27/11/44	RAAF 1949

Displacement (tons): *Standard* 23
Dimensions (feet): *Length* (oa) 63.0 *Beam* 15.3 *Draught* 4.0
Machinery: Two Hall Scott 'Defender' petrol engines, twin screws
Speed (knots): $33\frac{1}{2}$
Range (hours): $14\frac{1}{2}$
Manning: N/A
Armament: Two 0.5-inch MGs (2 × 2).

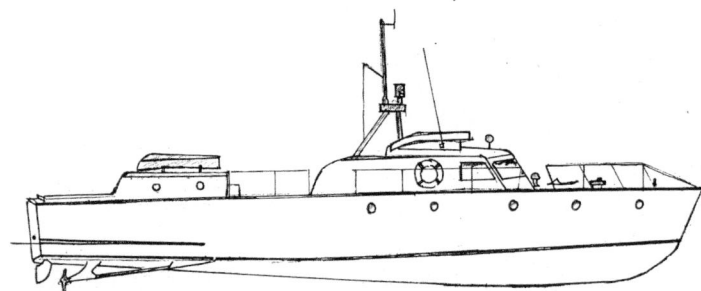

Sixty-three foot ASR: profile. (H. Adlam)

HMAS AIR CHIEF, 19th September 1944.

HMAS AIR MASTER during speed trials at Balikpapan, 12th September, 1945. Twin 0.5-inch machine guns are carried.

HMAS AIR MERCY post-war and with armament removed.

80 FOOT AIR-SEA RESCUE VESSELS – *Four Ships*

Twenty, 80 foot ASRs were approved for acquisition in July, 1943, at a total cost of £400,000 each. Only ten numbers, 969 to 978 were allotted. Eventually the funds were used up importing twenty 63 foot ASRs from the U.S.A.

Displacement (tons): *Standard* N/A
Dimensions (feet): *Length* (oa) 80
Machinery: N/A
Speed (knots): N/A
Range (hours): N/A
Armament: Two 0.5 inch MGs.

Pend. No.	Builder	Cons. Time	Comp.	Fate
969	Arcus Ltd.	–	–	Cancelled 12/1945
970	Arcus Ltd.	–	–	Cancelled 12/1945
971	M.H.T.	1y 3m	11/1945	–
972	M.H.T.	9m	1/1946	–

REQUISITIONED AIR-SEA RESCUE VESSEL – *One Ship*

Name	Details	Status
Fauro Chief (FY51)	*Ketch* 19½ gross tons 65 × 16 × 6.6 feet 35 h.p. = 8 knots 1 × .303 Vickers	Built – Commandeered 4/8/42 Comm. 4/9/42 Lost 5/1945

MOONRAY, 1936. (Photo – R. Gillett Collection)

REQUISITIONED VESSELS ATTACHED TO HMAS ASSAULT – *Ten Ships* (Combined Operations)

HMAS ASSAULT was commissioned as the combined operations school, Port Stephens, New South Wales on 4th September 1942. The base was allotted the following craft.

Name	Details	Status
Assault MB1	*Motor Yacht* 40 gross tons 45 × 12 feet 142 h.p.	Built 1936 Req. 4/8/42 Purchased 16/3/43 Sold 9/1945
GK MB5	18 gross tons 40 × 11.6 feet 234 h.p.	Built 1937–38 Req. 2/8/42 Purchased 3/3/43 Sold 4/1946
Goblin MB6	*Motor Cruiser* 38 × 11 feet	Built 1936 Req. 2/8/42 Purchased 23/12/43 Sold 4/1945
Gumleaf	*Trawler* 57 × 16 feet	Built – Req. 11/11/42 Comm. 1/6/43 Purchased 3/7/43 Sold 6/1946
Hulda	*Motor Launch* 38 × 9.6 feet	Built – Req. 2/8/42 Transferred to New Guinea 9/1942 Sunk 12/9/42 Raised & refitted 21/5/43 Sunk 22/9/43
Jackeroo MB9	*Motor Boat* 34 × 10 feet	Built – Req. 2/8/42 Purchased 23/3/43 Darwin 2/1944 Sold 5/1946
Jason MB7	32 × 10 feet	Built 1937 2/13 Battn AIF 5/8/42 Purchased 2/3/43 Sold 4/1945
Moonray MB8	*Motor Cruiser* 36 × 16.6 feet 95 h.p.	Built 1936 Req. 12/8/42 Purchased 15/3/43 Sold 3/1945
Unnamed	–	Built – Req. 8/8/42 Purchased 20/5/43
Unnamed	–	Built – Req. 19/8/42 Purchased 29/6/43

DIVING BOATS

Hunter, Otter

Fishing trawler type, OTTER was purchased from Mr. L. Wolf of Ulladulla, NSW, on 11th November, 1943 and used as auxiliary BDV. Both boats attached to Penguin in 1947.

HUNTER ex PEE BEE was acquired from U.S. forces on 14th May 1945 and was sold by auction on 25 October 1947. She was later lost in a storm.

Displacement (tons): 45
Dimensions (feet): *Length* 55 *Beam* 14.10 *Draught* 6.3
Machinery: Vivian 3 cylinder, 60 h.p.
Speed (knots): N/A
Range (miles): N/A
Manning: N/A
Armament: Small arms.

Ship	Pend. No.	Builder	Comp.	Fate
Hunter	DB3	W. Holmes Sydney	1942	Sold 1947
Otter	DB2	R. Adams Sydney	1942	Sold 1968

HMAS OTTER, early 1960s. (Photo – Navy & Marine Corps. Museum)

DIVING BOAT

Seal

Built for the Australian Army as AS 1803, PEEBINGA.
Acqired by the R.A.N. and allotted to Port Diving Officer, Sydney.

Displacement (tons): 45
Dimensions (feet): *Length* 66 *Beam* 16 *Draught* 8
Machinery: Hercules DNX6
Speed (knots): N/A
Range (miles): N/A
Manning: N/A
Armament: Small arms

Ship	Pend. No.	Builder	Comp.	Fate
Seal	DB1	–	1944	Sold 1968

SEAL, 29th January, 1979. (Photo – R. Gillett)

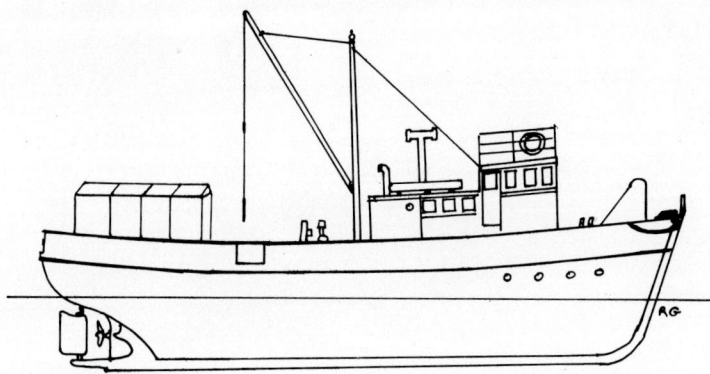
SEAL; profile. (R. Gillett)

GENERAL PURPOSE VESSELS
GPV Nos. 947–968

Twenty-two GPVs were constructed by the Green Point Shipyard. Nos. 969 to 978 were laid down but not completed. All were flush-deck types, except Nos. 953 and 954, which were fitted with raised forecastles. GPV No. 965 was completed on 16th January, 1946, but not commissioned until 12th May, 1949. PANDION allotted pendant number FY 09.

Four types of engines were fitted:
120 h.p. Atlas Imperial (Nos. 949 to 953)
 160 h.p. Blackstone E.V.F.M.G. (Nos. 948, 954 to 960, 962 to 964)
 150 h.p. Crossley D.R.6 (Nos. 961, 965 to 968)
 150 h.p. Euston 6 V.P.P.M. (No. 947)

Displacement (tons): *Standard* 77
Dimensions (feet): *Length* (oa) 75.1 *Beam* 19.3 *Draught* 7.2
Machinery: Diesel, 120/150/160 h.p. (see above)
Speed (knots): 8
Range (miles): 1,040 @ 8 knots (120 h.p.); 900 @ 8 knots (150 & 160 h.p.)
Manning: 8 to 12
Armament: One 20mm Oerlikon (1 × 1), (not fitted to 959 to 968).

Ship	Pend. No.	Role	Cons. Time	Comm.	Fate
Pandion	GPV 947	Loop Repair	6m	22/8/44	Broken Up 1950
Limicola	GPV 948	Loop Repair	6m	4/10/44	Sold 1958
Larus	GPV 949	Loop Repair	6m	19/12/44	Sold 1959
Limosa	GPV 950	Loop Repair	6m	3/11/44	Sold 1946
Tringa	GPV 951	ASDIC Repair	8m	19/3/45	Sold 1959
Sterna	GPV 952	Radar Repair	10m	30/5/45	Sold 1958
–	GPV 953	–	10m	28/8/45	Sold 1956
–	GPV 954	–	9m	17/8/45	Sold 1959
–	GPV 955	–	10m	17/8/45	Sold 1951
–	GPV 956	–	9m	20/8/45	Sold 1959
–	GPV 957	–	9m	28/8/45	Sold 1968
–	GPV 958	–	9m	6/9/45	Sold 1983
–	GPV 959	–	9m	19/9/45	Sold 1959
–	GPV 960	–	9m	5/10/45	Sold 1957
Albatross	GPV 961	–	7m	19/10/45	Sold 1971
Walrus	GPV 962	Water Tender	8m	5/11/45	Sold 1971
–	GPV 963	–	7m	26/11/45	Sold 1959
Mindari	GPV 964	–	8m	12/1945	Sold 1956
Nyanie	GPV 965	–	7m	12/5/49	Sold 1956
Brolga	GPV 966	Survey Tender	8m	7/5/46	Sold 1959
Jabiru	GPV 967	Survey Tender	10m	13/5/46	Sold 1959
Tallarook	GPV 968	Survey Tender	10m	28/5/46	Deleted 1969

GPV 965, NYANIA. (Photo – P. Britz)

GPV 968, post-war.

LAUNCHES/MOTOR BOATS
20 Ships

Four of the following boats were attached to combined operations and are marked with an asterisk.

Name	Details	Status
Ashodel	30 × 9.6 feet	Built 1934 Req. 17/5/43 Purch. 23/12/43 Sold 4/1945
Evelyn	31 × 8 × 3 feet	Built 1935 Sold 2/1946
Grey Ghost	–	Built – Sold 26/1/46
Gwen	–	Built – Purch. 3/1942 Sold 1/1948
Huon	38 × 9.6 feet	Built 1913 Sold 1946
Jackeroo	34 × 10 feet	Built – Req. 2/8/42 Purch. 23/3/43 RAN 2/1944 Sold 5/1946
June	43 × 12 feet	Built – Req. 9/1942 Purch. 7/1943 Sold 12/1945
Lil John*	37 × 10.6 feet	Built 1940 Req. 7/1942 USAFIA 4/1943 Purch. 6/1944 Sold 3/1946
Moonglo	–	–
Moreton	–	–
Natoonda*	–	Req. 23/7/42 Purch. 1/1943 USAFIA 4/1943
Neta*	36 × 10.6 feet 40 h.p.	Built 1912 Req. 19/7/42
Omar	–	NOIC – Sold 4/1945
Otter	–	–
Pagrus	–	–
Patricia	–	–
Potrero (FY36)	5 tons	Built – Comm. 7/1942
Rooana	–	–

Name	Details	Status
Ruel*	37 × 10.6 feet	Built 1940 Req. 21/7/42 Purch. 2/1943 NOIC – Sold 3/1946
Tritton	28 × 9 feet	Built – Sold 1/1946

In addition to the 20 craft listed here, hundreds of minor harbour craft including barges, motor dories, pinnaces, lighters, launches personnel boats and work boats were in use.

GREY GHOST before requisitioning. (Photo – K. Hughes)

120 FOOT MOTOR LIGHTERS
MRL Nos. 251–253, MSL Nos. 251–252 and MWL Nos. 251, 253–257

Eleven 120 foot motor lighters were constructed, three of which were refrigerated. Each lighter could transport more than 4,750 cubic feet of refrigerated cargo. Four derricks were provided to load and unload cargoes. MRL 254 and MRL 255 were cancelled in November, 1945.

Two stores lighters were completed. Cargo capacity was 180 tons in the hold. Like the refrigerated version, the MSLs carried four derricks.

The six water-lighters could carry 175 tons of fresh water, plus 50 tons of dry cargo. Two derricks and one derrick post were fitted. MWL 252, 258, and 259 were completed for private trade in 1946.

Other 120 foot lighters were constructed for the Royal Navy, United States Navy, Australian Army and Royal Australian Air Force. Machinery and accommodation spaces were provided aft.

Displacement (tons): *Standard* 350
Dimensions (feet): *Length* (oa) 122.3 *Beam* 24.6 *Draught* 8.0
Machinery: Two diesel engines, Ruston 6VCBM except MWL 256 Atlas Polar
Speed (knots): $9\frac{1}{2}$
Range (miles): 3,000 @ 8 knots
Manning: 4/5
Armament: Three 20mm (3 × 1).

Pend. No.	Builder	Cons. Time	Comp.	Fate
REFRIGERATED				
MRL 251	Tullochs	8m	10/3/46	Sold 1958
MRL 252	Johnsons	7m	5/3/46	Deleted Early 1960s
MRL 253	Johnsons	–	6/46	In service 1983 as TV GAYUNDAH (TV 282)
STORES				
MSL 251	Tullochs	–	1946	Wrecked 23/6/50 while on loan to Dept. of External Territories.
MSL 252	Tullochs	–	1946	Sold 1974
WATER				
MWL 251	Structural Eng.	10m	5/46	Sold 1960s
MWL 253	State Dockyard	6m	26/9/45	Sold 1960s
MWL 254	State Dockyard	5m	20/11/45	Active 1983
MWL 255	State Dockyard	6m	5/2/46	Sold
MWL 256	State Dockyard	5m	11/3/46	Papua New Guinea 1983
MWL 257	A.E. Goodwin	9m	3/46	Active 1983

MSL 703, BORONIA. (Photo – Navy and Marine Corp. Museum)

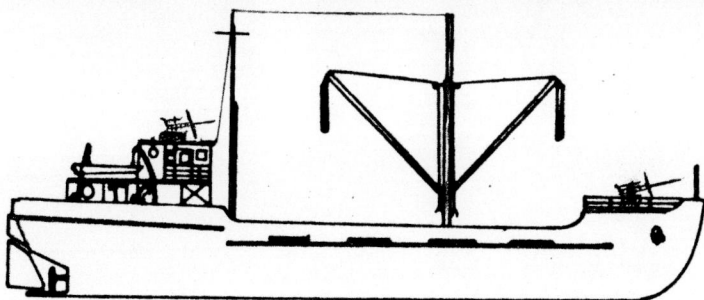

MWL; profile. (RAN)

MRL 252.

MWL 257, 1945. (Photo – P. Britz)

85 FOOT MOTOR STORES LIGHTERS
MSL Nos 701–708

Eight wooden MSLs were in service by the end of the Second World War. Each lighter could carry 600 gallons of water in the ship's tanks and was equipped with a 3-ton derrick. No. 709 was cancelled in 1945. No. 701 served in New Guinea; 702 at Darwin; 703 at Sydney; 704 at Fremantle; 705 to 707 in New Guinea; and 708 at Darwin.

Similar lighters were constructed for the Australian Army.

Displacement (tons): *Standard* 180
Dimensions (feet): *Length* (oa) 85.0 *Beam* 21.9 *Draught* 7.8
Machinery: Blackstone or Vivian diesels, 160 h.p.
Speed (knots): 8.75 knots
Range (miles): 1,000 @ $7\frac{1}{2}$ knots
Manning: 2 officers; 8 sailors
Armament: Nil.

MSL 707.

Ship	Pend. No.	Builder	Cons. Time	Comp.	Fate
Hixson	MSL 701	Botterill & Fraser	11m	22/3/44	Disposed of by burning 6/1964.
Beaver	MSL 702	Botterill & Fraser	1y 4m	26/8/44	Sold 1966
Boronia	MSL 703	Botterill & Fraser	1y	11/9/44	Sold 1971
–	MSL 704	Botterill & Fraser	11m	23/10/44	To Army 1958
–	MSL 705	Botterill & Fraser	1y 2m	11/4/45	Sold 1954
–	MSL 706	Botterill & Fraser	1y	11/5/45	Sold 1963
–	MSL 707	Botterill & Fraser	1y	4/6/45	Sold 1971
–	MSL 708	Botterill & Fraser	10m	7/7/45	Sold 1955

MSL 708.

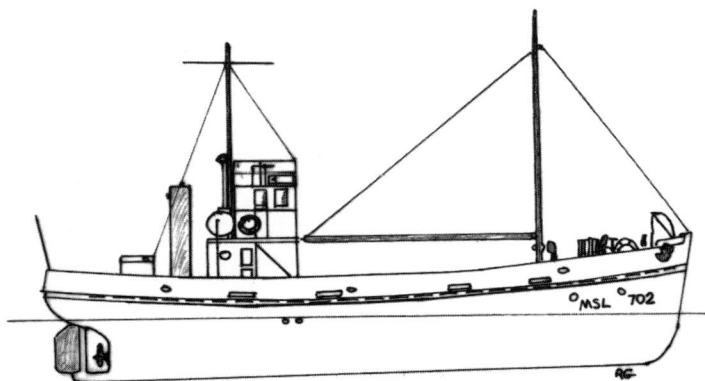

MSL 702; profile. (R. Gillett)

OIL FUEL LIGHTERS (DUMB) –
OFL Nos 1–4

Four old World War I oil fuel lighters (OFL Nos. 1, 2, 3 and 4) remained in service during World War II. Each lighter was fitted with ten tanks for a total capacity of 549.1 tons. OFL No. 3 was converted for sullage.

Displacement (tons): *Standard* N/A *Full Load* 944
Dimensions (feet): *Length* (oa) 156.0 *Beam* 30.0 *Draught* 9.3
Machinery: N/A
Speed (knots): N/A
Range (miles): N/A
Manning: N/A
Armament: N/A
Built: World War I.

OFL 1201, ROCKLEA, being launched in February, 1941.

OIL FUEL LIGHTERS (DUMB)
OFL Nos. 1201–1208

Each lighter could carry 1,204 tons of oil fuel and was fitted with four 2-ton pumps. To allow prolonged usage the lighter was fitted out with accommodation and galley spaces on the upper deck aft as well as a 15 foot dinghy. Only two OFLs were named.

Displacement (tons): *Gross* 803
Dimensions (feet): *Length* (oa) 187.9 *Beam* 37.3 *Draught* 12.3
Machinery: N/A
Speed (knots): N/A
Range (miles): N/A
Manning: N/A
Armament: N/A.

Ship	Pend. No.	Builder	Comp.	Fate
Rocklea	OFL 1201	Evans Deakin	23/11/40	In use 1983
–	OFL 1202	Morts Dock	22/2/45	In use 1983
–	OFL 1203	Morts Dock	22/3/45	In use 1983
–	OFL 1204	Poole & Steel	–	In use 1983
–	OFL 1205	Poole & Steel	29/10/45	Sold
–	OFL 1206	Williamstown	12/10/45	Mercantile 1968
–	OFL 1207	Williamstown	15/2/46	In use 1983
Karpoint	OFL 1208	Evans Deakin	22/9/45	In use 1983

OFL 1201, ROCKLEA.

1200 ton OFL; profile. (RAN)

REQUISITIONED LIGHTERS –
Sixteen Ships

From a peacetime fleet of only four WWI vintage OFLs, the navy found use for many old lighters in Australian and New Guinea waters. Three of their number were sunk.

Name	Details	Status
Agnes	–	–
Alc 3021	–	–
Ambon (FY35)	*Stores* 50 h.p. = $6\frac{1}{2}$ knots 1 × .303 Vickers	Built Comm. 21/9/42
Apa	*Coal* 267 gross tons 128.9 × 28 feet	Built 1882 Req. 17/4/41 Returned 13/2/47
Bosun	75 × 30 feet	Built – Req. 30/9/41 Purchased 20/5/42 Sold 12/1947
Carroo (FY47)	*Stores* 281 gross tons 130 × 25.1 feet 20 h.p. = 7 knots	Built 1897 Req. 9/6/42 Comm. 9/9/42 Returned 23/12/44
Florrie	*Torpedo lugger* 52 × 14 feet	Built – Req. 18/2/42 Torpedo Carrier 11/1943 Sold 12/1945
Iron Duke	*Water*	–
Kalaroo	*Water* 118 tons 96 × 23 feet	Built – Req. 26/2/41 Purchased 17/6/42 Petrol Lighter 1943 Sold 3/3/42
Karalee	*Water* 117 tons 103 × 23 feet	Built 1911 Req. 10/5/41 Sunk 3/3/42
Kelat	*Coal* 1,849 gross tons 261 × 41 feet	Built 1881 Req. 4/7/41 Sunk 24/2/42
Mombah	*Coal* 3,440 gross tons 315 × 50 feet	Built 1923 Req. 13/3/44 Sold 2/1948
No. 2 Lighter	–	Built – Req. 4/3/41 Returned 4/2/42 Sunk Darwin
Oura	110.6 × 25 feet	Built – Req. 15/4/42 Purchased 8/6/43 Sold 1948
Rona	*Coal* 610 gross 192.2 × 30.1 feet	Built 1885 Req. 12/8/43 Returned 11/9/46
Tiga (ex H.M. Monitor M16)	177.3 × 31 × 7 feet	Built 1915 Req. 30/7/42 Returned 4/8/42
Yampi Lass	*Stores* 45 gross tons 63 × 16 feet 40 h.p.	Built – Req. 23/1/42 Purchased 4/6/43 Sunk 11/4/43 Sold 26/10/46

HMAS CARROO

IRON DUKE alongside HMAS KINCHELA at Brisbane, 15th March, 1944.

MOMBAH at Morotai, 2nd June, 1945.

TIGA. (Photo – R. Gillett Collection)

DUMB LIGHTERS
16 Types

CAL 501, 50 ton ammunition lighter. (Photo – R. Gillett)

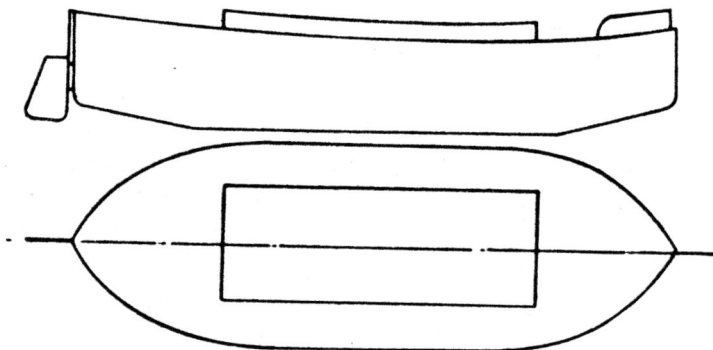

50 ton CAL; profile. (RAN)

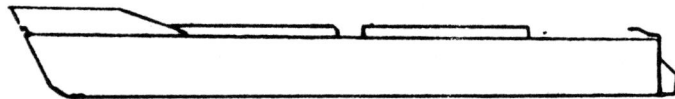

200 ton CAL; profile. (RAN)

Type	Details	Remarks
50 Ton Ammunition	45 × 17	One in use
100 Ton Ammunition	55 × 20	Twelve in use
120 Ton Ammunition	39 tons 60 × 24	
50 Ton Barge	50 × 17	
60 foot Cody Willis (flat top)	57 tons 60 × 26	
50 Ton Concrete Ammunition	69 × 18	Six in use
100 Ton Concrete Ammunition	90 × 21	Two in use
200 Ton Concrete Ammunition	107 × 25	Nine in use
100 Ton Phillipine	71 tons 60 × 25	Four in use (2 ex Army)
300 Ton Phillipine	100 × 27	Two in use (one ex Army)
35′ Steel	35 × 13	Five in use
54′ Sullage	54 × 20	Eleven in use
60′ Sydney Harbour	60 × 26	
Tobruk Lighter	28 tons 49.2 × 18	Seven in use
Victualling Yard	45 × 2.6	
50 Ton Welded Steel Lock Up	21.5 tons 55 × 16	One in use

REQUISITIONED LUGGERS
Fourteen Ships

The ubiquitous lugger provided yet another source of requisitioned craft to perform the all important odd jobs for the fleet, as well as a secondary patrol force.

Name	Details	Status
Arthur Rose (FY29)	*Tender* 21 gross tons 53 × 13.4 feet 27 h.p. = 3 knots 1 × .303 Vickers 2 rifles	Built – Comm. 9/9/42 Sold 24/10/45
Catherine R	18 gross tons	Built – Comm. 15/10/43 Sold 31/1/46
Francis	37.2 × 11.7 feet	Built 1908 Req. 4/1942 Sold 11/1945
Gloria	18 gross tons	Built – Req. 18/2/42 NAP 11/8/42 Comm. 15/10/43 Purchased 23/2/44 Sold 31/1/46
Griffoen (FY25)	*Transport* 45 h.p. = 6 knots 1 × .303 Vickers	Built – Comm. 27/5/42 Paid Off 15/2/44 USN 30/5/45
Heather	–	Built 1939 Req. 18/2/42 Sold 11/1945
Ibis (FY28)	*Tender* 21 gross tons 60 × 15 feet 20 h.p. = 7 knots 1 × .303 Vickers	Built 1931 Req. 2/1942 Comm. 6/1942 Sold 10/1945
Malanda (FY37)	*Net Layer* 57 tons 192 h.p. = 11 knots 1 × .303 Vickers	Built – Req. 23/3/42 Comm. 21/9/42
Mavie	19 tons	Built 1903 Appropriated 12/41 Comm. 31/12/41 Lost 19/2/42
Medic	–	Built – Seized 12/1941 Sold 3/1947
Red Bill (FY27)	21 gross tons 60 × 15 feet 8 h.p. = 4 knots 1 × .303 Vickers	Built 1933 Req. 20/4/42 Comm. 15/6/42 Sold 15/1/46

Name	Details	Status
St. Francis (FY26)	18 h.p. 1 × .303 Vickers	Built – Comm. 21/3/42
Tarneit	105.6 × 20 feet	Built 1942 Req. 2/6/43 Purchased 27/3/44 Sold 6/1946
Winnie	22 h.p. 58 × 14 feet	Built – Req. 18/2/42 Army 30/6/42 Sold 26/1/46

HEATHER.

FLEET OILER

Kurumba

KURUMBA served with the Royal Navy from 1916 and with the RAN from 1919. She paid off and was placed in reserve on 5th June, 1928. During World War II KURUMBA operated in Australian waters and sailed to New Guinea, the Netherlands East Indies and the Phillipines. From March, 1942, she was used as a U.S. fleet oiler.

KURUMBA was de-stored at Brisbane on 29th July, 1946, and in November, 1947, was sold for £27,500 to the Artemis Maritime Co. Inc. of Panama.

Displacement (tons): *Standard* 7,806
Dimensions (feet): *Length* (oa) 378.0 *Beam* 45.6 *Draught* 23.3
Machinery: 2 sets triple expansion steam, 2,300 h.p.
Speed (knots): 10
Range (miles): N/A
Manning: 60
Armament: One 4-inch (1 × 1), Four .303 Vickers

Ship	Pend. No.	Builder	Cons. Time	Comm.	Fate
Kurumba	X 36 (1.18) X 64 (1939)	Swan Hunter	1y 3m	4/9/39	Sold 20/11/47

KURUMBA, 1939. The water tender RIPPLE and oil ligher No. 4 lie alongside. (Photo – R. Wright Collection)

REQUISITIONED OILERS
Thirteen Ships

For a fleet at war, the lone KURUMBA was unable to satisfy all replenishment needs. To meet the increasing demand for oil products, 13 auxiliary oilers were placed at the disposal of the RAN for varying periods.

Name	Details	Status
Aase Maersk	6,184 gross tons 407 × 54.7 feet 489 h.p. = 11 knots 1 × 4-inch, 1 × 12 pdr. MGs	Built 1930 USN 6/10/42 RAN – WWII Returned 1945
Bishopdale (X66)	17,357 gross tons 481.7 × 61.9 490 n.h.p. = 11.5 knots 2 DCs	Built 1937 Req. 4/1942 RN 1945
British Sailor	–	Built – Req. 1/1/42 Returned 12/5/42 Req. 21/5/42 Returned 6/10/42
Capsa	–	Built – Req. 8/1942
Cedar Mills	–	–
Colina	–	–
Falkefjell	7,927 gross tons 462 × 59.7 feet 778 n.h.p. = $11\frac{1}{2}$ knots	Built 1931 Req. 11/12/41 Returned 20/4/42
Gadila	*Storage vessel*	Built – Req. 20/6/42 Returned 21/8/42
Madrono	*Storage vessel*	Built – Req. 25/5/42 Returned 4/6/42
Ostav	*Storage vessel*	Built – Req. 20/6/42 Returned 2/7/42
Peek	*Storage vessel*	Built – Req. 28/5/42 Returned 22/6/42
Vera	–	Built – Req. 9/1942
Yamhill	–	Built – Req. 4/1944

AASE MAERSK.

BISHOPDALE as a Royal Fleet Auxiliary. (Photo – S. Given)

BISHOPDALE, 20th February, 1943.

REPAIR AND BASE SHIP

Platypus

'PLATYPUS' was originally constructed as the fleet's submarine depot ship. In July, 1922, she was re-designated a destroyer depot and fleet repair ship, and in March, 1929, as a submarine tender. During 1930 she became the depot ship at Garden Island and was renamed PENGUIN. She continued in this capacity until 26th February, 1941, when she was recommissioned for sea-going service as a training ship.

In May, 1941, she proceeded to Darwin to act as a base ship and later to Cairns fulfilling a similar role. PLATYPUS underwent a major refit at the Williamstown dockyard between June and December, 1945. She sailed to New Guinea on 5th January, 1945 for service as a repair and maintenance vessel. These duties kept the ship busy until December, 1945. On 13th May, 1946, PLATYPUS paid off, but continued to give services as headquarters ship for vessels in reserve. She was sold in 1958.

Displacement (tons): *Standard* 3,476
Dimensions (feet): *Length* (oa) 325.0 *Beam* 44.0 *Draught* 15.8
Machinery: Triple expansion engines (2 sets), 3,500 h.p.
Speed (knots): 15.5
Range (miles): N/A
Manning: 304
Armament: Two 4-inch (2 × 1), Two 20mm (2 × 1), Two .303 Lewis.

Ship	Pend. No.	Builder	Cons. Time	Comm.	Fate
Platypus	D56 F123	John Brown	2y 4m	2/3/17	Sold 20/2/58

HMAS PENGUIN (ex PLATYPUS) as a depot ship, Garden Island.

HMAS PLATYPUS, New Guinea, 1945. HMA Ships BOWEN and AIR CLAN lie alongside with the Army workboat SOLLUM (AM 1629) outboard of the air-sea rescue vessel. (109365)

HMAS PLATYPUS, 1941.

Workshop interior of HMAS PLATYPUS at Morotai, 27th May, 1943. (109336).

REQUISITIONED REPAIR SHIPS
Two Ships

HMAS KOOPA, 25th October, 1943.

WHANG PU.

Name	Details	Status
Koopa **(FY49)**	*River Steamer* 416 gross tons 192.7 × 28.1 × 8.7 feet	Built 1911 Req. 10/8/42 Comm. 14/9/42 RN 26/7/45 RAN 24/9/45 Returned 10/1/49
Whang Pu **(FY03)**	*River Steamer* 3,204 gross tons 228 × 46 × 11.6 feet 11.5 knots 1 × 40mm, 3 × 20mm 2 × twin 0.5-inch Colt MGs	Built 1920 Req. 13/12/41 (RN) Comm. 1/10/43 (RAN) Repair Ship 5/1944 Stores Ship 1945 Paid Off 22/4/46

REQUISITIONED AMMUNITION & STORES SHIPS – *Ten Ships*

HMAS CHARON, Simpson Harbour, New Britain, 30th November, 1945.

Name	Details	Status
Baralba	*Steamer* 998 gross tons 211.6 × 33.9 feet 8 knots	Built 1921 Req. 31/5/42 Returned 11/2/43
Charon	*Steamer* 3,600 gross tons	Built 1936 Req. 18/3/42 Returned 1945
Franklin	(SEE EXAMINATION VESSELS)	
Mamutu	*Motor vessel* 300 gross tons 113 × 25 × 10 feet	Built 1938 Req. 16/12/41 Returned 1/1942
Matafele **(FY67)**	*Motor vessel* 335 gross tons 115.5 × 25.6 × 10.6 ft diesel	Built 1938 Req. 12/1942 Comm. 1/1/43 Sunk 20/6/44
Merkur	*Motor vessel* 5,952 tons 393.1 × 51.9 × 21.5 ft 12.5 knots 1 × 4-inch, 2 × 20mm 4 × .303 Vickers	Built 1924 Req. 12/12/41 Returned 1945
Mulcra	*Motor vessel* 1,200 gross tons 215.8 × 34.2 feet	Built 1925 Req. 1945 Comm. 11/6/45 Returned 10/1/46

HMAS POYANG: one 4-inch gun forward and 20mm gun before the mainmast.(Photo – J. Straczek)

Name	Details	Status
Ping Wo **(FL150)**	*River Steamer* 3,105 gross tons 300 × 48 × 13.6 feet Triple expansion engines = 14 knots 11 days @ 10 knots Crew 50 1 × 12 pdr., 2 × 20mm (later 4 × .303 Vickers, DCCs)	Built 1922 Req. 12/1941 (RN) Paid Off 19/5/42 Comm. 22/5/42 (RAN) Repair Ship 1945 Paid Off 24/6/46 Returned 1946
Poyang **(FY20)**	*Steamer* 2,873 gross tons 299.8 × 44.2 × 23 ft 13 knots 13½ days @ 11 knots 1 × 4-inch, 1 × 20mm 2 × .303 Vickers	Built 1941 Req. 12/5/42 Comm. 6/12/43 Returned 19/8/45
Poyrord	–	Built – Comm. 7/1942
Yunnan **(FL151)**	*Motor vessel* 2,812 gross tons 299.8 × 44.2 × 17.6 feet 11 knots 44 days @ 11 knots 2 × .303 Vickers 1 × 20mm	Built 1934 Req. 22/6/42 Comm. 20/9/44 Returned 31/1/46

HMAS MATAFELE.

HMAS PING WO, 1945; the forward gun has been deleted, although two small guns are carried behind the bridge and on the upper deck aft.

SURVEY BOATS

Blowfly, Sandfly

Survey motor-boat SANDFLY.

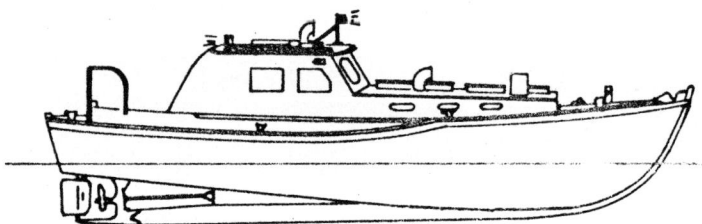

SANDFLY; profile. (RAN)

Both built at Garden Island 1944–45. SANDFLY later attached to WARREGO. Could also carry 10 passengers or 3/4 ton of cargo.

Displacement (tons): 6.9
Dimensions (feet): *Length* 34 *Beam* 8.3 *Draught* 4
Machinery: Diesel, Chrysler M12 (SANDFLY); Perkins S6M (BLOWFLY)
Speed (knots): 9½
Range (miles): 135
Manning: 2
Armament: Nil

REQUISITIONED SURVEY SHIPS
Seven Ships

The 1,320 ton MORESBY was acquired as a survey ship in 1925. Although active as an anti-submarine escort vessel from 1940 she resumed survey duties in late 1943.

BANGALOW, 1939.

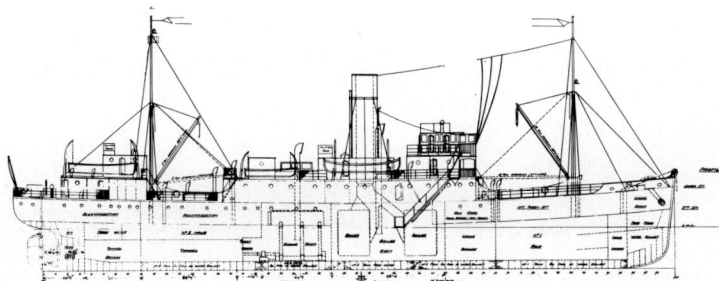

CAPE LEEUWIN; inboard profile as built. (Cockatoo Dockyard)

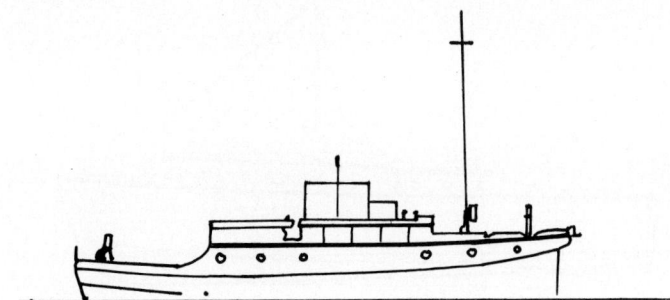

WINTER: profile. (R. Gillett)

HMAS STELLA: a small machine gun is carried at the bow and the 20mm Oerlikon aft.

Name	Details	Status
Alert	–	In use 1945
Bangalow (FY23)	Steamer 648 tons 162 × 36 × 11 feet Triple expansion reciprocating = 10 knots 1,800 miles @ 10 knots Crew 44 1 × 12 pdr., 2 × 20mm 2 × .303 Vickers	Built 1939 Req. 3/1942 Comm. 23/6/42 Returned 18/1/46
Cape Leeuwin (FY30)	Steamer 2,050 tons 235.5 × 35 × 14.8½ feet 11.5 knots 1 × 12 pdr., 1 × 20mm	Built 1924/25 Req. 27/8/43 Comm. 27/8/43 Paid Off 12/12/45 Returned 1945
Kwato (Q90)	Motor vessel 43 gross tons 43 × 14.8 × 6 feet Twin Widdgo diesels = 8 knots 2 × .303 Vickers	Built 1938 Req. 18/2/42 Comm. 7/1942 Purchased 3/1944 Deleted 1/1949
Polaris (FY63)	Motor vessel 50 gross tons 1 × .303 Vickers	Built – Comm. 11/1942 Returned 1944
Stella (FY43)	Motor vessel 111 gross tons 82 × 19 × 8 feet British Polar diesel, 200 b.h.p. = 8 knots 1 × 20mm	Built 1938 Req. 1/10/42 Comm. 22/10/42 Paid Off 19/12/45 Returned 29/10/46 Purchased 1951 Sold 3/1966
Winter (FY04)	Launch 60 × 17.6 × 11 feet Man marine diesel, 120 h.p.	Built 1942 Req. 9/9/42 Sold 25/1/46

TORPEDO RECOVERY VESSELS
TRV Nos 1–3

Three wooden torpedo recovery vessels were in service during the latter years of World War II. TRV 3, sold in 1968, survives as a cruise vessel in Sydney. TRV 2, the longest survivor, was reduced to reserve in 1970 and sold the following year.

Displacement (tons): *Standard* N/A
Dimensions (feet): *Length (oa)* 60.2 *Beam* 13.10
Machinery: Three Perkins 56-M diesels
Speed (knots): 12
Range (miles): 550
Manning: N/A
Armament: Nil

Pend. No.	Builder	Comp.	Fate
TRV 1	–	1944/45	Sold 1960s
TRV 2	–	1944/45	Sold 1971
TRV 3	–	1944/45	Sold 1968

TRV 2. (Photo – J. Mortimer)

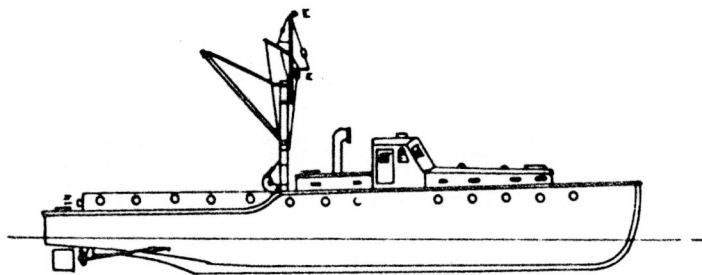

TRV 1; profile. (RAN)

TORPEDO RECOVERY BOATS
TRB Nos. 585–586

TRB 585, named LOCH LONG, and TRB 586, named BIN-CLEAVES, were ordered in 1942. Both craft operated from the Pittwater torpedo range, north of Sydney. LOCH LONG was sold in February, 1978.

Two smaller craft, GREENOCK and ALDWYCH, built in 1944, were also in service with the torpedo factory.

In total 147, 38 foot defence boats were constructed by Lars Halvorsen and Sons at Ryde, N.S.W. Fifty served with the Army, 43 with the RAAF, 50 in the US Army and two with Dutch forces.

Originally one 0.5-inch Browning or .303-inch twin Vickers machine gun could be mounted.

Displacement (tons): *Standard* 5 (approx.)
Dimensions (feet): *Length (oa)* 38.0 *Beam* 10.9 *Draught* 2.9
Machinery: Two Ford diesels, 225 h.p.
Speed (knots): 24
Range (hours): $28\frac{1}{2}$ hours @ 24 knots
Manning: 3
Armament: Small arms.

Pend. No.	Builder	Comp.	Fate
TRB 585	Halvorsens	1943	Sold 1978
TRB 586	Halvorsens	1943	Active

TRB 585. (Photo – G. Merlin)

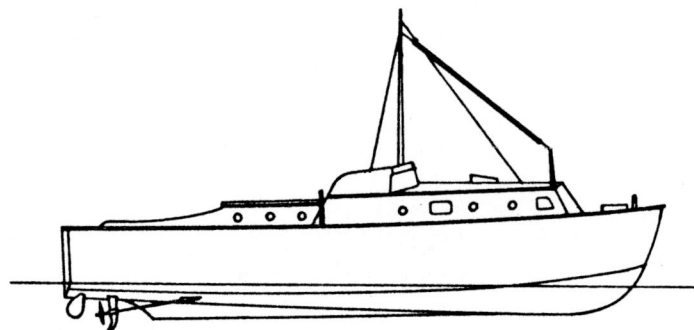

TRB 585; profile. (RAN)

FLEET TUGS

Reserve, Sprightly

RESERVE, SPRIGHTLY and their sister ship TANCRED (operated by the Commonwealth Salvage Board), were built in the U.S.A. to an Admiralty design on behalf of the Commonwealth Government. Each tug was designed to maintain a towing speed of 10 knots in fair weather, hauling a 10,000 ton vessel. Both were transferred to the RAN under the Lend-Lease Agreement. Their original names were BAT 11 (RESERVE) and BAT 12 (SPRIGHTLY).

Both RAN tugs saw service in waters in the north of Australia. RESERVE paid off on 19th October, 1953. SPRIGHTLY was laid up on 23rd February, 1946, recommissioned on 23rd November, 1953, and paid off in June, 1959. After being leased to a salvage company 1961–63, she was again laid up.

HMAS RESERVE post-war. (Photo – P. Britz)

Displacement (tons): *Full Load* 800
Dimensions (feet): *Length (oa)* 143.0 *Beam* 33.0 *Draught* 16.0
Machinery: Twin diesel-electric engines, 1,875 i.h.p.
Speed (knots): 14
Range (miles): N/A
Manning: 34
Armament: One 3-inch (1 × 1), Two 20 mm (2 × 1), One 0.5-inch MG.

Ship	Pend. No.	Builder	Cons. Time	Comm.	Fate
Reserve	W149	Levingstone	1y 3m	27/8/43	Sold 21/9/61
Sprightly	W103	Levingstone	1y 8m	23/2/44	Sold 29/8/69

HMAS SPRIGHTLY during the 1950s.

45 FOOT TOW BOATS
TB Nos 1–12

Ten wooden harbour tugs served in the RAN from 1945. The other two, TB 7, completed in January, 1946, and TB 11, also completed in 1946 and transferred in 1947, did not see war service. TB 5 was deleted in the late 1960s, after service at Tarangua with TB 6.

TB 10 (named CERBERUS IV) relieved KOORONGA at Western Port in 1948 and was sold in 1958. TB 9 (named SARDIUS) and AT 1536 (acquired in 1958 as replacement for TB 10) continue in service. AT 1536 was named CERBERUS V.

Similar craft were operated by the Australian Army, AT 1536 being originally christened DOOEN for Army service.

Displacement (tons): *Standard* 30
Dimensions (feet): *Length (oa)* 45.8 *Beam* 15.2 *Draught* 6.0
Machinery: Diesel, 270 h.p; Hercules DNX6 in Nos 5, 6, 7, 9, 11 & 12; Gray 6/71 in TB 10.
Speed (knots): 8
Range (miles): 500
Manning: 4
Armament: Nil.

TB 7.

TB 9 as rebuilt post-war. (Photo – B. J. Browne)

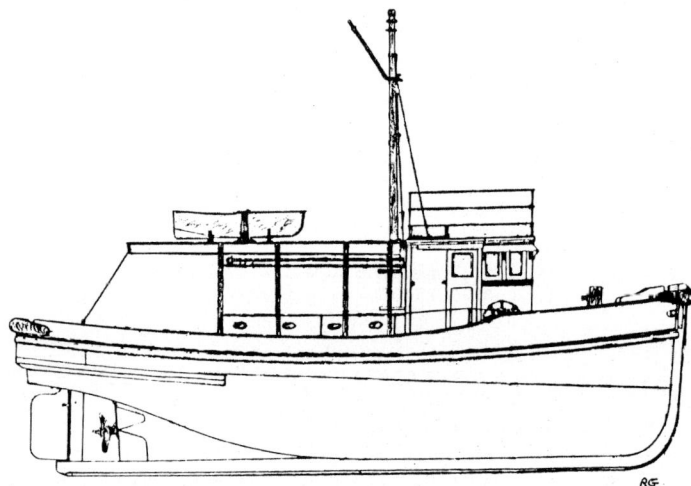

TB4; profile. (R. Gillett)

Pend. No.	Builder	Cons. Time	Comp.	Fate
TB 1	J. Wallace	7m	9/1945	RN 10/1945
TB 2	South Coast Co-Op	10m	12/1945	To Netherlands East Indies
TB 3	South Coast Co-Op	1y	12/1945	To Netherlands East Indies
TB 4	South Coast Co-Op	1y	1945	To Netherlands East Indies
TB 5	G. Green	–	1945	Sold 1960s
TB 6	Brooks Robinson	8m	8/1945	Sold
TB 7	W.C. Cone	11m	1/1946	Deleted 1960s
TB 8	Brooks Robinson	7m	10/1945	Sunk late 1940s
TB 9	Brooks Robinson	7m	10/1945	Active
TB 10	Brooks Robinson	–	1945	Sold 1958
TB 11	Slavengers	–	1946	Transferred 1947
TB 12	Barnes	6m	12/1945	–

REQUISITIONED TUGS
Eight Ships

WATO, one of eight tugs requisitioned by the RAN during 1939–45 held the distinction of the oldest commissioned vessel of the war.

Name	Details	Status
Elwing (FY42)	47 gross tons 63.8 × 15.7 × 6.5 feet Vivian diesel, 160 h.p. Crew 10	Built 1933 Req. 16/6/42 Comm. 16/6/42 Purchased 26/10/43 Sold 5/1947
Forceful (WI26)	288 gross tons 121 × 27.1 × 13.3 feet Triple expansion, 187 h.p. = 12 knots Crew 20 1 × 20mm, 1 × .303 Vickers	Built 1925 Req. 31/1/42 Comm. 16/2/42 Returned 11/10/43
George Dinsdale	–	Built – Req. 8/5/45 Comm. 5/1945
Heros (WI30) (FY87)	382 gross tons 135.4 × 29 × 13.6 feet Triple expansion = 12 kts Crew 32 1 × 12 pdr., 2 × .303 Vickers, 2 DCTs	Built 1919 Req. 2/11/39 Comm. 12/1/40 Returned 13/8/42 Req. 12/2/43 Comm. 25/2/43 Paid Off 12/2/46 Returned 5/11/47
James Wallace	192 gross tons 109 × 23.6 × 11.7 feet 80 h.p. steam engine, 750 i.h.p. = 10 knots	Built 1924 Req. 1945 Sold 26/4/47
St Giles (FY 86)	380 gross tons 135.4 × 29 × 13.6 feet Triple expansion, 208 h.p. = 12 knots 1 × 12 pdr.	Built 1919 Req. 2/11/39 Comm. 15/1/40 Returned 18/5/42 Req. 8/1945 Paid Off 11/3/46 Returned 4/6/47

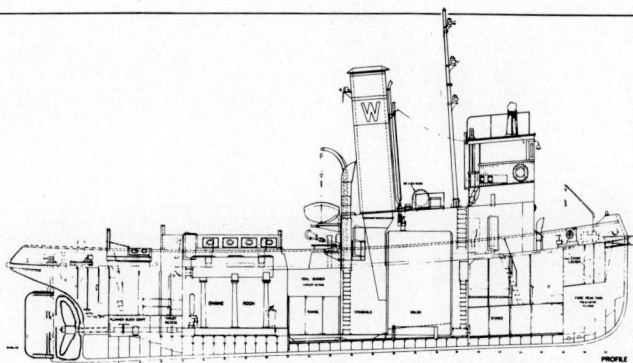

Name	Details	Status
Waree (WI28)	253 gross tons 95 × 25 × 13.5 feet 860 h.p. Crew 21 2 MGs	Built 1939 Req. 4/9/42 Comm. 18/9/42 Wrecked 17/10/46
Wato (WI27)	292 gross tons 125 × 23.7 × 13.9 feet Triple expansion steam, 660 h.p. = 11.5 knots 9 days @ 11.5 knots Crew 20 2 × .303 Vickers, 1 × 20mm	Built 1904 Req. 19/4/41 Comm. 11/5/41 Paid Off 12/11/45 Returned 27/5/46

WAREE, 1939; inboard profile. (P. Webb)

HMAS ST. GILES.

HMAS HEROS sailing from Sydney

HMAS WATO, Brisbane.

OTHER TUGS
Five Ships

BEAVER – Commercial Hire 4/10/41 to 19/11/41
CARLOCK – 8/5/42 to 13/5/42 and 21/5/42 to 29/5/42
TOORONGA – Chartered 23/10/43 to 15/12/43
UCO – 23/8/41 to 13/9/41
UTA – 2/1943

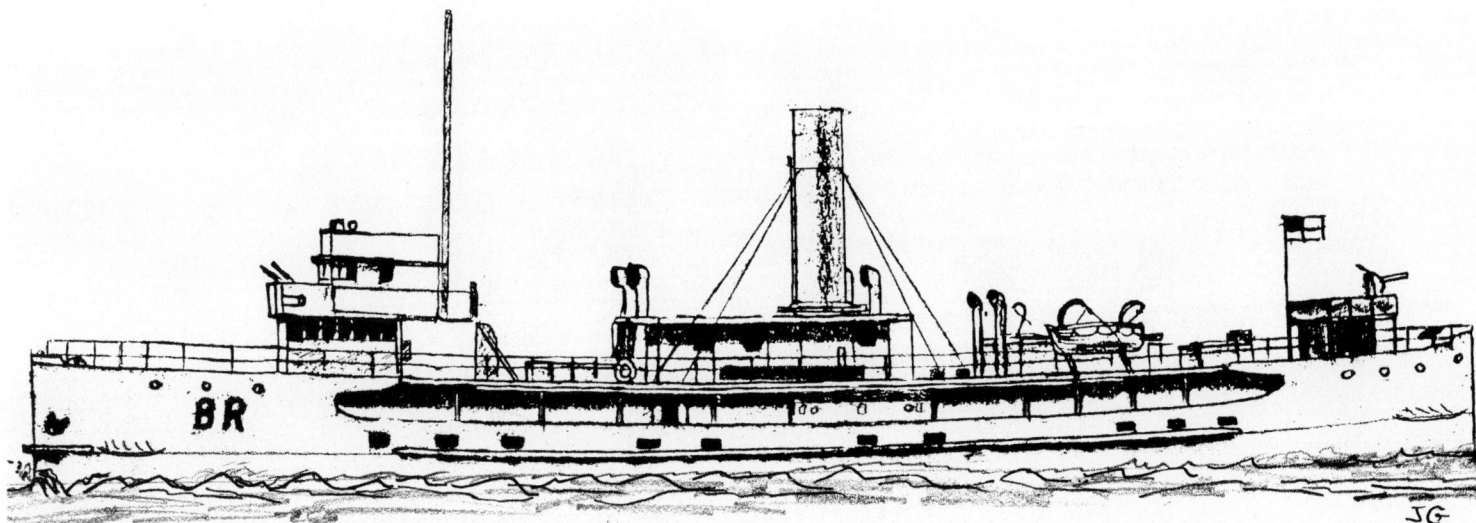

HMAS K9.

REQUISITIONED TRAINING SHIPS – *Three Ships*

Training was carried out on most major fleet units to increase the number of ships available for active service. BURRA BRA also operated as a target vessel, working in conjunction with the RAAF.

During her brief service with the RAN, K9 spent more time in dockyard hands than at sea. She was an unsuccessful acquisition due to her numerous mechanical defects.

Name	Details	Status
Burra Bra (FY69)	*Ferry* 458 gross tons 195.3 × 31.7 × 13.5 feet 3 cylinder triple expansion steam, 100 n.h.p. 13 knots 1 × 12 pdr., 2 × .303 Vickers, 2 DC	Built 1908 Req. 13/11/42 Comm. 1/2/43 Purchased 25/8/43 Paid Off 1/6/44 Sold 11/1947
K9 (N39)	*Submarine* 521 tons surfaced, 712 tons submerged 210.3 × 17.9 × 11.8 feet 2 Shelde–Sulzer diesels 15 knots surfaced, 9½ knots submerged 4 × 17.7-inch torpedo tubes	Built 1922 Comm. 22/6/43 Paid Off 31/3/44 Wrecked 7/6/45
Emlyn Castle	*Ketch* 18 gross tons 25 × 12 × 5 feet	Built 1938 Req. 18/2/42 Sold 11/1945

HMAS BURRA BRA, 1943; profile. (J. Gunter)

Right – BURRA BRA in Wooloomooloo Bay, 1945; the 12 pounder gun is mounted on a bandstand aft. A tug is manoeuvring BURRA BRA (serving as a steam supply vessel) into the berth. (Photo – R. Gillett collection).

Below – BURRA BRA alongside a Royal Navy escort carrier in Circular Quay, 1945. She still retains her original Manly Ferry bridge and single funnel. (Photo – R. Gillett collection).

TRANSPORTS, FUEL, STORE AND WATER CARRIERS – *37 Ships*

Requisitioned for short or intermittent periods.

Arkaba
Barossa
Burwah
Deagon (water)
Diggers
Duntroon
Edendale
Fiona
Giangann
Gorgon
Islander
James Cook (stores)
Jarrandale (water)
Katoomba
Koolana
Lakatoi
Macdhui
Mako
Mangola

Manutu
Mollyhawk
Moonta
Morinda
Muliana
Mundalla (stores)
Narbada
Neptuna
Nicol Bay
Orungal
Period
Port Tauraiga
Rockingham (water)
Southern Cross VII (stores)
Taroona
Toulouse
Urises
Zealandia

AWB 426. (Photo – R. Wright)

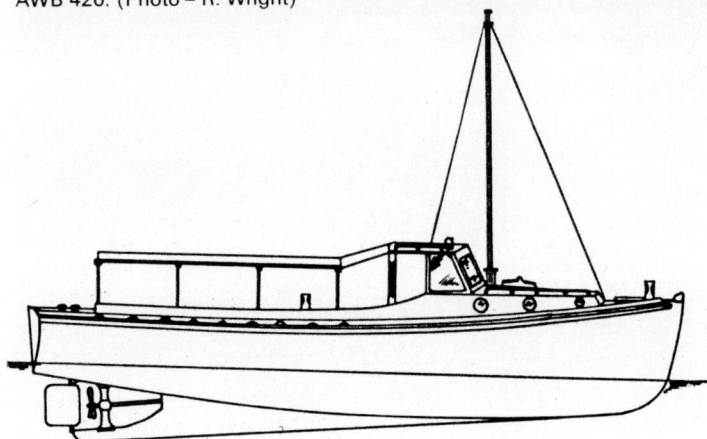

40 foot workboat; profile. (RAN)

40 FOOT WORKBOATS
50 Ships

About fifty 40 foot workboats were constructed for the RAN by various shipbuilders, including Brine, W.A., General Motors Holden, Ford Motor Co., Victoria, and Botterill & Fraser. Other boats were constructed for the Australian Army and R.A.A.F.

The Navy craft were on charge throughout Australia and New Guinea. Only two received names, AWB 404 TOPAZ and AWB 420, AMETHYST. Both were based in Sydney.

Forty-three remained in service or in reserve on 1st November, 1947.

In 1983 some 25 were still in use, a number of which had been rebuilt.

Displacement (tons): *Full load* 10 (approx)
Dimensions (feet): *Length* 40 *Beam* 12.5 *Draught* 4.6
Machinery: Cadillac petrol or Gray 64 HN9 diesel or Chrysler M8 petrol, 175 h.p.
Speed (knots): 9
Range (miles): 600
Manning: 1
Armament: Nil.

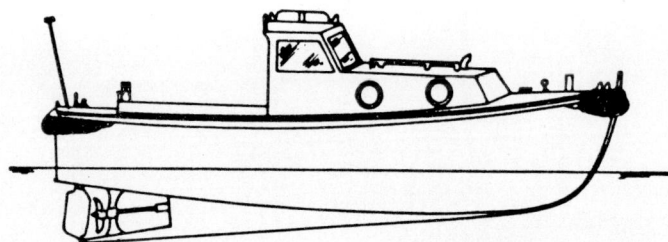

26 foot motor dory; profile. (RAN)

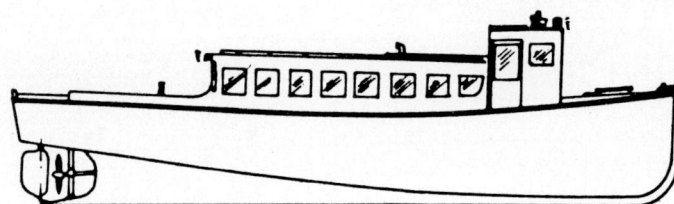

45 foot motor boat; profile. (RAN)

MISCELLANEOUS REQUISITIONED VESSELS
27 Ships

Name	Details	Status
Annaiawe	*Tender* at HMAS **ORION**	Built – Comm. 28/12/42
Ban Hong Liong	*Trawler* 1,671 gross tons 269.9 × 40.4 feet 10 knots	Built – Returned 1945/46
Beth	Tender to HMAS **TORRENS**	Built – Comm. 22/9/42
Caroline	*Auxiliary*	
Chinampa (FY31)	*Ketch* 60 tons 4 cylinder Vivian diesel, 80 h.p. 7.5 knots Endurance 8 days 1 × .303 Vickers, 2 rifles	Built 1938 Req. 18/2/42 Comm. 1/3/42 Purch. 28/8/42 Sold 21/2/46

Name	Details	Status
Everon II	*Ketch* 10 gross tons 36 × 10.6 × 4 feet 16/24 h.p. Ailsa Craig diesel	Built 1942 Req. 18/8/42 Purch. 26/2/43 Sold 1946
Innisfail (FY21)	*Steamer* 399 gross tons 144.6 × 32.3 × 7.1 10.5 knots 1 × 12 pdr., 1 × .303 Vickers, DCCs	Built 1912 Req. 3/9/41 Comm. 30/10/41 Decommissioned 1/3/46 Returned 28/6/46
Jon Jim (FY59)	*Trawler* Ex Iadava	Built – Req. 8/2/42 Comm. 1/4/43 Purch. 9/1944 Sold 6/1946

HMAS INNISFAIL.

Name	Details	Status
Kai Kai	*Ferry*	Built 1907
	Accomodation Vessel	Hired intermittently
	303 gross tons	1940–42
	152 × 33 × 11.9 feet	Purch. 4/3/43
		Sold 2/6/47
Kavite	*Ketch*	Built –
		Sold 1/1946
Kieth Cam	–	–
(FY45)		
Kuranda	*Ferry*	–
Kuttabul	*Ferry*	Built 1922
	Accomodation Vessel	Req. 7/11/40
	447 gross tons	Comm. 26/2/41
	182.6 × 36.9 × 13.9 feet	Sunk 1/6/42
Lookout	*Motor Vessel*	Built 1939
(FY70)	71.8 tons	Req. 12/1942
	93 × 18 × 5 feet	Comm. 1/5/43
	Diesel, 230 h.p.	Renamed 27/12/43
	11 knots	WATCHER
		Sunk 14/5/45
Lurgurena	*Punt*	–
M.M.44	*Deperming*	Built –
		Req. 30/11/42
		Purch. 14/4/43
Maroubra	*Cutter*	Built 1930
(FY40)	49 gross tons	Req. 20/3/42
	61.4 × 18.4 feet	Comm. 21/9/42
	72 h.p.	Sunk 10/5/43
	8 knots	
	1 × .303 Vickers	
Nepean	1 × .303 Vickers	Built 1925
	60 h.p. = 8 knots	Comm. 31/7/42
		Purch. 31/8/42
		Sold 1945

Name	Details	Status
Parvanger	*Motor Launch*	Built 1936
	Deperming	Req. 15/1/43
	36.9 × 11.5 feet	Purch. 17/9/43
	14 h.p.	BDV: 6/1944
		Sold 27/7/46
Protem	*Deperming*	–
30′ Punt	Not named	Built –
	Deperming	Req. 13/1/43
		Returned 31/3/43
Ripple	*Tank Vessel*	Built 1904
	390 gross tons	Acquired 1/7/13
	120 × 21 feet	Sold 1949
	triple expansion	Scrapped 1951
	8 knots	
South	–	Built –
Seaman		Req. 12/1941
		Sunk 2/12/42
		Raised 5/2/43
		Returned 2/1943
Springdale	*Deperming*	–
Sulituan	*Ketch*	Built –
(FY 39)	15 tons	Req. 20/4/42
	43 × 12.6 × 6 feet	P.O. 3/1943
		Sold 3/1948
Swiftsure	–	Built –
		Req. 21/5/42
		Purchased 26/1/42
Weerutta	–	Built –
		Comm. 16/9/42

RIPPLE alongside the auxiliary minelayer HMAS BUNGAREE.

Bottom – KUTTABUL, 1st June, 1942. (42975)

Interior damage to KUTTABUL following the midget submarine attack of 31st May/1st June, 1942.

HMAS MAROUBRA: with a single .303 Vickers mounted aft.

OTHER CRAFT
17 Ships

Active	Diamond Star	Goodwill	Phylos
Barter	Dolphin	Lanakin	Ranjani (FY52)
Condor	Flying	Laurose	Regina
Dacre	Gannet II	Lucky Star	Thorough
			Tonga 2

Australian army
Small Craft
1939–1945

Four examples of locally produced Army water transport craft in Sydney Harbour, 1945. From left to right, motor dory AM 2729, 40 foot workboat AM 1643 (LATRUN), 45 foot harbour tug AT 1520 (COMPARA) and 62 foot hospital launch AM 2833. (124577)

THE FIRST AUSTRALIAN Water Transport group (small craft) was formed on 4th November, 1942. The force originally comprised an odd assortment of craft. In the following year all requisitioned and built-for-the-purpose craft were allocated consecutive numbers.

After the impression of more than 120 vessels, orders were placed for a wide variety of craft to satisfy Army requirements. By October, 1943, 846 craft had been ordered. This number included wooden cargo vessels, lighters, tugs, repair ships, trawlers, launches, lighters and dinghys. Another 655 landing craft, steel cargo vessels and workboats were also ordered.

By 15th July, 1944, 2,276 numbers had been allotted, i.e. Nos. 1 to 12 and 14 to 2277. Each small craft was designated either AB (barge or lighter), AD (dinghy), AF (ferry), AH (sea ambulance), AK (ketch), AL (lugger), AM (launch), AS (trawler), AT (tug), or AV. (vessel)

The 2,276 craft were based throughout Australia at Melbourne, Toorbul Point, Thursday Island, Cairns, Townsville, Brisbane, Darwin, Wyndham, Bribie Island, Fremantle, Broome, Adelaide, Sydney, Newcastle, Hawkesbury River (NSW), Hobart and the 1st Australian Corps. Training Area. Bases were also established at Port Moresby, Milne Bay, Buna, Lae, Finschhafen, Madang and Meruake.

A selection of requisitioned vessels follows the built-for-the-purpose craft to illustrate the various types taken up for war service.

Unit Strengths – July, 1944
Built for the Purpose and Requisitioned Types

Army Barges, Landing Craft, Lighters, and Repair Ships	(AB)	836 craft
Army Powered Dinghys	(AD)	27 craft
Army Ferries	(AF)	–
Army Sea Ambulances	(AH)	6 craft
Army Ketches and Schooners	(AK)	42 craft
Army Luggers	(AL)	92 craft
Army Launches, Lifeboats and Seine Boats	(AM)	608 craft
Army Trawlers	(AS)	115 craft
Army Tugs, harbour and ocean	(AT)	107 craft
Army vessels	(AV)	78 craft
Total		**1911**

Nos. 704 to 1000 and 1218 to 1277 – type not known

BUILT FOR THE PURPOSE CRAFT
July, 1944

ABs

ALC 3

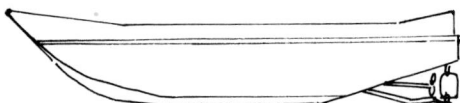

ALC 3; profile. (R. Gillett)

Nos. 103, 105, 110, 162, 306, 317, 318, 384, 385, 386, 393
Dimensions: 33 × 9.6 × 3 feet
Machinery: 170 h.p.
Speed: 7.5 knots
Range: 132 miles
Could carry one jeep.

AB 2175 (Photo – K. Hughes)

AB 2113, ALC 40. (Photo – K. Hughes)

ALC 5

Nos. 86, 106, 107, 160, 161, 176–185, 198–200, 275–277, 282–284, 286–291, 296–299, 301–305, 307, 319–322, 387–391, 434–437, 1001–1138, 1381, 1473
Dimensions: 39.6 × 9.6 × 3.6 feet
Machinery: 170 h.p.
Speed: 7.5 knots
Range: 132 miles
Some fitted for eight stretcher patients. Could transport 15 cwt. of cargo.

* * *

ALC 15

Nos. 87, 111, 175, 278, 285, 300, 308, 323, 392–394, 438, 439, 1139–1201
Dimensions: 50 × 13.6 × 3.9 feet
Machinery: 190 h.p.
Speed: 8 knots
Range: 120 miles
Could carry one jeep.

* * *

ALC 20

Nos. 61, 62, 1202–1217, 1382, 1384–1433
Dimensions: 60 × 13.6 × 3.6 feet
Machinery: 190 h.p.
Speed: 6 knots
Range: 96 miles
Could carry four jeeps maximum.

* * *

ALC 40

Nos. 395, 1474, 2017–2036, 2095–2195
Dimensions: 66.6 × 19.6 × 3.6 feet
Machinery: 380 h.p.
Speed: 8 knots
Range: 100 miles
Could transport four 3 ton vehicles or 200 passengers.

Floating Docks

Nos. 1283, 2242–2246

*　　*　　*

Higgins Barges

Nos. 579–582
Dimensions: 51 × 14 feet
Machinery: 500 h.p.

*　　*　　*

Lifeboats

Nos. 653–655
Dimensions: 28 × 7.9 × 3 feet

*　　*　　*

Lighters

Armco: Nos. 383, 398, 399, 402–421, 446–452
　　Dimensions 33 × 22.6 × 2.6 feet
Dumb: No. 669
　　Dimensions 35 × 18 × 3 feet

100 ton: Nos. 1672–1700
　　Dimensions 60 × 25 × 5.9 feet
Mackenzie: Nos. 2260, 2261
　　Steel
Phillipine: Nos. 1286–1303
　　Displacement 100 tons
　　Dimensions 60 × 25 × 6 feet
　　Nos. 1278–1282, 2262–2277
　　Displacement 300 tons
　　Dimensions 102 × 27 × 6.6 feet
　　Nos. 2216–2221, 2253–2258 (oil barges)
　　Displacement 300 tons
　　Dimensions 102 × 27 × 8.6 feet
Refrigerated: Nos. 2037–2048
　　Displacement 300 tons
　　Dimensions 100 × 27 × 5.6 feet
　　2 guns
Tobruk: Nos. 71, 310–314, 327–351, 1304–1348

　　Dimensions 48 × 18 × 4 feet
Steele: Nos. 590–629

*　　*　　*

Surfboats

Nos. 1443–1472, 2259
Dimensions: 30 × 8.3 × 1.9 feet
Could carry 30 passengers.

*　　*　　*

Symonds Barges

Nos. 372–381
Dimensions: 48 × 18 × 11.6 feet
Could carry 35 passengers.

AB 2044, (refrigerated lighter) and AB 2493. (123762).

REQUISITIONED ABs

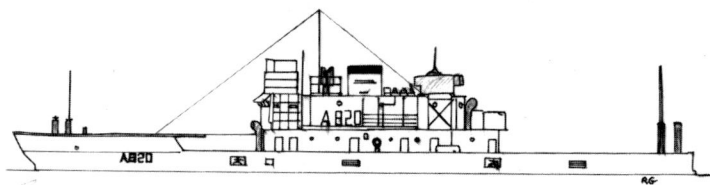

AB 20, GEORGE PEAT; profile. (R. Gillett)

AB 97, KALANG, in Sydney, 28th April, 1944, as mobile Army workshop. KALANG was reconstructed from a harbour showboat and was defensively armed. (66225).

AB 20, GEORGE PEAT under conversion in Sydney, December 1942. (275584).

AB 20, GEORGE PEAT, in Brisbane. Designated as a powered lighter, the former vehicular ferry could carry fourteen 3 ton vehicles or 50 jeeps at 6 knots over 4,000 miles. A stern door was provided for roll on/roll off operations. (Photo – K. Hughes)

Right – AM 163, the launch QUASTINA, alongside GEORGE PEAT. Note the 20mm Oerlikons and MGs arming the larger vessel. (Photo K. Hughes).

Below – AB 442, FRANCIS PEAT, was originally built as vehicular ferry (with GEORGE PEAT) for service on the Hawkesbury River. She is shown here in Jacquinot Bay, New Britain, on 6th November, 1944. A single 40mm Bofors is mounted forward. (76705).

ADs

16′ Power Dinghys

Nos. 63, 64, 152–159, 201–204
Dimensions: 15.6 × 5.6 × 1.9 feet
Machinery: $2\frac{1}{2}$ h.p.
Speed: 4 knots
Range: 16 miles
Could carry 5 passengers.

Nos. 670, 2237, 2238, 2251, 2252
Dimensions: 16 × 4.6 × 2.6 feet
Machinery: $3\frac{1}{2}$ h.p.
Speed: 4 knots
Could carry 8 passengers.

* * *

No. 630
Dimensions: 12.2 × 3 × 1.6 feet
Machinery: $2\frac{1}{2}$ h.p.

AD 2279, 21st November, 1944, a 16 foot powered surfboat built by Joyce Bros., Neutral Bay, Sydney. AT 1503, BOURBAH, lies alongside. (83359).

AHs

62' Launch

Nos. 2090–2094, 2751, 2830–2835
Dimensions: 62 × 14.6 × 3 feet
Machinery: 225 h.p.
Speed: 15 knots
Range: 2000 miles
Could carry 17 stretcher patients. Originally built as fast supply launches. Some not completed till after V-J Day.

* * *

80' H.D. Launch

Nos. 1730–1734
Displacement: 70 tons
Dimensions: 80 × 15.9 × 5.3 feet
Machinery: 300 h.p.
Speed: 12½ knots
Range: 1500 miles
Could carry 30 patients.

Left – AH 2831. Each launch was armed with three twin light machine guns and smaller weapons.

Below – AH 2831, a 62 foot hospital-launch, built by Lars Halvorsen & Sons, Ryde, NSW.

Bottom – AH 2090, BALIDA, was built as a 62 foot fast supply-boat, but used as a hospital-launch. The **photograph was taken on 31st August, 1945.**

REQUISITIONED AHs

Four large merchant ships were taken up for duties as hospital ships. These ships, CENTAUR, MANUNDA, ORANJE and WANGANELLA were converted by the RAN, crewed by civilians, staffed by Army medical personnel and maintained and routed by the RAN. MANUNDA carried 400 patients, WANGENELLA, 280. The maintenance cost of ORANJE was borne by the Netherlands.

AH 169, STRADBROKE II, at Chowder Bay, Sydney Harbour. Employed as a sea ambulance with a top speed (motor) of $4\frac{1}{2}$ knots and normal range of 1,000 miles. (122265).

ALs

Cutters

Nos. 700–703
Dimensions: 30 × 18 × 4 feet
Sail only.

REQUISITIONED ALs

Below left – AL 256, PEARL (left), and AL 255, SHEILAH, luggers converted at Brisbane by N. Wright & Co. for Army water transport. Both were sail-powered only. (Photo – K. Hughes)

Below – AL 255, SHEILAH. (Photo – K. Hughes)

Bottom – Hospital ship CENTAUR. (Photo – S. Given)

AMs

38 foot launches under construction at Lars Halvorsen & Sons on the Parramatta River.

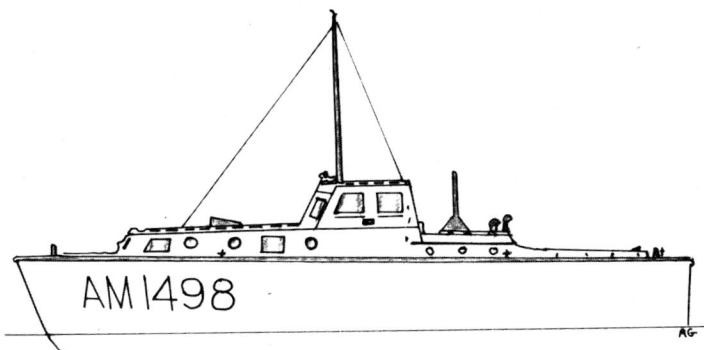

AM 1498, BOMORA; profile. (R. Gillett)

AM 2093, WANARRA, a fast supply-launch or hospital-boat for 17 stretcher patients. (See AH listing).

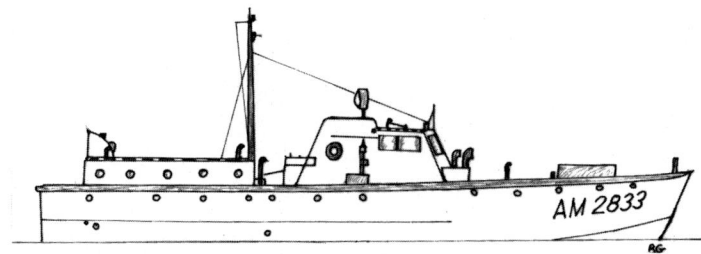

AM 1735, KYABRAM; profile. (R. Gillett)

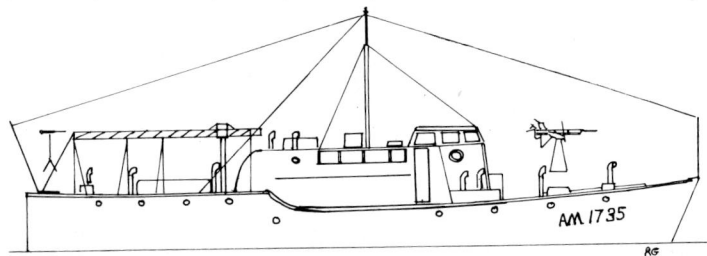

AM 2833; profile. (R. Gillett)

Launches

18′ Launch

Nos. 456–462, 675–678
Dimensions: 18 × 6.6 × 1.6 feet

Nos. 657–662
Dimensions: 18 × 7 × 2 feet

Nos. 583–587
Dimensions: 18 × 6.6 × 2 feet

Nos. 643–647
Dimensions: 18 × 7 × 1.6 feet

* * *

20′ Launch

Nos. 679–699
Dimensions: 20 × 7.6 × 2 feet

Nos. 352–371, 424–427
Dimensions: 20 × 6.9 × 2 feet
Machinery: 10 h.p.

* * *

62′ Launch

No. 1475 and others
Dimensions: 62 × 14.6 × 3 feet
Machinery: 216 h.p.
Speed: 15 knots
Range: 450 miles

* * *

Lighters

No. 2095 Experimental Dumb Lighter
Dimensions: 60 × 24 feet

* * *

26′ Motor Dory

No. 1721
Dimensions: 25.6 × 8.6 × 3.3 feet
Speed: 8.5 knots

* * *

25′ Launch

Nos. 2233, 2234
Dimensions: 25 × 8 × 3 feet
Machinery: 85 h.p.
Speed: 9 knots
Range: 400 miles

38′ Launch

Nos. 1476–1502 and others
Dimensions: 38 × 10.9 × 2.9 feet
Speed: 20 knots
Range: 250 miles
50 launches were built as fast supply/ command boats by Lars Halvorsen for the Australian Army. Another 43 were constructed for the RAAF, 2 for the RAN, 2 for the Royal Netherlands Navy and 50 for the U.S. Army.

* * *

Seine Boat

Nos. 2235, 2236, 2249, 2250

Work Boats

25′

Nos. 2247, 2248

* * *

40′

Nos. 1435–1442, 1558–1671, 1722–1729, 1820–2009
Dimensions: 40 × 12 × 5.6 feet
Machinery: 108 h.p.
Speed: 9 knots
Range: 600 miles
Could carry 25 passengers. Some used for stretchers (8) and refrigerated. Also used by RAN and RAAF.

AM 1488, BILOOLA, of the 53 Port Craft Company RAE, in Jacquinot Bay, New Britain, on 31st August, 1945. (95641).

AM 1643, LATRUN, under refit in Sydney 1945.

AM 1498, BOMORA, on speed trials.

AM 2419 and AM 1734, KURANDA. The latter, an 80 foot vessel, still with the AM prefix was employed as a hospital-launch, carrying 30 patients. A 40 foot workboat lies between the two boats.

REQUISITIONED AMs

AM 91, DONALD, capable of carrying one jeep and six passengers. Top speed of 15 knots and normal range of 100 miles. (Photo – K. Hughes)

AM 163, QUASTINA. (Photo – K. Hughes)

AM 113, MIRIMAR, towing the lighter EXCELSIOR on the Brisbane River. (Photo – K. Hughes)

AM 119, BARCE. (Photo – K. Hughes)

AM 164, JULUS, on acceptance trials following conversion.

PILGRIM, being refitted.

38 foot launch, 28th August, 1945, converted from an American landing Craft Vehicle by 55 Field Park Co. RAE. The work was performed in the Taut River area, New Britain. (95516).

ASs

Trawlers

Nos. 1735–1816, 1818, 1819
Dimensions: 66 × 17 × 8 feet
Speed: 10 knots
Range: 1500 miles
Bridge structure forward.

AS 1744, MANGANA; profile. (R. Gillett)

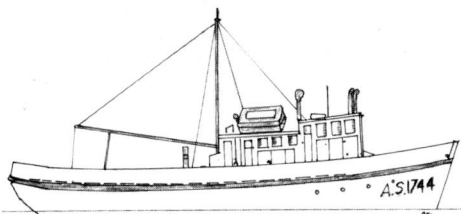

AS 1742, MACALVA, below the Storey Bridge, Brisbane. Trawler type and motor-power. (Photo – K. Hughes)

AS 1755, MINGELA; trawler with sail-power and motors. (123899).

REQUISITIONED ASs

AS 26, BALMAIN. (Photo – K. Hughes)

AS 29, BURRILL. (Photo K. Hughes)

Floating crane. (Photo – K. Hughes)

ATs

Harbour Tugs

Nos. 1503–1557, 1817, 2010–2015, 2239–2241

Dimensions: 45 × 14 × 6.6 feet
Speed: 8 knots
Range: 500 miles
Small towboats, also in RAN service, TB1 etc.

* * *

Ocean-Going Tugs

Nos. 2196–2216, 2223–2232
Dimensions: 75.8 × 18 × 7.9 feet
Machinery: 220 h.p.
Speed: 8 knots
Range: 3000 miles
Requisitioned Vessels.

FREDA, ocean-going tug as the Melbourne Harbour Trust's VIGOROUS, 29th December, 1974. (Photo – R. Wright)

AT 1520, COMPARA, with hulk COBAKI (AB431) in Sydney's Middle Harbour, 1945. (123771)

AT 1503, BOURBAH May 1945 at Bouganville beached after a cyclone. (92554)

AT 1520, COMPARA.

REQUISITIONED ATs

AT 80, ACTIVE, was employed on harbour duties. She could carry 20 passengers. Speed 7 knots, maximum range 900 miles. (Photo – K. Hughes)

AT 440 KOORA. (Photo – K. Hughes)

AT 1566, RADIO, on trials. (Photo – K. Hughes)

<u>AVs</u>

300 Tonners

106′

Nos. 2049, 2081–2089
Displacement: 350 tons
Dimensions: 106.6 × 26.6 × 6.9 feet
Machinery: 300 h.p.
Speed: 8½ knots
Range: 1000 miles
Could carry 5 × 3 ton vehicles or 60 passengers.

* * *

Nos. 2016
As above but 200 h.p.

* * *

120′

Nos. 2050–2080
Dimensions: 120 × 24 × 7.5 feet
Machinery: Two diesel engines
Speed: 9½ knots
Armament: 20mm guns
Similar vessels also in RAN and RAAF service.

* * *

125′

Nos. 1349–1380
Dimensions: 125 × 24 × 12.6 feet
Speed: 8–10 knots
Range: 2,400 miles

AV 2082, DORA, a 300 tonner, carrying AM 1705, GUNNEDAH, a 26 foot motor dory. DORA carries guns at both bow and stern. (Photo – K. Hughes)

300 tonner under construction at Prince of Wales Bay, Tasmania, 1944. (Photo – B. Johnson)

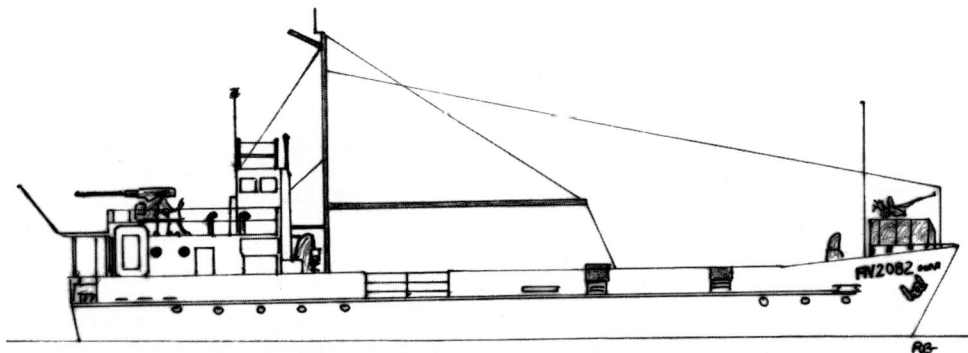

AV 2082, DORA; profile. (R. Gillett)

AV 1362, RANNAH, in New Guinea waters. The vessel's two 20mm Oerlikons are covered.

AV 2056, EVELYN, 21st November, 1944, was built by Commonwealth Shipbuilding Establishment No. 4. Employed as stores vessel and armed with two single 20mm Oerlikons (forward). (83358)

AV2767 *Crusader*

AV 2767, CRUSADER, under construction at the Melbourne Harbour Trust's yard at Williamstown, Victoria. (112581).

CRUSADER, the Army's largest ocean-going vessel of World War II, was designed by Major General C. S. Steele as a shallow-draft vessel to transport large military cargoes. All heavy equipment was loaded and unloaded by her six 30-ton cranes or driven aboard via six bridge-like structures, which were extended sideways from the vessel to the shore or wharf.

CRUSADER was powered by six propellors, with a top speed of 9 knots. For manoeuvring in tight areas she was fitted with four rudders. Cargo could be discharged at the rate of 90 tons at any one time. A sister ship AV 2768(?) was cancelled.

Not fully operational by VJ Day, CRUSADER was employed transporting equipment back to Australia. In 1947 she was purchased by the Queensland Cement & Lime Co. for conversion to a self-propelled coral barge. Renamed CEMENTCO, the wheel-house was cut free from the aft superstructure and sited about 50 feet from the bow. Conversion work was completed in late 1948. She remains active.

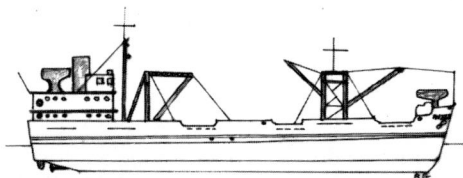

AV 2767, CRUSADER; profile. (R. Gillett)

AV 2767, CRUSADER. (112579).

AV 2767, CRUSADER, in service, late 1945. (119686).

Dimensions: 200 × 50 × 12 feet
Machinery: Ruston & Horsby engine
Speed: 9 knots
Endurance: 30 days
Manning: 31
Armament: Fitted for self-defence guns at bow at stern
Military Load: Main Deck 40 vehicles Internally 1,600 tons in 3 holds
Builder: M.H.T., Williamstown
Launched: 8/8/45
Completed: 1945
Fate: Sold 1947

AV 279, GUNDIAH, was taken up for war service as a cargo vessel. She carried a single 40mm Bofors aft. (Photo – K. Hughes)

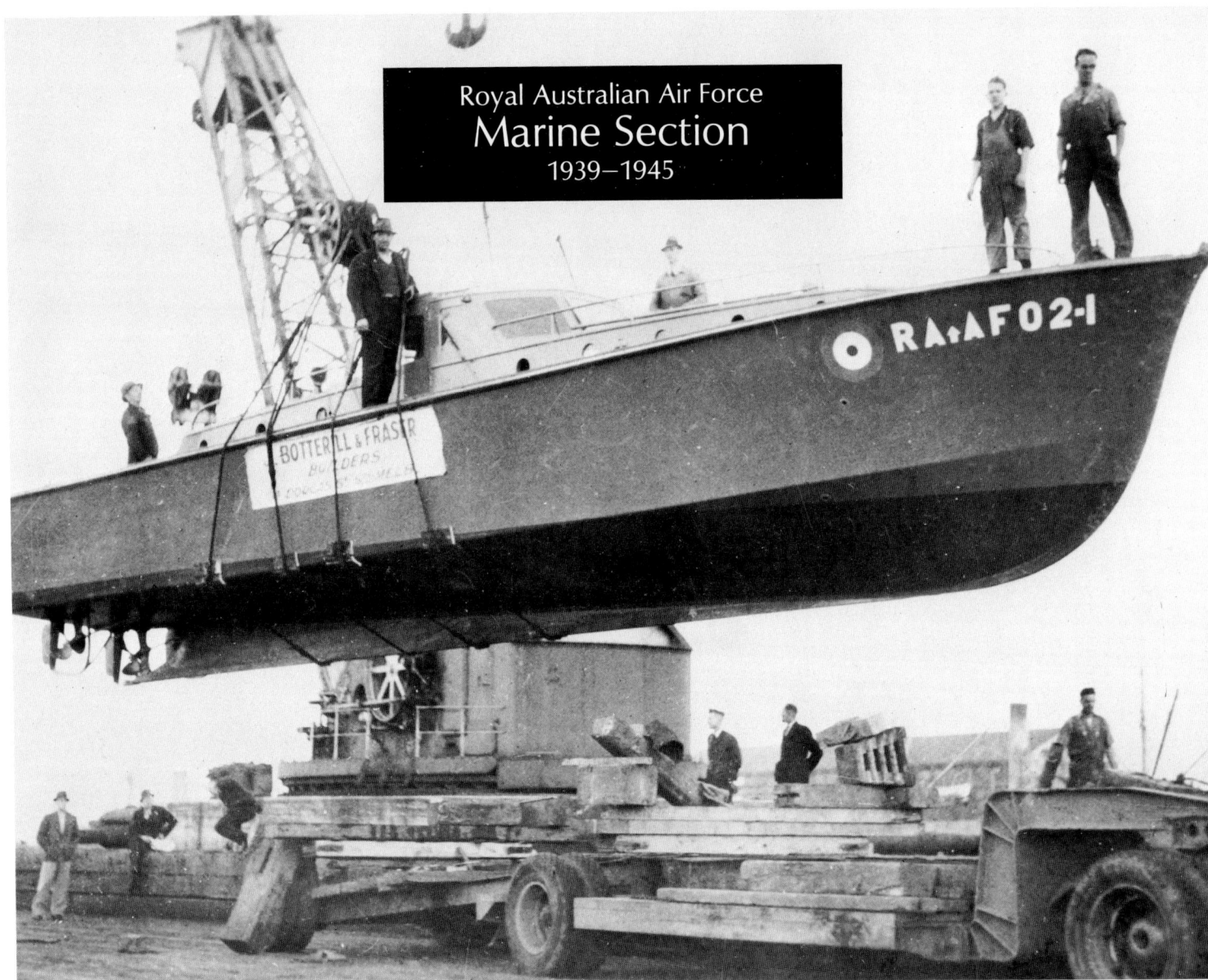

Royal Australian Air Force
Marine Section
1939–1945

02-1, rescue launch. (134495).

DURING THE SECOND WORLD WAR, the Royal Australian Air Force operated its own marine section, composed of requisitioned and built-for-the-purpose craft. Each vessel was numbered, e.g. 05-1 or 016-6, and in many instances was also named.

The acquisition of sea planes by the RAAF created the necessity to establish a marine support section. At first the need was satisfied by using all types of craft, but following the outbreak of war, the requirement for additional vessels to service aircraft alighting areas, to rescue downed airmen and to provide supplies to forward RAAF bases became urgent.

During October, 1943, Seagull amphibian aircraft were assigned to the ASR role. Later 08 type ASR vessels joined the force and subsequently 02 ASR vessels began entering service. By late in the war, small craft in service included armoured target launches, rescue launches, torpedo recovery launches, marine tenders, seaplane tenders and training and supply launches. All marine craft were painted standard grey and flew the RAAF Ensign.

In addition to the built-for-the-purpose craft listed here, hundreds of requisitioned vessels were used around Australia and New Guinea where forward bases were established.

BUILT-FOR-THE-PURPOSE CRAFT

01 Type – Target Launches

Dimensions: 40 × 8.9 × 3 feet
Machinery: Three power Meadows engines, 100 h.p.
Speed: 20 knots
Seven armoured target launches 01-1 to 01-7 completed for the Royal Air Force. Subsequently transferred to the R.A.A.F.

*　　*　　*

02 Type – Rescue Launches

Dimensions: 46 feet
Machinery: Chrysler Royal M8
Speed: 17 knots
Seven 46 foot rescue launches in service. Built by Botterill and Fraser, Melbourne and Spring & Dinard, Brisbane. Some launches armed with twin Vickers 0.5 inch machine guns.

*　　*　　*

Dimensions: 48 feet
Machinery: Chrysler Royal M8
Speed: 17 knots
Eight in service. Built by Botterill & Fraser, Melbourne and Spring & Dinard, Brisbane. Some boats carried twin Vickers 0.5 inch machine guns.
　02 boats carried nos. 1 to 15.

*　　*　　*

03 Type – Torpedo Recovery Vessels

Dimensions: 60 × 14.4 × 3.9 feet
Machinery: Chrysler Royal M8
Speed: 12 knots
Range: 550 miles
Thirteen, torpedo recovery vessels constructed by Crowley & Sons, Brisbane were in use from 1944. Various boats were employed as refuelling barges. All served in eastern Australian and New Guinea waters. Some boats were constructed in Sydney. Two 130 gallon fuel tanks. Three similiar units, TRVs 1, 2 and 3 were built for the RAN.

02-3 on trials after overhaul at Thursday Island, 23rd December 1943 (42803).

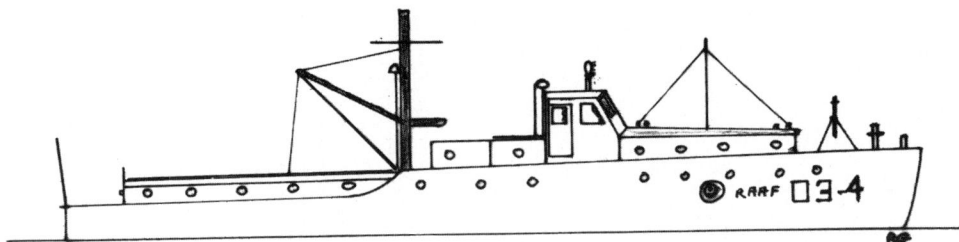

03-4, profile. (R. Gillett)

03-4

04 Type

1 known vessel, 04-5

* * *

05 Type

Numbers 05-1 to 05-21 active. Most employed as refuelling barges.

* * *

06 Type – Motor Lighters (steel)

Displacement: 350 tons
Dimensions: 122.3 × 24.6 × 8 feet
Machinery: Two diesel engines
Speed: 9.5 knots
Range: 3,000 miles @ 8 knots
Armament: machine guns
Eleven similar vessels served with the RAN as refrigerated, stores and water lighters. At least five including 06-12 to 06-16 were R.A.A.F. commissioned. All served in New Guinea waters during 1945.

Thirty-one also employed by Army and others by U.S. forces.

* * *

07 Type

Small motor boat with cabin forward – 07-10 Also GAYLESS JNR – 07-4

03-4, torpedo recovery vessel.

06-12, motor stores lighter.

07-10.

06-11, YALATA, a 70-foot-long ketch employed as a stores vessel. Top speed, 6 knots.

08 Type – Crash Boats

Dimensions: 38 × 10.9 × 2.9 feet
Machinery: Chrysler Royal M8
Speed: 20 knots

Number 08-1 to 08-45 were alloted, but only 44 were in R.A.A.F. service from 1943. No. 08-22 used as seaplane tender. Nos. 08-34 and 08-44 now named LEDA II and POSEIDON, remain active with the Royal Victorian Motor Yacht Club. Most 08 vessels were constructed by Lars Halvorsen & Sons, Sydney, for the Department of Munitions.

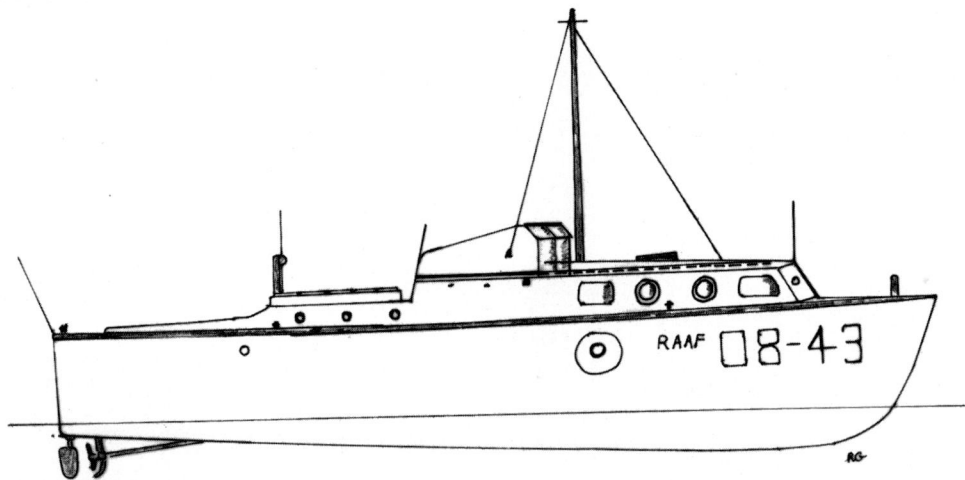

08-43, profile. (R. Gillett)

38 foot seaplane tenders (right) and torpedo recovery boats (left).

Nos. 33 and 34 crash boats.

08-43 crash boat.

09 Type

*   *   *

010 Type

Open-hull launches.

*   *   *

011 Type

Open-hull launches.

*   *   *

012 Type

*   *   *

013 Type

*   *   *

014 Type

011-29, seaplane tender (launch).

010-13, river lighter.

015 Type – Cargo Vessels

Displacement: 54 tons
Dimensions: 56 × 16 × 4.6 feet
Machinery: Gray marine diesel, single screw, 180 h.p.
Speed: 8½ knots
Range: 1200 miles
Armament: small arms

Approximately five scows were constructed late in the war, some by Slavengers (Australia) Pty. Ltd., on the Cooks River, Marrickville, NS.W. The boats were employed as bomb scows and harbour and island service boats, and could carry 2½ tons of cargo. Another five were built for the Australian Army. All vessels were flat bottomed for easy beaching in the absence of jetties.

015-75 and 015-73, were transferred to the RAN in 1962, renamed TORTOISE and TURTLE, and employed by the Navy as diving tenders until sold on 26/4/74.

015-91, prior to launching. (134600).

015-91 (134601).

REQUISITIONED 015 TYPE

015-5 SAPPHIRE, later redesignated 016-8. (134592).

015-56, ENA, three-masted schooner, employed as supply ship in Australian and New Guinea waters from 1940 to 1945. Built 1906. (134533).

015-69, three-masted schooner.

016 Type

* * *

017 Type – Work Boats

Dimensions: 40 × 12.6 × 5.6 feet
Machinery: Diesel or petrol engines
Speed: 9 knots
Range: 600 miles
As well as equipping the RAN and Army Water Transport squadrons the RAAF also received the 40 foot workboat for general harbour and island duties. The boats carried 215 gallons of fuel and 70 gallons of water.

* * *

018 Type

018-12
018-18
018-29
018-30
018-32 Invasion barge used for the transport of supplies.

* * *

019 Type

019-8; a small lighter equipped with one single derrick.

017-29, 40 foot workboat.

019-8, flat-top lighter with derrick. (134610).

018-32, invasion barge. (134605).

020 Type – Fire Boats

020-1 being one example

020-1, fire boat. (134622).

OTHER REQUISITIONED VESSELS

WANAKA, stores carrier, requisitioned from the Union Steamship Co. of New Zealand. (Photo – J. Millar)

Part II

New Zealand

HMNZS LEANDER and Fairmile B Motor Launch Q404 in the Cook Strait; a RNZAF Havard flies overhead.

New Zealand Government 1914–1921

New Zealand Division of the Royal Navy 1921–1941

Royal New Zealand Navy 1941–45

THE MAJOR SHIP OPERATED by New Zealand prior to the creation of the New Zealand Division of the Royal Navy was the 1891 vintage PHILOMEL. She had been initially employed as a seagoing training ship, but after 1917 was used as an alongside depot ship and training vessel.

During the Great War a number of New Zealanders served with the R.A.N. and R.N. and from 1921 aboard ships of the New Zealand Division. An important gesture on the part of New Zealand was the construction of the battlecruiser NEW ZEALAND in 1909, a gift from the Dominion to the Royal Navy. Because of manning and maintenance problems NEW ZEALAND was operated by the Royal Navy.

The sloop TORCH, built in Great Britain in 1895 and operational in Australia from 1897, was scheduled for transfer to New Zealand, but the deal was not proceeded with and she was finally sold in 1920.

The Government acquired the former gunboat HMS SPARROW and converted her to a boys' training ship, renamed AMOKURA. Unlike her Australian counterpart, TINGIRA, the Kiwi ship was sea-going between the years 1906 and 1922.

With the creation of the New Zealand Division in 1921, the alongside depot ship PHILOMEL continued in service and actually joined the RNZN in 1941.

Auckland naval dockyard. In the foreground are the two D class cruisers, DIOMEDE and DUNEDIN and the sloops LABURNUM and VERONICA (astern). PHILOMEL lies at the jetty, protruding from the Calliope Dock, with WAKAKURA opposite. The cable ship TUTUNEKAI is anchored above the jetty.

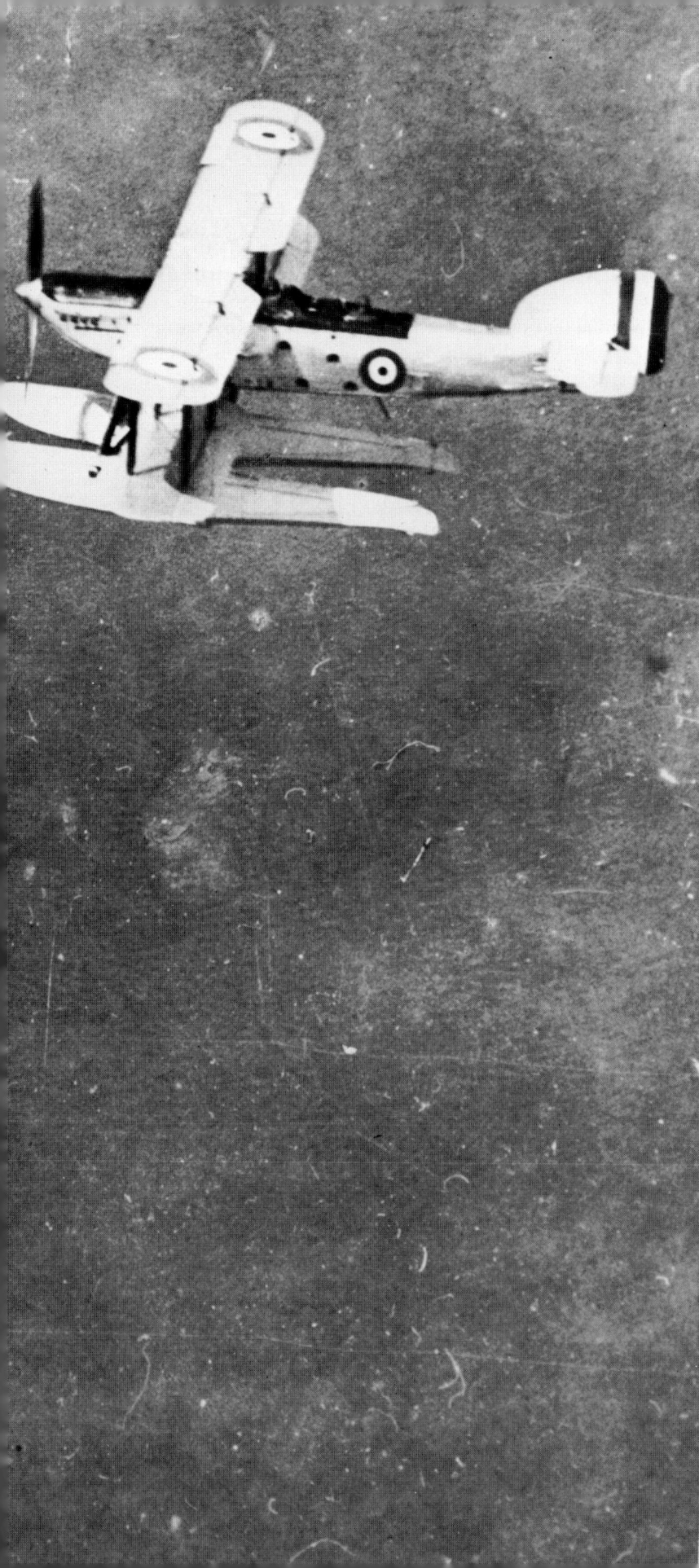

BETWEEN THE YEARS 1921 and 1937, the Royal Navy cruisers CHATHAM, DIOMEDE and DUNEDIN were active in New Zealand waters as part of the New Zealand Division of the Royal Navy. The first cruiser, CHATHAM, sailed from Chatham Dockyard in October 1920, and arrived in Auckland on 26th January, 1921. She operated until May, 1924, being employed on the more formal tasks such as goodwill island cruises before returning to the Royal Navy. CHATHAM was broken up in 1926.

To replace the ship, DUNEDIN, a member of the visiting Royal Navy Squadron (1924) remained in New Zealand waters, and on 10th May, assumed the duties of flagship. Later in January, 1924, DIOMEDE was offered to local authorities and arrived on 21st January, 1926. Both D class cruisers were eventually returned to the Royal Navy, DIOMEDE via the East Indies on 20th October, 1935. The ship paid off on 31st March, 1936, and her crew transferred to ACHILLES. DUNEDIN sailed for the mother country on 15th February, 1937, to be replaced by LEANDER.

DUNEDIN was sunk by a U Boat on 24th November, 1941, while DIOMEDE survived the war to be broken up.

During the inter-war period the Division also operated two pairs of sloops. The first, LABURNUM and VERONICA, were war-built units of the Acacia class, sister ships of MALLOW in the RAN. Both reached New Zealand waters in the early twenties and remained active until replaced in 1934 by LEITH (VERONICA) and WELLINGTON (LABURNUM). The second pair were members of the Grimsby class, closely resembling SWAN and YARRA. With war imminent LEITH and WELLINGTON were ordered from New Zealand waters on 25th August, 1939.

VERONICA was broken up after her arrival in Great Britain while LABURNUM was lost in February, 1942. LEITH and WELLINGTON survived the Second World War to be transferred to Denmark in 1949 (LEITH) and to the Master Mariners as a Headquarters ship in 1947 (WELLINGTON).

In addition to the five cruisers and four sloops, New Zealand took delivery of the reserve training ship WAKAKURA in 1926, the oiler NUCULA in 1924 and the first of three oil barges, 01, in 1936.

Upon the outbreak of war in September, 1939, the Government organised available private tonnage for quick conversion to minesweepers, and established a flotilla and three groups. The flotilla comprised COASTGUARD, GALE, MATAI, MURITA and PURIRI. The first group (based at Auckland) included WAKAKURA, DUCHESS and HUMPHREY, the second (at Wellington) SOUTH SEA and FUTURIST and the third JAMES COSGROVE and THOMAS CURRELL.

Although requisitioned prior to the official establishment of the R.N.Z.N., these auxiliary mine warfare ships and other private tonnage (used in a multitude of roles) are included in the R.N.Z.N. section where they served out most of their war commissions.

THE NEED FOR AN independant naval force, as distinct from Royal Navy ships on loan to the Division, was satisfied in July, 1941, when the R.N.Z.N. was formally established by Royal Decree.

As a first step, all ships currently serving with the New Zealand Division and those ordered and active with the Government for war service, were integrated into the new Navy. These included all built-for-the-purpose and requisitioned craft.

During the period up to 1945 the navy remained a small ship force, equipped with numerous locally-built patrol and minesweeping vessels. As with RAN, the Fairmile B motor launch was produced locally, although all Harbour Defence Motor Launches were imported.

From only six active units in September, 1939, and 29 in July, 1941, the fleet operated 81 warships and auxiliaries by late 1945. Sufficient warships and auxiliaries were now available for active service or in reserve for future use.

HMS NEW ZEALAND at Lyttleton, 2nd September, 1919, during the visit of Admiral Jellicoe.

1912

NOVEMBER

A GIFT WARSHIP

The battlecruiser HMS NEW ZEALAND, paid for by New Zealand, commissioned for service in the Royal Navy. Her first voyage to New Zealand occurred during 1913 and again in 1919 with Admiral Jellicoe embarked.

1914

JULY

FIRST CRUISER

PHILOMEL, the 22 year old 2nd class cruiser was presented to the New Zealand Government by the Royal Navy for use as a sea-going training ship in 1913 and commissioned on 15th July, 1914. However, her service was cut short by the outbreak of the Great War. During 1914–18 PHILOMEL was active around New Caledonia, the South Pacific, Indian Ocean and Mediterranean Sea. In the latter she landed parties ashore against Turkish positions.

HMS PHILOMEL.

1920

NEW SLOOPS

The first of two Acacia class minesweeping sloops, VERONICA, arrived in Auckland, followed by LABURNUM in March, 1922. Both were maintained by the Admiralty, although they were under the orders of the Chief of New Zealand Naval Staff. VERONICA left in February, 1934 and LABURNUM in February, 1935. Both were replaced by new sloops.

1921

MARCH

'PHILOMEL' COMMISSIONS AS TRAINING SHIP

Following her war service overseas with the Royal Navy and duties as a minesweeper depot ship in Wellington, PHILOMEL assumed the role of training ship, moored in Devonport Dockyard, Auckland. During the following years numerous buildings would be erected on her main deck.

JUNE

NEW ZEALAND DIVISION CREATED

20th June witnessed the Order in Council for the formation of the New Zealand Division of the Royal Navy. The Chatham class light cruiser, HMS CHATHAM, became the first flagship and served until 1924, when she was replaced by HMS DUNEDIN. She was assisted in the force by the sloops VERONICA and LABURNUM.

HMS DUNEDIN, 1938.

1924

MAY

ADDITIONAL TONNAGE

The five year old D class cruiser DUNEDIN was offered to the New Zealand Government as a replacement for the older Division flagship CHATHAM. DUNEDIN had been a member of the visiting Royal Navy Squadron and in January, 1926, was joined by her sister ship DIOMEDE, (offered to the Division in January, 1924).

HMS PHILOMEL as a base and depot ship, Auckland.

1926

APRIL

RESERVE TRAINING

The trawler WAKAKURA, built during the Great War, was commissioned in Great Britain for service as a training ship for local reservists. The vessel left Britain on 14th June, 1926. Defects in her engines necessitated repairs in the West Indies and later in Trinidad. During her transit of the Pacific Ocean, WAKAKURA had to be towed by the US cruiser PITTSBURGH to Pearl Harbour, where she was thoroughly refitted. WAKAKURA finally arrived in Auckland on 16th January, 1927.

1934

FEBRUARY

SHORT SERVICE

To replace the old sloops VERONICA

HMS LEANDER as completed, 1933.

and LABURNUM, LEITH arrived to take over the duties of VERONICA and WELLINGTON for LABURNUM in May, 1935. However, before the outbreak of war, both ships reverted to Admiralty control and in August 1939 were ordered to Singapore without delay.

1936

MARCH

THE LASTEST FROM BRITAIN

As a consequence of the 1935 Italian Invasion of Abyssinia, DIOMEDE left New Zealand waters for Aden on 20th October, 1925. Although intending to return it was decided to take up the Admiralty offer of the new Leander class cruiser HMS ACHILLES. DIOMEDE paid off on 31st March, 1936, the same day ACHILLES was commissioned for duties with the Division. The new cruiser arrived on 6th September. DUNEDIN followed on 15th February, 1937, and was replaced by LEANDER, which arrived during the following August.

1939

MAY

CORVETTE ORDER PLACED

HMNZS KIWI in drydock, 26th March, 1943, after ramming the submarine I-1.

On 2nd May, the New Zealand Government placed orders for three minesweeping corvettes to be named KIWI, MOA and TUI. All were built in British yards and completed in time for the Pacific war.

DECEMBER

BATTLE OF THE RIVER PLATE

ACHILLES, joined by the heavy cruiser EXETER and light cruiser AJAX, encountered and eventually forced the destruction of the Nazi 'Pocket' battleship ADMIRAL GRAF VON SPEE at the entrance of Montevideo Harbour, Uraguay. Unable to ascertain the strength of his enemy and believing the three cruisers had been rein-

ADMIRAL GRAF SPEE. (Photo – P. Britz)

forced, the German Captain scuttled his ship on 17th December. Prior to abandoning the ship, ADMIRAL GRAF VON SPEE, had been under attack by the trio of cruisers, all of which approached for their attack from varying angles. Although EXETER took much of the damage during the sea battle, ACHILLES fired over 200 broadsides. Although she suffered no direct hits, splinters killed four men and damaged the signal platform.

1940

AUGUST

FIRST KIWI ARMED MERCHANT CRUISER

Fitted out as an Armed Merchant Cruiser, the liner MONOWAI was commissioned on 30th August, for patrol escort and transport duties.

1941

FEBRUARY

RAIDER SUNK

LEANDER achieved success when she detected and sank the Italian commerce raider RAMBI in the Indian Ocean. Eleven officers and 92 ratings were taken prisoner.

MAY

MINESWEEPER LOST

On 14th May, 1941, the mine warfare ships PURIRI and GALE were ordered to locate a drifting mine laid by the raider ORION. The mine had been attached to a buoy the previous day, but conditions were too poor for it to be found. One and a half miles from its recorded position PURIRI struck the mine and sank in a violent explosion. Twenty-six survivors were picked up by GALE.

ROYAL NEW ZEALAND NAVY ESTABLISHED

From 1st October, 1941, the New Zealand Division of the Royal Navy was, by Royal decree, to be known as the Royal New Zealand Navy, with the ships names prefixed by HMNZS instead of HMS. The new navy comprised 27 major vessels.

1942

JANUARY

JAPANESE LANDING CRAFT SUNK

While patrolling off Cape Esperance late in the month, MOA and TUI engaged four enemy landing craft and sank two of them.

DECEMBER

'SOUTH SEA' LOST

On 19th December, the requisitioned trawler SOUTH SEA, serving as an auxiliary minesweeper, sank after colliding with the Union Steamship Co. vessel WAHINE while on patrol with RATA in Wellington.

1943

JANUARY

'KIWI' AND 'MOA' IN ACTION

During the night of 29th–30th January, KIWI and MOA, operating around the Solomon Islands with the 25th Minesweeping Flotilla, fought a successful action against the large Japanese submarine I-1. I-1, forced to the surface after being depth charged, was engaged by gunfire from KIWI and MOA. KIWI rammed

Fleet strength 1st October, 1941 – Major units

Ships	Type	Origin	Age Years	Main Armament
Achilles	Cruisers	RN	8	Eight 6 inch Four 4 inch
Leander		RN	8	Eight 6 inch Eight 4 inch
Monowai		Req.	16	Eight 6 inch Two 3 inch
Kiwi	Corvettes	NZ Govt	1	One 4 inch
Moa		NZ Govt	1	One 4 inch
Tui		NZ Govt	1	One 4 inch
Wakakura	Mine Warfare Ships	NZ Govt	34	One 4 inch
Humphrey		Req.	24	One 4 inch
James Cosgrove		Req.	23	One 4 inch
Thomas Currell		Req.	22	One 4 inch
Duchess		Req.	43	–
Futurist		Req.	21	One 4 inch

Ships	Type	Origin	Age Years	Main Armament
Gale		Req.	6	–
Kaiwaka		Req.	4	–
Kapuni		Req.	32	–
Matai		Req.	11	–
Muritai		Req.	18	–
Rata		Req.	12	–
South Sea		Req.	18	One 4 inch
Coastguard	Dan Layers	Req.	6	–
Kaiwaka		Req.	4	–
Awanui	Examination Vessels	Req.	34	–
Hauiti		Req.	30	–
Ikatere		Req.	1	–
Janie Seddon		Req.	40	–
John Anderson		Req.	50	–
Philomel	Depot Ship	RN	50	Removed

the sub three times and forced it onto a reef. KIWI, in need of refit, was docked in March for repairs.

'ACHILLES' HIT

With her sister ship LEANDER, ACHILLES operated under the Commander of United States Naval Forces, South Pacific Area, and was employed as a convoy escort in the Solomon Islands area. On 5th January, 1943, while covering the passage of allied reinforcements to Guadalcanal, ACHILLES was struck by a bomb on X gun turret. Thirteen of the crew were killed and eight wounded. The cruiser was paid off on 21st September, 1943, for repairs in Portsmouth, England, over the ensuing fourteen months.

APRIL

'MOA' LOST

The minesweeping corvette MOA fought her last battle at Tulagi in the Solomons on 7th April, when she was attacked by enemy aircraft. She sank in four minutes.

JULY

SECOND CRUISER OUT OF ACTION

During operations in the Pacific as a unit of a USN task force, LEANDER was struck by a torpedo fired by a Japanese warship during the Battle of Kula Gulf on 13th July. A hole 27 × 18 feet in the forward boiler room necessitated temporary repairs at Tulagi and completion of the work at Auckland. The ship then proceeded to Boston for a complete overhaul. To replace the two Leander class ships, arrangements were set in motion to acquire GAMBIA.

1944

FEBRUARY

'MONOWAI' ASSUMES NEW ROLE

With less need for armed merchant cruisers it was decided to convert the liner MONOWAI into an Infantry Landing Ship. In her new role she operated until July, 1946, before returning to her owners.

MAY

'GAMBIA' ARRIVES

The officers and ship's company of LEANDER turned over to man the new GAMBIA in May, 1944. Later on 22nd September, she commissioned as a New Zealand unit. Initially GAMBIA served with the Eastern Fleet based at Trincomalee. After refitting in New Zealand the cruiser joined Task Force 57.

RNZN Fleet strength

Type	Strength	Lost 1939–45
Cruisers	2	–
Corvettes	4	1
LSI	1	–
MWS	8	–
MWS Req.	10	2
Dan Layer	3	–
Fairmile B MLS	12	–
HDMLS	16	–
Patrol Craft (Req.)	9	–
Examination Vessels	3	–
BDVs	4	–
Depot Ship	1	–
Harbour Service	5	–
Transport	1	–
Miscellaneous	8	–
Tugs	2	–

PEARL CLASS TRAINING CRUISER

Philomel

PHILOMEL arrived in New Zealand waters during 1913 as a gift from the Admiralty and commissioned at Wellington. She commenced training at sea but upon the outbreak of war took up her cruiser duties, initially as an escort from New Zealand and later bombarding Turkish forces in the Mediterranean.

PHILOMEL returned to New Zealand in April 1917 to become a minesweeper depot ship at Wellington. From January 1921, she was used as a training ship at Auckland. During 1924 her boilers and machinery were removed and the armament gradually reduced. The ship survived the Second World War but as a base ship and was not deleted until 1947. Her hull was sunk at sea on 6th August 1949.

PHILOMEL was originally completed on 10th November 1891. In April 1917 she lost her major calibre guns but in later years carried one 6 inch, one 4 inch and two 12 pdr guns. These weapons were used for drill purposes only.

Displacement (tons): 2,575
Dimensions (feet): *Length* (oa) 278 *Beam* 41 *Draught* 16.10
Machinery: 2 shafts, 4,000 ihp
Speed (knots): 17
Range (miles): N/A
Manning: 217 (as built)
Armament: Eight 4.7 inch (8 × 1), Eight 3 pdr (8 × 1), Four MGs, Two 14 inch torpedo tubes (2 × 1).

Ship	Pend. No.	Builder	Cons. Time	Comm.	Fate
Philomel	–	Devonport	2y 6m	15/7/14	Paid Off 16/1/47

HMS PHILOMEL at Malta, prior to the Great War.

Above – PHILOMEL being towed into the training jetty, Devonport; all her armament has been removed save one gun abreast the bridge on the port and starboard beams...

Left – HMNZS PHILOMEL at Devonport, 1946.

TRAINING SHIP

Amokura

Constructed in Scotland as the Redbreast (or Goldfinch) class composite gunboat, HMS SPARROW, AMOKURA operated on the Cape of Good Hope Station before sailing to Australia in March, 1901. The ship was paid off at Sydney on 31st March, 1904, and remained in reserve at Garden Island until 28th February, 1905, when she was presented to the Government of New Zealand and renamed.

AMOKURA was converted to a boys training ship bearing the title NZS (New Zealand Ship) and on 10th July, 1906, was purchased from the Admiralty for £800. Training of boys for the navy continued until December, 1921, when the vessel was ordered for disposal.

AMOKURA was purchased for conversion to a coal hulk and was finally broken up in 1955. Her remains are still visible in Pelorus Sound, near Picton.

Displacement (tons): 805
Dimensions (feet): *Length* 165 *Beam* 30 *Draught* 13.9
Machinery: 1,200 h.p.
Speed (knots): 13
Range (miles): N/A
Manning: 76 (RN)
Armament: Two 4 inch (2 × 1), Two 3 pdr (2 × 1).

Ship	Pend. No.	Builder	Cons. Time	Comm.	Fate
Amokura	–	Scott	–	13/5/90	Sold 1922

AMOKURA as HMS SPARROW. (Photo – Alexander Turnbull Library)

CABLE SHIP
One Ship

Owned by the New Zealand Government. Originally built in Port Glasgow.

Name	Details	Status
Tutanekai	*Steamer* 811 gross 205.6 × 33.7 × 15.9 1,600 h.p. = 14 knots	Built 1896 NZ WWI

YACHT
One Ship

Name	Details	Status
Hinemoa	–	NZ WWI

NZTS AMOKURA.

NEW ZEALAND DIVISION
Five Light Cruisers

Name	Details	Status
Chatham	5,400 tons 457 × 49.10 × 17.8 25,000 shp = 25.5 knots 8 × 6 inch (8 × 1), 1 × 3 inch (1 × 1), 4 × 2 pdr, 2 MGs, 2 × 21 inch torpedo tubes (2 × 1)	Built 1912 NZ 1/21 RN 5/25
Diomede (I92–WWII)	4,765 tons 472.6 × 46.6 × 16.6 feet 40,000 shp = 29 knots 6 × 6 inch (6 × 1), 3 × 4 inch (3 × 1), 4 × 3 pdr, 2 × 2 pdr, 2 MGs, 8 Lewis, 12 × 21 inch torpedo tubes (4 × 3)	Built 1922 NZ 10/25 RN 31/3/36
Dunedin (I93–WWII)	4,650 tons 472.6 × 46.6 × 16.6 feet 6 × 6 inch (6 × 1), 3 × 4 inch (3 × 1), 4 × 3 pdr, 2 × 2 pdr, 2 MGs, 8 Lewis, 12 × 21 inch torpedo tubes (4 × 3)	Built 1919 NZ 5/24 RN 3/37
Achilles	SEE ROYAL NEW ZEALAND NAVY	
Leander	SEE ROYAL NEW ZEALAND NAVY	

HMS CHATHAM.

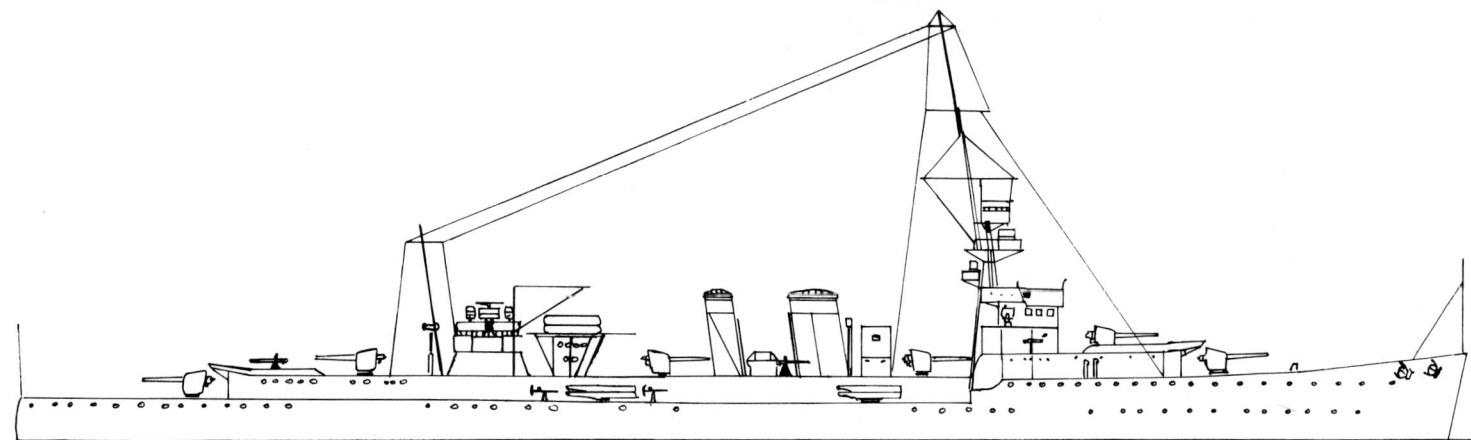

HMS DUNEDIN; profile. (R. Gillett)

Above right – HMS DIOMEDE in Wellington during the 1930s. Each 6-inch gun was allotted 200 rounds of ammunition and 300 rounds per 3-inch weapon. (Photo – Wellington Harbour Board)

Above left – HMS DUNEDIN, Sydney, 1924; 6-inch guns are carried in A, B, X and Y positions and two amidships before the fore and abaft the second funnels; 3-inch guns abreast the funnels and aft between the 6-inch mounts on the superstructure; torpedo tubes are on the main deck in four triple mounts. The revolving triple tubes were the first to be carried in a British warship.

Below – HMS CHATHAM, January, 1921; 6-inch guns are mounted on the centreline fore and aft, two abreast the bridge and amidships on the lower deck aft; two searchlights are carried between second and third funnels and abaft the mainmast.

FOUR SLOOPS

Name	Details	Status
Laburnum	1,325 full load 262.6 × 33 × 11 feet 1,800 hp = 16½ knots 2 × 4 inch (2 × 1), 4 × 3 pdr (4 × 1), 2 × 2 pdr (2 × 1), MGs	Built 1915 NZ 1922 RN 1935
Veronica	1,325 full load 262.6 × 33 × 11 feet 1,800 hp = 16½ knots 2 × 4 inch (2 × 1), 4 × 3 pdr (4 × 1), 2 × 2 pdr (2 × 1), MGs	Built 1915 NZ 1920 RN 1934

Name	Details	Status
Leith **(L36–WWII)**	990 tons 266 × 34 × 8.6 feet 2,000 shp = 16½ knots 2 × 4.7 inch (2 × 1), 1 × 3 inch (1 × 1), 4 × 3 pdr (4 × 1), 10 MGs	Built 1934 NZ 1934 RN 1940
Wellington **(L65–WWII)**	990 tons 266 × 34 × 8.6 feet 2,000 shp = 16½ knots 2 × 4.7 inch (2 × 1) 1 × 3 inch (1 × 1) 4 × 3 pdr (4 × 1) 10 MGs	Built 1935 NZ 1935 RN 1940

HM Ships VERONICA and LABURNUM: single 4-inch gun forward of the mast; searchlights on bridge-wings.

HMS LABURNUM, Wellington, early 1930s. A second 4-inch gun is visible aft. (Photo – Wellington Harbour Board)

HMS WELLINGTON: 4.7-inch gun in A position and 3-inch gun in B position.

HMS LEITH.

RESERVE TRAINING SHIP

Wakakura

Originally built for the Canadian Navy as TR 1 and completed on 17th October 1917. A total of 60 Castle class minesweeping trawlers were constructed in Canadian yards. Sold to Captain Munro in 1920 and to the New Zealand Government in April 1926 for use as a training ship for the Royal Navy Volunteer Reserve.

In September 1939 she resumed minesweeping duties and from July 1944 as a danlayer. WAKAKURA was sold in 1947 to the Tasman Steamship Company.

WAKAKURA's original armament comprised one 12 pdr., 12 cwt 10w angle gun.

Ship	Pend. No.	Builder	Cons. Time	Comp.	Fate
Wakakura	–	Port Arthur Shipbuilding Co., Ontario	–	17/10/17	Paid Off 10/45

HMS WAKAKURA, Wellington.

LEANDER CLASS

Achilles, Leander

Five ships of the Leander class were completed for the Royal Navy between March, 1933, and April, 1935. Although all five were constructed as flagships, only LEANDER and two others, were fitted out for the role.

The class mounted four twin six inch gun turrets, with 200 rounds per gun. Four single four inch guns (250 rounds) were sited amidships abaft the bridge structure and abreast the single funnel. Immediately behind the funnel and on the upper deck were the two quadruple 21 inch torpedo tubes.

It was decided in the mid 1930s that two new cruisers would replace the older DIOMEDE and DUNEDIN. The scheme was put into effect on 31st March, 1936, (ACHILLES), and April, 1937, (LEANDER). ACHILLES arrived in New Zealand on 6th September, 1936, and LEANDER in April, 1937. Upon the formation of the RNZN on 1st October, 1941, both ships automatically assumed HMNZS status.

Prior to the outbreak of war in 1939, LEANDER received new four inch twin gun mounts to replace the single mounts. Each ship was also fitted for the Walrus amphibian carried amidships on a platform behind the stack.

During 1943/44 ACHILLES was re-armed to six 6 inch (3 × 2), eight 4 inch (4 × 2) and sixteen 20mm guns (5 × 2, 6 × 1). Her twin 6 inch guns in X position were deleted due to damage sustained by Japanese aircraft. At the same time her aircraft catapult was also removed and four quad pom-poms installed.

LEANDER's aircraft and catapult were removed in Alexandria in June, 1941, and a quadruple pom-pom from HMS LIVERPOOL fitted in the vacant position. The pom-pom was removed in New Zealand later in the year. At the same time the opportunity was taken to fit five 20mm guns (5 × 1).

During 1943, an additional four single 20mm guns were fitted.

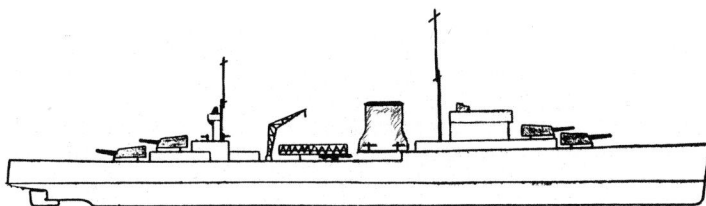

Following severe damage inflicted by a Japanese torpedo on 13th July, 1943, LEANDER proceeded to Boston, USA, for repairs. By May, 1944, when she reverted to the Royal Navy, LEANDER'S armament included six 6 inch, eight 4 inch, two quad Bofors, three twin and four single 20mm guns. Her final outfit in late 1946 saw the replacement of the quad bofors by two twin mounts, the loss of all single and one twin 20mm guns and the fitting of three single Bofors.

ACHILLES reverted to the Royal Navy in September, 1946, and in 1948 was sold to India. She was broken up in 1978. LEANDER was sold for scrap on 15th December, 1949.

Displacement (tons): 7,030 (ACHILLES), 7,270 (LEANDER)
Dimensions (feet): *Length* (oa) 554.6 *Beam* 55 (LEANDER) 56 (ACHILLES) *Draught* 16
Machinery: Parsons geared turbines, 4 shafts, 72,000 s.h.p.
Speed (knots): 32.5
Range (miles): N/A
Manning: 550
Armament: Eight 6-inch (4 ×), Eight 4-inch (4 × 2) (except ACHILLES Four 4-inch (4 × 1), Four 3 pdr., Ten smaller, Eight 21-inch torpedo tubes (2 × 4).

Ship	Pend. No.	Builder	Cons. Time	Comm.	Fate
Achilles	C70	Cammell Laird	2y 4m	10/10/33	Paid Off 9/1946
Leander	C75	Devonport	2y 6m	23/3/33	Paid Off 5/1944

HMNZS ACHILLES; armament profile. (R. Gillett)

HMS ACHILLES with original armament. Note the seaplane on catapult abaft the single funnel and searchlights against the funnel.

HMS ACHILLES, pre 1939; she still retains her single 4-inch guns. (Photo – P. Britz)

HMNZS LEANDER with twin 4-inch mounts. (Photo – C.W. Collins, copyright B. Collins)

HMNZS LEANDER.

HMNZS LEANDER leaving the Calliope Dock after repair work to damage inflicted by the Japanese torpedo in the Kula Gulf battle. Note the Harbour Defence Motor Launch (right) on the stocks undergoing refit.

HMNZS ACHILLES paying off at Auckland, 17th July 1946.

MAURITIUS CLASS

Gambia

GAMBIA was constructed for the Royal Navy under the 1938 programme. After commissioning she began service with the Eastern Fleet and on 22nd September, 1943, was transferred to the RNZN for manning.

As built, the cruiser carried a main armament of twelve 6-inch, eight 4-inch and eight 2 pdr. guns (two quad), and six 21-inch torpedoes. For close-range defence, two 2 pdr. pom-pom single mounts were available.

From 16th June, to 22nd September, 1943, GAMBIA was refitted at Liverpool. During her time in dockyard hands the aircraft and catapult were deleted. Six single 20mm, fitted at Rosyth in February, 1942, were removed, along with the two single 2 pdr. To provide a credible air defence ten twin 20mm guns were fitted.

During her short Kiwi commission GAMBIA was detailed to patrol work and was returned to the Royol Navy in July, 1946. She was eventually broken up in Inverkeithing from December, 1968.

Displacement (tons): 8,000
Dimensions (feet): *Length* (oa) 555.6 *Beam* 62 *Draught* 16.6
Machinery: Parsons geared turbines, 4 shafts, 80,000 shp
Speed (knots): 32.25
Range (miles): N/A
Manning: 900
Armament: Twelve 6-inch (4 × 3), Eight 4-inch (4 × 2), Eight 2 pdr. (2 × 4), Twenty 20mm (10 × 2), Six 21-inch torpedo tubes (2 × 3).

HMS GAMBIA; four enclosed twin 4-inch guns are mounted abreast the after-funnel and mainmast; 2 pounder pom-poms abreast the forefunnel. (Photo – C.W. Collins, copyright B. Collins)

HMS GAMBIA.

Ship	Pend. No.	Builder	Cons. Time	Comm.	Fate
Gambia	C48	Swan Hunter	2y 7m	2/1942	Paid Off 1/7/46

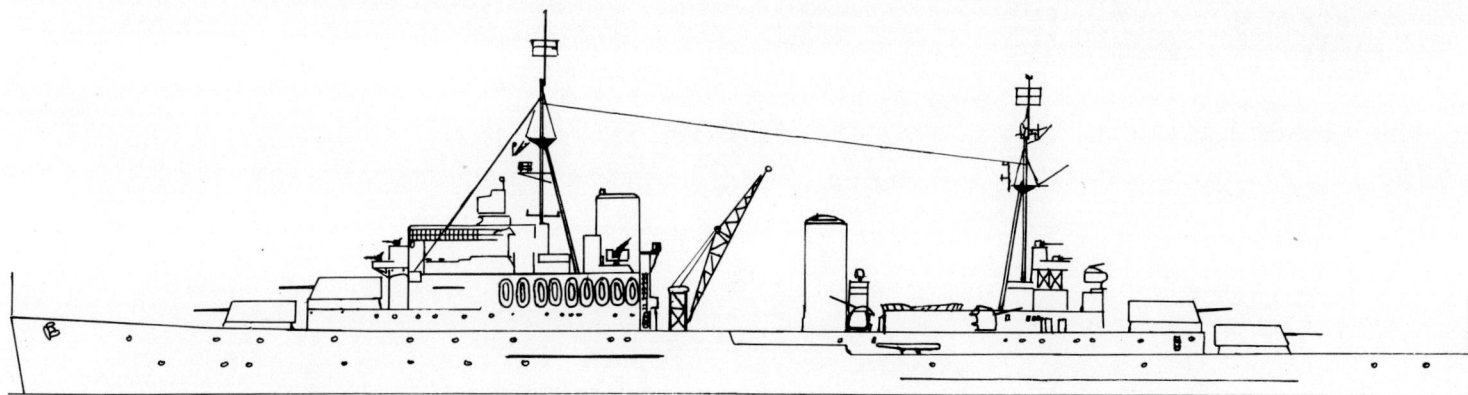

HMNZS GAMBIA; profile. (R. Gillett)

ARMED MERCHANT CRUISER
1 Ship

The 14 year old trans-Tasman passenger steamer MONOWAI was employed as an AMC and later converted to an infantry landing ship. The conversion was undertaken in Auckland and she commissioned in August, 1940.

HMNZS MONOWAI.

Name	Details	States
Monowai (F59)	*Steamer* *10,852 gross* *519 × 63.3 × 26* 14,740 BHP = 18 knots 8 × 6-inch, 2 × 3-inch	Built 1925 RN 23/10/39 PO 6/1943 LSI 2/1944 Returned 7/1946

HMNZS MONOWAI as an armed merchant-cruiser.

BIRD CLASS

Kiwi, Moa, Tui

Ship	Pend. No.	Builder	Cons. Time	Comm.	Fate
Kiwi	T102	Henry Robb	1y 7m	20/10/41	Paid Off 1949
Moa	T233	Henry Robb	1y 5m	12/8/41	Sunk 7/4/43
Tui	T234	Henry Robb	1y 5m	12/8/41	Paid Off 1946

The three Bird class corvettes were ordered by the New Zealand Government on 2nd May, 1939, to satisfy minesweeping, torpedo training and gunnery requirements. The trio were grouped as the 25th Minesweeping Flotilla RNZN. MOA was lost on 7th April, 1943, after attacks by Japanese aircraft at Tulagi.

Post-war, KIWI operated as a training ship until 1949 and again from 1951 to 1956. She was sold in 1964. TUI was also employed in the training role after recommissioning in 1952. She was converted to a trials vessel in 1955 and was sold in 1969 after paying off two years earlier.

Displacement (tons): 825 full load
Dimensions (feet): *Length* (oa) 156 *Beam* 30 *Draught* 13
Machinery: Triple expansion, 1 shaft, 1,000 ihp
Speed (knots): 14
Range (miles): N/A
Manning: 35
Armament: One 4-inch (1 × 1), One 20mm.

HMNZS MOA, as built.

HMNZS KIWI, post-war (Photo – P. Britz)

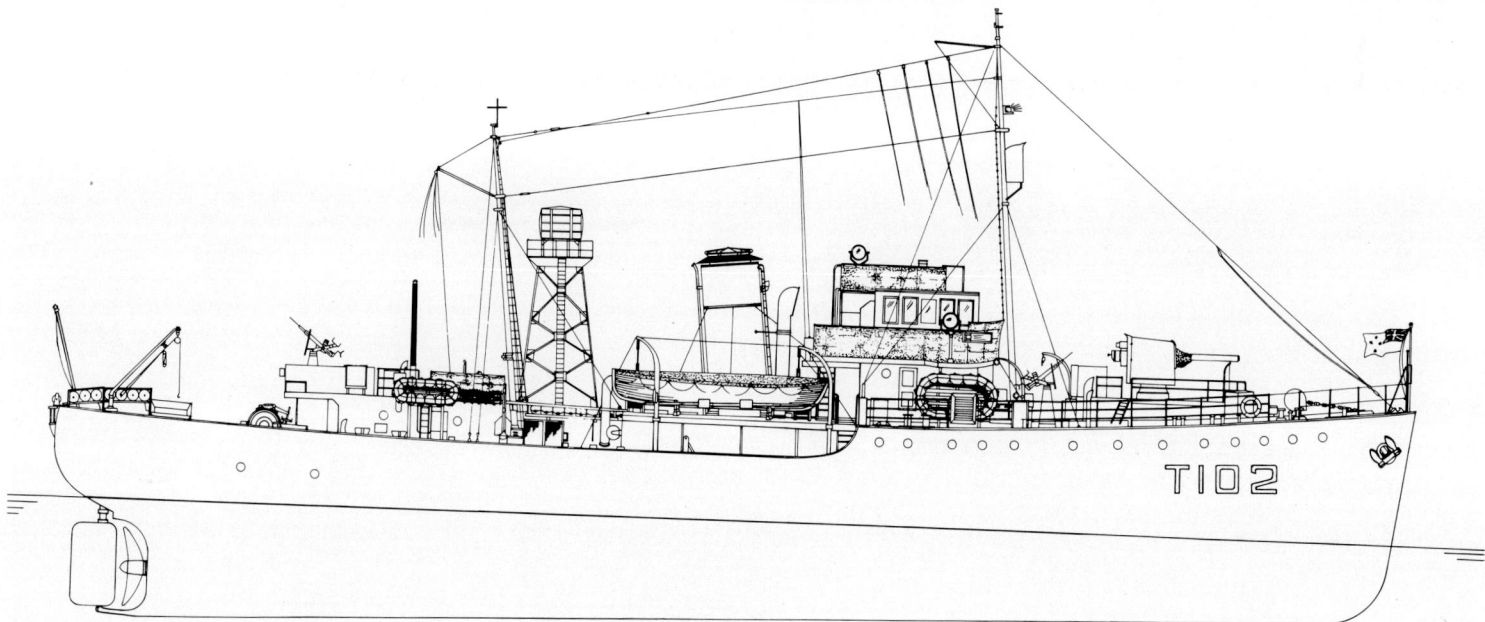
HMNZS KIWI, January, 1943; profile. (P. Webb)

MODIFIED FLOWER CLASS

Arabis, Arbutus

ARABIS and ARBUTUS were transferred to the RNZN upon completion, entering service on 22nd February, 1944, and 16th June, 1944, respectively. During their service with New Zealand both were equipped for minesweeping duties. ARBUTUS also operated as a radar and radio maintenance vessel from June to October, 1945, with the British Pacific Fleet.

Both corvettes were broken up in Great Britain from 1951.

Displacement (tons): 925
Dimensions (feet): *Length* (oa) 205 *Beam* 33 *Draught* 13
Machinery: Triple expansion, 2,800 ihp
Speed (knots): 16
Range (miles): N/A
Manning: 85
Armament: One 4-inch (1 × 1), Eight 20mm (6 × 1, 1 × 2)

Ship	Pend. No.	Builder	Launched	Comp.	Fate
Arabis	K385	George Brown	28/10/43	3/1944	Paid Off 7/1948
Arbutus	K403	George Brown	26/1/44	7/1944	Paid Off 7/1948

HMNZS ARBUTUS: note the twin 20mm Oerlikon on the bandstand aft.

HMNZS ARABISI: forward 4-inch gun; two 20mm Oerlikons on the bridge wings.

HMNZS ARABISI paying off, July, 1948.

INFANTRY LANDING SHIP –
1 Ship

Originally taken up for service as an Armed Merchant Cruiser and converted to LSI at Liverpool, U.K., from June, 1943, to February, 1944. Fitted with landing craft.

Name	Details	Status
Monowai (F59)	*Steamer* 10,852 gross 519 × 63.3 × 26 14,740 bhp = 18 knots 1 × 4-inch, 2× 12 pdr. 2 × 40mm, 8 × 20mm	Built 1925 RN 23/10/39 PO 6/1943 LSI 2/1944 Returned 7/1946

MONOWAI as a trans-Tasman steamer. (Photo – Dufty Collection)

ISLES CLASS MINESWEEPING TRAWLERS

Inchkeith, Killegray, Sanda, Scarba

One hundred and forty-five vessels of the Isles class were constructed during the Second World War for service in the Royal, Dominion and Allied navies.

During early 1942 all Kiwi vessels commissioned with local crews. The four RNZN ships paid off during January and February, 1946, and remained laid up in reserve until sold in August, 1958. SANDA survived to 1970 as a merchant ship.

Displacement (tons): 560
Dimensions (feet): *Length* (oa) 164 *Beam* 27.6 *Draught* 10.6
Machinery: Triple expansion, 1 shaft, 850 ihp
Speed (knots): 12
Range (miles): N/A
Manning: 40
Armament: One 12 pdr (1 × 1), Three 20mm (3 × 1), DCs

Ship	Pend. No.	Builder	Cons. Time	Comp.	Fate
Inchkeith	T155	Lewis	11m	24/10/41	Paid Off 1946
Killegray	T174	Cook	10m	7/11/41	Paid Off 1946
Sanda	T160	Goole	10m	4/11/41	Paid Off 1946
Scarba	T175	Cook	8m	25/11/41	Paid Off 1946

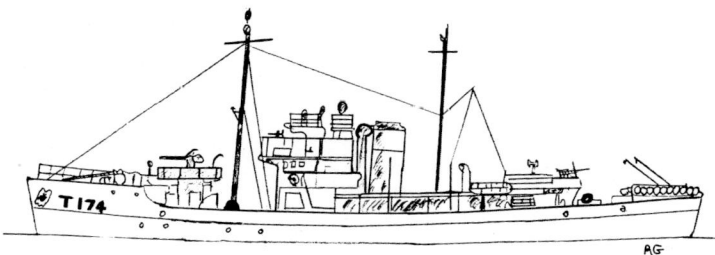

HMNZS KILLEGRAY; profile. (R. Gillett)

HMNZS KILLEGRAY. (Photo – C.W. Collins, copyright B. Collins)

HMNZS SCARBA. (Photo – C.W. Collins, copyright B. Collins)

HMNZS KILLEGRAY, November, 1942.

CASTLE CLASS MINESWEEPERS

Hinau, Manuka, Rimu, Tawhai

Generally similar to vessels in the Royal Navy. All built of Kauri planking upon steel frames. Seventeen vessels were originally planned, including these four magnetic minesweepers and nine anti-submarine minesweepers. Another four were cancelled.

HINAU remained in reserve until her sale in 1955, as did RIMU. The latter's hull was eventually sunk for target practice off Cavier Island by the RAZAF on 21st August, 1958. TAWHAI used by United Nations in China as a relief boat, post 1947.

Displacement (tons): *Full load* 612
Dimensions (feet): *Length* (oa) 134 *Beam* 23.6 *Draught* 13.6
Machinery: Triple expansion, 1 shaft, 480 ihp
Speed (knots): 10
Range (miles): N/A
Manning: 32
Armament: One 12 pdr (1 × 1), Two MGs

HMNZS HINAU,

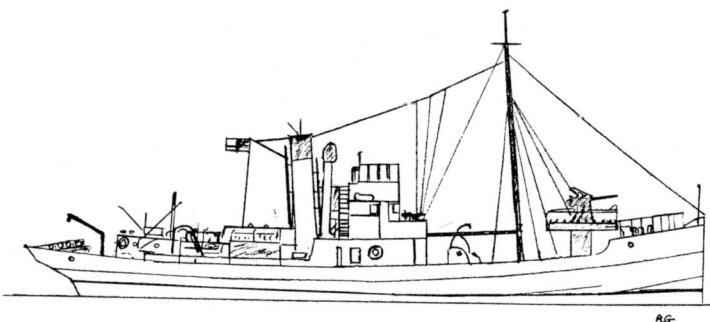

Castle class minesweeper; profile. (R. Gillett)

Ship	Pend. No.	Builder	Cons. Time	Comm.	Fate
Hinau	T17	Senior Foundry	–	15/7/42	Paid Off 1946
Manuka	T19	Mason	5m	30/3/42	NZ Govt 1946
Rimu	T18	Seager	–	15/7/42	Paid Off 1946
Tawhai	T348	Seager	–	24/4/44	Paid Off 1946

REQUISITIONED MINESWEEPERS
3 Ships

These vessels were originally constructed as minesweepers for service with the Royal Navy in the Great War. Like many others, they were subsequently employed as fishing boats, but were still considered suitable for the second conflict. HUMPHREY and THOMAS CURRELL were originally units of the Strath class and JAMES GOSEROVE of the Castle class. The former served with Sanford Ltd., Auckland, NZ, from 1929, JAMES COSGROVE in 1923 and THOMAS CURRELL in 1919.

THOMAS CURRELL, post-war. (Photo – I.J. Farquhar)

Name	Details	Status
Humphrey (6)	Trawler 207 gross 115.7 × 22.1 × 12.2 57 nhp = 10 knots 1 × 4-inch, MGs, DCs	Built 1917 NZ 16/10/39 Paid Off 8/1944
James Cosgrove (T10)	Trawler 277 gross 125.6 × 23.5 × 12.8 480 hp = 10 knots 1 × 4-inch, MGs, DCs	Built 1918 NZ 10/10/39 BDV 4/1944 Paid Off 1946
Thomas Currell	Trawler 204 gross 115.2 × 22.1 × 12.2 430 hp = 11 knots 1 × 4-inch, MGs, DCs	Built 1919 NZ 16/10/39 Paid Off 1944 Ret. 11/1945

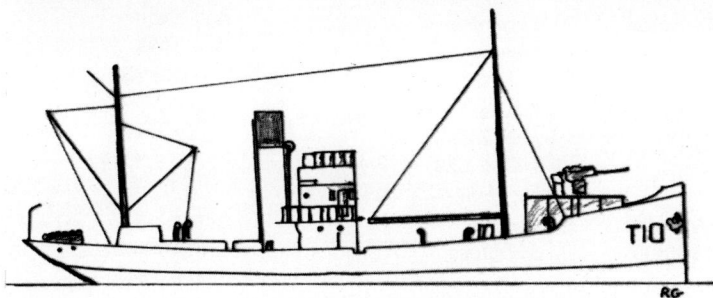

HMNZS JAMES COSGROVE: profile. (R. Gillett)

HMNZS HUMPHREY.

REQUISITIONED MINESWEEPERS
14 Ships

The following craft were requisitioned by the New Zealand Government or RNZN for service in local waters to fill the obvious lack of tonnage in this area. Some vessels operated around Fiji and the Solomon Islands. Like their RAN contemporaries, the requisitioned ships gave extremely useful service and also satisfied other requirements later in the war. The conversion of MURITAI to minelayer was not completed. SOUTH SEA was lost after a collision with the WAHINE in Wellington Harbour on 19th December, 1942. PURIRI was sunk by a mine in the Hauraki Gulf during May, 1941.

HMNZS KAPUNI (T15) with other minor war-vessels. (Photo – C.W. Collins, copyright B. Collins)

Name	Details	Status
Breeze **(T371)**	*Steamer* 622 tons 175.1 × 30.1 × 12.5 156 hp 1 × 4-inch, 20mm guns, DCs	Built 1933 RNZN 26/10/42 Ret. 1946
Duchess	*Steamer* 314 tons 133.6 × 26 × 10.3 81 hp	Built 1897 NZ 6/1940 Gate Vessel 1/1944 Harbour 1946 Deleted 1947
Futurist	*Trawler* 234 gross 128.8 × 23.4 × 10.1 550 hp = 10 knots 1 × 4-inch, MGs, DCs	Built 1920 NZ 8/1940 Ret. 1945
Gale	*Motor vessel* 622 tons 175 × 30.1 × 10.3 725 bhp	Built 1935 RNZN 3/4/41 Paid Off 10/1944 Ret. 1945
Hawera	*Motor vessel* 188 tons 106 × 20 × 7.9 140 hp	Built 1912 RNZN 1942 Paid Off 1946 Ret. 1/1946

Name	Details	Status
Kaiwaka **(T14)**	*Motor vessel* 169 gross 88.3 × 23 × 7.75 145 bhp	Built 1937 NZ 25/5/41 Paid Off 1946 Ret. 1946
Kapuni **(T15)**	*Motor vessel* 190 tons 100.6 × 19.9 × 10.7 140 hp	Built 1909 NZ 4/1941 Paid Off 1946 Ret. 1946
Matai **(T372)**	*Steamer* 1,050 tons 219 × 35.1 × 13.6 178 hp	Built 1930 NZ 1/1941 Transport 1944 Paid Off 1945 Ret. 1946
Muritai **(M)**	*Steamer* 462 tons 165.3 × 30.1 × 11.3 90 hp	Built 1923 NZ 8/1940 Minelayer 1945 Ret. 1946
Puriri	927 tons	Built 1938 RNZN 1941 Sunk 14/5/41
Rata	*Steamer* 974 tons 209.7 × 34.4 × 10.8 196 hp	Built 1929 NZ 11/1940 Paid Off 11/10/43 Ret. 1944
Simplon	*Steamer* 69 tons	Built 1929 Hulk 1934 RNZN WWII
South Sea **(T08)**	*Trawler* 322 gross 140 × 23.8 × 12.4 1 × 4-inch, MGs, DCs	Built 1912 NZ 12/8/40 Sunk 19/12/42
Wairua **(T364)**	*Steamer* 352 gross	Built 1913 RNZN 1942 Sold 3/1945

HMNZS MATAI; profile. (R. Gillett)

HMNZS BREEZE, 1942; note the 20mm Oerlikons on bandstands before the bridge, aft and on the bridge wings; depth-charges are also stored aft.

HMNZS KAIWAKA.

HMNZS SOUTH SEA.

REQUISITIONED DANLAYERS
4 Ships

Danlayers were employed to work with the minesweepers, marking buoys, areas swept clear of mines, and areas to be cleared. The training vessel WAKAKURA commenced danlaying operations in July 1944 and paid off in October 1945.

HMNZS PHYLLIS, 1942.

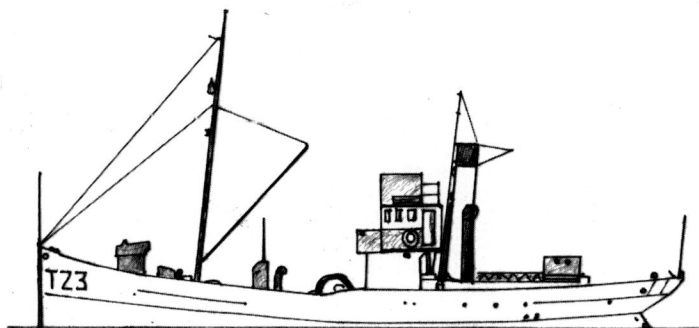

HMNZS NORA NIVEN: profile. (R. Gillett)

Name	Details	Status
Coastguard (T)	*Ketch* 49 gross 62 × 16.7 × 7.8 feet 100 b.h.p.	Built 1935 NZ 1940 Tender 1946 Sold 1961
Kaiwaka (T14)	*Motor vessel* 169 gross 88.3 × 23 × 7.75 feet 145 b.h.p.	Built 1937 NZ 25/5/41 Sold 1946
Nora Niven (T23)	*Steamer* 166 gross 96 × 20.6 × 10.8 feet 35 h.p.	Built 1907 RNZN 10/42 Ret. 2/44
Phyllis (T22)	*Steamer* 148 gross 96.1 × 19.5 × 12.8 feet 43 n.h.p.	Built 1912 RNZN 10/42 Paid Off 2/44 Ret. 1944

FAIRMILE B MOTOR LAUNCHES
Q 400–411

For the relatively modest price of £35,000 each, the Royal New Zealand Navy was equipped with twelve mass produced Fairmile B motor launches. The flotilla was originally intended to serve in the anti-submarine role but instead formed two ML groups in the Solomon Islands from the beginning of 1944.

Fairmile No 400, the only launch to suffer damage during the war, was incapacitated by an engine room fire and explosion. All boats were sold between 1946 and 1947.

No 411 recommissioned into the fleet during 1947. Six years later she was designated P3571 and renamed KAHU until she was sold again in 1965. In 1953 No 409 reverted to the RNZN and was renamed IRIS MOANA (P3570). In 1956 she was renamed MAORI and was sold for the second time in 1963.

Displacement (tons): 80
Dimensions (feet): *Length* (oa) 112 *Beam* 17.10 *Draught* 4.10
Machinery: 2 Hall Scott 12 cylinder petrol engines, 2 shafts, 1,260 hp
Speed (knots): $18\frac{1}{2}$
Range (miles): N/A
Manning: 16
Armament: One 2 pdr (1 × 1), One 20mm (1 × 1), Two MGs, One Y gun (1 × 1), DCs. (One 20mm later replaced the 2 pdr).

Pend. No.	Builder	Cons. Time	Comm.	Fate
Q400–411	Auckland	2/42	20/12/43	All sold 1946–47 except No 411

Fairmile B. MLs in the dockyard basin at Devonport, Auckland. Note lack of armament on the MLs.

HARBOUR DEFENCE MOTOR LAUNCHES
Q 1183–1194 and Q1348–1351

Harbour Defence MLs at Devonport with the danlayer PHYLLIS and auxiliary patrol vessel Q47 to the left. (Photo – C.W. Collins, copyright B. Collins).

Sixteen Harbour Defence Motor Launches entered service during 1943–44, but in 1945 all were laid up. Ten were retained, five sold and one transferred to the Army. During the mid-fifties the surviving boats were fitted with radar and lattice masts and re-engined with Foden diesels.

All boats were subsequently renamed and allotted new pendant numbers. Two were converted to survey launches whilst others operated as fishery protection and volunteer reserve training vessels.

Displacement (tons): 54 full load
Dimensions (feet): *Length* (oa) 72 *Beam* 15.10 *Draught* 5.4
Machinery: Diesels, 2 shafts, 550 hp
Speed (knots): 10–12
Range (miles): N/A
Manning: 10
Armament: One 20mm (1 × 1), One .5 inch Browning MG (1 × 1), Two .303 inch MGs, DCs.

Pend. No.	Builder	Cons. Time	Comp.	Fate
Q1183–94 & Q1348–51	U.S.A.	1942	From 1943	See Notes

HDML Q1190 on 12th November, 1943.

Q1191 (R. Gillett)

HDML Q1187 under refit. (Photo – C.W. Collins, copyright B. Collins)

CASTLE CLASS ANTI-SUBMARINE MINESWEEPERS

Aroha, Awatere, Hautapu, Maimai, Pahau, Waiho, Waikato, Waima, Waipu

Sister ships of the four magnetic minesweepers built of Kauri planking on steel frames. All decommissioned in 1946 and sold to the fishing industry within two years.

Four additional units, WAIAU (Mason, Auckland), WAUTI (Mason), WAIKAKA (Stevenson and Cook), and WAIKANAE (Stevenson and Cook) were cancelled in October 1943.

Displacement (tons): 612 full load
Dimensions (feet): *Length* (oa) 134 *Beam* 23.6 *Draught* 13.6
Machinery: Triple expansion, 1 shaft, 480 ihp
Speed (knots): 10
Range (miles): N/A
Manning: 28
Armament: One 12 pdr (1 × 1), Two MGs, DCs.

Ship	Pend. No.	Builder	Launched	Comm.	Fate
Aroha	T24	Stevenson	8/9/42	12/5/43	Paid Off 1946
Awatere	T25	Patent Slip	26/9/42	26/6/43	Paid Off 1946
Hautapu	T26	Stevenson	18/11/42	12/2/44	Paid Off –
Maimai	T27	Stevenson	25/2/43	–	Paid Off 1946
Pahau	T28	Stevenson	3/4/43	–	Paid Off –
Waiho	T34	Stevenson	19/2/44	3/6/44	Paid Off 1946
Waikato	–	Mason	16/10/43	–	Incomplete
Waima	T33	Stevenson	11/12/43	28/3/44	Paid Off 1946
Waipu	T32	Stevenson	31/7/43	17/11/43	Paid Off 1946

HMNZS WAIHO.

Right – HMNZS HAUTAPU, January, 1946.

Below right – HMNZS AROHA: note the machine gun tubs before the bridge.

Bottom left – HMNZS WAIHO.

Bottom right – WAIPU, post 1945. (Photo – I.J. Farquhar)

Below – AWATERE being launched, 26th September, 1942.

EXAMINATION VESSELS
Seven Ships

Requisitioned ships, some lightly armed, were employed in the examination service at principal ports.

Name	Details	Status
Awanui	*Cutter*	Built 1907
	170 gross	Req. 1941
		Ret. 1944
Hauiti	*Steamer*	Built 1911
	148 gross	Req. 1941
	106.2 × 20 × 7.4 feet	Harbour Service 1944
	32 h.p.	Deleted 1950
Ikatere	*Motor boat*	Built 1940
	43 gross	Req. 1941
	58.6 × 14.8 × 6.6 feet	Ret. 1944
	150 h.p.	
Janie	*Steamer*	Built 1901
Seddon ﹜	*126 gross*	Req. 5/41
	90 × 18.9 × 9.3 feet	Base Ship 1944
	360 i.h.p.	Sold 1947
John	*Steamer*	Built 1891
Anderson	58 gross	NZ 1939
	83.7 × 14 × 6.7 feet	Sold 1947
	25 h.p.	
Lyttleton	*Steamer*	Built 1907
	292 gross	Req. 1942
	115.5 × 25.1 × 13.5 feet	Ret. 1945
	133 h.p.	
Tuirangi	*Motor vessel*	Built 1908
	114 gross	Req. 1942
	85 × 18.3 × 9.6 feet	Ret. 1945
	145 b.h.p.	

HMNZS MOUAIRE.

NAVAL AUXILIARY PATROL SERVICE

In common with most nations, including Australia, New Zealand established an NAP in the four main ports employing pleasure-cruiser type vessels which easily adapted to patrol work.

Each boat carried a Q pendant number and was armed with small calibre weapons, some also carried depth charges. Many of the boats carried the prefix 'Lady'; one was named after the former New Zealand Government Training Ship AMOKURA. The accompanying photographs illustrate some of the boats taken up for war duties.

HMNZS AMOKURA.

HMNZS MOUAIRE.

AUXILIARY BOOM DEFENCE VESSELS – *4 Ships*

No built-for-the-purpose boom defence vessels were constructed either locally or overseas for the Royal New Zealand Navy up to 1945. Ports depended upon the following four craft to carry out all necessary boom defence work.

Name	Details	Status
Claymore	*Steamer* 260 gross 133.2 × 21.1 × 9.8 feet 54 h.p.	Built 1902 Purchased 10/43 Sold 1953
Duchess	*Steamer* 314 gross 133.6 × 26 × 10.3 feet 81 h.p.	Built 1897 NZ 6/40 Gate Vessel 1/44 Harbour Service 1946 Deleted 1947
James Cosgrove (T10)	*Trawler* 277 gross 125.6 × 23.5 × 12.8 feet 480 h.p. = 10 knots 1 × 4 inch MGs	Built 1918 NZ 10/10/39 BDV 4/44 Paid Off 1946
Whakaire	*Steamer* 819 gross 180.2 × 36 × 13.1 feet 120 h.p.	Built 1903 RNZN WWII

SUPPORT

Numerous privately owned vessels were requisitioned for war service. These craft fulfilled the roles of tugs, surveying, cable laying and ammunition resupply.

The largest support vessels was NUCULA, a replenishment ship built in 1906 and capable of storing over 9,600 tons of fuel. Numerous other small craft were taken over 1939–45 but lack of detail precludes them from being listed.

DEPOT AND RECEIVING SHIP

Philomel

Since 1921 PHILOMEL was moored at the training jetty, Devonport, Auckland and employed as a depot and training ship. For full details see earlier listing.

Displacement (tons): 2,575
Dimensions (feet): *Length* (oa) 278 *Beam* 41 *Draught* 16.10
Machinery: Inactive
Speed (knots): N/A
Range (miles): N/A
Manning: 220
Armament: One 6 inch (1 × 1), One 4 inch (1 × 1), Two 12 pdr (2 × 1).

Ship	Pend. No.	Builder	Cons. Time	Comm.	Fate
Philomel	–	Devonport	2y 6m	15/7/14	Paid Off 16/1/47

Harbour Defence ML Nos. Q1184, Q1187 and Q1186 alongside the depot ship HMNZS PHILOMEL at Devonport. (Photo – C.W. Collins, copyright B. Collins)

OIL BARGES
Two Ships

Three oil barges built specifically for naval use were ordered from 1936, with the Wellington Patent Ship Co. The first, '01', was launched sidewards in 1936.

HINUWAKA and HINUPAHI followed in 1943 and 1947 respectively. All three required tugs for harbour movements. The superstructure was located amidships.

HINUWAKA being launched Evans Bay, 24th September, 1943.

NUCULA.

REQUISITIONED SUPPORT SHIPS

Name	Details	Status
DEGAUSSING		
Kiritona	*Ketch* 136 gross 87 × 24.5 × 8.5 feet 150 hp	Built 1909 RNZN 1942 Ret. 1946
HARBOUR SERVICE		
Endeavour	*Schooner* 82 gross 74.6 × 21.5 × 6.5 feet 50 hp	Built 1904 Req. 1942 Purchased 1943 Renamed HAURAKI 1956 Sold 1963
Hipi	*Motor Boat* 39 gross 56.6 × 14.4 × 6.3 feet 100 hp	Built 1909 Req. 1942 Purchased 1943 Sold 1958
Nucula	*Oiler-Hulk* 9,830 tons 370 × 48.6 feet	Built 1906 NZ 4.24 Deleted
MISCELLANEOUS		
Arataka	–	
Kaianui	–	
Kawau	*Steamer* 55 gross 78.6 × 14.8 × 6.5 feet 15 hp	Built 1891
Onewa	*Steamer* 74 gross 70.6 × 14.6 × 6.4 feet $18\frac{1}{2}$ hp	Built 1910
Tu Atu	*Streamer* 42 gross 65 × 15 × 6.3 feet 54 hp	Built 1903
Vesper	*Schooner* 47 gross 76.8 × 21.2 × 3.5 feet 60 bhp	Built 1902
Viti	700 gross	Built 1940 Req. 1941 Ret. 1946
Wairangi		

TRAINING
One Ship

A number of small requisitioned craft were also employed in the training role.

Name	Details	Status
Wakakura (T00)	*Trawler* 360 tons 134 × 23.6 × 12 feet 480 ihp = 10½ knots 1 × 4 inch MGs, DCs.	Built 1917 NZ 1926 M/S 9/39 D/L 7/44 Paid Off 10/45 Sold 1947

TOIA.

TOWING
Two Ships

Name	Details	Status
Kahanui	*Steamer* 207 gross 110.3 × 24.2 × 11.1 feet 800 ihp	Built 1926 Req. 1.43 Ret. 1946
Toia	570 tons 135.6 × 29 × 14.6 feet 1,250 ihp = 12 knots	Built 1919 NZ 18/3/25 RNZN 1941 Ret. 1947

OTHER CRAFT

During the Second World War, the Royal New Zealand Navy also operated lighters and small craft such as workboats and launches. Requisitioned craft carried out small towing jobs and personnel movements within harbour.

Part III

Appendices

HMAS VAMPIRE under refit in dry dock, Malta, March, 1940. (133584)

NAVAL ORDNANCE

8-inch Mk VIII BL guns firing on the heavy cruiser
HMAS AUSTRALIA. (Photo H. Adlam)

B.L. GUNS

Gun	Bore	Length In Calibres	Weight Gun	Weight Projectile	Weight Full Charge	Muzzle Velocity in P/S	Max Range Yards	Elevation	Mounting*	Notes	Carried In
12 Inch Mk X	12″	45	58 Tons	850 lbs	258 lb	2000	18,630	$13\frac{1}{2}°$	B MK VIII Twin Turret	Heaviest Gun used by RAN	AUSTRALIA (I)
8 inch MK VIII*	8″	50	17.2 Tons	251 lbs	66 lbs	2805	30,000	60°	Twin Turret	Entered service with County class cruisers in 1927	AUSTRALIA (II) CANBERRA SHROPSHIRE ENCOUNTER AMC's 1939–45
6 inch MK VII	6″	45	7 Tons	100 lbs	29 lbs	2493	12,000	16°	PII	Entered service in 1896. Still in use as coast defence gun in 1945.	
6 inch MK XI*	6″	50	8.5 Tons	100 lbs	32 lbs	2800	18,000	$22\frac{1}{2}°$	PIII	Most of these guns were used in coast defence, 1939–45.	SYDNEY (I) MELBOURNE BRISBANE ADELAIDE
6 inch MK XIII	6″	50	8.6 Tons	100 lbs	33 lbs	2800	18,000	30°	PIII	Mounted as single in ADELAIDE only.	
6 inch MK XXIII	6″	50	6.9 Tons	112 lbs	30 lbs	2758	25,000	60°	Twin Turret	Turret mounted, twin	SYDNEY (II) HOBART GAMBIA, PERTH ACHILLES, LEANDER
5 inch MK III	5″	23	2 Tons	50 lbs	4 lb $7\frac{1}{2}$ ozs	1750	8,000	15°	VCP I	Guns dated from 1887.	PALUMA (I)
4.7 inch BL MK I	4.742″	50	2 Tons 10 cwt	50 lbs	9 lbs	2600	14,000	30°	CPIV	Came into service 1918 as gun for flotilla leaders.	STUART
4 inch MK VII	4″	45	42 cwt	31 lbs	9 lbs 15 ozs	2852	12,000	15°	PII P	High velocity gun, short recoil	AUSTRALIA (I)
4 inch MK VIII	4″	40	26 cwt	31 lbs	5 lbs 4 ozs	2287	10,000	20°	PV P	Low velocity gun, long recoil	River class Destroyers
4 inch MK IX*	4″	45	42 cwt	31 lbs	5 lbs 14 ozs	2625	12,000	30°	CPI	High velocity gun. BL version of 4″ QF MK V Entered service 1916.	Early AMS

*NOTE FOR MOUNTINGS: P = Pedestal, CP = Central Pivot, VCP = Vavasseur Central Pivot

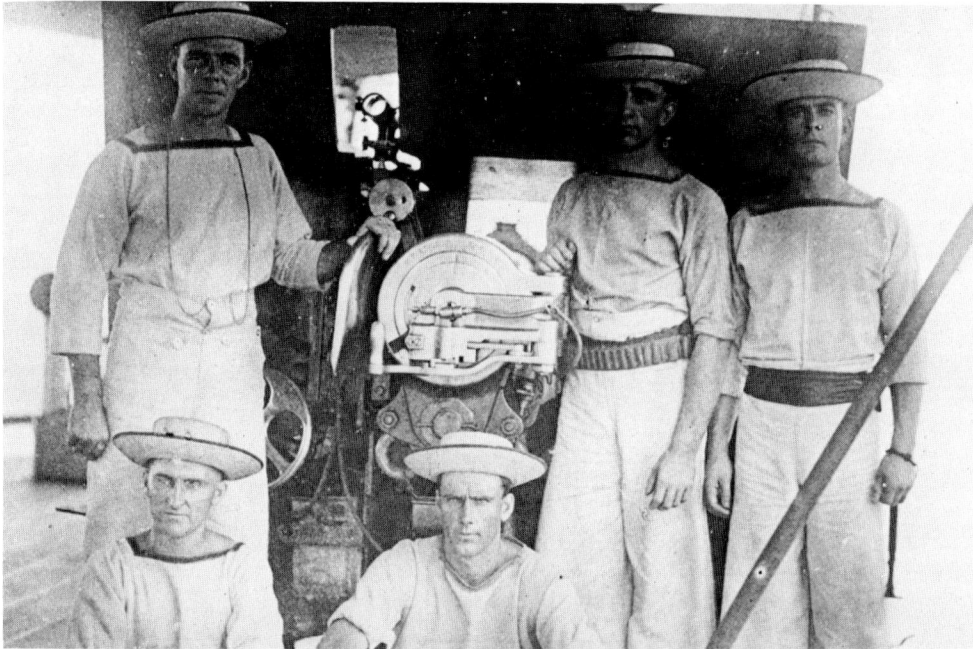
Starboard III gun-crew of 4-inch Mk III single mount on HMAS PIONEER, 1916. (Photo – L. Forsythe)

12-inch MkX BL guns. (Photo – H. Adlam).

Forward 8-inch guns on HMAS AUSTRALIA.

4-inch Mk VIII gun aboard HMAS TORRENS in the Mediterranean Sea during the Great War.

HMAS HOBART at Tawi Tawi, 16th April, 1945. HMA Ships YUNNAN (left), and MERKUR (right), lie alongside the cruiser. On the centreline are the X and Y 6-inch Mk XXIII guns. A single 40mm bofors is sited above the 6-inch guns. (112327).

4.7-inch Mk XII quick-firing guns aboard HMAS ARUNTA, 21st July, 1945.

One of HMAS SYDNEY's four 4-inch Mk V quick-firing single mounts. Note the 31lb projectile being loaded.

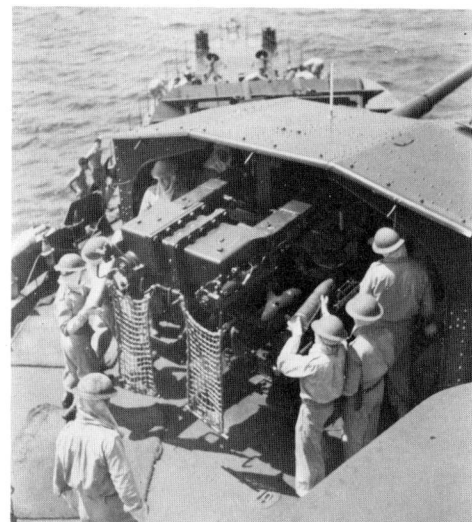

Starboard 2 pounder Mk VIII pom-pom. (112339).

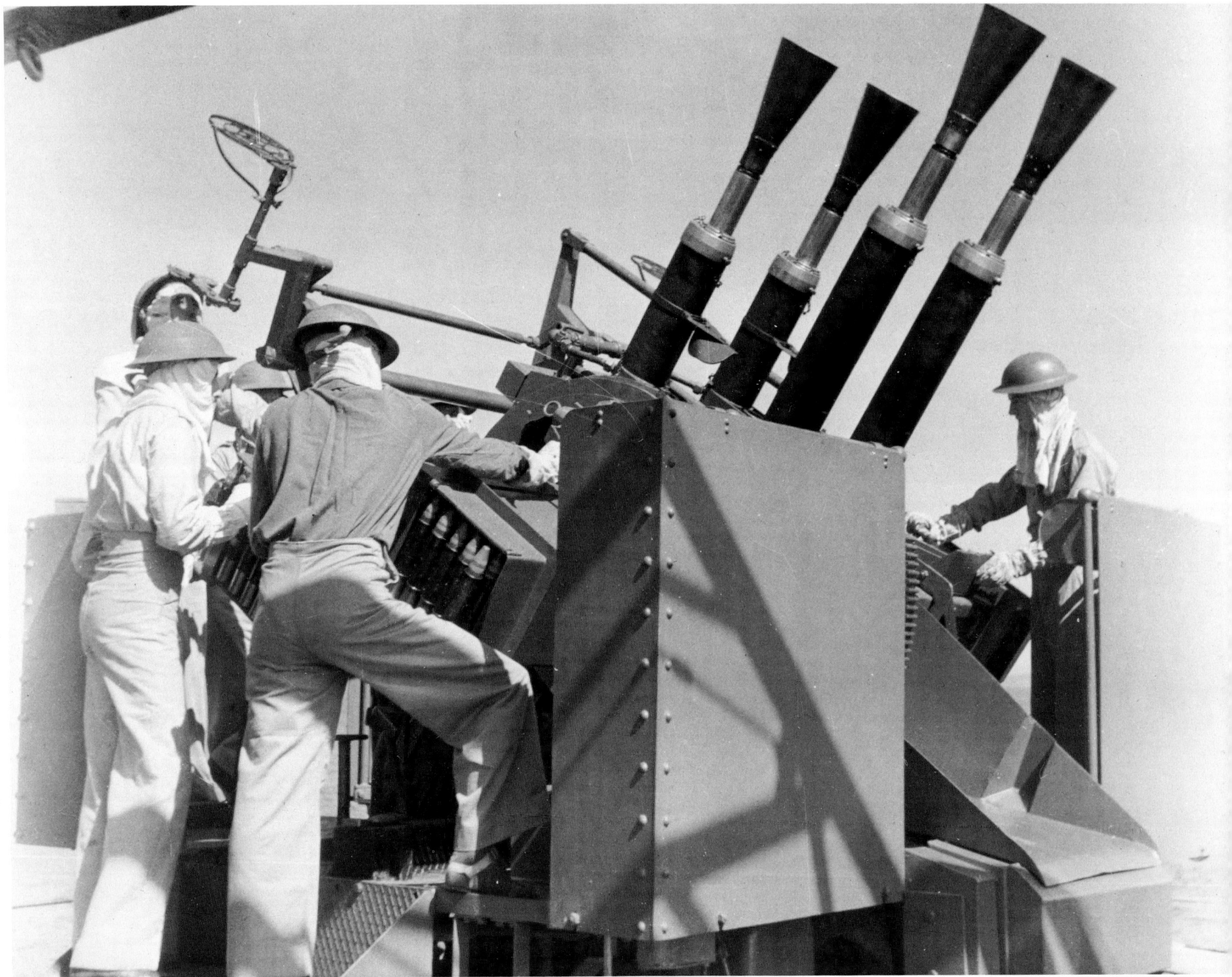

QF GUNS

Gun	Bore	Length In Calibres	Weight Gun	Weight Projectile	Weight Full Charge	Muzzle Velocity F/P/S	Max Range Yards	Elevation	Mounting*	Notes	Carried In
4.7 inch MK II	4.742"	40	42 cwt	45 lbs	5 lbs 7 ozs	2150	11,800	20°	PIII		GAYUNDAH PALUMA
4.7 inch MK IX	4.742"	45	2.97 Tons	50 lbs	10 lbs	2650	17,200	40°	CPXVIII		Q class
4.7 inch MK XII	4.742"	50	3 Tons	50 lbs	10 lbs	2650	17,800	40°	CPXIX		N class Tribal class
4.7 inch MK VIII	4.742"	45	2.9 Tons	50 lbs	9 lbs	2600	16,000	90°	HA MK XII	AA Armament, fixed ammunition	ALBATROSS
4 inch MK III	4"	40	26 cwt	25 lbs	3 lbs 9 ozs	2090	7,500	20°	PI		PIONEER PSYCHE FANTOME
4 inch MK IV	4"	40	26 cwt	31 lbs	5 lbs 1¾ ozs	2225	13,000	30°	CPIII		S class
4 inch MK IV	4"	40	24 cwt	31 lbs	5 lbs 9 ozs	2225	10,000	20°	PIX	Early mounting for MK IV gun	DOOMBA AUXS.
4 inch MK V	4"	45	42 cwt	31 lbs	7 lbs 11 ozs	2625	14,000	30°	CPII		V & W class
4 inch MK V	4"	45	42 cwt	31 lbs	7 lbs 11 ozs	3000	14,000	85°	HAIII		SWAN (II) YARRA (II) CANBERRA SYDNEY (II)
4 inch MK XVI	4"	45	2 Tons 1 cwt	35 lbs	9 lbs	2650	18,000	80°	CP MKXIX		Tribal class Cruisers, Sloops, AA Frigates
4 inch MK XVI	4"	45	2 Tons 1 cwt	35 lbs	9 lbs	2650	18,000	80°	CP MK XX		AMS, Sloops Frigates
4 inch MK XIX	4"	40	1 Ton 5 cwt	31 lbs	4 lbs	1275	9,500	60°	CP MK XXIII	Woolworth gun, fixed ammunition	AMS
3 inch 20 cwt	3"	45	20 cwt	12.5 lbs	2.5 lbs	2500	Ceiling 23,000 ft	90°	HA II to V		STUART AMC
3 inch 50 Cal MK 21 MODO	3"	50	11 cwt	13 lbs	4 lbs	2700	14,600	-13° +85°	MK 22 MODO	U.S. Model	RESERVE SPRIGHTLY
12 pdr. 12 cwt.	3"	40	12 cwt	12.5 lbs	2 lbs	2258		80°	HA III	AA version of earlier gun	V & W class BDVs, Auxs.
12 pdr. 12 cwt.	3"	40	12 cwt	12.5 lbs	2 lbs	2258	8,000	-15° +20°	PI	Introduced in 1894	Various ships
6 pdr. Hotchkiss	2.244"	40	8 cwt	6 lbs	7¾ ozs	1818	7,600	-20° +20°	PI		MALLOW
3 pdr. Hotchkiss	1.85"	40	5 cwt	3 lbs	6½ ozs	1873	4,000	-35° +25°	PI	Originally for anti-TB defence. Later as saluting gun.	Most ships except destroyers to 1939
2 pdr. MK XIV	40mm	45	2 cwt	2 lbs		2000	3,000	30°	P	Fired pom-pom ammunition. Known as Rolls Royce gun	MLs

*NOTE FOR MOUNTINGS: P = Pedestal, CP = Central Pivot, VCP = Vavaseur Central Pivot, HA = High Angle

Quick-firing 4-inch Mk V anti-aircraft gun on HMAS CANBERRA. (Photo – I. Cowie)

H.A. guns HMAS WARREGO. The quick-firing weapons are 4-inch MK XVI on a CP Mk XIX twin-mounting. (Photo V. Hutchison).

A 12 pounder gun aboard HMAS MALLOW in the Hawkesbury River, 1925.

6 pounder Hotchkiss aboard HMAS MALLOW, 1925.

Two single 2 pounder pom-poms on HMAS AUSTRALIA. Gibraltar is in the background. (Photo – B. Worthington)

20mm Oerlikon gun, HMAS WARREGO. (Photo – V. Hutchison)

Quad 0.5-inch Vickers, HMAS WARREGO. (Photo – V. Hutchison)

CLOSE RANGE WEAPONS

Gun	Bore	Length Cal	Muzzle Velocity ft/sec	Effective Range Yards	Rate of Fire rpm	Weight Gun	Projectile Weight	Elevation	Feed	Notes
40mm Bofors	40mm	60	2720	2,500	120	202 Bar 616 lbs	2 lbs	−5° +90°	Clip	Mounted as single or twins. Widely used. Singles MK III. HOBART had three MK VI Hazemeyer mountings (twin)
2 pdr. MK VIII Pom-Pom	40mm	39	2000	1,200	115	530 lbs	2 lbs	−10° +80°	Belt	Either single or four barrel units. Gradually replaced by 40mm Bofors. Pom-Pom was much less powerful than Bofors.
20 mm Oerlikon	20mm	65		1,000	450			85°	Drum	Single or twin mounts. Widely used.
.5 inch Vickers	0.5″		2520	800	600			80°	Belt	Carried in a 4 barrel mounting. Fitted in cruisers, destroyers, sloops, etc. Replaced by 20 mm Oerlikon.
.5 inch Browning	0.5″		2800	1,200	600			85°	Belt	Standard U.S. heavy M.G. Widely used.
.303 inch Vickers	0.303″		2600	800	600				Belt	Standard MMG in 1934. Widely used. Used MKVIIIZ ammunition.
.303 inch Lewis	0.303″		2240	600	450				Drum	Standard LMG in 1939. Widely used. For AA fire normally used as twin mounting.
.303 inch V.B.	0.303″		2440	600	550				Drum	Vickers-Berthier model, known as 'K' gun or 'GO' (gas operated). In MLs, HDMLs etc.
.303 inch Bren	0.303″		2440	600	550				Box Mag	Standard British LMG in 1934. Entry into RAN slightly later.
.303 inch Maxim	0.303″		2440	500	500				Belt	Standard MG in 1914. Some still in use in 1939.
0.45 inch Maxim	0.45″		2000		500				Belt	Obsolete but still in use in 1914–18. Fired 0.45 inch Martini-Henry round.
0.45 inch Gatling	0.45″		1800		800			60°	Strip or Drum	Fired 0.45″ GG (Gatling-Gardiner) cartridge. Obsolete in 1914 but some retained. 10 Barrel unit.

NOTES: 1. Combinations of these weapons carried by most ships.
2. Elevations of M.G.s depended on the type of mounting used.

Browning 0.5 inch machine gun, aboard HMAS SEA MIST at Morotai, 24th June, 1945.

Vickers 0.303-inch MMG, HMAS WARREGO (Photo – V. Hutchison)

Twin Lewis 0.303 LMG on anti-aircraft mounting, HMAS WARREGO. (Photo – V. Hutchison)

SHIPBOARD AVIATION

HMAS AUSTRALIA, 1918, with aircraft being retrieved. (EN 542).

SOPWITH BABY – *Scout/Seaplane*

One Sopwith 'Baby' was operated by the light cruiser BRISBANE on loan from HMS RAVEN II between April and May 1917. Seventy one aircraft were originally built by the Blackburn Aeroplane and Motor Co. Ltd.

The seaplane was carried between BRISBANE's aft funnel and mast and lowered overboard by a derrick for take-off. The reverse applied for retrieval. During its brief period of service the 'Baby' was employed in the search for the German commerce raider WOLF.

In total 185 'Babys' were constructed.

Crew: One
Weights (lbs): 1,715 (loaded)
Dimensions (feet): *Length* 23 *Wing Span* 25.8 *Height* 10
Engines: Clerget rotary tractor engine, 130 hp
Speed (mph): 98
Endurance (hours): $2\frac{1}{4}$
Ceiling (feet): 7,600
Guns: One Lewis MG
Payload: Two 65 lb bombs.

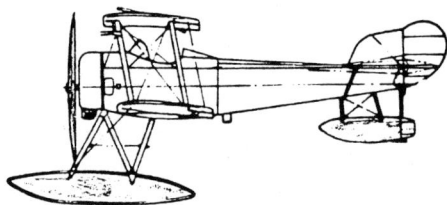

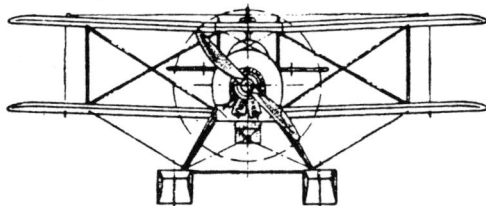

Sopwith 'Baby' being hoisted aboard HMAS BRISBANE.

Sopwith 'Baby' taking off.

Sopwith Baby. (R. Gillett)

SOPWITH PUP – *Fighter/Scout*

Sopwith 'Pups' were originally flown in RAN service from the Town class light cruiser SYDNEY. The acquisition of the aircraft was in response to the menace of German Zepplins which attacked allied ships at will, beyond the range of anti-aircraft defences.

Approximately 290 'Pups' were built for the Royal Naval Air Service. In mid-1917 SYDNEY was fitted with a revolving aircraft platform behind and partly over the forrard 6 inch gun mount. The initial flight was made from the ship on 8th December 1917 using 'Pup' borrowed from HMS DUBLIN. This was the first time an aircraft had taken off from an RAN warship.

On 17th December SYDNEY launched the 'Pup' into the wind, the first time an aircraft had been launched from a revolving platform.

The flagship AUSTRALIA, based at Rosyth, also operated a 'Pup' during December 1917 when an example was flown off the deck. During the following January a 'Pup' was again launched on the 30th of the month.

Crew: One
Weight (lbs): 1,225 (loaded)
Dimensions (feet): *Length* 19.4 *Wing Span* 26.6 *Height* 9.5
Engines: One Le Rhone, 80 hp
Speed (mph): 111 at sea level
Endurance (hours): 3
Ceiling (feet): 17,500
Guns: One Lewis MG (foreward)
Payload: N/A.

Sopwith 'Pup', HMAS AUSTRALIA, 1917.

Sopwith 'Pup' taking off from the flagship.

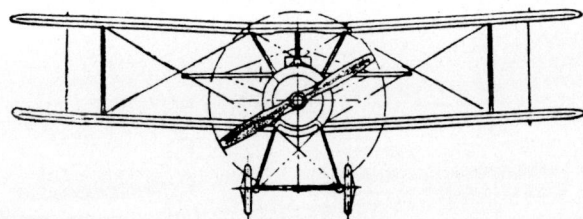

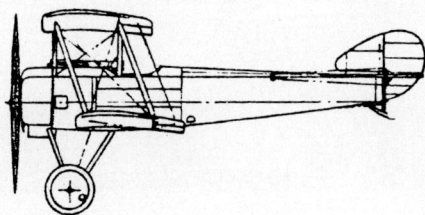

Sopwith Pup. (R. Gillett)

SOPWITH CAMEL – *Fighter/Scout*

A development of the Sopwith FI 'Camel' the 2FI version first joined AUSTRALIA and SYDNEY in February 1918. Both warships began flying operations immediately, the former from an aircraft platform over Q turret amidships (starboard) and subsequently from the P turret (port). SYDNEY worked her 'Camel' from the revolving platform originally erected for the 'Pup'.

For a time, AUSTRALIA's midship turrets were both provided with aircraft, one being the 'Camel' and the other a '1$\frac{1}{2}$ Strutter'. On 22nd October 1918 AUSTRALIA operated two 'Camels'.

A revolving platform was fitted to MELBOURNE in March 1918 with the first flight, by a 'Camel' on 10th May. 'Camels' from both SYDNEY and MELBOURNE commenced their initial operational flights in January 1919.

All 'Camels' were returned to the Royal Air Force in early 1919.

Crew: One
Weight (lbs): 1,530 (loaded)
Dimensions (feet): *Length* 18.8 *Wing Span* 26.11 *Height* 9.1
Engines: One Clerget, 130 hp
Speed (mph): 124
Range (miles): N/A
Ceiling (feet): 17,300
Guns: One Vickers MG (above fuselage), One Lewis MG (above wing centre section)
Payload: Two 50 lb bombs.

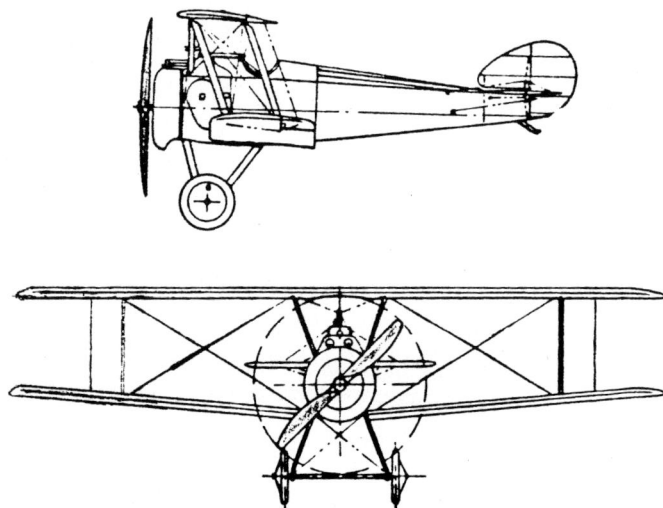

Sopwith Camel. (R. Gillett)

Sopwith 'Camel' aboard the light cruiser HMAS SYDNEY.

Sopwith Camel.

Sopwith Camel.

SOPWITH 1½ STRUTTER –
Bomber/Fighter/Reconaissance

The Strutter was originally developed for the Royal Naval Air Service in 1915. Approximately 550 aircraft, including 420 two-seat versions, were built.

Experiments aboard Royal Navy warships began in late 1917. The battle cruiser AUSTRALIA, which had been fitted with a large launching platform, made the first launch in March, 1918. A two-seat Strutter was successfully launched from a short deck constructed above Q turret on 8th March, 1918 and again on 14th May.

Crew: Two
Weight (lbs): 2,149 (loaded)
Dimensions (feet): *Length* 25.3 *Wing Span* 33.6 *Height* 10.3
Engines: One Clerget, 110 hp
Speed (mph): 106
Endurance (hours): 4
Ceiling (feet): 13,000
Guns: One Vickers MG (forward), One Lewis MG (aft)
Payload: Two 65 lb bombs.

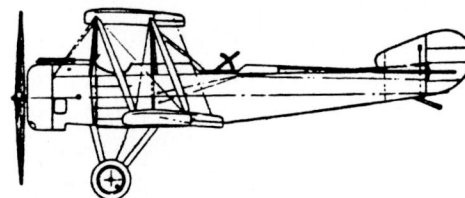

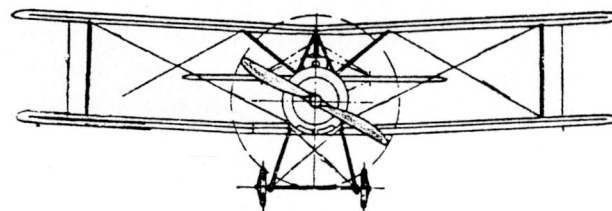

Sopwith 1½ Strutter. (R. Gillett)

Sopwith 1½ Strutter, HMAS AUSTRALIA, 1918.

AVRO 504L – *Bomber/Seaplane*

A standard trainer for the British services, the Avro 504 was built from July 1913 and employed by the Royal Naval Air Service until the late 1920s.

In 1920 an Australian Army Aviation Corps seaplane (504L) was embarked in AUSTRALIA for a trial period. The aircraft was stowed abreast the funnel and lifted out via the coal derrick. With the impending decommissioning of AUSTRALIA in 1921 it was decided to transfer the 504L to the light cruiser MELBOURNE.

The resultant tropic trails caused many problems and the aircraft was landed in November, 1920.

Crew: One
Weight (lbs): 1,574
Dimensions (feet): *Length* 29.5 *Wing Span* 36 *Height* 10.5
Engines: Gnome Monosoupape, 100 hp
Speed (mph): 82
Endurance (hours): $4\frac{1}{2}$
Ceiling (feet): N/A
Guns: One Lewis
Payload: Four 20 lb bombs.

Avro 504L at Cairns, operating from HMAS MELBOURNE.

Fairy IIID with her original RAN markings. "ANA" stood for Australian Naval Aircraft.

FAIRY IIID – *Reconnaissance/Seaplane*

Six Fairy IIIDs were purchased by the RAAF in 1921 for operations from the RAN's cruisers and sloops. The aircraft were designated ANA (Australian Naval Aircraft).

However the only RAN ship to embark the IIID was the survey sloop GERANIUM for operations on the Great Barrier Reef.

Later the aircraft were re-designated with RAAF numbers, A10–1 to A10–6.

Crew: Three
Weight (lbs): 5,050
Dimensions: *Length* 37 *Wing Span* 46.1 *Height* 11.4
Engines: One Rolls Royce Eagle VIII, 375 hp
Speed (mph): 106
Range (miles): 550 @ 100 mph
Ceiling (feet): 16,500
Guns: One Vickers MG (forward), One Lewis MG (aft)
Payload: N/A.

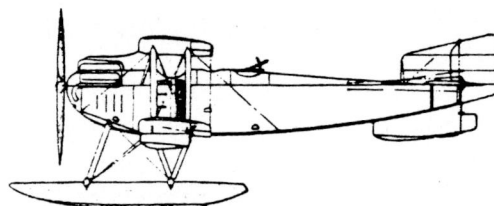

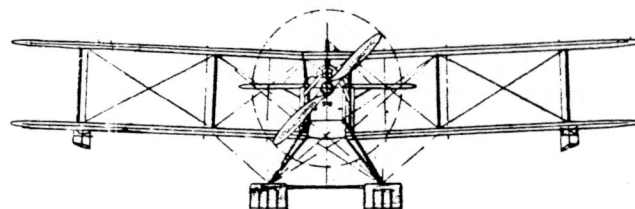

Fairy IIID. (R. Gillett)

Fairy IIID stored aboard HMAS GERANIUM, the first British survey ship to embark a seaplane.

Fairy IIID aboard the heavy cruiser, HMAS AUSTRALIA.

Fairy IIID.

SEAGULL III –
Reconnaissance/Seaplane

Six Supermarine Seagull III Mark 3 (wooden boat hulled bi-plane amphibians) were ordered in 1925 to be used for survey and training with the Royal Australian Air Force. Between 1925 and 1928 the aircraft operated with No. 101 Fleet co-operation flight, surveying the Barrier Reef from shore bases.

The aircraft were retained and embarked in the seaplane carrier ALBATROSS when that ship commissioned in 1929. As Finance for newer amphibians had not been forthcoming the Seagull IIIs were used and a further three purchased at scrap value.

After the decommissioning of ALBATROSS in 1933 the aircraft joined the heavy cruisers AUSTRALIA and CANBERRA. As both ships lacked the catapult necessary to launch the Seagull IIIs their use was entirely dependent on the prevailing state of the sea. The Seagull III was eventually replaced by Seagull V.

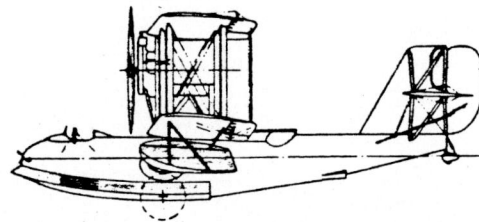

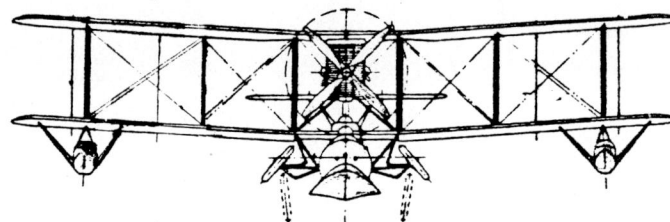

Seagull III. (R. Gillett)

Seagull III aboard the seaplane carrier HMAS ALBATROSS. The Seagull landed on her hull in lieu of floats.

Crew: Three
Weight (lbs): 5,688
Dimensions (feet): *Length* 37 *Wing Span* 46 *Height* 12
Engines: One Napier Lion V, 450 hp
Speed (mph): 108
Range (miles): N/A
Ceiling (feet): 5,000
Guns: One Lewis MG (amidships, aft)
Payload: N/A.

SEAGULL III.

WACKETT WIDGEON Mk1 –
Seaplane

The single seat Widgeon was carried by ALBATROSS for tropic trials during 1929.

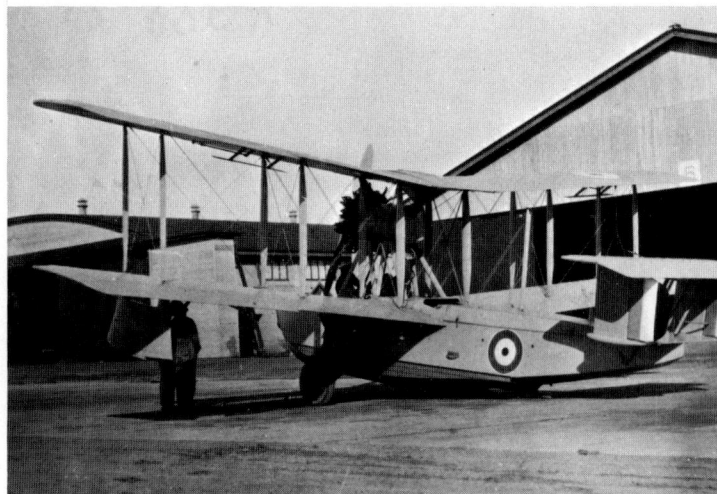

Wackett Widgeon Mk I.

SEAGULL V (WALRUS) –
Reconnaissance/Seaplane

In June 1933, shortly after the paying off of ALBATROSS the prototype Seagull Mk V amphibian flew. The aircraft was first ordered by the Australian Government for embarkation aboard her cruisers. Twenty-four were delivered to Australia by 1937.

During the Second World War, the heavy cruisers AUSTRALIA and CANBERRA and light cruisers HOBART, PERTH and SYDNEY were each equipped with an aircraft and catapult. For a short time CANBERRA operated a second aircraft. The armed merchant cruisers WESTRALIA and MANOORA also carried the aircraft but without a catapult.

The New Zealand ships ACHILLES and LEANDER were equipped with the Seagull V. Both planes were lost.

The last RAN ship to carry the Seagull V, AUSTRALIA landed her amphibian in October 1944 at Manus Island.

During Royal Navy service, ALBATROSS carried Seagull Vs during her deployment to the South Atlantic and Indian Oceans. A total of 744 Seagull V (Walrus) aircraft were built between 1935 and 1944.

Crew: Three
Weight (lbs): 7,200
Dimensions (feet): *Length* 37.3 *Wing Span* 45.10 *Height* 15.3
Engines: One Bristol Pegasus II, 775 hp
Speed (mph): 135
Range (miles): 600
Ceiling (feet): 18,500
Guns: Two Vickers
Payload: Small bombs.

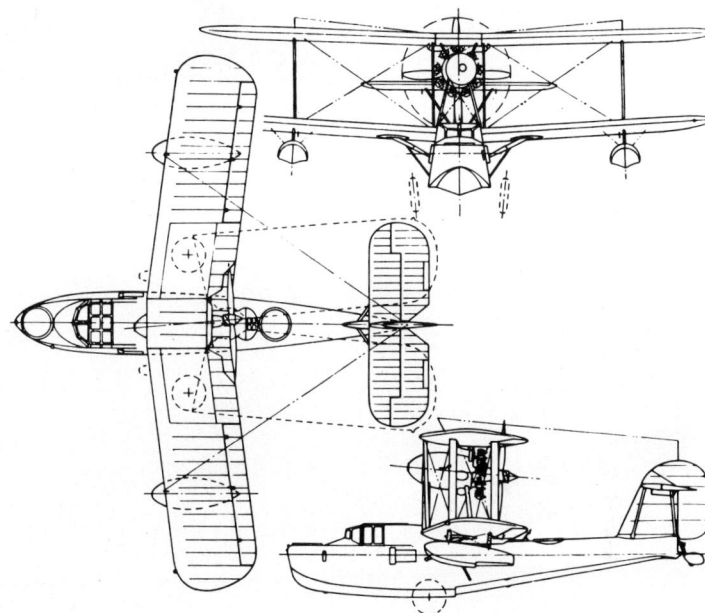

Seagull V. (RAN)

Seagull V, A2-1, on its catpult, HMAS HOBART.

Seagull V A2-1 after a mishap aboard HMAS AUSTRALIA. (Photo – J. Sanderson)

Seagull V, HMAS CANBERRA. The Seagull Vs principal advantage over its predecessor was that the ship could catapult the aircraft, instead of stopping dead in the water to make the launch. However, it still had to stop to recover.

HMAS MANOORA as an armed merchant cruiser with Seagull V embarked between the bridge and funnel. No catapult was fitted.

Seagull V on its catapult between the funnels of HMAS PERTH, 1941.

RAN PENDANT NUMBERS 1914–1918

Note: Where no year is given, pendant number is as built/as requisitioned/or first allotted.

1–AEI
H02 – SUCCESS (1920)
A1 – SYDNEY (1.18)
F1A – SUCCESS (4.19)
2 – AE2
F2A – TATTOO (4.19)
F3A – SWORDSMAN (3.19)
F4A – STALWART (4.19)
C6 – AUSTRALIA (2.15)
C8 – PLATYPUS (1.18)
YA8 – GRANTALA (1914)
O9 – AUSTRALIA (1.18)

H11 – SWORDSMAN (1920)
H14 – STALWART (1920)
H25 – TASMANIA (1920)
H26 – TATTOO (1920)
T27 – MALLOW
X36 – KURUMBA (1.18)
T37 – GERANIUM (1.18)
50 – HUON
G50 – ANZAC (1.18)
T51 – MARGUERITE (1.16)
52 – SYDNEY (4.18)
55 – PARRAMATTA
T56 – GERANIUM
T59 – MALLOW (1.18)
G60 – ANZAC (4.17)
T60 – MARGUERITE (1.18)

61 – SWAN
F61 – ANZAC (2.17)
67 – TORRENS
M68 – MALLOW
70 – WARREGO
G70 – ANZAC (4.18)
79 – YARRA
80 – AE1
81 – AE2
81 – AUSTRALIA (4.18)
86 – MELBOURNE (1.18)
G90 – ANZAC
93 – MELBOURNE (4.18)
G97 – TASMANIA (2.19)

RAN PENDANT NUMBERS 1939–1945

D00 – STUART
FY00 – TOLGA
I00 – STUART (1940)
FY01 – TOORIE
J01 – DOOMBA (1941)
N01 – DOOMBA
FY02 – FALIE
G02 – NESTOR
FY03 – WHANG PU
FY04 – WINTER
D5 – ARUNTA (1943)
FY05 – THREE CHEERS
FY06 – SLEUTH (ex Vigilant)
Z06 – KINCHELA
FY07 – NARANI
FY08 – COOMBAR
D9 – BATAAN
FY09 – PANDION
D10 – WARRAMUNGA (1943)
FY10 – PATERSON

Q10 – SEA MIST
Q11 – LEILANI
FY12 – BOMBO
Q12 – STEADY HOUR
D13 – NAPIER (1945)
D14 – NEPAL (1945)
Q14 – LOLITA
D15 – NIZAM (1945)
FY15 – BIRCHGROVE PARK
P15 – KOOKABURRA
Q15 – ESMERALDA
Z15 – KOOKABURRA (1940)
D16 – NORMAN (1945)
FY16 – WARRAWEE
Q16 – MAKO
FY17 – SOUTHERN CROSS
Q17 – MORUYA
FY18 – ALLENWOOD
Q18 – COONGOOLA
FY19 – KIANGA

Q19 – NEREUS
D20 – QUIBERON (1945)
FY20 – POYANG
Q20 – MARLEAN
D21 – QUICKMATCH (1945)
FY21 – INNISFAIL
Q21 – SIROCCO
D22 – WATERHEN
I22 – WATERHEN (1940)
Q22 – SAGITTAS
F23 – KANIMBLA (AMC)
FY23 – BANGALOW
Q23 – TASMA
FY24 – ALATNA
Q24 – ARCADIA
FY25 – GRIFFOEN
G25 – NEPAL
J25 – COOLEBAR
FY26 – ST FRANCIS
Q26 – GRELKA

FY27 – RED BILL
Q27 – NOKOMIS
FY28 – IBIS
D29 – PERTH (1940)
FY29 – ARTHUR ROSE
I29 – PERTH
M29 – BUNGAREE
FY30 – CAPE LEEUWIN
I30 – ARUNTA
D31 – VOYAGER
FY31 – CHINAMPA
I31 – VOYAGER (1940)
Q31 – WESTWIND
FY32 – MEDEA
Q32 – GRELKA
D33 – CANBERRA (1940)
FY33 – URALBA
I33 – CANBERRA
Q33 – MARTINDALE
FY34 – MERCEDES
K34 – ARARAT
Q34 – CYGNUS
FY35 – AMBON
FY36 – POTRERO
Q36 – NEPEAN
FY37 – MALANDA
FY38 – GIPPSLAND
G38 – NIZAM
FY39 – SULITUAN
N39 – K9
FY40 – MAROUBRA
FY42 – ELWING
Q42 – MIRO
FY43 – STELLA
I44 – WARRAMUNGA
L44 – PARRAMATTA
U44 – PARRAMATTA (1940)
FY45 – KIETH CAM
FY46 – KURAMIA
FY47 – CARROO
D47 – ADELAIDE (1940)
I47 – ADELAIDE
D48 – SYDNEY (1940)
F48 – MANOORA (AMC)
FY48 – MARY CAM
I48 – SYDNEY
FY49 – KOOPA
G49 – NORMAN
Q50 – MIRAMAR

FY51 – FAURO CHIEF
Q51 – YARROMA
FY52 – RANDJANI
Q52 – SILVER CLOUD
Q53 – FAY C
J54 – MORESBY
Q54 – SAN MICHELLE
FY55 – ABRAHAM CRIJNSSEN
Q55 – WINBAH
D56 – PLATYPUS
FY56 – ARCADIA
FY57 – ELLAN
Z57 – MARY CAM
FY58 – ARCADIA
FY59 – LADAVA (ex Jon Jim)
FY60 – GUMLEAF
C61 – WESTRALIA (LSI)
FY62 – GERARD
D63 – HOBART (1940)
FY63 – POLARIS
I63 – HOBART
FY64 – LAURABADA
X64 – KURUMBA
FY65 – JOHN OXLEY
Q65 – TOOMAREE
FY66 – MATTHEW FLINDERS
X66 – BISHOPDALE
FY67 – MATAFELE
D68 – VAMPIRE
I68 – VAMPIRE (1940)
D69 – VENDETTA
FY69 – BURRA BRA
I69 – VENDETTA (1940)
P69 – KOALA
Z69 – KOALA (1942)
FY70 – WATCHER
Q70 – JOHN HARDY
FY71 – BERYL II
Q71 – LUCY STAR
FY72 – TONGKOL
U73 – WARREGO
FY74 – GOORANGAI
L74 – SWAN
U74 – SWAN (1940)
FY75 – GOOLGWAI
FY76 – OLIVE CAM
C77 – MANOORA (LSI)
L77 – YARRA
U77 – YARRA (1940)

C78 – KANIMBLA (LSI)
FY78 – WONGALA
FY79 – KOROWA
FY80 – UKI
P80 – KANGAROO
Q80 – VIGILANT
Z80 – KANGAROO (1940)
FY81 – BERMAGUI
G81 – QUIBERON
Q81 – LARRAKIA
Q82 – KIARA
Q83 – KURU
Z83 – TAMBAR
D84 – AUSTRALIA (1940)
FY84 – COOLEBAR
I84 – AUSTRALIA
FY85 – BONTHORPE
FY86 – ST GILES
FY87 – HEROS
FY88 – BINGERA
KY89 – ADELE
FY90 – KYBRA
Q90 – KWATO
FY91 – YANDRA
Q91 – LYSANDER
FY92 – WILCANNIA
G92 – QUICKMATCH
FY93 – DURRAWEEN
Q93 – PALUMA
FY94 – GOONAMBEE
F95 – WESTRALIA (AMC)
FY95 – SAMUEL BENBOW
FY96 – KING BAY
Z96 – KINCHELA
FY97 – ALFIE CAM
G97 – NAPIER
FY98 – GUNBAR
FY99 – TERKA
Z101 – BERYL II
W103 – SPRIGHTLY
F123 – PLATYPUS
W126 – FORCEFUL
W127 – WATO
J128 – GERALDTON
W128 – WAREE
W129 – ELWING
J130 – ORARA
W130 – HEROS
J137 – TONGKOL

J141 – TAMBAR
J145 – LISMORE
W149 – RESERVE
FL150 – PING WO
FL151 – YUNNAN
J153 – WHYALLA
J157 – TOOWOOMBA
J158 – BATHURST
J167 – GOULBURN
J172 – WOLLONGONG
J175 – CESSNOCK
J179 – LAUNCESTON
J181 – TAMWORTH
J183 – CAIRNS
J184 – BALLARAT
J186 – IPSWICH
J187 – BENDIGO
J188 – GAWLER
J189 – PIRIE
J191 – BROOME
J192 – KALGOOLIE
J195 – MARYBOROUGH
J198 – BURNIE
J201 – GEELONG
J202 – WARRNAMBOOL
J203 – ROCKHAMPTON
J204 – KATOOMBA
J205 – TOWNSVILLE
J206 – LITHGOW
J207 – MILDURA
Z216 – KARANGI (1942)

J218 – KAPUNDA
Z221 – KARA KARA
J222 – WALLAROO
J231 – BUNDABERG
J232 – DELORAINE
J233 – INVERELL
J234 – LATROBE
J235 – HORSHAM
B236 – BALLARAT (1945)
J236 – GLENELG
B237 – BENDIGO (1944)
B238 – BURNIE (1944)
J238 – GYMPIE
B239 – CAIRNS (1945)
B240 – CESSNOCK (1945)
J240 – ARMIDALE
B241 – GAWLER (1945)
J241 – BUNBURY
B242 – GERALDTON (1944)
J242 – COLAC
B243 – GOULBURN (1944)
B244 – IPSWICH (1944)
J244 – CASTLEMAINE
B245 – KALGOOLIE (1944)
B246 – LAUNCESTON (1944)
J246 – FREMANTLE
B247 – LISMORE (1944)
B248 – MARYBOROUGH (1944)
J248 – SHEPPARTON
B249 – PIRIE (1944)
B250 – TAMWORTH (1944)

B251 – TOOWOOMBA (1944)
J251 – DUBBO
B252 – WHYALLA (1944)
J252 – ECHUCA
B253 – WOLLONGONG (1944)
Z253 – LANIKAI
Z256 – KOOMPARTOO
Z270 – GUNBAR
P282 – KARANGI
J285 – BOWEN
J315 – WAGGA
J316 – COOTAMUNDRA
J323 – BENALLA
J324 – GLADSTONE
J348 – STAWELL
J351 – COWRA
J353 – KIAMA
K354 – GASCOYNE
J361 – PARKES
J362 – JUNEE
J363 – STRAHAN
K363 – HAWKESBURY
K364 – LACHLAN
K375 – BARCOO
K376 – BURDEKIN
K377 – DIAMANTINA
521 – SEABIRD
AM1475 – ALATNA
MFV2045 – EDUARDO

RAN DISTINGUISHING LETTERS 1939–1945

AC – ALFIE CAM
BB – BOMBO
BP – BIRCHGROVE PARK
BR – BURRA BRA
BT – BERYL II
CB – COOLEBAR
DW – DURRAWEEN
FC – FAURO CHIEF
FE – FALIE
GB – GOONAMBEE
GD – GERARD

GG – GOOLGWAI
GL – GUMLEAF
GN – GUNBAR
GP – GIPPSLAND
GR – GOORANGAI
IF – INNISFAIL
IS – IBIS
JJ – JON JIM
JO – JOHN OXLEY
KB – KING BAY
KN – KIANGA

KO – KOROWA
KP – KOOPA
KU – KURAMIA
KY – KYBRA
LD – LADAVA
LU – LAURABADA
MB – MERBADOE
MC – MARY CAM
MD – MALANDA
ME – MEDEA
MF – MATAFELE

MR – MAROUBRA
MS – MERCEDES
MW – MARRAWA
MW – MATTHEW FLINDERS
NB – NAMBUCCA
NR – NARANI
OC – OLIVE CAM
PN – PANDION
PO – POTRERO
PS – POLARIS
PT – PATERSON
PY – POYANG
RB – RED BILL

RJ – RANDJANI
SB – SAMUEL BENBOW
SF – ST FRANCIS
SG – ST GILES
SL – STELLA
SM – SMEROE
SU – SULITUAN
SX – SOUTHERN CROSS
TA – TERKA
TC – THREE CHEERS
TK – TONGKOL
TL – TOLGA
TO – TOORIE

TR – TERKA
UK – UKI
UR – URALBA
VG – VIGILANT
WA – WATCHER
WG – WONGALA
WN – WILCANNIA
WP – WHANG PU
WR – WINTER
WW – WARRAWEE
YD – YANDRA

RNZN PENDANT NUMBERS 1941–1945

M – MURTIAI
T00 – WAKAKURA
W04 – TOIA
T05 –
T08 – SOUTH SEA
T10 – JAMES COSGROVE
T14 – KAIWAKA
T15 – KAPUNI
T17 – HINAU
T18 – RIMU
T19 – MANUKA
T22 – PHYLLIS
T23 – NORA NIVEN
T24 – AROHA
T25 – AWATERE
T26 – HAUTAPU
T27 – MAIMAI
T28 – PAHAU
T32 – WAIPU
T33 – WAIMA

T34 – WAIHO
L36 – LEITH
C48 – GAMBIA
F59 – MONOWAI
L65 – WELLINGTON
C70 – ACHILLES
K73 – ARABIS
C75 – LEANDER
K86 – ARBUTUS
T102 – KIWI
T155 – INCHKEITH
T160 – SANDA
T174 – KILLEGRAY
T175 – SCARBA
T233 – MOA
T234 – TUI
T338 – MAIMAI
T340 – HAUTAPU
T343 – WAIKATO
T348 – TAWHAI

T349 – WAIMA
T351 – PAHAU
T357 – WAIPU
T364 – WAIAU (Cancelled)
T364 – WAIRUA
T371 – BREEZE
T372 – MATAI
K385 – ARABIS
T396 – AROHA
T397 – AWATERE
T398 – HAWERA
T399 – HINAU
T400 – KAPUNI
T401 – MANUKA
T402 – RIMU
K403 – ARBUTUS
T403 – WAIHO
Q – NAP boats (prefix)

RAN SHIPBUILDING PRIOR TO 1914

HUON (left) and TORRENS (right) under construction at Cockatoo Island, Sydney, 22nd April, 1913.

HUON and TORRENS, 29th July, 1913. Note the cruiser HMAS PROTECTOR in the Fitzroy dock.

HUON, 29th September, 1913. The sign below her bow shows her original name of DERWENT.

HUON, 19th January, 1914.

TORRENS, stern view, 22nd October, 1914.

HUON nearing completion, 1st December, 1914.

Launching of HUON, 19th December, 1914.

RAN SHIPBUILDING POLICY 1939–45

In the Second World War the RAN comprised a large proportion of requisitioned tonnage, Local shipyards produced 198 vessels, ranging in size from the Tribal class destroyers to small 45 foot tow boats. A building programme instituted in 1939 saw 56 Bathurst class AMS completed and in service by mid 1944. Twenty of the class were on account of the British Admiralty, the first ten being ordered in January, 1940.

The second largest group to be built locally were the 35 Fairmile B motor launches, laid down between March, 1942, and August, 1943, an average of two launches per month. The following table illustrates the origin and fate of all vessels built for the purpose, including numbers cancelled during the course of the war.

Class	Built in Aust.	Built in U.K.	Cancelled	Lost	Retained by RAN
Tribal	3	–	5	–	3
'N'	–	5	–	1	–
'Q'	–	2	–	–	2
Grimsby	2	–	–	1	1
River	8	–	–	–	8
Bay	4	–	10	–	4
AMS	56	–	–	3	53
Fairmile B	35	–	–	2	33
HDML	9	19*	2	–	9
SRD	8	–	1	–	–
Bar	3	–	–	–	3
ASR	4	20**	2	–	20
GPV	22	–	10	–	22
120′ Lighters	11	–	5	–	11
85′ Lighters	8	–	1	–	8
OFL	8	–	1	–	8
TRV/TRB	5	–	–	–	5
Tugs	–	2**	–	–	2
45′ Tow Boat	12	–	–	–	6

*16-USA   **Built USA

The Tribal class destroyer ARUNTA immediately prior to launching at Cockatoo, 30th November, 1940 (80820).

WARSHIPS

Commissioned	Tribal	N	Q	Grimsby	River	AMS	Fairmile	HDML	SRD	BDV
1939 – 1st Half	1	–	–	–	–	–	–	–	–	1
– 2nd Half	1	–	–	–	–	–	–	–	–	–
1940 – 1st Half	–	–	–	1	–	–	–	–	–	1
– 2nd Half	–	1	–	1	–	2	–	–	–	1
1941 – 1st Half	–	2	–	–	–	6	–	–	–	–
– 2nd Half	–	1	–	–	–	8	–	–	–	1
1942 – 1st Half	–	1	–	–	–	12	–	–	–	–
– 2nd Half	–	–	2	–	–	15	1	2	–	–
1943 – 1st Half	–	–	–	–	–	7	17	1	–	–
– 2nd Half	–	–	–	–	1	2	14	2	–	–
1944 – 1st Half	–	–	–	–	2	4	3	10	–	–
– 2nd Half	–	–	–	–	1	–	–	10	1	–
1945 – 1st Half	1	–	–	–	2	–	–	3	3	–
– 2nd Half	–	–	–	–	–	–	–	–	4	–

ROCKHAMPTON under construction by Walkers.

SUPPORT CRAFT

Completed	ASR	GPV	120′ Lighters	85′ Lighters	OFLs	TRV/TRB	Tugs	45′ Tow Boat
1939 – 1st Half	–	–	–	–	–	–	–	–
– 2nd Half	–	–	–	–	–	–	–	–
1940 – 1st Half	–	–	–	–	–	–	–	–
– 2nd Half	–	–	–	–	1	–	–	–
1941 – 1st Half	–	–	–	–	–	–	–	–
– 2nd Half	–	–	–	–	–	–	–	–
1942 – 1st Half	–	–	–	–	–	–	–	–
– 2nd Half	–	–	–	–	–	–	–	–
1943 – 1st Half	–	–	–	–	–	–	–	–
– 2nd Half	–	–	–	–	–	2	1	–
1944 – 1st Half	–	–	–	1	–	–	1	–
– 2nd Half	11	4	–	3	–	3	–	–
1945 – 1st Half	8	4	–	3	2	–	–	–
– 2nd Half	2	10	2	1	3	–	–	10
1946 – 1st Half	1	4	9	–	1	–	–	2

RAAF stores lighter 06-15 with other craft in various stages of fitting out. (134543).

Left - AB 442, FRANCIS PEAT, re-arming in Morts Bay, Sydney, 1944.

AV 2767, CRUSADER, under construction at the Williamstown yards of the Melbourne Harbour Trust, 1945. Note the six propellers and four rudders. (112582).

RNZN SHIPBUILDING POLICY 1939–45

	Built in NZ	Built in UK	Cancelled	Lost	Retained by RNZN
Leander	–	2	–	–	–
Gambia	–	1	–	–	–
Bird	–	3	–	1	2
Flower	–	2	–	–	–
Isles	–	4	–	–	4
Castle (M/S)	4	–	–	–	4
Fairmile B	12	–	–	–	2
HDML	–	16 (USA)	–	–	10
Castle (A/S)	8	–	5	–	–

TAWHAI being launched, 20th July 1943.

WARSHIPS

	LEAN	GAMB	BIRD	FLOWER	ISLES	CASTLE (M/S)	FAIRMILE	HDML	CASTLE (A/S)
1939 1st half	–	–	–	–	–	–	–	–	–
2nd half	–	–	–	–	–	–	–	–	–
1940 1st half	–	–	–	–	–	–	–	–	–
2nd half	–	–	–	–	–	–	–	–	–
1941 1st half	–	–	–	–	–	–	–	–	–
2nd half	2	–	3	–	4	–	–	–	–
1942 1st half	–	–	–	–	–	1	–	–	–
2nd half	–	–	–	–	–	2	–	–	–
1943 1st half	–	–	–	–	–	–	1	4?	2
2nd half	–	–	–	–	–	–	11	4?	3
1944 1st half	–	–	–	1	–	1	–	4?	3
2nd half	–	–	–	1	–	–	–	4?	–
1945 1st half	–	–	–	–	–	–	–	–	–
2nd half	–	–	–	–	–	–	–	–	–

LOSSES OF RAN SHIPS, 1914–45

Ship	Date Lost	Type	How & Where Lost
AE 1	14/9/14	Submarine	Struck unchartered reef near Cape Gazelle, New Guinea
AE 2	30/4/15	Submarine	Sunk by Turkish warship, Sea of Marmora, Turkey.
Goorangai	20/11/40	Auxiliary Minesweeper	Collided with MV DUNTROON in Port Phillip.
Waterhen	30/6/41	Destroyer	Sank off Libya after German air attack.
Sydney	19/11/41	Light Cruiser	Sunk by German auxiliary cruiser KORMORAN off Western Australia.
Parramatta	27/11/41	Sloop	Sunk by German submarine off Libya.
Sirocco	26/1/42	NAP	Destroyed by fire, Hobart.
Mavie	19/2/42	Lugger	Destroyed by Japanese aircraft, Darwin.
Kelat	24/2/42	Lighter	Sank as a result of Japanese air attack on 19/2/42 in Darwin.
Perth	1/3/42	Light Cruiser	Sunk by Japanese naval forces in Sunda Strait.
Karalee	3/3/42	Light	Sunk as a result of Japanese air attack on 19/2/42 in Darwin.
Yarra	4/3/42	Sloop	Sunk by Japanese cruisers south of Java.
Vampire	9/4/42	Destroyer	Sunk by Japanese aircraft ESE of Ceylon.
Kuttabul	1/6/42	Depot Ship	Sunk by Japanese midget submarine in Sydney.
Nestor	16/6/42	Destroyer	Sunk by depth charges from HMS JAVELIN after bomb damage by German aircraft SW of Crete.
Nereus	2/7/42	NAP	Destroyed by fire, Sydney.
Canberra	9/8/42	Heavy Cruiser	Sunk by Japanese cruisers off Savo Island.
Siesta	23/9/42	NAP	Destroyed by fire, Sydney.
Voyager	25/9/42	Destroyer	Grounded on coast of Timor. Destroyed by crew.
Armidale	1/12/42	AMS	Sunk by Japanese aircraft off Timor.
Patricia Cam	22/1/43	Auxiliary Minesweeper	Sunk by Japanese aircraft off Wessel Island, N.T.
Yampi Lass	11/4/43	Lighter	Wrecked by storm, Darwin.
Adele	7/5/43	Stores Vessel	Wrecked by storm, Port Kembla.
Maroubra	10/5/43	Misc.	Destroyed by Japanese aircraft, N.T.
Wallaroo	11/6/43	AMS	Collided with US Liberty Ship and sank off Fremantle.
Silver Cloud	12/7/43	NAP	Destroyed by fire, Sydney.
Starfish	7/9/43	NAP	Ex CORSAIR. Grounded and wrecked Wollongong.
Hulda	21/9/43	Attached to Assault	Destroyed by Japanese, Buna, New Guinea.
Gladmore	17/10/43	NAP	Destroyed by fire, Fremantle.
Terka	26/3/44	Auxiliary Minesweeper	Foundered off Madang, New Guinea.
Matafele	20/6/44	Store Carrier	Presumed foundered en-route Townsville to Milne Bay.
ML 430	13/8/44	Fairmile B	Accidentally sunk by ML 819 north of Biak, New Guinea.
Geelong	18/10/44	AMS	Sank after collision with US tanker north of Langemak, New Guinea.
Marlean	12/11/44	Patrol	Destroyed by fire, Sydney.
ML 827	20/11/44	Fairmile B	Capsized under tow and sank after grounding near Cape Kawai, New Britain.
Steady Hour	3/3/45	NAP	Destroyed by fire, N.T.
Watcher	14/5/45	Misc.	Wrecked on Harvey Rocks, NE of Thursday Island.
Fauro Chief	16/5/45	Exam.	Sunk by collapse of jetty whilst moored alongside, Milne Bay, New Guinea.
Lolita	13/6/45	NAP	Wrecked following explosion and fire, Madang, New Guinea.
Warrnambool	13/9/47	AMS	Sank after striking mine near Cockburn Reef, Qld., (classed as war loss).

SHIPBUILDERS ABBREVIATIONS

BHP – Broken Hil Pty. Co. Ltd., Whyalla, S.A.

Barclay Curle – Barclay Curle & Co. Ltd., Glasgow, Scotland

Wm. Beardmore – Wm. Beardmore & Co. Ltd., Dalmuire, U.K.

John Brown – John Brown & Co. Ltd.

Cammell Land – Clydebank, Scotland.

Cockatoo – Cockatoo Island Dockyard, Sydney, NSW.

W. C. Cone – W. C. Cone......

Cook – Cook Welton & Gemmell, U.K.

Devonport – Devonport Dockyard, U.K.

Elscot – Elscot Boats, City Island, USA.

Evans Deakin – Evans Deakin & Co. Ltd., Brisbane, Qld.

Fairfield – Fairfield Shipbuilding & Engineering Co. Ltd., Govan, Scotland.

Fellows & Stewart – Fellows & Stewart Inc., U.S.A.

Freeport – Freeport Port Shipyard, Lond Island, USA.

George Brown – George Brown and Co.

A. E. Goodwin – A.E. Goodwin Ltd., Port Kembla, NSW.

Green Point – Green Point Naval Boatyard, Mortlake, NSW.

Halvorsen – Lars Halvorsen & Sons Pty. Ltd., Sydney, NSW.

Harbour Boat – Harbour Boat Building Co., U.S.A.

Henry Robb – Henry Robb Ltd., U.K.

E. Jack – E. Jack, Launceston, Tasmania.

Johnsons – Johnsons Tyne Foundry, Melbourne, Vic.

C.P. Leek – Charles P. Leek, New Jersey, U.S.A.

Hawthorn Leslie – Hawthorn Leslie & Co. Ltd., Heburn-on-Tyne, U.K.

Levingstone – Levingstone Shipbuilding Co., Orange, Texas, U.S.A.

Lewis – Lewis, Aberdeen, Scotland.

MacFarlane – MacFarlane & Sons, Birkenhead, S.A.

Mason – Mason Bros, Aucklord.

Morts – Morts Dock, Balmain, N.S.W.

Palmers – Palmers Shipbuilding & Iron Co. Ltd., U.K.

Patent Slip –

Poole & Steel – Poole & Steel Ltd., Balmain, N.S.W.

Portsmouth – Portsmouth Dockyard, U.K.

Purdon – Purdon & Featherstone Ltd., Hobart, Tasmania

L. Robinson – Leo Robinson, Gloucestshire, U.K.

Seager – Seager Bros, Shipbuilders Ltd., N.Z.

Senior Faondry – Senior Faondry Co., Auckland.

Sittinghouse – Sittinghouse Shipbuilding Co., U.K.

Slazengers – Slazengers Australia, Sydney, NSW.

South Coast – South Coast Co., U.S.A.

South Coast Co-Op – South Coast Co-Op, Moruya, N.S.W.

State Dockyard – N.S.W. State Dockyard, Newcastle, N.S.W.

Alex Stephen – Alex Stephen & Sons Ltd., Govan, Scotland.

Stevenson – Stevenson & Cook, Port Chalmers

Structural Engineering – Structural Engineering Co. Ltd., Perth, W.A.

Swan Hunter – Swan Hunter Wigham Richardson Ltd., Wallsend-on-Tyne, U.K.

Thornycroft – John I. Thornycroft Co. Ltd. Southhampton, U.K.

L. S. Thorson – L.S. Thorson, Ellesworth, U.S.A.

Truscott – Truscott Boat & Dock Co., St. Joseph, U.S.A.

Tullochs – Tullochs Shipyard, Sydney, N.S.W.

Walkers – Walkers Ltd., Maryborough, QLD.

J. Wallace – J. Wallace, Australia

Wellington – Wellington Patent Slip, Wellington

J. Samuel White – J. Samuel White & Co., Cowes, Isle of White

Williamstown – Williamstown Naval Dockyard, Williamstown, VIC.

N. Wright – Norman Wright, Bulimba, QLD.

LIST OF ABBREVIATIONS

AIB – Allied Intelligence Bureau
AMC – Armed Merchant Cruiser
AMS – Australian Minesweeper (corvette)
A/S – Anti-submarine
ASR – Air Sea Rescue Vessel
ASSAULT – HMAS ASSAULT
BDV – Boom Defence Vessel
Comm – Commissioned
Dan – Danlayer
DC – Depth Charge
DCC – Depth Charge Chute
DCR – Depth Charge Rail
DCT – Depth Charge Thrower
Exam. – Examination Vessel
GPV – General Purpose Vessel
Har – Harbour service
HDML – Harbour Defence Motor Launch
HMAS – His Majesty's Australian Ship
HMNZS – His Majesty's New Zealand Ship
HMS – His Majesty's Ship
LSI – Landing Ship Infantry
M – Month/s
MG – machine gun
Misc – Miscellaneous
Ml – Minelayer
MRL – Motor Refrigerated Lighter

Ms – Minesweeper
MSL – Motor Stores Lighter
MWL – Motor Water Lighter
MWS – Mine Warfare Ship
N/A – Not Available
NAP – Naval Auxiliary Patrol
OFL – Oil Fuel Lighter
PO – Paid Off
Pt – Part time
Purch. – Purchased
RAAF – Royal Australian Air Force
Req. – Requisitioned
Ret. – Returned
RN – Royal Navy
RAN – Royal Australian Navy
RNN – Royal Netherlands Navy
RNZN – Royal New Zealand Navy
SRD – Service Reconnaissance Department
SSV – Special Service Vessel
TCV – Tank Cleaning Vessel
TRB – Torpedo Recovery Boat
TRV – Torpedo Recovery Vessel
TT – Torpedo Tube
USN – United States Navy
USS – United States Ship
Y – Year/s

SECRETIVE CRAFT

After being formed in January, 1944, the Services Reconnaissance Department aquired fifteen 'Sleeping Beauties', (SBs), one man Motorised Submersible Canoes for operation 'Rimau', a second Singapore raid.

These 498 lb craft were 12.6 feet long with a beam of 2.2 feet and speed of 3.1

knots. Each SB was powered by a 24v motor plus a paddle. Limpet mines were carried. The above photographs show the 'SB' in and out of its container (Photo – The Australian Archives)

Another unusual type used by the SRD was the Welfreighter, in appearance a variation of the Royal Navy's X craft. (Photo – Australian Archives)

BIBLIOGRAPHY

Australia's Colonial Navies – Ross Gillett.
Australia's Ships of War – John Bastock.
British Warships 1914–19 – F. Dittmar and J. Colledge.
Conways All the Worlds Fighting Ships 1860–1905.
Conways All the Worlds Fighting Ships 1922–46.
Historical Studies and Research Section, Department of Defence.

Janes Fighting Ships – Various years.
The Royal Australian Navy 1914–18 – A. W. Jose.
The Royal Australian Navy 1939–45 – G. Herman Gill.
The Royal New Zealand Navy – Michael Burgess.
Ships of the Royal Navy Vol. 2 – J.J. Colledge.
Warships of Australia – Ross Gillett.

INDEX

ROYAL AUSTRALIAN NAVY 1914-45

AUSTRALIAN ARMY SMALL CRAFT 1939-45

ROYAL AUSTRALIAN AIR FORCE MARINE SECTION 1939-45

NEW ZEALAND GOVERNMENT 1914-21
NEW ZEALAND DIVISION OF
THE ROYAL NAVY 1921-41
ROYAL NEW ZEALAND NAVY 1941-45